Critical Thinking
About Psychology

Hidden Assumptions and
Plausible Alternatives

LEARNING RESOURCES
CENTRE
Havering College
of Further and Higher Education

Edited by

Brent D. Slife
Jeffrey S. Reber
Frank C. Richardson

American Psychological Association • Washington, DC

Published by
American Psychological Association
750 First Street, NE
Washington, DC 20002
www.apa.org

To order
APA Order Department
P.O. Box 92984
Washington, DC 20090-2984
Tel: (800) 374-2721; Direct: (202) 336-5510
Fax: (202) 336-5502; TDD/TTY: (202) 336-6123
Online: www.apa.org/books/
E-mail: order@apa.org

In the U.K., Europe, Africa, and the Middle East, copies may be ordered from
American Psychological Association
3 Henrietta Street
Covent Garden, London
WC2E 8LU England

Typeset in Goudy by Stephen McDougal, Mechanicsville, MD

Printer: United Book Press, Inc., Baltimore, MD
Cover Designer: Naylor Design, Washington, DC
Technical/Production Editors: Rosemary Moulton and Devon Bourexis

The opinions and statements published are the responsibility of the authors, and such opinions and statements do not necessarily represent the policies of the American Psychological Association.

Library of Congress Cataloging-in-Publication Data

Slife, Brent D.
  Critical thinking about psychology: hidden assumptions and plausible alternatives / Brent D. Slife, Jeffrey S. Reber, Frank C. Richardson.
      p. cm.
  Includes bibliographical references and index.
  ISBN 1-59147-187-7 (alk. paper)
  1. Psychology—Philosophy. 2. Psychotherapy—Philosophy. I. Reber, Jeffrey S.
II. Richardson, Frank C. III. Title.

BF38.S5817 2004
150'.1—dc22   2004013990

British Library Cataloguing-in-Publication Data
A CIP record is available from the British Library.

Printed in the United States of America
First Edition

Critical Thinking
About Psychology

CONTENTS

CONTRIBUTORS

Robert C. Bishop, PhD, Department of Philosophy, Logic and Scientific Method, London School of Economics and Political Science, England

Colin Burchfield, Captain, United States Air Force, 74th Medical Group, Wright-Patterson Air Force Base, OH

John Chambers Christopher, PhD, Department of Health and Human Development, Montana State University, Bozeman

Blaine J. Fowers, PhD, Department of Educational and Psychological Studies, University of Miami, FL

Edwin E. Gantt, PhD, Department of Psychology, Brigham Young University, Provo, UT

Dawson Hedges, MD, Department of Psychology, Brigham Young University, Provo, UT

Ramona O. Hopkins, PhD, Department of Psychology, Brigham Young University, Provo, UT

Suzanne R. Kirschner, PhD, Department of Psychology, College of the Holy Cross, Worcester, MA

Jack Martin, PhD, Faculty of Education, Simon Fraser University, Burnaby, British Columbia, Canada

Shawn P. O'Connor, Department of Psychology, University of Missouri, St. Louis

Lisa M. Osbeck, PhD, Department of Psychology, State University of West Georgia, Carrollton

Jeffrey S. Reber, PhD, Department of Psychology, State University of West Georgia, Carrollton

Frank C. Richardson, PhD, Department of Educational Psychology, University of Texas, Austin

Brent D. Slife, PhD, Department of Psychology, Brigham Young University, Provo, UT

Jeff Sugarman, PhD, Faculty of Education, Simon Fraser University, Burnaby, British Columbia, Canada

Brian Vandenberg, PhD, Department of Psychology, University of Missouri—St. Louis

Richard N. Williams, PhD, Department of Psychology, Brigham Young University, Provo, UT

Stephen C. Yanchar, PhD, Department of Instructional Psychology and Technology, Brigham Young University, Provo, UT

Critical Thinking
About Psychology

INTRODUCTION: THINKING CRITICALLY ABOUT CRITICAL THINKING

BRENT D. SLIFE, STEPHEN C. YANCHAR, AND JEFFREY S. REBER

Critical thinking has long been acclaimed as an essential skill for any academic or professional endeavor. Within psychology, especially, critical thinking has been consistently championed for all students and professionals (Benjafield, 1994; Bensley, 1998; Griggs, Jackson, Marek, & Christopher, 1998; Halpern, 1998; Halpern & Nummedal, 1995; Levy, 1997; Meltzoff, 1998; Smith, 2002; Yanchar & Slife, 2004). Psychologists are taught early in their careers to use their research findings to critically examine common myths and urban legends as well as debunk false beliefs and advertising ploys (e.g., Tavris, 2001). Yet, in spite of this obvious emphasis, psychologists do not typically subject psychology itself to critical evaluation. As many outside observers of psychology have noted (e.g., Bohman, 1993; MacIntyre, 1984; Taylor, 1985), mainstream psychologists often take for granted their philosophies, research methods, and professional practices. Even the tacit assumptions that guide psychological research on critical thinking are rarely critically analyzed or systematically examined. Why?

A primary reason for this neglect is that many psychologists have misunderstood critical thinking. Critical thinking has too often been mistaken for rigorous thinking. Rigorous thinking is frequently identified with "scientific analytic reasoning" (Dick, 1991, p. 84), which focuses on methodological concerns such as quality of research design, appropriateness of statistical analyses, and rigor of general reasoning. Psychologists are well known to engage skillfully in this type of thinking. Rigorous reasoning and methods are used not only to conduct psychological investigations but also to administer therapeutic practice. With few exceptions, investigators are supposed to follow the logic of their science, and clients are supposed to follow the rationality of their therapists. This commitment to rigorous reasoning is so widespread that psychologists conceptualize most of their activities in these terms. Students of psychology are taught this type of rigor in virtually all their courses.

One of the main problems with this sort of rigorous thinking is that it selectively excludes certain topics from critical examination. For example, scientific reasoning and empirical methods are often themselves taken for granted, exempting from critical analysis one of the core activities of psychologists. Philosophers of science point to many hidden assumptions and values in scientific methods and practices (Bem & de Jong, 1997; Bernstein, 1983; Bohman, 1993; Curd & Cover, 1998; Slife & Williams, 1995; Taylor, 1985; Toulmin, 1972). Yet, these assumptions and values are rarely included in texts or discussions of research and therapy methods in psychology. Consequently, the foundations of these methods and these practices are not themselves subjected to critical scrutiny.

This volume attempts to rectify such oversight and selectivity. It does so by adopting a conception of critical thinking that a number of philosophers and educators have contended is broader and deeper than previous conceptions. Perhaps most notably, recognized critical thinking theorists and researchers, such as Stephen Brookfield (1987) from education and Richard Paul (Paul & Elder, 2001) and Robert Ennis (1982) from philosophy, have emphasized a reformulation of critical thinking that moves beyond mere scientific analytic reasoning. If applied to psychology, this approach would inevitably lead to a critical analysis of all aspects of the discipline, including psychological research on critical thinking itself.

This reformulation of critical thinking has two parts. The first requires knowledge of the assumptions and underlying worldviews of a particular discipline or field of inquiry. In our case, this means knowledge of the *current* assumptions and values underlying psychology, including ideas concerning psychology's proper methods. Sometimes students of psychology are surprised or even disappointed to discover the assumptions underlying psychology's cherished ideas and explanations. When brought into the light of day, these fundamental ideas often seem less compelling and certain than they once did. For this reason, explicating these assumptions and understanding their implications is the first step in these students becoming critical evaluators of their discipline.

The second part of this reformulation of critical thinking involves developing ideas and assumptions that are *alternative* to our present views. To engage seriously in critical thinking about psychology, we must seek out and ponder the most credible and convincing alternatives to psychology's currently favored ideas and methods. Often, the assumptions and guiding values of mainstream psychology are so familiar that they seem like the only possible premises for our work. Indeed, they seem more like axioms and truisms than the working assumptions or fruitful perspectives they are. Knowing there are alternative possibilities, however, allows students to question the often taken-for-granted assumptions of their field. This questioning is important because these assumptions may themselves need to be reevaluated—a possibility that cannot even be seriously entertained without having alternatives with which to compare present assumptions.

ILLUSTRATING THE NEW CONCEPTION OF CRITICAL THINKING

To illustrate these issues, consider two examples, one from everyday life and the other from the world of professional psychology.

Danny and His Mother, Jill

Consider first the situation of young Danny and his mother, Jill. Jill wants to critically evaluate the problems that Danny is having at school. She spends considerable time taking a rigorous reasoning approach to the problem. She reads about what scientists and psychologists have to say about Danny's behavior and symptoms, and even investigates recent empirical studies. Jill eventually comes to the conclusion that Danny might be diagnosed with attention-deficit hyperactivity disorder (ADHD). When she questions her family physician about this possibility, he immediately confirms Jill's suspicions and prescribes a drug to "correct" Danny's problem. The importance of rigorous thinking in Jill's solution to her problem is undeniable, both in the process of Jill's thinking and in the scientists' investigations of these behaviors.

However, there is a great deal more to a thoroughly critical analysis of this situation. Truly critical thinking would also examine some of the assumptions made in this process of diagnosis and prescription as well as consider possible alternative perspectives that might be helpful to the problem. In fact, recent interview studies show that many people like Danny and his mother take for granted that the prescribed medication is largely, if not solely, responsible for the decrease in Danny's ADHD behaviors (e.g., Burchfield & Slife, 2004). In other words, they make the common but thoroughly debatable assumption that Danny's biology (with the drug changes) strongly determines these behaviors—the assumption of *biological determinism*. As a result, Danny believes that he has little or no *personal* responsibility or choice about his "bad" (ADHD) behaviors at school, because personal responsibility and choice are typically associated with an *alternative* set of assumptions, namely that Danny has some capacity for free will and personal responsibility that is usually an important dimension of his behavior. For this reason, Danny gives up making any effort to control his problematic behaviors.

Danny's mother has similar ideas about her responsibilities as a parent. She assumes, for instance, that his diagnosis and treatment mean that his problems at school cannot be blamed on her faulty parenting. After all, she cannot be held responsible for Danny's difficulties if his biology is responsible for them. Her experiences with Danny's diagnosis and treatment also teach her that she has limited parental responsibility for any of Danny's future difficulties, because neither Danny nor her parenting controls them (see chap. 6, this volume, for more on this assumption). The point of this illustration is to ask several vital questions: Is it not important to identify and examine such assumptions when diagnosing and treating children for ADHD? Might not the assumption of biological determinism lead Jill and Danny to overlook other possibly valuable resources in their struggle for Danny's well-being? Could the tacit assumption of biological determinism lead them to overlook important dimensions of the problem and direct them, perhaps without full awareness, to view themselves as somewhat passive and unable to control the situation?

Empirically Supported Treatments

Consider another example of critical thinking in the heart of professional psychology. Many psychologists today believe that counselors and psychotherapists should only use therapeutic strategies that have been critically evaluated (see Messer, 2001). According to the conventional idea of critical thinking in psychology—rigorous thinking—the proper evaluation of counseling strategies or techniques consists of using scientific reasoning and testing to demonstrate their effectiveness. Indeed, a list of these strategies has now been drawn up as *empirically supported treatments* (ESTs), with some psychologists proposing that these should be the only treatments permitted in psychotherapy (Division 12 Task Force, 1995). Should therapeutic approaches be restricted in this manner?

Many critics of ESTs, including many psychologists, believe that this approach is too narrow, limited, and mechanical (e.g., Bohart, O'Hara, & Leitner, 1998; Messer, 2001). However, many EST supporters view these critics as better at protesting the EST movement than stating clearly what is wrong with the movement or proposing constructively a better alternative. Indeed, from the perspective of many EST advocates, the critics of ESTs have little to recommend other than an unsystematic, "anything goes" approach. This unsystematic approach appears to return psychology to the same chaotic situation that gave rise to the use of rigorous thinking and methods in the first place—a situation in which psychotherapists were not properly held accountable. Thus, the critics of ESTs often fan the fires of their own discontent.

This controversy presents a classic case of the need for a truly critical analysis in the expanded sense recommended in this book. Of course, a complete analysis of this controversy is not appropriate or even possible here, though aspects of this issue and a number of others like it are examined in some detail in the chapters that follow (e.g., chaps. 3 and 4). For the purpose of illustration, however, it may be sufficient here to point to one of the many unexamined, and possibly quite problematic, assumptions underlying the EST controversy: the assumption that effectiveness is needed. Is there anymore frequently used concept in professional psychology than "effectiveness"? Effectiveness is often touted as professional psychology's highest ideal, but what is it really?

The Meaning of Effectiveness

Perhaps the core meaning of effectiveness is that some method or technique reliably and predictably produces some desired end or result. If we want a therapeutic method to be effective, we must first specify the end or outcome of the technique we desire. The problem is that merely wanting effectiveness tells us nothing about what ends or goals are truly worthwhile. There are effective terrorists and thieves just as there are effective teachers and clergy. The profound differences among these types of effectiveness involve the human and moral quality of the ends they serve, not their productivity or efficiency. In this sense, rigorous reasoning and empirical methods are perhaps best suited for assessing the effectiveness of means, not for judging the quality or worth of ends. Surely a comprehensive approach to understanding and improving human life has to include both. Surely critical thinking requires an evaluation of the ideas associated with means *and* ends, even if the latter are less empirically accessible.

To take the matter a step further, the enormous emphasis placed on effectiveness in professional psychology often reflects an assumption that much of everyday life is a matter of maximizing effectiveness and control over our environments and ourselves. However, many critics in recent decades—including psychologists such as Erich Fromm (1941/1969) and John Schumaker (2001) as well as philosophers such as Christopher Lasch (1991), Jürgen Habermas (1973), and Alasdair MacIntyre (1984), to mention just a few—have argued that our emphasis on mastery, control, and cost–benefit (effectiveness) analyses are actually a major source of emotional problems, mental illness, and relationship problems. In the minds of these thinkers, mastery and effectiveness are often splendid things, but they need to be subordinated to more worthy and lasting purposes in living. If psychology does not take such *critical* perspectives into account, it runs the risk of inadvertently perpetuating some of the ills it tries to cure.

Of course, everyone has their own values and biases. However, the purpose of this brief illustration on ESTs is not to argue for one moral outlook or philosophy over another. Rather, it is to point out that the extensive discussion of effectiveness in psychology is based on a number of unexamined assumptions and tacit values that are worthy of serious reconsideration. As needed and helpful as rigorous and scientific thinking is, it is inadequate to the tasks associated with truly critical thinking. Paul Wachtel (1997), a psychotherapist noted for critical thinking in the fullest sense, put it this way:

> We need a good deal more critical thought about how to conceptualize the issues, about what is worth knowing, and about the various ways in which what has been observed thus far can be understood. We need to examine more closely the assumptions that underlie our questions. For our questions are our destiny; once we have framed a question, the answer already lies in wait, concealed as the statue is in the sculptor's block of marble. . . . Psychology has been obsessed with answers. This book is concerned mainly with questions. (p. xvii)

The present volume, too, is concerned mainly with questions. However, as Wachtel observed, good questions—which already frame good answers—originate from critical thinking that examines "more closely the assumptions that underlie our questions."

THE LITERATURE ON CRITICAL THINKING

Does the research literature on critical thinking in psychology address the importance of unexamined assumptions? How do specialists in this research conceptualize critical thinking? A review of this literature reveals careful empirical studies as well as instructive theoretical insights. However, few if any of the investigators working in this area have advocated the need to think critically about fundamental assumptions. Although these authors invariably endorse the need to think critically about and thus empirically investigate all sorts of claims (e.g., folk psychology, advertising), they rarely recommend that the assumptions underlying these investigations be critically examined.

Many specific texts *appear*, particularly in their titles, to critically evaluate psychology's methods, such as Meltzoff's (1998) *Critical Thinking About Research* and Benjafield's (1994) *Thinking Critically About Research Methods.* However, these texts concentrate almost exclusively on showing how the tools of traditional science can rigorously assess claims and test hypotheses. They do not cast critical light on the nature of these methods, nor do they bring to this light their historical context, assumptions, and implications. Critical thinking is thus couched rather narrowly in terms of rigorous reasoning, namely, the quantity and quality of empirical support for claims, theories, and therapies. Critical thinking as discussed by Brookfield (1987) and the authors of this book is largely ignored.

The general literature on critical thinking in psychology also champions rigorous reasoning (Bensley, 1998; Halpern, 1984, 1998; Halpern & Nummedal, 1995; Lehman, Lempert, & Nisbett, 1988; Levy, 1997; McGovern, Furumoto, Halpern, Kimble, & McKeachie, 1991; Smith, 2002; Stanovich, 1998; Zechmeister & Johnson, 1992). A review of this literature suggests that scientific analytic reasoning has shaped much of our discipline's consciousness about the nature of excellent thinking: Excellent thinkers are professionals and students who can reason well about methods, variables, and the logicality of their thinking within the cannons of empirical science.

This view of excellent thinking is also reflected in the reasoning and methods of many approaches to psychotherapy and counseling—in at least three ways. First, a critical appraisal of therapeutic methods is almost always considered complete with scientific analytic reasoning, such as testing their effectiveness through the methods of science (Messer, 2001). Second, therapeutic methods are themselves thought to be administered rigorously and rationally, as indicated by the use of therapy manuals and standardized diagnoses (Division 12 Task Force, 1995). Third, rigorous reasoning has itself become a standard for identifying client problems and desired treatment outcomes, such as in cognitive–behavioral therapy (e.g., Beck, Rush, Shaw, & Emery, 1984). A lack of rigorous reasoning is frequently viewed as an important problem for clients, because they are viewed as "irrational," whereas rigorous reasoning about the conduct of their lives is often considered a preferred method and outcome of treatment.

If psychologists seek to champion critical thinking and grant it prominent status in the discipline, why is critical discussion confined to the rigor of reasoning and methods alone? Analysis of fundamental assumptions is virtually nonexistent in psychology's general textbooks and the more specific critical thinking literature. On the relatively few occasions that assumptions are mentioned in this literature, they are treated in only a cursory way (e.g., Bensley, 1998; Halpern, 1998). Fundamental questions about the very nature and purpose of commonly accepted psychological methods, theories, and therapies simply are not addressed (e.g., Smith, 2002). These authors seem to assume that rigorous reasoning is all that is required to deal with the challenges of understanding psychological life and facilitating human flourishing. Or perhaps critical thinking in the broader sense of this book seems unnecessary to these authors because the only alternative to careful, rigorous reasoning—as they conceive of it—is blind intuition, irrational dogma, or ineffable mysticism.

The authors of this volume believe otherwise. We believe there are profound and pressing reasons for taking a richer view of critical thinking and making it a routine part of our work as social scientists and professional psychologists. Restricting ourselves to rigorous reasoning alone is a fool's errand, even in our practical lives. Our difficulties in coping with some person or problem do not always result from overt tactics or conscious reasoning about the situation. They may also stem from faulty assumptions about another's motives or the way the world works, which a moment of insight or a good word from a friend helps us understand. Indeed, as we go about our daily lives, we are constantly revising our assumptions (often realizing that we are making them for the first time), considering alternatives, and beginning to make progress instead of just spinning our wheels. Critical thinking in this reformulated sense is part of thoughtful, meaningful living.

CONTENT OVERVIEW

To help psychologists advance their discipline in thoughtful and meaningful ways, the content of this book is organized into six parts, each part corresponding to a major subdiscipline of psychology: clinical/counseling, social, neuroscience/experimental, cognitive, developmental, and statistical/methodological. Each part consists of two chapters that critically examine several important topics or issues within a subdiscipline. Because truly critical thinking involves an understanding of both the current and alternative assumptions underlying each topic or issue, one chapter excavates current assumptions and the other explores plausible alternative assumptions.

The book opens with a critical examination of several pivotal issues in the subdiscipline of *clinical/counseling psychology*. In the first chapter of this pair, Frank Richardson, himself a counseling psychologist, identifies tacit assumptions and values that underpin professional psychology and may be the source of often-discussed problems and blind spots in this field. Blaine Fowers, also a counseling psychologist, sketches an alternative to psychotherapy assumptions, drawing on the field of virtue ethics, that portrays personal development, psychological well-being, and the good life in a fresh and potentially fruitful way.

The chapters of Part II address issues in *social psychology*. To begin this part, social psychologists Jeff Reber and Lisa Osbeck investigate the strengths and limitations of the traditional assumptions underlying social psychology topics such as sociality, love, and helping behavior. In light of these limitations, theoretical psychologist Ed Gantt provides alternatives to these assumptions by borrowing from social constructionist psychology, hermeneutic philosophy, and ethical phenomenology.

Part III is concerned with several important issues and themes of *experimental psychology*, specifically *neuroscience*. In the first chapter, neuroscientist and pharmacologist Dawson Hedges collaborates with Colin Burchfield to outline the main current assumptions of neuroscience research on mental disorders, especially research on depression and antidepressants. The next chapter contains a proposal for reframing these assumptions of neuroscience. Theoretical psychologist Brent Slife teams up with neuroscientist Ramona Hopkins to discuss how this alternative proposal might better fit neuroscience data and provide valuable new insights into neuroscience investigations of children diagnosed with ADHD.

The fourth part of the book investigates several key issues in *cognitive psychology*. In the first chapter, Robert Bishop, a philosopher of science and mind, explicates the assumptions underlying current understandings of memory, traditional models of reasoning, and the computer metaphor for the human mind. In the second chapter, cognitive psychologist Stephen Yanchar explores interesting and fruitful alternative ways to understand how people experience the world and engage in activities such as acting and remembering.

Part V addresses significant topics in *developmental psychology*. In the current assumptions chapter, developmental psychologists Brian Vandenberg and Shawn O'Connor use Piaget's theory to cast light on some of the deepest presuppositions of this subdiscipline. They discuss the broader historical context of cosmological, geological, and biological theories of development. Developmentalist John Christopher analyzes in the second chapter how our Western cultural understandings have deeply colored familiar theories of development. He then outlines an alternative approach that might overcome this Western bias while still speaking to common features of human development across cultures.

The final part of the book evaluates several pivotal topics in the subdiscipline concerned with *statistics and methods*, including hypothesis testing, measurement, and the interpretation of results. Statistician and methodologist Richard Williams describes the current assumptions that underlie these notions, whereas two psychological researchers with expertise in the philosophy of science, Jeff Sugarman and Jack Martin, propose alternative conceptions of human science inquiry.

Suzanne Kirschner, a theoretical psychologist, concludes the book by identifying many of the common ideas that cut across the chapters. She points to some fascinating thematic connections both across the chapters describing current assumptions and across the chapters that discuss alternative conceptions of each subdiscipline. These themes include issues of mind/body dualism, social atomism, individualism, meaning-centeredness, free will/determinism, contextualism, and many others. Ultimately, as Kirschner observes, the purpose of all 12 chapters is to help the students of psychology reflect more deeply on the premises and methods of the field.

The authors believe that this reflection will help students in three important ways. First, students will realize that psychological theories and ideas, including those that initially seemed unquestionable, are based on fallible assumptions and subject to critical examination. Second, students will learn the advantages and disadvantages of available ideas, allowing them to become sophisticated consumers of these ideas as well as take more care in formulating their own positions on psychological issues. Third, students will understand these ideas within a broader intellectual framework, situating psychology within the larger enterprise of science and the humanities.

REFERENCES

Beck, A., Rush, A., Shaw, F., & Emery, G. (1984). *The cognitive therapy of depression*. New York: Guilford Press.

Bem, S., & de Jong, H. L. (1997). *Theoretical issues in psychology: An introduction*. London: Sage.

Benjafield, J. G. (1994). *Thinking critically about research methods*. Boston: Allyn & Bacon.

Bensley, D. A. (1998). *Critical thinking in psychology: A unified skills approach*. Pacific Grove, CA: Brooks/Cole.

Bernstein, R. J. (1983). *Beyond objectivism and relativism: Science, hermeneutics, and praxis*. Philadelphia: University of Pennsylvania Press.

Bohart, A. C., O'Hara, M., & Leitner, L. M. (1998). Empirically violated treatments: Disenfranchisement of humanistic and other psychotherapies. *Psychotherapy Research, 8*, 141–157.

Bohman, J. (1993). *New philosophy of social science*. Cambridge, MA: MIT Press.

Brookfield, S. (1987). *Developing critical thinkers: Challenging adults to explore alternative ways of thinking*. San Francisco: Jossey-Bass.

Burchfield, C. M., & Slife, B. D. (2004). *The meaning of being diagnosed as and prescribed medication for ADHD*. Unpublished doctoral dissertaton.

Curd, M., & Cover, J. A. (1998). *Philosophy of science: The central issues*. New York: Norton.

Dick, R. D. (1991). An empirical taxonomy of critical thinking. *Journal of Instructional Psychology, 18*, 79–92.

Division 12 Task Force. (1995). Training in and dissemination of empirically validated psychological treatments: Report and recommendations. *The Clinical Psychologist, 48*, 3–23.

Ennis, R. H. (1982). Identifying implicit assumptions. *Syntheses, 51*, 61–86.

Fromm, E. (1969). *Escape from freedom*. New York: Avon (Original work published 1941)

Griggs, R. A., Jackson, S. L., Marek, P., & Christopher, A. N. (1998). Critical thinking in introductory psychology texts and supplements. *Teaching of Psychology, 25*, 254–266.

Habermas, J. (1973). *Theory and practice*. Boston: Beacon Press.

Halpern, D. F. (1984). *Thought and knowledge: An introduction to critical thinking*. Hillsdale, NJ: Erlbaum.

Halpern, D. F. (1998). Teaching critical thinking for transfer across domains: Dispositions, skills, structure training, and metacognitive monitoring. *American Psychologist, 53,* 449–455.

Halpern, D. F., & Nummedal, S. G. (Eds.). (1995). Psychologists teach critical thinking [Special issue]. *Teaching of Psychology, 22*(1).

Lasch, C. (1991). *The true and only heaven: Progress and its critics*. New York: Norton.

Lehman, D. R., Lempert, R. O., & Nisbett, R. E. (1988). The effects of graduate training on reasoning: Formal discipline and thinking about everyday-life events. *American Psychologist, 43,* 431–442.

Levy, D. A. (1997). *Tools of critical thinking: Metathoughts for psychology*. Boston: Allyn & Bacon.

MacIntyre, A. (1984). *After virtue* (2nd ed.). Notre Dame, IN: Notre Dame University Press.

McGovern, T. V., Furumoto, L., Halpern, D. F., Kimble, G. A., & McKeachie, W. J. (1991). Liberal education, study in depth, and the arts and sciences major—psychology. *American Psychologist, 46,* 598–605.

Meltzoff, J. (1998). *Critical thinking about research: Psychology and related fields*. Washington, DC: American Psychological Association.

Messer, S. (2001). Empirically supported treatments: What's a nonbehaviorist to do? In B. Slife, R. Williams, & S. Barlow (Eds.), *Critical issues in psychotherapy: Translating new ideas into practice* (pp. 3–19). Thousand Oaks, CA: Sage.

Paul, R., & Elder, L. (2001). *Critical thinking: Tools for taking charge of your learning and your life*. Upper Saddle River, NJ: Prentice Hall.

Schumaker, J. (2001). *The age of insanity: Modernity and mental health*. Westport, CT: Praeger.

Slife, B. D., & Williams, R. N. (1995). *What's behind the research? Discovering hidden assumptions in the behavioral sciences*. Thousand Oaks, CA: Sage.

Smith, R. A. (2002). *Challenging your preconceptions: Thinking critically about psychology* (2nd ed.). Belmont, CA: Wadsworth/Thomson.

Stanovich, K. E. (1998). *How to think straight about psychology* (5th ed.). New York: Longman.

Tavris, C. (2001). *Psychobabble and biobunk: Using psychology to think critically about issues in the news* (2nd ed.). Upper Saddle River, NJ: Prentice Hall.

Taylor, C. (1985). *Philosophy and the human sciences: Philosophical papers*. Cambridge, England: Cambridge University Press.

Toulmin, S. (1972). *Human understanding*. Princeton, NJ: Princeton University Press.

Wachtel, P. (1997). *Psychoanalysis, behavior therapy, and the relational world*. Washington, DC: American Psychological Association.

Yanchar, S., & Slife, B. (2004). Teaching critical thinking by examining assumptions: An instructional framework. *Teaching Psychology, 31*(2), 85–90.

Zechmeister, E. B., & Johnson, J. E. (1992). *Critical thinking: A functional approach.* Pacific Grove, CA: Brooks/Cole.

I

CLINICAL AND COUNSELING PSYCHOLOGY

1

PSYCHOTHERAPY AND MODERN DILEMMAS

FRANK C. RICHARDSON

Men and women today are haunted by a sense that in the midst of plenty, our lives seem barren. We are hungry for a greater nourishment of the soul. In the England of today, a businessman turned philosopher, Charles Handy, has won a widespread following with his writing. Capitalism, he argues, delivers the means but not the point of life. Now that we are satisfying our outer needs, we must pay more attention to those within— for beauty, spiritual growth, and human connection. "In Africa," Handy writes, "they say there are two hungers . . . the lesser hunger is for the things that sustain life, the goods and services, and the money to pay for them, which we all need. The greater hunger is for an answer to the question 'why?,' for some understanding of what life is for."
—David Gergen, editorial, *U.S. News & World Report*, August 23, 1999

In the 1960s, the sociologist Peter Berger (1977, p. 23) called our attention to a "social phenomenon of truly astounding scope" that he saw taking place. He was talking about the emergence of what he called a new "psychological society" dominated by "an assortment of ideas and activities derived in one way or another from the Freudian revolution in psychology." This "institutionalized psychology" is so well suited to our contemporary situation, Berger wittily suggested, that "if Freud had not existed, he would have had to be invented" (p. 23). He pointed out that as traditional religious belief has lost its authority for many people, a host of psychotherapists, social workers, career counselors, psychiatrists, management trainers, organizational development consultants, and other mental health specialists come to play a pivotal role in providing guidance and direction in our society. In addition, quite novel concepts and ideals, such as self-esteem, adjustment, self-actualization, defenses, repression, projection, personal growth, and a host of others, have become part of our everyday vocabulary. More than that, they have become part of the very way we think about our lives and make important decisions about them. Thus, Philip Rieff (1966, p. 232) could speak of a veritable "triumph of the therapeutic" in our era.

What are we to make of this astounding social phenomenon? Is it a good thing or a bad thing? This chapter and the next attempt, cautiously, to address these questions. It is difficult to make sense of this enormous and significant cultural development because it is quite complex and we are so close to it. But just because it is so important, we are obligated to make the effort. In this chapter, I try to contribute to this effort by identifying what I think are some of the crucial assumptions and values that underlie the theory and practice of modern counseling and psychotherapy. It is quite striking how these assumptions and values shape psychology and psychotherapy at their very core at the same time that they go largely unnoticed by most of us.

We all know that many different kinds of psychology and psychotherapy over the last century have become virtual cults with ardent and unquestioning worshippers. Many of us are aware that, in contrast, the modern therapy enterprise has had many detractors from the beginning. In the early years of the 20th century, for example, the noted Austrian essayist Karl Kraus remarked that "Psychoanalysis is that disease of which it purports to be the cure." Surely, the truth lies somewhere in the middle between worship and scorn. In my view, we ought to look a lot more favorably than unfavorably on what has taken place. But there also are reasons to think that a great deal of chaff is mixed in with the wheat of this explosion of therapeutic ideas and activities that has directly touched many of us and become a part of all our lives.

CONCERNS ABOUT PSYCHOTHERAPY

Throughout the 20th century, a number of thoughtful critics have voiced sharp concerns about the entanglement of modern therapy theory and practice with questionable values and social trends in contemporary society. It seems remarkable how astute their observations are, how much they seem to be saying similar things about developments in this area, and yet how uncertain they are about what to do about the problems they may have brought to light. So, perhaps these critics have identified some real blind spots in the modern therapy venture but have not yet gotten to the bottom of what causes them, and therefore find it difficult to imagine effective mid-course corrections or creative revisions of the status quo.

Here are some representative expressions of concern about psychotherapy from over the years. In the 1960s, C. Marshall Lowe (1976) argued that modern people often experience a severe "crisis of values" because at the same time that the authority of traditional morals and customs is waning, the uncertainty and flux of modern life tend to prevent the crystallization of any new beliefs and values to serve as a basis for living. One result is that increasing numbers of people turn to counselors and therapists as what Lowe termed "new moral authorities" or "secular priests," as guides who are asked to "make moral pronouncements in the name of science in the way the clergy was called upon for religious directives" (pp. 16–17). Unfortunately, he believed, this "solution" to our confusion and need for direction creates as many problems as it solves.

First of all, if we think of psychotherapy mainly as a kind of applied science, it is not going to be of much help to individuals who are faced with moral or existential questions concerning their lives and choices. Such an applied science might help one find more effective or efficient means to already established ends or goals. But it is of little value in determining what sorts of purposes or directions in living are worth pursuing in the first place or are good in themselves (see Vandenberg & O'Connor, chap. 9, this volume). Second, according to Lowe (1976), although we have lost both the guidance of tradition and the rugged individualism of earlier modern times, we still have a basic human need for standards of some sort, a need to belong to something, and a great "need for approval" (p. 15). As a result, we become "other-directed" personalities whose lives we can only evaluate not so much "by conformity to the will of God or by economic achievement," but by our "ability to adjust to contemporary social customs" in a manner that is congruent with public views about "mental health and . . . other social values" (pp. 16–17). Life becomes more of a popularity contest than a pathway of achievement or character formation. However, the quest for popularity or approval is an uncertain and unstable business, as anyone knows who appreciates how fickle people can be or has experienced the kind of relationship in which two or more people desperately want one another's approval but resent having to conform to the will of the other to obtain it.[1]

In the end, Lowe (1976) felt that therapists must "take sides in complex issues of . . . social and moral direction" (p. 22). But he did not indicate any clear way counseling and therapy might guide us in coping with the emotional confusion of the present situation beyond the inadequate alternatives he identified, namely applied science, blind adherence to tradition, or the kind of rugged individualism that underestimates human interdependence and the need for some lasting social ties and loyalties.

In the 1970s, Jerome Frank (1978, pp. 6–7) thoughtfully observed that as "institutions of American society, all psychotherapies . . . share a value system that accords primacy to individual self-fulfillment," including "maximum self-awareness, unlimited access to one's own feelings, increased autonomy and creativity." The individual is seen as "the center of his moral universe, and concern for others is believed to follow from his own self-realization" (p. 6). In Frank's view, these values are admirable in many ways, and

---

[1]Of course, the answer of much professional and pop psychology to this problem in recent decades has been to sever one's sense of self-worth or importance entirely from social standards or the approval of others. However, for reasons that may become clearer as this chapter proceeds, for the deeply social animals we are, this may be more of a recipe for emotional isolation and emptiness than for a sense of dignity and emotional stability.

modern therapies are often beneficial, even life saving. Nevertheless, he noted, the implicit value system of modern psychotherapy "can easily become a source of misery in itself" (p. 6) because of its unrealistic expectations for personal happiness and the burden of resentment it imposes when inevitable disappointments occur. In his opinion, the literature of psychotherapy gives little attention to such traditional, possibly worthwhile values or virtues as "the redemptive power of suffering, acceptance of one's lot in life, adherence to tradition, self-restraint and moderation" (p. 7). I find these remarks of Frank quite moving, but he did not have much to say about how to bring the best of these more traditional ideals to life again in a skeptical and pluralistic age.

In their engaging book, *We've Had a Hundred Years of Psychotherapy and the World's Getting Worse*, James Hillman and Michael Ventura (1992) analyzed the contemporary overpsychologizing of life and its struggles. They felt that psychotherapy, valuable as it can be, tends to reinforce some of the most problematic aspects of modern life. In particular, it perpetuates a view of the person as a self-encapsulated entity and places a heavy stress on inwardness. For example, these authors contended that therapeutic thinking tends to "internalize emotions" (p. 23). It takes powerful emotions and passions, like outrage and indignation over injustice, that bind us to the world and other people and can give us a sense of purpose, and converts them into inner feelings, like anxiety, hostility, or depression, which we ought to process and work through to free the inner citadel of the self from disturbance.

A corollary of internalizing emotions, according to Hillman and Ventura (1992), is a certain "developmental" perspective that is the "principle content of American psychology" (p. 67). This perspective underlies the widespread therapeutic belief that because personality and behavior are determined mainly by one's family relationships during childhood, the proper focus of therapy is the past personal history of the individual as this has influenced his or her inner life. Such an internal focus on healing the effects of the past might seem like the ideal way to undercut false dependencies and foster autonomy and self-responsibility. To some extent it does, of course. But, Hillman and Ventura felt that it also represents an excessively narrow and inward focus that blinds us to the real social and cultural patterns that are a major source of human miseries. It cuts us off from awareness of our need to work together as a community to confront dehumanizing and unjust structures within our world, and from experiencing our deep-rootedness and participation in the larger history of our nation or traditions. Hillman and Ventura worried that certain psychotherapeutic myths are "turning us into children" (p. 98) who are preoccupied with issues of dependence on and need for protection from powerful parentlike figures, which encourages them to see themselves as victims rather than agents in their own life stories.

Philip Cushman (1990, p. 604) argued that our society defines the mature or ideal individual as a "bounded, masterful self" that is expected to "function in a highly autonomous, isolated way" and "to be self-soothing, self-loving, and self-sufficient." Unfortunately, Cushman thought there is evidence that this inflated, would-be autonomous self almost inevitably collapses into an "empty self," whose characteristics of fragility, sense of emptiness, and proneness to fluctuation between feelings of worthlessness and grandiosity are often said to be the hallmarks of neurotic psychopathology in our day (Kohut, 1977). Cushman (1990, p. 604) defined emptiness as, "in part, an absence of communal forms and beliefs" that leaves individuals quite vulnerable to influence from cultural forms such as advertising and psychology, both professional and "pop," which emanate authority and certainty. So it is telling that the goals of psychotherapy are usually rendered in terms of more effective individual behavior, enhanced self-realization, or personal authenticity. Little is said about ethical qualities of character or commitment that many feel are essential to a worthwhile or fulfilled life. Their absence may be a virtual recipe for personal shallowness and social fragmentation. Moreover, in their absence it is unclear why such autonomous, self-interested individuals would ever "choose to undergo the self-sacrifice and suffering necessary" (Cushman, 1990, p. 605) to raise children in modern America.

A danger in all this, Cushman (1990, p. 605) believes, is that academic and professional psychology may reinforce a one-sided "preoccupation with the inner self" that "causes the social world to be devalued or ignored" except to the degree that it simply mirrors or serves the purposes of "the self." As a result, the social and cultural milieu "loses its impact as a material force, and social problems lose their relation to political action" (p. 605). But both Hillman and Ventura (1992) and Cushman are much clearer about these problems of excessive inwardness and emptiness than about credible antidotes for them. Is political action called for? Surely, in part, it is. But bringing about a more fair and just society by itself will not correct the kind of turning inward and loss of a sense of wider purpose these concerned critics speak about. Also, any sort of deeper cultural renewal seems beyond the scope and competence of psychology as a field. (An article of Cushman's [2002], however, pointed in the direction of supplementing social reform with the kind of "virtue ethics" that the following chapter explores as a framework for rethinking psychotherapy.)

CONCEALED VALUES, HIDDEN ASSUMPTIONS

One common denominator among these and many other observers seems to be that modern psychology and psychotherapy *both* creatively address emotional problems in living *and* inadvertently perpetuate ideals and practices of our way of life that may actually contribute to those very problems. We can get to the source of this somewhat paradoxical state of affairs only by unearthing some of the usually unexamined assumptions and largely tacit values that really power the psychotherapy enterprise as we know it. After decades of ruminating over this situation, it now seems possible to get closer, at least, to the root of the problem.

Value-Freedom

Near the beginning of the recent upsurge of psychotherapeutic activities in American society, the distinguished researcher Paul Meehl (1959) expressed a sharp concern that therapists would behave like "crypto-missionaries" (p. 257) seeking to convert their clients to their own preferred cultural, moral, or religious values. To prevent this from happening, Slife, Smith, and Burchfield (2003, p. 56) in their recent, incisive review of this issue pointed out that just as "good scientists are assumed to be objective and value-free observers of psychological facts, good therapists are assumed to be objective and value-free observers of therapeutic facts." Moreover, "if therapists do not strive for objectivity and value-freeness, they are considered unethical" (p. 56). This kind of *value-freedom* or *value-neutrality* is a defining characteristic and a pillar of modern psychotherapy.[2] It has allowed therapists to share in the prestige of the natural scientist who is thought to operate on a higher plane of objectivity, above the fray of ordinary moral debate and cultural politics, at the same time that they offer understanding and guidance concerning the most pressing problems and choices in living.

There is no doubt that this commitment to value-freedom, value-neutrality, or objectivity has fostered much in the way of honesty, fairness, careful thinking, respect for diversity, and courage and daring in pursuit of the truth. However, value-freedom makes a strange stalking horse for these weighty virtues and ideals given that it is supposed to make all such moral and cultural values largely irrelevant to understanding human behavior and to the good work of psychotherapy! Slife et al. (2003) drove home the point that the notion of value-freedom embroils psychologists and therapists in paradoxes that have caused them a great deal of discomfort and confusion at times. Many sincere efforts have been made to think this problem through by theorists and therapists who are concerned about intellectual and moral clarity. But it looks like it may not be possible to straighten things out without questioning some of our most prized assumptions.

To begin with, Slife et al. (2003) pointed out that dedication to value-freedom or value-neutrality embroils therapists in the paradox of firmly believing that they *should* or *ought* to be neutral or objective. In other words, they ought to "value being value-free" (p. 60) in a way that seems quite contradictory. This is not just a conceptual inconsistency but a concrete, exis-

---

[2]Ask undergraduate students what the difference is between talking over a problem with a parent or relative and with a counselor and the first thing most of them will say is not that the counselor is knowledgeable or wise but "objective."

tential one. The kind of whole-hearted dedication to the ideal of value-freedom demanded of therapists is exactly the same kind of allegiance to particular values they are morally charged to spurn or avoid.[3] Now the common sense or practical wisdom of both therapists and clients can often be counted on to take this ideal with a grain of salt, appreciate the fact that there are good and bad values, and find a way to advocate for better ones while respecting the clients' right and ability to draw their own conclusions about such matters. However, therapeutic communication is a tricky and artful business, and the ideal of value-freedom is at best a confusing guide to practicing that art.

Dozens of research studies on values and therapy over the years confirm that counseling and psychotherapy are anything but value-neutral (Beutler & Bergan, 1991; Kelly & Strupp, 1992; Tjeltveit, 1986, 1999). Some of the most interesting findings concern what has been come to be known as *value convergence* between therapist and client over the course of therapy. Slife et al. (2003, p. 63) argued that this research shows that value convergence "is even more important to therapy improvement than a host of other factors, such as therapist credibility and competence." As a matter of fact, "all sorts of values seem to be important to perceived client improvement—professional values, moral values, and in many studies religious values were pivotal." But what is this convergence? It might sound "like a mutual and reciprocal relationship between client and therapist." However, it does not appear to be an innocent blending of perspectives. According to Slife et al. (2003),

> Overwhelmingly, this research indicates that therapists do not change their values during therapy; only clients change their values (Tjeltveit, 1986). One might say that therapists only perceive success in therapy when their clients have come to have values like their own. (p. 63)

The basis for saying this lies in evidence reviewed by Kelly (1990) indicating that "values convergence . . . does not apply to clients' ratings of their own improvement; it only applies to therapists' rating of improvement and normality" (Slife et al., 2003, p. 64). So, one might ask, are we talking about value *convergence* or value *conversion*, the very thing Meehl feared in the 1950s?

One way therapy theorists have tried to preserve value-neutrality is to base clinical interventions on purely "objective" principles or findings, relying on and trying to imitate the supposedly value-free status of scientific methods. The trouble is, very few philosophers of science any longer view science as strictly value-free. Currently, we tend to view natural science inquiry as a creative, interpretive endeavor in which even "objective facts" depend in part on the theories we hammer out and in which theory selection

---

[3]Indeed, there are clear ethical injunctions against imposing values on clients (American Psychological Association, 2002).

depends on such "values" as parsimony or fruitfulness (Bernstein, 1983; Kuhn, 1970). To adopt the model of the natural sciences as the only or main way to study human action and social life is to make an even more value-laden and partisan choice. To place a high value on what is observable and replicable in human affairs, and on the sorts of techniques that allow us to manipulate the world or ourselves more efficiently or effectively, is to adopt and recommend an approach to life and living that does appeal to many in the modern world. But it is a value program, not a value-free stance toward the world. There are both moral philosophies and therapeutic approaches (humanistic, existentialist, those that stress spiritual values, and others) that not only encourage very different attitudes and kinds of living but vigorously contend that just such a one-sided stress on technique and control is actually a major source of emotional difficulties in our kind of society (Schumaker, 2001).

There is no space to discuss it adequately in this chapter, but it should be mentioned that in the view of many contemporary philosophers of social science (Root, 1993; Taylor, 1985), the natural sciences represent a deep and valuable but narrow and limited approach to understanding the world, especially the human realm. In everyday life, humans pursue a number of kinds of knowledge and understanding (ethical, cultural, spiritual) that are different from that pursued in the natural sciences. In studying humans, therefore, we often are concerned not with impersonal causal explanation or even with producing certain reliable results, but with grasping the *meaning* of people's actions and the *quality* of their motives and aims. Those who take a phenomenological or interpretive approach to social science inquiry of this kind are likely to view significant change in personal or social life as taking place less through gaining mastery over the internal or external causes of behavior than through reinterpreting and reevaluating the meanings and goals that channel our living.

To insist that the social sciences should confine themselves to a knowledge of lawful regularities in human behavior and ways of maximizing mastery and control over events is not science but pure ideology. For one thing, it is a wide open question as to whether such invariant regularities exist at all. Kenneth Gergen (1982) asserted that a

> fundamental difference exists between the bulk of the phenomena of concern to the natural as opposed to the sociobehavioral scientist. . . . [T]here appears to be little justification for the immense effort devoted to the empirical substantiation of fundamental laws of human conduct. There would seem to be few patterns of human action, regardless of their durability to date, that are not subject to significant alteration. (p. 12)

In any case, to place an overriding emphasis on reengineering human behavior in more effective or efficient ways is not dictated by reality or science—it is a moral choice. If so, then the recent movements in psychology of *technical eclecticism* and *empirically supported treatments*, which try to identify therapy techniques that are most effective for specific problems, represent not value-neutral science but a philosophical and moral stance. As Slife et al. (2003) put it, there is "no empirical justification for empiricism, no scientific validation for science" (p. 60).

Another strategy for preserving value-neutrality is to adopt a thoroughgoing relativism concerning values, holding that "therapists ought to be nonjudgmental and nonpartisan about the values their clients should have" (Slife et al., 2003, p. 61). Of course, this approach shipwrecks on the paradox of morally enjoining therapists to be neutral! The obligation to approach clients in a nonjudgmental manner is anything but neutral. To be tolerant or open to someone's values is to endorse the values of tolerance and openness. More than that, it seems clear that therapists who adopt relativism are going to more or less subtly steer their clients in the direction of these values. Most of them will interpret the problems of someone who is dogmatic and closed-minded as a symptom, in part, of their inability to endorse and practice tolerance and openness. In many cases, that may be appropriate. But what happened to value-neutrality? In the same vein, it has been argued that advocates of the very popular multiculturalism movement in psychology are famous for adamantly, at times outright dogmatically, insisting on the relativistic tolerance of diverse worldviews (Fowers & Richardson, 1996).

Objectivism and relativism may appear to be polar opposite viewpoints, but like so many antagonists, their opposition covers over the fact that they share some key underlying assumptions and values. They both tacitly assume that *either* we have pristine, timeless standards of truth and goodness *or* we have no valid standards at all for judging scientific or ethical merit (Bernstein, 1983). Much of modern culture has been marked by this kind of "give me certainty or give me death" attitude, which upon reflection seems to be neither realistic, mature, nor wise. In the real world of both scientific practice and the moral life, we always have to make do without final or certain truth, our understanding or insights improve fitfully (it is hoped) over time, and our imperfect standards themselves have to be thrashed out in a concrete, practical, often intuitive process of living that we can never fully objectify or control (Gadamer, 1960/1989; Heidegger, 1962). We arrive at many important insights with our whole being, so to speak, not just cerebral activity.

Also, both objectivism and relativism portray human agents as disconnected or detached from their cultural and moral values in a way that just does not ring true. We do not possess our basic moral convictions so much as they possess us. They define us as historical and cultural beings. We cannot simply reject them because a supposedly objective social science finds evidence to the contrary. If it were discovered that values of honesty and integrity were associated with greater stress and decreased longevity, we likely would not abandon those values but reevaluate the price of living a decent life.[4] And we cannot treat our most sincere ideals, as relativists tend to do, as mere preferences or "lifestyle choices" that we can discard relatively easily when our goals or tastes happen to alter. Thus, we cannot be absolutely tolerant without, as the saying goes, being so open-minded that our brains fall out.

Individualism

How did psychology become embroiled in such a paradoxical understanding of values and their role in life? Slife et al. (2003, p. 56) pointed us in the right direction by noting that the ideal of value-neutrality, along with the doctrines of objectivism and relativism that are used to shore up this ideal, are a product of modern culture's profound reaction against what it saw as arbitrary, tyrannical abuses of power in earlier times, and against the dogmatic, absolutist belief systems that justified or rationalized tyranny and oppression. It has seemed to many that the only way to avoid these abuses is to allow our beliefs and values to be justified only by pristine objective methods, or perhaps to get rid of false authority by undermining all authority—perhaps, thereby, throwing out the baby with the bath water—with a thoroughgoing relativism. I would like to develop this idea by suggesting that psychology and psychotherapy as we know them are animated at their core by a moral outlook and ethical program often termed *individualism* or *liberal individualism* that supplies much of the cultural force of the modern therapy enterprise (Bellah, Madsen, Sullivan, Swidler, & Tipton, 1985; Richardson, Fowers, & Guignon, 1999). Liberal individualism's many virtues together with its notable ethical blind spots help explain what has troubled many critics, even if they admired it, about modern psychology.

From Premodern to Modern

It is essential to recall the historical rise of individualism to its intellectual and moral ascendancy in today's world. Most of us have a sense of how people in premodern or traditional societies took for granted that they belonged to a hierarchical and meaningful cosmic drama or order of being. As a result, men and women acquire meaningful roles to play in everyday life as well as the cosmic plane. They acquire what Anton Antonovsky (1979, p. 23) called "a sense of coherence" that helps make "affectively comprehensible" the uncontrollable and tragic aspects of human life. The collapse of the traditional vision of a meaningful cosmic order went hand in hand with

---

[4]Or, we might refine or adjust our ideals because they really do seem to cause pointless pain and suffering. These are matters of judgment of the sort I am suggesting we can neither make with certainty nor excuse ourselves from making. The main point is, however, that we would not allow our ideals to modify simply *because* they involved painful or inconvenient consequences. The testimony of the ages is not only that there can be meaning in suffering but that suffering is inevitable and there may be no deeper or lasting meaningfulness without learning from it.

the rise of what we might call the "objectifying outlook of modern science" (Richardson et al., 1999, p. 32). Much of natural science proceeds by ignoring or abstracting away from the rich appearance of things, including the values and meaningful relationships of our ordinary experience. By doing so, science can regard the world in an objectified way, as made up of inherently meaningless objects in causal interaction with one another—a "disenchanted" universe, as Max Weber famously put it.

The corollary of this kind of objectivity is subjectivity. Now our experiences of things like beauty, relevance to our purposes, and goodness are regarded as merely human fabrications, products of our varying interpretations and purposes, which must be located in and confined to a private, purely subjective realm. This idea of subjectivity gives birth to our distinctive modern emphasis on personal inwardness and inward depths, which is enriching but also tends to leave us deeply disconnected from one another and the social world. This new picture of things is sometimes called a *subject–object ontology*, an outlook on the world that underpins and shapes much of our modern way of life. But it may also significantly distort human experience. Our concrete existence of intertwined lives, shared purposes, and moral struggles is still there, even if it is ignored or set aside in the pursuit of one narrow, albeit valuable, kind of knowledge.

This new scientific outlook and subject–object ontology reinforces and is reinforced by the distinctive moral temper of the modern age, one we might describe as *antiauthoritarian* and *emancipatory*. The concept of a disengaged subject of scientific knowledge confronting a separate material universe greatly resembles the moral ideal of the autonomous and free modern individual who distances herself or himself from the past and the social world and seeks above all "to be self-responsible, to rely on one's own judgment, to find one's purpose in oneself" (Taylor, 1995, p. 7). Commitment to resisting arbitrary authority and an unyielding insistence on respect for the dignity and rights of every individual set an ethical standard that we still strive to attain. This approach makes people the responsible center of their own moral universe. But it also risks emotional isolation and debilitating alienation by significantly downplaying lasting social ties, a sense of tradition, or wider purposes beyond individual self-realization.

The Dynamics of Liberal Individualism

Robert Coles (1980), when he toured the United States, found that no matter where he went, people were all too ready to speak in a psychologically charged vocabulary of their "problems" and "issues." "The hallmark of our time," he wrote, is "lots of psychological chatter, lots of self-consciousness, lots of 'interpretation'" (p. 189). Psychology here means "a concentration, persistent, if not feverish, upon one's thoughts, feelings, wishes, worries— bordering on, if not embracing, solipsism: the self as the only or main form of (existential) reality" (p. 189). Robert Bellah and his colleagues (Bellah et al.,

1985, p. 143) used the term *ontological individualism* to describe this widespread modern notion that the basic unit of human reality is the individual person, who is assumed to exist and have determinate characteristics prior to and independent of his or her social existence. Social systems, in this view, must be understood as artificial aggregates of individuals that are set up to satisfy the needs of those individuals. Ontological individualism serves as the cornerstone of a modern way of life with its stress on personal autonomy and self-realization, its sharp distinction between public and private realms, and its tendency to privilege and idealize relatively distant, mainly contractual ties between individuals who cooperate or compete for ultimately individual ends.

It is hard to imagine the theories and practices of 20th-century psychotherapy theory and practice without a healthy dose of ontological individualism. Robert Fancher (1995) argued that modern therapy systems claim to be based on some kind of "science" of psychopathology but in reality reflect and surreptitiously promote a particular view of the good life, a value system, or a "culture." Concerning psychoanalysis, for example, Fancher (1995) wrote:

> There is no inherent reason why internal dynamics, rather than one's place in society, must be the principle source of health or illness. For most of history, in most civilized cultures, the kind of internal fulfillment that psychoanalysis values has been suspect, and fidelity to "one's station and its duties" has generally been a higher value. (p. 124)

For some, psychoanalysis "may offer a superior way to live, or a way of living that makes more sense in a highly mobile, modern society" (Fancher, 1995, p. 125). But psychoanalysts promulgate "a set of values that they rarely defend on moral or social grounds—though the moral and social ramifications of these values are immense." Instead, they deceptively justify these values by claiming "that this is what 'health' is" (p. 125).

However, it must be emphasized that there is more to the modern outlook and modern ethics than just ontological individualism. Modern individualism, or liberal individualism[5], typically counterbalances its heavy stress on self-interest and self-realization with a serious ethical emphasis on regarding human agents as imbued with dignity and inherent worth, and as possessed of natural or human rights. It is clear that ontological individualism's view of things runs a high risk of deteriorating into an amoral clash of will

---

[5]It is important to remember, in the view I am taking here, that the political doctrines of the conventional liberal and conservative camps in today's politics, from this perspective, are more alike than different. They are different versions of the same underlying modern individualistic doctrine. One advocates large-scale social programs and a high degree of personal or lifestyle autonomy, the other stresses reliance on broad market forces and celebrates individual economic freedom. Both political viewpoints make individuals and individual freedom or rights the cornerstone of their approach, even though they cannot ever agree on what that freedom means or what those essential rights are. Both tend to rely on large-scale impersonal mechanisms, either the state or market, to sort out our differences, and downplay more traditional notions of community, civil society, or reasoning together about the public interest or common good (Etzioni, 1996; Sarason, 1986; Wolfe, 1989).

against will, power against power. To prevent such a calamity, the modern moral outlook supplements an uncompromising stress on autonomy and self-interest with a serious commitment to respecting individual dignity and rights. Needless to say, there is considerable tension between these two ethical poles of radical self-interest and deep obligation to respecting the rights of others. We experience this tension in different ways quite often in everyday life.

Liberal individualism links together the ideals of self-interest and respect for the rights of others in a unique modern approach to ethics. First formulated by the philosopher Immanuel Kant, this approach centers on *formal* principles of *procedural* justice or fairness (Neal, 1990; Rawls, 1971). Such principles "constitute a fair framework within which individuals and groups can choose their own values and ends, consistent with a similar liberty for others" (Sandel, 1996, p. 11). The purpose of this scheme is to avoid designating any particular ends in living or ways of life as superior while still assuring respect for individuals and their choices. In the mental health arena, we adopt this approach by talking about more or less "effective" therapeutic means to reaching ends that we often label *health* or *well-being*, as if these ends were purely given by nature or chosen by clients without any outside influence. We maintain *both* our neutrality about others' choices *and* our dedication to their welfare by obscuring how much "health" is always, in part, defined by cultural and moral norms, and how much we influence clients in adopting or reworking the meanings they live by (Christopher, 1999; Fancher, 1995; Richardson et al., 1999). These meanings are assumed to exist inside the client, rather than being something constructed in interaction with others and given shape in the social world. Therapists who think in these terms can blithely assume that they are merely facilitating a natural developmental process that is unaffected by their personal influence. However, as Hoffman (1998) observed, this is simply not the case:

> When we interpret the transference, we like to think that we are merely bringing to the surface what is already "there," rather than that we are cultivating something in the patient and in the relationship that might not have developed in the same way otherwise . . . our hands are not clean. (p. 109)

Liberal individualism represents a sincere effort to affirm freedom without dissolving responsibility, or to eliminate dogmatism without abandoning our moral duties to others. Nevertheless, this approach is one-sided. It is embroiled in the paradox of advocating (as we have seen) a thoroughgoing *neutrality* toward all values as a way of *promoting* certain basic values of liberty, tolerance, and human rights. Justice is strictly procedural, which means that the focus is on *formal* rules or codes that we hope will protect our rights and prerogatives while ensuring that no one can define the good life for anyone else. However, there is reason to worry that if we cannot reason together meaningfully about the worth of ends, we also cannot defend liberal individualism's own vision of a way of life characterized by dignity and re-spect (Sullivan, 1986, p. 39). A serious commitment to human dignity and rights clearly sketches out a way of life that is taken to be morally superior or *good in itself*. But what is to prevent a principled neutrality toward all notions of the good life from extending to those basic values of liberty and human dignity as well, undermining their credibility, and stripping them of any pos-sibility of rational defense (Kolakowski, 1986; Sarason, 1986)? A slide to-ward moral relativism and social fragmentation seems inevitable.

On a practical level, liberal individualism's insistent characterization of human action and motivation as exclusively self-interested is very likely a self-fulfilling prophecy. The direct pursuit of security and happiness seems progressively to dissolve the capacity to respect and cherish others (Bell, 1978, p. xv ff). It erodes our capacity for devotion not just to traditional values of the sort Jerome Frank (1978) mentioned, such as "the redemptive power of suffering" and "self-restraint and moderation" (p. 7), but even to the best modern ideals of freedom and justice as well. In the opinion of many thoughtful critics from Tocqueville to the present day, those ideals by them-selves engender a social order that is too "thin" to ensure even their own survival. According to Michael Sandel (1996), the individualistic public philosophy by which we live "cannot secure the liberty it promises, because it cannot inspire the sense of community and civic engagement that liberty requires" (p. 6).

Psychology and Disguised Ideology

Over the course of the modern era, individualism appears to have taken several distinct forms. I suggest that these types of individualism, their strengths and weaknesses alike, form "disguised ideologies" (Bernstein, 1983) that supply a great deal of the conceptual and moral underpinnings of con-temporary psychotherapies. Bellah et al. (1985) identified two main forms of individualism in modern times. The first they term *utilitarian individualism*, which "takes as given certain basic human appetites and fears . . . and sees human life as an effort by individuals to maximize their self-interest relative to these given ends" (p. 336). It assumes that the ends of human life are either inbuilt pleasures and satisfactions or whatever goals or desires we just happen to prefer. Human thought and action are essentially tools for effec-tively and efficiently pursuing survival, security, and satisfaction. The ego in Freudian or classical psychoanalytic theory is almost a pure utilitarian, prag-matic calculator of such limited gratifications as are possible under the heavy constraints of social living. Interestingly, even though the behavioral and cognitive therapies are often sharp antagonists of psychoanalytic theory and practices, a utilitarian individualist vision also seems to lie at their core, con-cerned as they are with more effective controlling or self-controlling sequences of behavior and thought.

The second form of individualism Bellah et al. (1985) identified is *expressive individualism*, which is guided by the belief that "each person has a unique core of feeling and intuition that should unfold or be expressed if individuality is to be realized" (p. 334). It arose out of the Romantic movement of the late 18th and 19th century as a reaction against the overly rationalistic, calculating, deadening aspects of utilitarian views and has reverberated throughout our culture down to the present day. Romanticism celebrates closeness to nature, instinct, mythical consciousness, and beauty and art. Romantic notions have a large presence in the world of psychotherapy. They are client-centered, humanistic, Gestalt, and a host of therapeutic approaches. They are expressed richly in Heinz Kohut's rebellion against the classical Freudian viewpoint. His ideas resonate with a contemporary sensibility so much that if Kohut, too, had not existed, he probably would have had to be invented. In Kohut's (1977) theory, the self, far from the beleaguered, calculating ego that Freud depicted, becomes, if properly nurtured, an artist of its own life. The self follows a universal "narcissistic line of development" (p. 54) from birth to maturity. Its goal is a "healthy narcissism" that includes pride, assertiveness, vitality, joyfulness, creativity, and, eventually, mature wisdom and acceptance of one's mortality. Both meaningful social ties and life-guiding values play a more significant role in Kohut's view than Freud's, because empathic parental "self-objects" are essential to this development and "twinship experiences" with others are an enduring part of a full life. But such relationships and values seem to many (Cushman, 1990; Eagle, 1984) to serve mainly as means to the end of self-enhancement, or what Kohut (1977) called an "intensification of the inner life" (p. 139).

I suggest that there is a third type of modern individualism that figures prominently in therapy theory and practice. Let us call it *existential individualism*. Like the expressive variety, it represents a protest against the scientism, technicism, and conformism in modern society. But existential individualism also is skeptical of the expressivist idea of getting in touch with core feelings or impulses as the main way to find integrity and direction in life. Sartre's (1956) classic formulation of existential freedom involves repudiating any notion of pregiven inner directives or objective values as inauthentic "bad faith." Instead, we can take a kind of total responsibility for the de facto basic choices that "invent" the ultimate values and "fundamental project" of our lives as a whole. Indeed, we should strive to realize both our own practical freedom and that of all others as well. Numerous modern therapy theories incorporate a version of this ideal of existential freedom, including Gestalt therapy and many influential "existential" accounts of psychotherapy (May, 1958; Yalom, 1980). For example, Roy Schafer's (1976) radical revision of psychoanalytic theory incorporates an interesting and original version of existential philosophy. Schafer argued that psychoanalysis must ground itself in an "action language" that more fully captures the dynamic of lived experience. Schafer rejected the tendency of many therapy theories to (a) "disown responsibility" for our actions by attributing them to inner or outer causes other than our own choice—"my feelings or hang-ups made me do it"—and insisted that we should (b) accept our ultimate responsibility as authors of ourselves, others, and our world through what he called "optional ways of telling the stories of human lives" (p. 41). Schafer celebrated the "joyfulness" and "integrity" this kind of freedom and autonomy can bring.

Elsewhere (Richardson & Zeddies, 2001), I have argued that influential new postmodern or social constructionist views in psychology (e.g., Gergen, 1985; Gergen & Kaye, 1992; McNamee & Gergen, 1992) reflect many of the themes of existential individualism. To be sure, these theorists often sharply criticize what they call *self-contained individualism*. They argue that there is no universal, decontextualized self or truth about the self. Rather, notions of self and world, as well as all the meanings or values we live by, are social artifacts that are not grounded in any kind of transcendent realities, natural or ethical, but are endlessly shaped and reshaped through ongoing "negotiations of meaning" in social life. Contrary to modern individualism, constructionist thinkers stress how deeply we are embedded in and shaped by history and culture. However, they insist that the only basis for evaluating our beliefs or values, in everyday life, science, or psychotherapy, is according to their "pragmatic implications" (Gergen, 1985, p. 275). Any claim to hold "true" moral beliefs or values only gets in the way of what truly "works" in the business of living. One difficulty with this view is that the agent of such purely pragmatic calculations sounds very much like a sovereign, disengaged modern self. Indeed, the kind of choice of values and goals in living they recommend seems to closely resemble the highly individualistic sort of radical freedom touted by existentialists like Sartre.[6] Another problem is that constructionist writers give every evidence that they believe strongly their view of things is truly liberating and the most conducive to human happiness and well-being! In this way, they seem to reproduce the paradox of ethical commitment to value-neutrality in a new form.

Instrumentalism

Finally, it seems to me that another crucial, usually taken-for-granted assumption of much modern psychology might be labeled *instrumentalism*. No one has analyzed instrumentalism and its effects in our civilization more astutely than the critical theorist Jürgen Habermas. According to Habermas, modern society to a great extent is built on a harmful confusion of *praxis* with *techne*, Greek words meaning roughly culturally meaningful activities and

---

[6]Thus, Jane Flax (1990) pointed out inconsistencies in the work of postmodern thinkers who claim to dismantle modern notions of selfhood but still embrace a profoundly modern romantic/aesthetic vision of the "constant remaking of the self" (p. 216). They "presuppose a socially isolated and individualistic view of the self" that seems impossible to reconcile "with, for example, the care of children or with participation in a political community" (p. 217).

technical capacity. Specifically, we tend to collapse the cultural and moral dimensions of life into merely technical and instrumental considerations. As a result, according to Habermas (1973, p. 254), we imagine applying theory to practice chiefly as a matter of applying principles uncovered by empirical science in a manipulative or instrumental manner to gain control over natural and social processes and produce desired results. Unfortunately, according to Habermas, even as we grow in instrumental prowess, we progressively lose our ability to evaluate the worth of ends on any basis other than the sheer, arbitrary fact that they are preferred or desired. We become adept at discerning means–ends relationships and performing cost–benefit analyses, but weaken our ability to reason together about the inherent quality of our way of life and about what goals or ends we might best seek. I believe that Habermas has identified a principle source of the social fragmentation, loss of community, and increased sense of personal alienation complained about by so many cultural critics over the last century.

More than half a century ago, Erich Fromm (1941/1969) richly portrayed the kind of personal disorientation that accompanies a hyper-instrumentalized, turbo-capitalist way of life, something he thought was a major source of emotional problems in living in our day. Discussing what he called the *ambiguity of freedom* in modern times, Fromm argued that we have a well-developed sense of "freedom from" arbitrary authority and from dogmatic or irrational impediments to freedom and to exercising greater control over nature and ourselves. However, we sorely lack a corresponding sense of "freedom to" or "freedom for" that would give some context, direction, or deeper purpose to our increased freedom and opportunity. The result, Fromm felt, is that we tend to become interchangeable cogs in the social machinery, to become directionless and empty, to be led by the nose by whatever "sells" in the marketplace, including a widespread "personality market" in which even personal qualities must be revised to accommodate the impulses or preferences of others, and to treat others and ourselves as depersonalized objects. Hungry for substance but unable to find it, in Fromm's view, we tend to sell out our freedom to fascism, fanaticism, the illusion of total fulfillment in romantic love, craving and seeking the approval of others at all costs, numerous escapisms, or just going shopping.

A problematic instrumentalism, I believe, shows up at the heart of psychotherapy theories and practices. Those theories and approaches colored by utilitarian individualism clearly give prominence to a calculating, means–end rationality that may expand our mastery in important ways (like assertive training, new techniques for curtailing obsessive thoughts, and others) but can undermine our ability to evaluate the worth of the ends we seek, to set priorities and needed limits in personal and social life, and to achieve integrity as well as mastery in living. Expressive individualism tends to view the world and others very heavily as aids or impediments to our projects and self-actualization. This cuts against the grain of our common sense notion of moral commitment as something, in part, that sets a limit to the exercise of our freedom. By itself, self-actualization of this sort seems insufficient for overcoming egoism, resolving conflict, and achieving lasting social ties among mature individuals.

Existential individualism does argue, admirably, for the need for a more substantial kind of authenticity and integrity in an impersonal, highly bureaucratized world. However, in line with Fromm's critique, existential thinkers seem much clearer about what they are *against* than what they are *for*. They oppose arbitrary authority and copping out on one's responsibilities, but they offer no way to articulate the superiority of one way of life over another. In the end, radical choice of our ultimate values seems to come down to simply registering brute preferences or just arbitrarily settling on one option over others (Guignon, 1986). In fact, there seems to be no good reason, from within this perspective, why we *should* elect a life of authenticity or integrity at all, or even why we *should* nurture our own or others' existential freedom. Such wide open options undermine meaningful choice, not enhance it, and would seem actually to erode genuine autonomy over the long run.

The theory and discourse of modern psychotherapy are pervaded with instrumental terminology, like *mastery, effectiveness, reality testing, control, management, function*, and a host of others. We are comfortable with such language and concepts because in many ways instrumentalism in the sense of enhanced control, efficiency, and security are our credo in modern times. But a one-sided instrumentalism would seem to reinforce some of the worst moral blind spots in our kind of society and help foster many of the emotional problems in living that people characteristically develop in such a way of life. The following chapter argues, as well, that the instrumental view fails to capture the reality of good psychotherapy, which is as least as much about finding ends or goals in living that are worthy or meaningful in themselves as about finding means to whatever ends we just happen to desire. I have no doubt that good therapists appreciate this fact and have enough of what the next chapter calls *practical wisdom* to help clients find greater integrity, authenticity, and responsibility in living, not just raw effectiveness in controlling circumstances or outcomes. But I think we all suffer because we are so inarticulate about such practical wisdom and the good life. Often, it seems to me, therapists are forced to discuss values and directions in living with their clients in coarse, politically correct, and rather narrow terms like greater *realism* or enhanced *self-efficacy* when they are trying in part to identify and nurture character strengths and greater maturity in the face of life's joys and tragedies.

CONCLUSION

Value-freedom, individualism, and instrumentalism involve interlocking assumptions and values. A perhaps reactive or one-sided individualism embraces value-freedom to protect individuals from cultural and moral entanglements that may all too easily revert to dogmatism and domination. Also, it welcomes the idea of casting the relations between individuals and their world in largely instrumental terms, because this view seems to empower individuals, support their autonomy, and further protect them from unwanted or unjust intrusion by others or the state. But many critics have argued that this complex of ideas and values is too thin an ethical credo to live by. It is too thin to support even its own best values and is somewhat self-undermining over time.

William Doherty (1995) argued that modern psychology and psychotherapy have adopted as their own much of the overweening individualism and instrumentalism described in this chapter and, therefore, that they inadvertently perpetuate some of their less desirable features. Doherty felt that 20th-century psychotherapy approaches, by and large, enshrine ideals of autonomy and self-realization that have often served well to liberate people from a narrow ethic of blind self-sacrifice and inauthenticity. In what he called the "golden years" of psychotherapy from the 1960s into the 1980s, therapists commonly "saw the oppressiveness of cultural norms dressed up as moral principles" and saw "themselves as agents of emancipation" (Doherty, 1995, p. 11). Psychology and psychologists often scoff at what they see as conventional morality, he noted, but generally afford little to put in its place. Therefore, they tend to foster, or at least not deter, our slide into what has famously been described as a "culture of narcissism" (Lasch, 1978), with its irresponsible "nonjudgmentalism," excessive self-preoccupation, decay of community, and neglect of obligations to family and others that are often "followed by justifications based on personal entitlement, doing one's own thing, or victimization" (Doherty, 1995, p. 11). During psychotherapy's golden years, Doherty suggested, we were still able to do much good because, however imperfect, many of the "moral rules of conventional society . . . could be counted on to provide the scaffolding upon which the client could build a more authentic life." Unfortunately, by "the 1990's . . . whatever has served as the moral center of mainstream culture seems not to be holding" (p. 11).

How might psychology and psychotherapy best respond to these human and cultural dilemmas? I believe it is important to appreciate how limited are the conventional tools of the mental health establishment for making a dent in this problem. Far more narcissistic personality disorders are being produced by our culture on an annual basis than can ever be treated by available counselors and therapists—and their treatment is typically protracted, difficult, and of uncertain outcome. Moreover, a somewhat weakened or depleted culture often makes personal change difficult for clients in general and therapeutic endeavor less rewarding for therapists, to boot. We would do well to heed the words of Augsburger (1986), who noted that one helpful way to think of psychotherapy and counseling is as a "sanctioned retreat" from "the normal social obligations and from the social, spiritual, and communal context" to which the patient or client must return. However, he cautioned, if "there is no moral context from which to distance oneself in times of personal transformation, and none to rejoin," then both therapist and patient "suffer from confusion, isolation, and a loss of healing power" (p. 352).

I have argued (see Zeddies & Richardson, 1999) that the therapy context is not the main or best setting in which to explore ways to revitalize our way of life. That is a matter for citizens, including psychologists and therapists, who in the coming decades "may have to give as much attention to restoring the cultural and moral context of the therapy they offer as to therapy itself" (p. 598). But it seems likely that there will always be a genuine need for various kinds of counseling and therapy in a dynamic, pluralistic world such as ours. Therefore, it is just as important for therapists qua therapists as it is for ordinary citizens and those with greater influence to pay attention to issues of character, community, and the pursuit of cultural and moral excellence. The following chapter explores some ways that might be done.

REFERENCES

American Psychological Association. (2002). Ethical principles of psychologists and code of conduct. *American Psychologist, 57,* 1060–1073.

Antonovsky, A. (1979). *Health, stress, and coping.* San Francisco: Jossey-Bass.

Augsburger, D. (1986). *Pastoral counseling across cultures.* Philadelphia: Westminster Press.

Bell, D. (1978). *The cultural contradictions of capitalism.* New York: Basic Books.

Bellah, R., Madsen, R., Sullivan, W., Swidler, A., & Tipton, S. (1985). *Habits of the heart: Individualism and community in American life.* Berkeley: University of California Press.

Berger, P. (1977). *Facing up to modernity.* New York: Basic Books.

Bernstein, R. J. (1983). *Beyond objectivism and relativism.* Philadelphia: University of Pennsylvania Press.

Beutler, L., & Bergan, J. (1991). Value change in counseling and psychotherapy: A search for scientific credibility. *Journal of Consulting and Clinical Psychology, 43,* 16–24.

Christopher, J. (1999). Situating psychological well-being: Exploring the cultural roots of its theory and research. *Journal of Counseling & Development, 77,* 141–152.

Coles, R. (1980, Summer). Civility and psychology. *Daedalus, 109*(3), 136–137.

Cushman, P. (1990). Why the self is empty. *American Psychologist, 45,* 599–611.

Cushman, P. (2002). How psychology erodes personhood. *Journal of Theoretical and Philosophical Psychology, 22,* 101–113.

Doherty, W. (1995). *Soul searching: Why psychotherapy must promote moral responsibility.* New York: Basic Books.

Eagle, M. (1984). *Recent developments in psychoanalysis.* New York: McGraw-Hill.

Etzioni, A. (1996). *The new golden rule: Morality and community in a democratic society.* New York: Basic Books.

Fancher, R. (1995). *Cultures of healing: Correcting the image of American mental health care.* New York: Freeman.

Flax, J. (1990). *Thinking fragments: Psychoanalysis, terminism, and postmodernism in the contemporary west.* Berkley: University of California Press.

Fowers, B., & Richardson, F. C. (1996). Why is multiculturalism good? *American Psychologist, 51,* 609–621.

Frank, J. (1978). *Psychotherapy and the human predicament.* New York: Schocken.

Fromm, E. (1969). *Escape from freedom.* New York: Avon. (Original work published 1941)

Gadamer, H.-G. (1989). *Truth and method* (2nd ed., rev.) (J. Weinsheimer & D. Marshall, Trans.). New York: Continuum. (Original work published 1960)

Gergen, K. (1982). *Toward transformation in social knowledge.* New York: Springer-Verlag.

Gergen, K. (1985). The social constructionist movement in modern psychology. *American Psychologist, 40,* 266–275.

Gergen, K., & Kaye, J. (1992). Beyond narrative in the negotiation of therapeutic meaning. In S. McNamee & K. Gergen (Eds.), *Therapy as social construction* (pp. 166–185). London: Sage.

Guignon, C. (1986). Existentialist ethics. In J. DeMarco & R. Fox (Eds.), *New directions in ethics: The challenge of applied ethics* (pp. 73–91). New York: Routledge & Kegan Paul.

Habermas, J. (1973). *Theory and practice.* Boston: Beacon Press.

Heidegger, M. (1962). *Being and time.* New York: Harper & Row.

Hillman, J., & Ventura, M. (1992). *We've had a hundred years of psychotherapy and the world's getting worse.* San Francisco: HarperCollins.

Hoffman, I. Z. (1998). *Ritual and spontaneity in the psychoanalytic process: A dialectical–constructivist view.* Hillsdale, NJ: Analytic Press.

Kelly, T. (1990). The role of values in psychotherapy: A critical review of process and outcome effects. *Clinical Psychology Review, 10,* 171–186.

Kelly, T., & Strupp, H. (1992). Patient and therapist values in psychotherapy: Perceived changes, assimilation, similarity, and outcome. *Journal of Consulting and Clinical Psychology, 60,* 34–40.

Kohut, H. (1977). *The restoration of the self.* New York: International Universities Press.

Kolakowski, L. (1986, June 16). The idolatry of politics. *The New Republic,* pp. 29–36.

Kuhn, T. (1970). *The structure of scientific revolutions* (2nd ed.). Chicago: University of Chicago Press.

Lasch, C. (1978). *The culture of narcissism.* New York: Norton.

Lowe, C. (1976). *Value orientations in counseling and psychotherapy: The meanings of mental health* (2nd ed.). Cranston, RI: Carroll Press.

May, R. (1958). Contributions of existential psychotherapy. In R. May, E. Angel, & H. F. Ellenberger (Eds.), *Existence: A new dimension in psychiatry and psychology* (pp. 3–42). New York: Basic Books.

McNamee, S., & Gergen, K. (1992). *Therapy as social construction*. London: Sage.

Meehl, P. (1959). Some technical and axiological problems in the therapeutic handling of religious and valuational material. *Journal of Counseling Psychology, 6,* 255–259.

Neal, P. (1990). Justice as fairness. *Political Theory, 18,* 24–50.

Rawls, J. (1971). *A theory of justice*. Cambridge, MA: Harvard University Press.

Richardson, F., Fowers, B., & Guignon, C. (1999). *Re-envisioning psychology: Moral dimensions of theory and practice*. San Francisco: Jossey-Bass.

Richardson, F., & Zeddies, T. (2001). Individualism and modern psychotherapy. In B. Slife, R. Williams, & S. Barlow (Eds.), *Critical issues in psychotherapy: Translating new ideas into practice* (pp. 147–164). Thousand Oaks, CA: Sage.

Rieff, P. (1966). *The triumph of the therapeutic*. New York: HarperCollins.

Root, M. (1993). *Philosophy of social science*. Oxford, England: Blackwell.

Sandel, M. (1996). *Democracy's discontent: America in search of a public philosophy*. Cambridge, MA: Belknap/Harvard University Press.

Sarason, S. (1986). And what is the public interest? *American Psychologist, 41,* 899–905.

Sartre, J. (1956). *Being and nothingness*. New York: Philosophical Library.

Schafer, R. (1976). *A new language for psychoanalysis*. New Haven, CT: Yale University Press.

Schumaker, J. (2001). *The age of insanity: Modernity and mental health*. Westport, CT: Praeger Publishers.

Slife, B., Smith, A., & Burchfield, C. (2003). Psychotherapists as crypto-missionaries: An exemplar on the crossroads of history, theory, and philosophy. In D. Hill & M. Krall (Eds.), *About psychology: At the crossroads of history, theory, and philosophy* (pp. 55–72). Albany: State University of New York Press.

Sullivan, W. (1986). *Reconstructing public philosophy*. Berkeley: University of California Press.

Taylor, C. (1985). *Philosophy and the human sciences: Philosophical papers* (Vol. 2). Cambridge, England: Cambridge University Press.

Taylor, C. (1995). *Philosophical arguments*. Cambridge, MA: Harvard University Press.

Tjeltveit, A. (1986). The ethic of value conversion in psychotherapy: Appropriate and inappropriate therapist on client values. *Clinical Psychology Review, 6,* 515–537.

Tjeltveit, A. (1999). *Ethics and values in psychotherapy*. London: Routledge.

Wolfe, A. (1989). *Whose keeper? Social science and moral obligation*. Berkeley: University of California Press.

Yalom, I. (1980). *Existential psychotherapy*. New York: Basic Books.

Zeddies, T., & Richardson, F. (1999). Analytic authority in historical and critical perspective: Beyond objectivism and relativism. *Contemporary Psychoanalysis, 35,* 581–601.

2

PSYCHOTHERAPY, CHARACTER, AND THE GOOD LIFE

BLAINE J. FOWERS

Thinking critically about psychotherapy is a complex endeavor, given its multiplicity of voices and varied manifestations and ramifications. In the previous chapter, Richardson zeroed in on several key assumptions that seem to undergird much psychotherapeutic theory and practice, particularly instrumentalism and various forms of individualism. He showed that these value biases constitute a modern cultural morality that contradicts the self-described objectivity of classical conceptions of psychotherapy. Moreover, he argued that individualism itself might be the source of many of the difficulties that psychotherapy seeks to ameliorate. To the degree that the anxiety, depression, relationship difficulties, and other maladies are outgrowths of this individualism, current approaches to psychotherapy might make matters worse rather than better.

My goal in this chapter is to offer a reformulation of psychotherapy that allows us to move beyond the paradoxes that result from the attempt to create a value-neutral psychotherapy and from our focus on freedom from interference. This alternative reinterprets the aim of psychotherapy as a process of helping clients to cultivate the best in themselves and to live the best kind of life available to them. I present this as a frankly moral dialogue, in which therapists assist clients to pursue the worthwhile aims clients identify. I argue that we do not find the best kind of life in private satisfactions, but in participation in shared endeavors that imbue our lives with significance and make it possible to attain the kind of goods that we can only hold in common with others (e.g., friendship, harmony, democracy). Virtue ethics, an ancient approach to living well that has undergone a significant renaissance in recent years, provides the framework for this reinterpretation. My reformulation of psychotherapy has two aims: to capture what is best in therapeutic practice as it is and to illuminate some generally neglected dimensions of human flourishing to which therapists should attend. Thus, some of this reformulation will look familiar, even if presented in a new light, and some of it will suggest new therapeutic foci and activities.

DEFINING VIRTUE

Aristotle initiated virtue ethics proper in the 4th century B.C.E. He begins his famous inquiry in the *Nicomachean Ethics* (Aristotle, 1998) with a focus on living the best kind of life as a human being. I will have much more to say about it below, but roughly speaking, living well involves the full expression of our human capacities for reason, choice, and social engagement. Virtues such as generosity, honesty, and courage are the character traits that make it possible to pursue what is good in life. From this point of view, psychotherapy can be seen as a process in which individuals reflect on and alter their way of living to be better able to seek what they see as genuinely good. The pursuit of these goods becomes a matter of becoming the kind of person who is capable of succeeding in those endeavors.

The *Nicomachean Ethics* provides the groundwork for applying a virtue framework for psychotherapy. In this chapter, I discuss six interwoven themes of virtue and relate them to psychotherapy. Virtue ethics portrays human activity as (a) pursuing what we see as worthwhile goals, (b) which requires virtues or well-established patterns of character. (c) Virtues manifest themselves behaviorally in actions (d) that are pursued willingly and spontaneously, (e) based on a clear understanding of how best to act. (f) Enacting virtues involves wise choices about how to pursue the good in specific circumstances. Thus, virtue is multifaceted, with dispositional, goal-directed, behavioral, affective, cognitive, and wisdom-based aspects. One of the interesting features of a virtue framework for psychotherapy is that the development of good character is equally important for both therapists and clients.

There are many traditions from which we could draw for a definition of virtue, including warrior societies like the Lakota (Sioux) and Homeric Greeks, Eastern traditions such as the Buddhist and Confucian views, and more recent Christian and Victorian versions. I have chosen to focus on Aristotle for several reasons. The most important is that Aristotle has the most systematic and wide-ranging account of virtue per se. His presentation of virtue and its role in human flourishing is subtle, powerful, and, in my view, unsurpassed. He is the originator of virtue theory in Western civilization, and all subsequent approaches owe a very large debt to his views. In addition, the Aristotelian tradition has received a great deal of historical and recent scholarly attention, making it a rich and well-articulated source for an examination of virtue and psychotherapy. Although Aristotle's thought was incorporated into the Judeo-Christian tradition, his views predate Christianity and modern Judaism and therefore do not rely on those religious doctrines. This chapter provides the briefest of introductions to virtue ethics in psychotherapy. (For a more thorough treatment of virtue and psychology, see Fowers, in press.) Even if expository space were unlimited, Aristotle did not have the last word on virtue and neither will I. My hope is that this chapter will encourage readers to see the contribution that virtue ethics can make and pursue this line of inquiry in their own way.

CASE EXAMPLE: JULIE'S CHOICES

Julie, a 41-year-old woman, came to therapy seeking assistance with her sense that her life was "out of control." She had been married for 15 years to Ron, and although she said that she loved him and thought that they had a good marriage, she had recently become involved with Jake, a coworker in the marketing department of a major firm. The dalliance had only just begun and was limited to a strong emotional response between them, a lot of sexual excitement, and several short instances of intense kissing and embraces. Julie said that she had not slept with Jake but that they had begun to talk about arranging an opportunity to do so. She did not want to take the affair any further, but she did not think she could decline Jake's advances much longer.

At a recent company party, Julie's husband Ron had noticed the emotional and sexual connection between her and Jake. Ron questioned her about it at length after the party. She denied any involvement with Jake, but Ron did not believe her. The conversation ended in a tense stalemate of denial and disbelief.

Julie was also troubled by a recent development in her relationship with Ron. He earned substantially more money than she did and had been paying for their household expenses. From the beginning of their marriage, they had agreed to keep their finances separate, with individual checking accounts and credit cards. This left Julie free to spend her earnings as she wished. Ron had recently developed some serious health problems and his doctor had strongly recommended that he reduce his workload in his financial advising business to avoid exacerbating his health difficulties. He asked Julie to begin to pay some of their expenses so that he could work less without impairing their financial status and plans.

She was willing to pay for more of their expenses, but she did not have the money to do so. Over time, Julie had accumulated a number of major and department store credit cards, many of which she had charged up to her credit limit. At that point, it took most of her income just to make the minimum payments. The remainder of her money went toward the lease payment on her car and incidental expenses. Ron knew that she had significant credit card debt, but she had hidden the extent of the problem from him.

Julie wanted help to regain a sense of control in her life. She felt that she was unable to manage all the important choices she had to make. She felt very badly about deceiving Ron, but she could not imagine how to talk to him about Jake and her serious financial problems. We return to Julie's struggles and growth below as a way to exemplify how the six aspects of virtue ethics can clarify her progress in psychotherapy.

VIRTUE AND THE GOOD LIFE

The most basic premise of virtue ethics is that humans are goal-seeking beings who act to accomplish meaningful aims. Virtues are the character strengths that make it possible for us to pursue characteristically human aims or goods. From this perspective, a trait is valuable to the extent that it facilitates the accomplishment of worthwhile goals. For example, most psychotherapies require the ability to reflect on oneself as an important avenue of change. The value of self-reflection is found not so much in having that ability for its own sake. Rather it is valuable as a characteristic that makes it possible to recognize which aspects of one's thinking or behavior should be changed. Because the capacity to self-reflect is helpful in pursuing our valued aims (e. g., happiness or productivity), it is a trait worth having.

Aristotle begins the *Nicomachean Ethics* with the reflection that all of our activities have some goal: The end of medicine is health, of shipbuilding a vessel, and of war victory. We engage in some of our activities for their own sake and in some activities for the sake of other aims. Both the building of warships and the exercise of courage in battle serve the higher end of victory in war and ultimately security for the state and the populace. Another example of this is that psychotherapists seek to help clients change some aspect of their thinking or acting as a way to improve self-esteem, reduce depression, and so forth. Changing one's cognitions or behavior requires the capacity for taking responsibility for oneself. Clients who blame others for their problems have to learn first how to recognize and accept their responsibility for their own choices and actions before it is possible for them to change. We have now identified two "virtues" of standard psychotherapy: the capacities for self-reflection and self-responsibility.

The abilities to self-reflect and to take responsibility for oneself serve higher order goals, such as being able to work productively to earn money, pay one's bills, manage a household, and so on. These intermediate goals make it possible to own a home, which in turn provides the private space we see as important for living well. These aims are arranged in a hierarchy in that we seek some goals primarily for the sake of others.

Flourishing

Aristotle claims that there is a highest good, which is the aim that we seek only for its own sake and not for the sake of any other good. He calls the ultimate good in life *flourishing*, which is not just a positive feeling or even an overall sense of well-being (Broadie, 1991; Hursthouse, 1999). Mere emotional well-being cannot suffice as the human good because our affect is so changeable. It seems obvious that managing a fragile sense of happiness is insufficient as an ultimate aim in our lives. Aristotle defines flourishing as an activity rather than a subjective experience. His point is that living the best kind of life is a matter of acting in the best ways possible as a human being. In other words, living well in general has similar formal properties to understanding what it is to be a good musician or a good carpenter. Excellence in music or carpentry means that one is able to *do* these activities in an excellent manner. Similarly, we find the human good in acting with excellence in characteristically human activities.

We find what is good neither in an ethereal, otherworldly experience nor in pleasures taken as a reward for and respite from ordinary tasks. Flourishing is thoroughly intertwined with our everyday lives, with our work and our leisure, our personal relationships and our public involvements. Virtue ethics focuses on *how* we participate in ordinary affairs, and those activities form an interrelated whole. We find what is good by exercising our full capacities in meaningful activity toward worthwhile aims and in the pleasure we take in that exercise and its ends. Thus, human excellence emerges in the exemplary exercise of natural human capacities.

This overt emphasis on the good we pursue as human beings runs counter to a steadfast commitment in most psychotherapy approaches to identifying and elaborating the behavioral "strategies" that promote the accomplishment of clients' self-chosen goals. The relative inattention to goals in mental health disciplines is based on the individualistic premise that ends in life are properly seen as subjective, and therapeutic attention to goals would be an unwarranted intrusion on the individual's prerogatives (Richardson, Fowers, & Guignon, 1999).

Every therapeutic approach claims to relegate goals to client choice, but this assertion is more rhetoric than reality, growing out of professionals' commitment to individualism rather than out of their actual work. Both everyday practice and common sense refute the idea that therapists can take a hands-off approach to client goals. Many clients seek therapy without clear goals in mind other than the reduction of their misery. Therapists widely recognize that it is almost impossible to accomplish goals that are conceptualized in negatives, so they must help clients to formulate a more positive goal toward which they can work. Other clients have goals that are unworkable, such as being liked by everyone or being universally successful in everything they undertake. Therapists must question such goals and help clients to reformulate them. Some clients will present goals that therapists may find ethically difficult, such as a wish to dominate others or a plan to punish an ex-spouse by refusing child-support payments. Therapists simply cannot ignore their participation in formulating client goals in these common scenarios. Attempting to downplay this important therapeutic activity illustrates the power of an individualistic ideology more than the actual process of goal setting.

Given the importance of individual autonomy in modern Western culture, frankly acknowledging therapist involvement in goal choice raises anxiety about therapeutic coercion or untoward influence. I do not believe that therapists are in the business of specifying how their clients should live and what aims they should adopt. The therapist's role in goal choice is similar to how a good friend or caring mentor might help someone to carefully consider what is possible, what is in the person's best interests, the consequences of seeking a particular goal, and what is required for pursuing particular goals. This dialogue can only occur with the client's full participation and willing agreement, but it is a joint endeavor that requires therapists' involvement. Virtue ethics highlights the therapist's role in this goal-setting guidance.

Aristotle wisely left the concept of flourishing open-ended, because no one can possibly define what is best for everyone in a final or conclusive way. Although all of us have some ideas about what is in our best interests and we pursue the aims that attend those views, it is essential to remain open to questions, challenges, and input from others. All of us can learn from other perspectives, and changing circumstances and unforeseen constraints require new insights regarding our pursuit of what is good. The key virtues for therapists in goal setting with clients are a robust recognition of our own limitations and a respect for our clients' ability to make the final choices. Interested readers can find excellent descriptions of the capacity to acknowledge one's limits and thereby avoid abusing power in Woodruff (2001) and Richardson (2003).

Individualism and the Good

The astute reader will notice that there is some similarity between the concept of flourishing and the personal growth that is so important to more humanistic forms of therapy. According to virtue ethics, however, the best kind of life is not lived or experienced as a separate individual. This perspective emphasizes the essentially social nature of humans who are born into and live within ongoing communities. As social creatures, our ability to flourish is partly dependent on our social circumstances and whether they foster the best in us and provide opportunities for us to exercise our human capacities. Because we inevitably seek our ultimate aims in our social settings, some of the most important intermediate goals we pursue are those that involve endeavors in which no one can succeed individually: good personal relationships, well-functioning communities, academic institutions that foster the shared pursuit of knowledge, and so forth. Moreover, the goods that we seek in these endeavors are also held in common with others: solidarity, democracy, truth-seeking dialogue, and so on. No one possesses a relationship, a community, democracy, or dialogue—they are shared achievements. These shared goods are only available when people are able to coordinate their aims and activities in an ongoing way and with significant concordance about what they are seeking. Thus, there is a set of goods, perhaps the most precious goods, that can only be held in common (MacIntyre, 1999). These communal goods constitute a crucial, but neglected component of a life well lived. There are many shared goods, and their obviousness renders them easy to take for granted, but virtually no one would choose to live without them.

Participation in genuinely shared goods grows out of humans' social nature, which predisposes us to long-term affiliations in families, friendship networks, communities, and tribal or national groups. Shared goods do not ensue from simple membership in any of these groups. Rather, these goods are consequent to mutual participation in ongoing practices that constitute the group in a particular way and make it possible to experience shared benefits. For example, genuinely democratic government is only possible when there are practices including regularly occurring elections, accessibility to elective office, voting, secret ballots, trustworthy vote counting, a willingness to abide by the majority decision, a loyal opposition, and so on. The goods of democratic self-rule are dependent on the degree to which citizens engage in such practices.

One of the essential aspects of shared goods is that all of the participants possess them multilaterally. For this reason, there is no competition for shared goods, and no one can possess more of them than anyone else. It is meaningless to say that I have more democracy, solidarity, or friendship than others who are involved in these shared goods. These goods only exist if we hold them in common with others.

The idea of shared goods makes it clear that in some crucial respects what is good for me is inseparable from what is good for others. There is no neat dividing line between us when it comes to living within a well-functioning community. Most citizens have to participate with goodwill in the community most of the time for it to thrive, and the flourishing of each individual citizen is to some degree dependent on the order, safety, attractiveness, and cooperativeness upheld by the community as a whole.

Unfortunately, shared goods are entirely opaque in contemporary psychotherapy, which is almost wholly oriented to portraying individuals in a self-interested manner and focusing its attention on identifying strategies that make it possible to succeed in their pursuit of individually chosen and possessed goods. This narrow disciplinary focus may inadvertently undermine the communal pursuits and ends that are necessary for human flourishing. Therefore, it is vital for us to expand our understanding of psychotherapy to include shared goods and their cooperative pursuit so that we do not promote an excessive form of self-interested individualism.

Internal and External Goods

There is a prominent tendency in psychotherapy theories to characterize individuals as self-interested actors who seek to maximize their outcomes with the flexible employment of available strategies. A good deal of human activity is best understood as instrumental in just this way. Buying groceries, maintaining one's living quarters, and performing many work tasks are simply means to the end of having the wherewithal to live comfortably and pursue higher order goals.

Humans frequently seek what can be called *external ends*, such as pleasure, fame, popularity, honor, or wealth through various strategies. I am calling these ends external because there is no necessary connection between the methods used to attain the goal and the goal itself. External goods are the outcomes or products of some activity but are separable from the activity (MacIntyre, 1981; Sherman, 1989). For example, a financier arranges a merger between companies for the sake of the profit it will bring, a factory worker builds automobiles to make the product available, and we go grocery shopping so that we will have food to eat. The success of these kinds of activities is solely evident in whether they produce the desired result. If the production of the end fails or miscarries, then the efforts were misspent.

We can only attain *internal ends*, by contrast, in specific ways that are intrinsically related to the nature of the goal. There are some highly valued goals we can only pursue in this way. For example, the best kind of friendships can be cultivated only by acting as a good friend does. I cannot purchase these friendships, hire someone to do the work for me, achieve them through deception or pretense, or by any means other than by mutually acting in my friend's best interests. The distinction between external and internal goods can help us to see another important way that virtue ethics expands our grasp of the full range of human activity—by taking us beyond instrumental activity.

The difficulty is that most psychology theories exclude the possibility that some goals can only be pursued through actions that are intrinsically related to the goal, and success in goal attainment is largely a matter of pursuing the goal in a particular manner. For example, some portrayals of friendship suggest that friendship is no more than the exchange of favors, rewards, and assistance in an instrumental fashion. Of course, there are friendships of this kind and they are well worth having in some circumstances. But to insist that all human relationships are based solely on such exchanges is to rule out the richest possibilities of friendship. Such a thoroughgoing instrumental approach to life is incompatible with admirable instances of parenting, marriage, and friendship. Moreover, the predominance of an instrumental portrayal of human action also seems likely to reduce the likelihood that we will recognize noninstrumental activity and support it appropriately in psychotherapy.

A purely instrumental portrayal of human activity may create a kind of self-fulfilling prophecy of highly effective, but exploitive individuals who seek the most efficient means to satisfy their desires regardless of the costs to others. Because individualism portrays the goals in life as individually chosen, there is little common ground for seeking any sort of shared good, unless it benefits the individual directly or cooperation appears to be a better strategy for each individual involved. On an instrumental view, personal, social, and political relationships take on a contractual cast in which we engage in mutual involvement and attachment solely because the relationship provides benefits to us as individuals. If those benefits fail to compensate for the costs of the relationship or compare favorably with other alternatives in the present and foreseeable future, the only rational response is to terminate it.

In contrast, the ends of virtue are internally connected to virtuous activity. With external goods, the goal of the action is something that is separate from the activity itself, whereas we find internal goods in the worth and enjoyment of the activity itself. What counts most in virtue ethics is *how* one acts, whether one acts courageously or justly. For example, we characterize courage more in the way that someone undertakes a risk than in whether the venture is successful. Of course, soldiers act courageously for the sake of victory and winning the battle or the war is not a matter of indifference, but the key point is that an act is courageous whether or not victory is forthcoming. Courage is, in this sense, its own end, because what the virtuous agent cares most about is whether he or she is acting nobly. That does not mean that victory is irrelevant to the brave soldier or scientific progress is meaningless to the honest scientist. What it does mean is that victory or scientific progress is only praiseworthy if gained through courageous or honest actions (Sherman, 1989).

As Guignon (1993) explained, to the extent that one's life is characterized by a sequence of instrumental pursuits of external ends, that life will have an episodic nature that lacks cumulative worth or larger purpose. The activities themselves do not have any meaning and may be onerous chores. I might detest running but suffer through it because it is the most efficient way to stay fit, or I might dislike someone but cultivate his friendship only for what he can do for me. In contrast, a higher quality of life can be attained when one's actions are an integral part of being a certain kind of person. If I exercise as part of being a healthy person or do a favor because that is what it means to be a good friend, my actions help to make me that kind of person. My actions and my goals are one and the same, and this gives my activity continuity, wholeness, and cumulativeness that is not possible if I see my actions as mere means to some reward.

External goods are also goods of competition in that the supply is limited, and the more one individual has, the less others can have. Money, possessions, fame, and honors are goals for which individuals compete. In contrast, the shared goals I discussed above, such as friendship, solidarity, and a well-ordered community, are only held in common. They are also internal goals that can only be attained by acting as a friend, by standing together, and by being a good citizen.

This distinction between internal and external ends takes us back to the first aspect of goal seeking: We seek some goals for their own sake (internal) and others for the sake of other goals (external). Virtue ethics suggests a hierarchy of aims in life that are arranged in a way that our internal goals, those we think are good in themselves, have the highest place in our lives, and our efforts toward external goals promote the ultimate attainment of our internal aims. These concepts can help therapists to question the dominance and exclusiveness of instrumental reasoning. Therapists can move beyond instrumentalism and foster their clients' flourishing by helping them to order their priorities in a way that helps them focus on what is most important to them rather than being distracted by the endless pursuit of secondary aims.

Julie's Goals

Julie came to therapy feeling a great deal of confusion and pain. She had a clear sense that she needed to make changes in her life, but she did not know what she wanted to change. As we explored the sources of her pain, it seemed to have two primary origins, both of which were strongly related to her relationship with Ron. The first problem was that she felt defensive and guilty about deceiving him regarding her involvement with Jake and about her finances. The second problem was that Julie also felt inadequate about being unable to contribute more money to their household now that Ron needed her help.

It was clear to Julie that she loved Ron very much and wanted to remain married to him. She felt very torn about the emotional excitement she felt with Jake. On the one hand, it felt very good to be desired, and the passion and possibilities of this involvement left her feeling very alive. On the other hand, she did not want to hurt Ron and put their marriage at risk for the sake of this dalliance. As she explored what was most important in her life, she decided that her marriage was much more important than any future she could imagine with her coworker. Therefore, her first goal was to put an end to the involvement with Jake. She did not want to talk with Ron about it at this point and thought that simply ending the flirtation would be sufficient. Although the distinction was not discussed explicitly, the excitement and pleasure that she felt with Jake was an external good, because it could be sought with many men. In contrast, her ongoing marriage involved internal goods relating strongly to her long-term flourishing and to the quality of her life as a whole.

The discussion about how central her marriage was in her life also led to a decision on Julie's part to rework her finances so that she could contribute more to household expenses. It was clear to her that she had to tell Ron about her credit card debt, because he had to know why she could not begin paying for things immediately. The next goal was to talk with Ron about her financial situation.

She knew that he could help her rearrange her finances, because he was so good at it, but it galled her to need his help. An exploration of her negative reaction to seeking his help opened up a key dilemma in her marriage. She really liked the way that Ron took care of her financially and in other ways, but she had been feeling less and less comfortable with the sense that she had become a pampered child. Over time, it became clearer and clearer to her that her involvement with Jake was motivated by a complex mixture of feeling angry at Ron for his paternalism and fearing Ron's mortality and being abandoned by him. As this awareness emerged, Julie decided that her third goal was to become a more equal partner in their relationship by taking on more adult responsibilities. She believed that her dependence on Ron had restricted her capacities and that it was time to take on more responsibility. This pursuit of greater maturity and the improvement of her marital relationship became her overarching goals. Financially speaking, becoming a more responsible partner was an internal goal that took priority over the external goal of spending money to acquire more possessions. A full-fledged partnership is a shared good that can only be pursued by acting as a full partner, whereas treating Ron's financial prowess as a means to be exploited represents an external, individualistic goal (cf. Fowers, 2000, 2001).

VIRTUE IN ACTION

Action is critical to virtue, because there is no virtue without concrete activity. This is immediately clear if we imagine someone claiming to have courageous thoughts or generous feelings that are not reflected in that individual's actions. Honesty includes recognizing what is truthful and having a desire to act truthfully. This inner experience does not count as honesty if we fail to act honestly by expressing ourselves clearly, keeping our promises, speaking and acting in a consistent manner, and so forth. Honesty is an activity, a way of acting and speaking truthfully. Of course, we do commonly speak of being honest with oneself, but self-honesty would count for little if it were coupled with deceiving those who have a claim on the truth from us.

This emphasis on observable action is an important affinity between virtue ethics and mainstream psychology. Psychotherapists are also concerned with seeing improvements in concrete, observable actions. Good training in psychotherapy involves teaching students how to formulate therapeutic goals in terms of visible actions rather than vague construals of inner change. Similarly, excellence as a therapist is reflected in the ways that a professional acts rather than in his or her inner experience or unexpressed aspirations.

The capacity for honesty was particularly salient for Julie, both for being a more responsible, mature adult and for improving her marriage. It took her some time to prepare herself to disclose her financial difficulties to Ron. It was obvious to her that she had to act honestly, but her fears of his response and her reluctance to give up her comfortable world made honesty difficult. Thus, she also had to cultivate some degree of courage on the way to honesty. Although this part of the work with her will sound familiar to most therapists, the explicit use of ethical terms such as honesty and courage and the understanding of them as traits that are necessary for flourishing put them in a very different light than do standard therapy theories.

COGNITION AND VIRTUE

Acting in a way that appears generous or courageous is not enough to make those actions virtuous, however. We also have to act for the right reasons. Let me illustrate this with generosity. If someone gives money for a worthy project but does so for the purposes of self-aggrandizement or for a tax break, we do not consider that individual generous. The reasons for the gift disqualify the action as generous and define it as self-interested. Of course, self-seeking activity has its place, but we only count the gift as generosity when the giver acts primarily for the benefit of those who receive it; that is, gives for the right reasons. It is also possible that someone's actions may be accidentally similar to courage or justice, and these behaviors would not be praiseworthy because they were not done for good reasons.

Acting for the right reasons grows out of three sources. First, our understanding of the praiseworthy ends we seek guides our action. If we do not have a clear concept of our aims, we will be more likely to flounder and flail about than to pursue goodness in a focused and decisive manner. Second, our grasp of what is vital in the situations we face informs our actions. When we see clearly what is central rather than what is trivial, we will be able to act for the sake of what is important. Finally, understanding the specific character strengths will help us to better enact them. The more clearly we understand what it means to be just or generous, the better our actions will represent those qualities.

As Julie reflected on the reasons for her actions in sessions, she gradually found the resolve to discuss her finances with Ron. It became increasingly clear to her that she could not respect herself when she acted out of fear and a desire for him to take responsibility for her. As she came to value the goals of self-respect and maturity, she could see that she had to face the consequences of her previous decisions and to deal with them squarely. When she presented this information to Ron, he was not nearly as surprised as she thought he would be by her financial situation. The surprise for him was her acceptance of responsibility for the problem and her willingness to change her spending habits to get out of debt and contribute financially to the household.

Julie also struggled with taking action to break off her relationship with Jake. It had been very exciting to have someone else interested in her romantically, and she had enjoyed the thrill of new sexual possibilities. Consideration of her reasons for maintaining the extramarital involvement proved decisive in this area as well. Although the excitement she experienced with this dalliance was potent, she kept coming back to the idea that this involvement was a way for her to free herself from feeling controlled by Ron. For many years, she had felt like Ron was managing her; that she was very much in the position of being a child in the relationship. As she gave expression to this pent-up feeling, she was surprised by how much she resented feeling controlled and how strongly her growing rejection of her role as a child was involved in her nascent infidelity with Jake. The more she thought about it, the more convinced she became that both her extramarital interest and her excessive spending were means she used to combat feeling controlled by Ron. This underhanded way of asserting her independence became distinctly unpalatable to Julie as a reason for acting, and her shift in motives eliminated her ambivalence about ending her affair.

EMOTIONS AND VIRTUE

Although a good intellectual grasp of virtue is essential, having good character does not come down to an intellectual exercise any more than it is simply a matter of behavior. It is our desire to reach a worthy end that moves us to act well. Virtue ethics emphasizes the importance of our actions flowing from both our best reasons and our heartfelt emotions. This emphasis on the interrelationship of our intellectual and emotional sides illustrates the psychological holism of this perspective. We can, to some extent, separate our emotional reactions from our thinking about things, but this is an abstraction from our ordinary lives rather than the truth about us. From a virtue ethics point of view, the best kind of life is one in which there is very little separation or conflict between what we know, what we feel, and how we act.

Part of the pain and disorder of Julie's situation was that she had so thoroughly separated her reasons for action, her feelings, and her overall aims in life. She allowed herself to become caught up in the pleasures of spending money, being desired sexually, and defying Ron's control over her without really recognizing the reasons for her actions. As she pondered her motives, she found them in dramatic conflict with her overall goals for her life and began to see that persisting in those activities could destroy what she valued most. By reviewing her reasons for acting in the ways that she had, she found her desires shifting to be more in accord with her higher order goals of becoming more mature and of having a better relationship with Ron. She found herself wanting to talk to him about her finances and to break off the relationship with Jake. She still had some fears about taking these steps, but she was no longer ambivalent about doing these things.

The ideal of harmony between one's goals, thoughts, and emotions is one of the most attractive aspects of virtue ethics. A central premise of this outlook is that we are drawn to what we love. When we learn to love what is good, we seek it naturally and wholeheartedly. The concept of acting well because we are attracted to certain aims and ideals stands in stark contrast to most accounts of ethics that portray moral behavior in terms of acting out of duty or obligation and against our inclinations.

At our best, our feelings and desires accord with acting in the best ways, which leads us to spontaneously and gladly pursue what is good. This harmony of affect, cognition, and behavior is, of course, an achievement. Aristotle, unlike many moral philosophers, understands that becoming a moral person is a developmental process, and he discusses the educational activities that cultivate virtue and a love of what is good. Unfortunately, the limited space in this chapter precludes me from discussing that education in detail, but excellent accounts of it can be found elsewhere (Annas, 1993; MacIntyre, 1999; Nussbaum, 1986; Sherman, 1989).

There are, of course, times when even the best of us have mixed or unworthy feelings about something or someone in our lives. When we are hurt, we might entertain thoughts of revenge, or we may become caught up in envying someone else's possessions or accomplishments. In those circumstances, there is a way to bring our emotions into harmony with our overall pursuit of the good. We can do this by reviewing for ourselves what is most important in our lives and reminding ourselves about what we want our lives to amount to as a whole. This kind of reconsideration of what we most love in life is clarifying for us, allowing us to let go of emotions that are incompatible with our ideals. For example, a certain professor who is interested in virtue ethics might find himself envious of an acquaintance's 70-inch plasma television and begin to entertain angry feelings stemming from thoughts of social injustice regarding the distribution of wealth. On a good day, this professor can reconsider the reasons he has pursued an academic calling rather than a career that produces a higher level of wealth. As he recalls his love of the pursuit of knowledge and of sharing that knowledge with students and the myriad choices he has made to make this central in his life, he is able to sigh and let go of envious and revolutionary feelings about the spotty distribution of large plasma TVs and continue his scholarly pursuits gladly and wholeheartedly.

Paying attention to what we love can help us to order our lives to make it possible to pursue the goods we value. In psychotherapy, the process of identifying and clarifying goals helps clients to transform their emotional process to become motivated to act in new ways to seek goals that are now clearer and more attractive than they have been before. The pursuit of these goals often includes the development of necessary character strengths. As Julie clarified what was important to her, it became obvious that she had to develop a new capacity for honesty on the way to greater maturity and partnership in her marriage. In addition, she saw that it would take courage to disclose her financial dilemma to her husband, because it would be embarrassing to her and she would have to confront the consequences of having deceived him. Julie understood that her feelings of fear were related to having a childlike role in her marriage, and exercising the courage to confront her worries was part of becoming more of an adult with Ron.

VIRTUE AS A SETTLED DISPOSITION

One of the key aspects of virtue is that it goes beyond acting well on an occasional basis and refers to characteristic excellence, a habit of acting in ways that embody virtue. That is why the term *virtue* is synonymous with the word *character*. We find virtue in people who act well characteristically rather than intermittently. For example, we would not consider people who give away money or time episodically, whimsically, or under duress to be generous, whereas individuals who give consistently possess the virtue of generosity because they practice that excellence reliably. Although occasional acts of generosity, loyalty, and fairness are beneficial, we would not consider them evidence of character because they are not part of a reliable pattern of action that indicates a settled disposition to pursue what is good.

If we are to construct lives that amount to something worthwhile, that allow us to engage our essential human capacities, we must be able to act well consistently. For example, the development of strong personal relationships requires trust, which grows out of consistent honesty and dependability. I cannot be honest on isolated occasions or only when it suits my other purposes if I want to be trusted. Similarly, effective psychotherapists are able to act with characteristic courage, temperance (the ability to moderate one's actions appropriately), and good judgment. Therapists must express these capacities consistently to develop and maintain a context in which clients can trust them and work toward positive change. An individual of character is not easily dissuaded from courageous or temperate action by difficulties, distractions, or temptations, is firm in what he or she does, and stands by it (Broadie, 1991). Encouraging trainees to have this kind of reliable disposition to act well ethically and therapeutically is a central goal of all psychology training programs, even if we do not generally describe excellence as a psychologist in terms of virtue.

Virtues such as courage or generosity are acquired through practice. That is, one becomes courageous by acting bravely, just by doing justice, and so forth. The process is analogous to learning a skill in that the initial attempts to do something like wood working tend to be halting and lead to mixed results. It is only through practice and guidance that one can become adept at making attractive objects with wood. Creating a few pieces of furniture would not qualify one as a furniture maker. Similarly, the beginning of practicing courage or generosity would not be considered virtue because these actions have not yet become second nature, but are consciously done because they seem good. The cultivation of excellence in character is a result of developing habitually virtuous responses to such a degree that it becomes second nature to do them. Acting courageously or justly becomes a part of the individual who does so consistently. Indeed, we *characterize* ourselves through our habitual actions as someone who is generous or miserly, just or exploitive, temperate or self-indulgent.

Psychotherapy aims at the kind of stable change that grows out of cultivating new habits and dispositions to action. The goal is not to just alter one behavior or thought but to help clients develop new modes of action in problematic areas. Therapists want their clients to develop new capacities that will, with ongoing practice, become second nature for their clients.

Julie discussed her financial situation with her husband and they developed a plan to get her out of debt and in a position to contribute more to the household financially. She was proud of her ability to deal honestly and straightforwardly with Ron in this way. She was surprised by feeling stronger and enlivened by taking this responsibility. She was not surprised that sticking with the financial plan they had outlined required self-restraint initially. As we talked about her impulses to spend in light of her increasingly responsible role in her marriage and her growing ability to speak her mind to Ron, she found that the urge to spend irresponsibly had diminished considerably. Along the way to pursuing her goals, she had begun to develop the virtue of temperance—her appetite for spending had moderated and come into line with what was fitting to her more mature participation in reaching their financial goals.

There was another consequence of Julie's exercise of honesty. Once she had disclosed her financial situation and found that she could be honest and actually be glad about it, she recognized that she had to decide whether she would be honest in a selective way or to become an honest person overall. This question was particularly salient, because Ron continued to be troubled by his perception that something had occurred with Jake. There was an awkward reserve and a sense of hurt between Julie and Jake now, whereas there was palpable electricity between them before. Ron continued to ask Julie about this, and she decided that it was important to disclose her involvement with Jake, because she wanted to be honest with Ron generally, not just about some things. Divulging her involvement with Jake was obviously more momentous and difficult than sharing her fiscal peccadilloes with her husband. He was very hurt and angry about her infidelity, and the process of restoring trust and forgiveness took some time. Significantly, the pain that she had inflicted on Ron by deceiving him and being unfaithful to him actually reinforced Julie's resolve to take more responsibility for her actions and to endeavor to be honest with and loyal to him.

PRACTICAL WISDOM

One of the most neglected topics in psychotherapy is the degree to which good therapeutic work depends on making wise choices in the moment with clients. Choosing wisely about where to place the focus involves separating the central from the peripheral in therapy.

T. F. Tenney's (1993) book title *The Main Thing Is to Keep the Main Thing the Main Thing* provides an apt directive for the psychotherapist's daily work. Although this goal sounds straightforward, it is anything but simple. One of the most striking things about the therapeutic situation is the overwhelming amount of verbal and nonverbal information that is present at any given moment. Making sense of this information is very difficult because therapy clients are confused and bewildered, and they usually describe their situation to therapists in a jumble. Moreover, one of the primary reasons many people need therapists is that they have learned to cope by avoiding, obfuscating, or complicating the central issues in their lives. In the face of these complications, therapists must sift through and organize the information they receive, as well as decide what else we need to know to be helpful. The central problem that every therapist must resolve in every session is: What is the most important thing on which to focus with this client at this time?

The truly remarkable thing is that there is virtually no explicit, systematic training about how to recognize and respond to what is most important in a client's presentation. This capacity is often referred to as *clinical judgment*, without being well defined, and this judgment is believed to be rather mysteriously accrued through "experience." The problem is that good judgment does not magically arise from spending time with clients any more than musical skill arises from spending time in front of a piano. The development of good judgment requires instruction, feedback, and informed practice.

The first step in making wise choices is to perceive what is important in a situation. After all, circumstances do not come to us in a prelabeled way (Sherman, 1989). We have to construe what we encounter—to recognize that a particular occasion offers an opportunity to help a client to work on a particular goal.

This moral perception will often result in a clear and immediate response, and we do not have to ponder the appropriate course of action. In many circumstances, however, the most fitting response is not so obvious and requires deliberation. We deliberate to ascertain how to best realize our aims in a given situation. Each situation has a multitude of features, and we come to them with many interests and considerations. It is easy to see why we often err in our judgments about how to act because there is seldom a one-to-one correspondence between our aims and the features of a particular occasion. Thus, we find ourselves at times regretting missed opportunities to encourage a friend, offer guidance to a student, or to stand up to an injustice. Deliberating well depends on a practiced acuity in focusing on the most relevant elements of a situation in such a way that the appropriate concerns about the best kind of life are activated in us (Wiggins, 1980).

Once we see the possibility of pursuing an aim, we have to consider how best to bring it about in these particular circumstances. What is practicably best will inevitably differ from one state of affairs to another, which means that we have to tailor our actions to the specifics of the situation. To complicate matters further, there are no set rules or definite procedures for arriving at this judgment, and we must rely on our sense of what is proper or fitting to choose the best course of action.

Psychotherapy theories can be helpful in identifying what is important, but there are always many ways to construe a client's difficulties. The question is, which concepts are most relevant to the particular situation? Similarly, there are a vast number of techniques that are frequently effective in helping clients. Yet therapists must decide which technique is appropriate for a particular circumstance. Clinicians also have to determine how to apply a given technique to their client's situation, for each interpretation of a defense or challenge to a cognitive distortion or reflection of a feeling must be attuned to *this* particular client at *this* time and in *this* circumstance. In general, this problem can be summed up as: How do we apply abstract, generalized concepts and techniques to specific situations with a real person?

Our deliberations lead us to make choices about the appropriate actions in a given situation. In general, we deliberate to make choices among available options, to choose between what is better and worse, for choosing the best course means selecting from among several alternatives (Sherman, 1989). These deliberations are not just about the concrete situation but also related centrally to our overall aims. Practical wisdom is the ability to see how to pursue our essential goals in the specific circumstances we encounter. Although it sounds complex, all of us make this kind of judgment on a daily basis. The capacity to choose wisely is equally central to living well and to good therapeutic practice. Cultivating the ability to see what is most important, to deliberate well, and to choose the best available course of action is necessary to successfully pursue our aims. Extended discussions of practical wisdom and psychotherapy are available elsewhere (Fowers, 2003, in press).

CONCLUSION

Thinking critically about psychotherapy requires us to recognize and evaluate the background assumptions of this endeavor. The purpose of this chapter has been to provide an alternative perspective on psychotherapy that shows that standard background assumptions are not the only ones on which therapeutic work can be founded. The virtue ethical perspective provides a sharp contrast to the instrumental individualism found in most psychotherapeutic approaches.

The first contrast is in how we define the goals of therapy. In cognitive–behavioral therapies, success is generally equated with an increase in a client's instrumental capacities to use effective strategies to attain their goals. We have seen that this approach is fitting for attaining individual and external goals but that it is inappropriate for shared goals, which are held in common with others, and for internal goals, the attainment of which is intrinsically tied to the goal. Moreover, virtue ethics suggests that internal and shared goals are generally of a higher order and that external aims are best seen as providing the infrastructure for seeking more important goods. Humanistic approaches to therapy emphasize internal goods such as self-congruence and authenticity, but these tend to reside primarily in the inner experience of individuals, and it is difficult to see the richness of the intersubjective world through the humanistic lens. Virtue ethics views the social world as the primary arena in which individuals learn to appreciate what is good, learn how to act in the service of those goods, and practice virtues that are beneficial to themselves and others. In contrast, humanists tend to see the social context suspiciously, as an adversary that corrupts the natural goodness of the individual.

Virtue ethics also emphasizes that human flourishing is an outgrowth of becoming one's best self. This involves cultivating character strengths that make it possible to embody human excellence. Virtues are settled dispositions to act in admirable ways, and they help to define an individual. Virtues stand in contrast to behavioral strategies that are adopted or set aside depending on whether they are seen as effective. These character strengths are not just a matter of allowing the individual's inherent goodness to develop naturally, as in humanistic thought. Rather, virtues are consciously cultivated potentialities in beings who are equally equipped to act virtuously or viciously, depending on which possibilities are fostered.

Virtues involve the harmonious interplay of cultivated disposition, affect, cognition, and behavior. This perspective emphasizes that humans pursue what they love. The key to living well is to understand and be attracted by what is best. In that happy circumstance, the individual acts for the best reasons out of wholehearted desire for what is good. The good for humans cannot be definitively or finally stated because of the open-ended nature of human experience and reason. In fact, a large part of the good for human beings is the effort to define and clarify what is good.

Finally, virtue ethics stresses the importance of practical wisdom, the capacity to recognize what is central to our circumstances and our lives and to choose how to act to pursue our aims in light of the specific situation. This wisdom is crucial to living well and to therapeutic success. Because it is a thoroughly neglected topic in the psychotherapy literature, it is a crucial contribution of virtue ethics to our understanding of how to be a good therapist.

REFERENCES

Annas, J. (1993). *The morality of happiness.* Oxford, England: Oxford University Press.

Aristotle. (1998). *The Nicomachean ethics* (D. Ross, Trans.). Oxford, England: Oxford University Press.

Broadie, S. (1991). *Ethics with Aristotle.* Oxford, England: Oxford University Press.

Fowers, B. J. (2000). *Beyond the myth of marital happiness.* San Francisco: Jossey-Bass.

Fowers, B. J. (2001). The limits of a technical concept of a good marriage: Examining the role of virtues in communication skills. *Journal of Marital and Family Therapy, 27,* 327–340.

Fowers, B. J. (2003). Reason and human finitude: In praise of practical wisdom. *American Behavioral Scientist, 47,* 415–426.

Fowers, B. J. (in press). *Finding virtue in psychology.* Washington, DC: American Psychological Association.

Guignon, C. B. (1993). Authenticity, moral values, and psychotherapy. In C. B. Guignon (Ed.), *Cambridge companion to Heidegger* (pp. 215–239). Cambridge, England: Cambridge University Press.

Hursthouse, R. (1999). *On virtue ethics.* Oxford, England: Oxford University Press.

MacIntyre, A. (1981). *After virtue: A study in moral theory.* Notre Dame, IN: University of Notre Dame Press.

MacIntyre, A. (1999). *Dependent rational animals: Why human beings need the virtues.* Chicago: Open Court.

Nussbaum, M. C. (1986). *The fragility of goodness: Luck and ethics in Greek tragedy and philosophy.* Cambridge, England: Cambridge University Press.

Richardson, F. C. (2003). Virtue ethics, dialogue, and "reverence." *American Behavioral Scientist, 47,* 442–458.

Richardson, F. C., Fowers, B. J., & Guignon, C. (1999). *Re-envisioning psychology: Moral dimensions of theory and practice.* San Francisco: Jossey-Bass.

Sherman, N. (1989). *The fabric of character: Aristotle's theory of virtue*. Oxford, England: Oxford University Press.

Tenney, T. F. (1993). *The main thing is to keep the main thing the main thing*. New York: World Aflame Press.

Wiggins, D. (1980). Deliberation and practical reason. In A. O. Rorty (Ed.), *Essays on Aristotle's ethics* (pp. 221–240). Berkeley: University of California Press.

Woodruff, P. (2001). *Reverence: Renewing a forgotten virtue*. Oxford, England: Oxford University Press.

II

SOCIAL PSYCHOLOGY

3

SOCIAL PSYCHOLOGY: KEY ISSUES, ASSUMPTIONS, AND IMPLICATIONS

JEFFREY S. REBER AND LISA M. OSBECK

Many of the topics social psychology addresses reflect perennially and profoundly significant human experiences and concerns. The deeply disturbing loyalty and obedience of the Nazis led Stanley Milgram (1965) to investigate the conditions under which obedience to an authority is most likely to occur. Racism across cultures and within the United States spurred Gordon Allport's (1954) investigation of stereotyping, prejudice, and discrimination. Indeed, it was Norm Triplett's (1898) century-old observation that bicyclists raced faster against a competitor than against the clock that prompted him to investigate how the presence of others might facilitate improved performance and to publish one of the earliest social psychological studies.

Consistent with this tradition, this chapter seeks to facilitate critical thinking around three topics that are centrally important research agendas within the subdiscipline of social psychology as well as key concerns for most human beings. Specifically, we examine the basis of human sociality, love, and helping behavior. We focus on some principal assumptions underlying the social psychological methodology and theoretical approach to each topic and discuss some of the advantages and limitations of those assumptions for understanding human relatedness.

ISSUE NO. 1: THE SOCIALITY OF HUMAN BEINGS

Social psychology was established on the premise that human beings are inherently social. As Aristotle put it over 2,000 years ago, "man is by nature a social animal" and "society is something in nature that precedes the individual" (cited in Aronson, 1999, p. xix). Studies that follow from this premise have called into question the individuality and stability of many psychological constructs previously thought of as innate personality characteristics or traits. Milgram's classic studies, for example, showed that destructive obedience was produced by a variety of social (e.g., external authority) rather than individual (e.g., personality) forces, notwithstanding variations of this exhibited by different participants in the study. Similarly, Sherif (1966) showed that prejudice is not something with which a person is born; it is created under conditions of social competition and diffused in social cooperation. Attitudes, self-concept, perceptions, beliefs, love, aggression, and many other aspects of humanity are now understood to be socially formed and situation specific, despite the fact that we experience them privately and subjectively.

More broadly, to claim that humans are inherently social is to acknowledge the social nature of *mind* itself. What does this mean? For one thing, it means that phenomena traditionally regarded as properties of mind, such as personality, self-concept, and knowledge of the world, develop through social interaction and through the mores that support the way of life within a community (the "sociogenetic" view of mind, reviewed in Valsiner & van der Veer, 2000). That is, the nature and character of the social interaction established within the culture into which an individual is born have a profound effect on her or his perceptions, concepts, and personal style (personality). Consider self-concept as an example. Cross-cultural research on the self suggests that the character of self-concept varies from culture to culture. Thus, any understanding of an individual's self-concept requires understanding the culture that person inhabits. To understand the self-concepts of U.S. citizens, for instance, one would have to appreciate the cultural values that lead people to emphasize uniqueness and independence, whereas understanding self-concepts of Chinese citizens would necessitate an appreciation of the collectivistic culture that engenders a focus on group membership and interdependence (Trafimow, Triandis, & Goto, 1991).

This notion that humans are inherently social raises an important question for social psychologists: Isn't social psychology a contradiction in terms? That is, how does one reconcile psychology—usually thought of as the study of individuals (e.g., Zimbardo, Weber, & Johnson, 2003)—with the notion that humans are fundamentally social beings, especially when it seems too difficult to detect where the individual begins and society ends?

The Assumption

For much of contemporary social psychology, this dilemma is minimized by reliance on an implicit assumption of atomism (also discussed in chaps. 5 and 7 of this volume). Atomism is the idea that regardless of how something is formed and influenced, the explanation of its functioning (the account of why it does what it is observed to do) ultimately lies within the thing itself, in its self-contained fundamental properties. If we want to explain the functions of a hydrogen atom, for example, we need look no further than the atom's unique inherent properties—perhaps the property of having one proton and one electron. Similarly, on this account, the actions and experiences of people can be explained by their particular self-contained properties. For some psychologists, these properties are thought to be genetic code, for others they are reinforcement history. A growing number of social psychologists have come to favor the now dominant paradigm of *social cognition*, which emphasizes the representational content and information-processing particularities of individuals as these relate to traditional topics of social psychology like social perception, attribution, and attitude (e.g., Blair & Banaji, 1996; Smith & DeCoster, 1998).

Although social psychologists recognize that the self-contained properties with explanatory power develop in social circumstances and are continually affected by other people, they see the properties as inherent to the individual, not the dyad, group, or community (Aronson, Wilson, & Akert, 2002; Brehm, Kassin, & Fein, 2002; Feldman, 2001; Franzoi, 2000; Taylor, Peplau, & Sears, 2003). Thus, although a person's self-concept may have developed through socialization into a collectivistic or individualistic culture, it is now a property of the individual and therefore manifests itself in the individual's thoughts, feelings, and behaviors.

This focus on individual properties has important implications for methodology and explanation. For example, an atomist orientation on intimate relationships leads to a focus on the thoughts, feelings, and behaviors of each party, for it is assumed that these factors ultimately determine whether and how the relationship is maintained. Social exchange theory, for instance, suggests that relationships depend on each individual's thoughts about the equity of benefits and contributions. If, on the one hand, both individuals think that they are getting about what they give, they will continue in the relationship. If, on the other hand, one or both of them perceive themselves as "under" or "over" benefited, they will be unhappy and may end the relationship (Homans, 1958; Thibaut & Kelley, 1959). According to social exchange theory, the existence and quality of the social relationship depend on each individual's atomistic (self-contained) perceptions of his or her interaction. Other social psychologists might emphasize each individual's feelings (e.g., passion, jealousy) or behaviors (self-disclosure, flirtation). Some prefer a biochemical theory of intimacy wherein the relationship depends on each individual's production of and tolerance for oxytocin, vasopressin, and endorphins (Fisher, 1994). In each case, the research focus and the explanation of sociality are firmly rooted in individual properties or processes.[1]

Advantages

This reliance on atomism is advantageous in many ways. It allows social psychologists to study what appear to be complex social phenomena (e.g., intimacy) in a systematic way by simplifying them into observable, or at least operationalizable, individual properties (e.g., perceptions, scores on a questionnaire). Variables can be isolated much more easily on the individual level, and therefore experimental control is maximized, particularly in a laboratory setting. Using a version of the scientific method, researchers can observe, survey or interview participants, and expose them differentially to various circumstances. Their physiological responses to stimuli such as questions about their partner can be precisely measured. All of this can be done without the intimate partner present because the feelings, thoughts, and behaviors of the relationship are all contained within the participating individuals. Granted, the partner should also be studied to ensure that there is a correlation between measures of their feelings, cognitions, and behaviors, but it is not necessary to study them together. In fact, studying them together would only cloud the results to the extent that participants might be less honest or behave less naturally in front of each other.

The individual's scores on various measures can be compared with his or her scores on other occasions and with the scores of other people in similar conditions. This control, isolation, and systematic comparison of variables allows social psychologists more confidence in making statements about cause and effect in relation to social functioning (e.g., what, specifically, causes us to fall in love). Knowing something about the cause of a phenomenon allows for prediction of the conditions under which it is likely to occur again. Control, explanation in terms of causal relationships, and prediction have long been recognized as the important elements of science (e.g., Slife & Williams, 1995). Psychology has for over 100 years attempted to establish its own scientific standing (see, e.g., Koch & Leary, 1992). Therefore, the atomistic focus helps to promote the scientific standing of social psychology, enhancing its credibility and viability within the broader discipline and within a culture that upholds science as an unimpeachable authority.

---

[1]It is interesting that the broader field of cognitive science from which research on social cognition draws displays evidence of rethinking the traditional construal of cognition as a self-contained phenomenon in favor of a view of cognition as "socially distributed" in meaningful ways (e.g., Hutchins, 1995). However, these developments have yet to filter into the study of social cognition on a wide-scale basis, and thus have not radically altered the atomistic assumptions and corresponding research practices of social psychologists adopting this paradigm.

Limitations

As helpful as atomism might be for attaining scientific status, psychology's individualistic and scientific context offers severe limitations for understanding the complexities of human sociality. In fact, it works against a properly *social* psychology because it ascribes properties to individuals that can only be understood as properties of the relationship itself. Kurt Lewin, frequently considered the father of social psychology, recognized this momentous problem. Drawing on his background in Gestalt psychology, Lewin (1951) noted that "the organization of a group is not the same as the organization of individuals of which it is composed" and that "a social unit of a certain size has properties of its own" (p. 161). Consistent with the Gestalt perspective, this means that the social whole is not only greater than but also qualitatively different from the sum of its individualistic parts. It cannot, therefore, be explained in terms of the contributing properties of these parts. Therefore, according to Lewin's thinking, a full understanding of an intimate relationship cannot be achieved through an atomistic examination of each individual's thoughts, feelings, or behaviors. Rather, it requires a holistic examination of how the participants, by virtue of being with each other, are transformed in important and meaningful ways.

To fully explain social phenomena, Lewin (1951) argued that the *life space*—a social whole that includes not only the person but also the social environment as it exists for and in relation to that person—is the proper subject of social psychology. Lewin recognized that to understand human sociality one must abandon the concept of self-contained properties altogether, because those "properties" are not really properties of the individual at all. They are properly *relational*, not individual. Consider, as a mundane example, the phenomenon of speaking English with an accent. Obviously, the condition of "having an accent" depends on whether one is speaking to people who share one's geographical or cultural origin or people who originate somewhere else. In terms of self-contained properties, nothing about the individual's speech changes. The perception of accent is a function of the relational space. From a holistic perspective, everything about the relational context is different and, therefore, so is the speaking. True to Lewin's theorizing, an understanding of speech accents simply cannot be achieved atomistically. It requires a holistic examination of the social relationship. Curiously, it would appear that many social psychologists have either deemphasized or forgotten this very important aspect of human sociality.

ISSUE NO. 2: LOVE

In 1958, the renowned psychologist and then president of the American Psychological Association, Harry Harlow, lamented in his presidential address that "so far as love or affection is concerned, psychologists have failed in their mission. The little we know about love does not transcend simple observation, and the little we write about it has been written better by poets and novelists" (quoted in Sternberg & Barnes, 1988, p. vii). Love, it seemed to Harlow and others of his time, must be one of those human phenomena that simply does not lend itself to scientific investigation. In fact, scientific studies failed to yield substantive explanations of love, its causes remained unknown, and no universal laws could be identified that accounted for it. Still, because love is such a fundamental and significant human experience, social psychologists have been unwilling to give up their efforts to study it scientifically. Now, almost 50 years later, social psychologists are finding reasons to be much more optimistic about the scientific investigation of love.

The Assumption

Social psychologists' newfound optimism stems from the assumption of naturalism and the increased capacity to apply naturalistic explanations to intimate relationships. *Naturalism* refers to the idea that human beings are fundamentally the same as other objects of nature and as such are subject to the same laws that determine the behavior of those objects (Griffin, 2000). Gravity, for example, influences human behavior just as it acts on boulders, animals, and planets. Natural laws are universally applicable to all people in all times and all places; they are inescapable. Given the universal applicability and causal power of natural laws, it is possible to empirically examine, manipulate, and measure their effects on natural objects under a variety of conditions, and thus draw generalizations that enable predictions of future behavior.

Thus to the extent that social psychologists can identify a universal natural law regulating the experience of love, they will be able to achieve the explanatory power, predictability, and control necessary to validate love as the proper subject of a scientific social psychology. Consequently, whether psychologists study love in Papua New Guinea or New York City, in the year 2003 or 1763, they will inevitably find similarities in terms of attraction, mate selection, and parenting. In fact, because natural laws affect all objects of nature in the same fundamental way, psychologists will find similarities between human and animal species as well. In this sense, scientific research on animal populations, which is far more extensive, more convenient, and typically less complicated than the study of human beings, can be used to predict the behaviors of human beings. As such, it is often the case that evolutionary psychologists, for example, cite studies of mammals, birds, and even insects along with studies of past, present, primitive, and more civilized human populations to support their predictions about the attraction, love, and jealousy found among human beings (e.g., Buss, 1994; Fisher, 1994).

Evolutionary psychology, which claims to be a more formidable and polished evolutionary approach to social behavior than previous renditions (e.g., sociobiology; Buss, 1995), has successfully permeated social psychological theorizing and research on a variety of topics and has become an especially popular naturalistic strategy for investigating love. Essentially, the position of evolutionary psychology is that love is an adaptive, biologically based psychological mechanism that facilitates the proliferation of genes within a given species according to the law of natural selection. As a natural law, natural selection is assumed to apply to human beings as it applies to other living organisms, all of which are determined toward maximizing genetic survivability and adaptability within the particular selective pressures of the environment they inhabit. Love, because it is a ubiquitous byproduct of natural selection among human beings, would have to be an especially advantageous psychological mechanism helping us to meet the demands of this natural law. As such, it warrants the best of social psychological investigative efforts.

Advantages

Naturalism facilitates scientific research on love and meets its demand for predictability. Such predictability offers the potential to understand what for centuries has been regarded as being among the greatest of human mysteries, that which defies explanation or understanding. The mystery of romantic love has been attributable in large part to its seemingly whimsical nature. People seemed to fall into it and out of it in a fairly random or capricious way, which perplexed a discipline in search of predictability and explanation. Herein lies the greatest appeal of naturalism. By grounding explanations of love in a lawful naturalistic framework, psychologists move love from the realm of complex and confusing fancy to the straightforward domain of natural, predictable sequences of inherited and functional inclinations. For example, evolutionary explanations for why we love the way we do now and the predictions of how we will love in the future are clearly indicated by the ways in which natural selection has acted on our ancestors in the past. We marry or establish partnerships, divorce, cheat, and raise our children the way we do because of the ways in which natural selection inclined our ancestors to behave. Insofar as we can understand those past behaviors, we can fully explain our current activities.

In a related way, naturalism benefits the social psychological investigation of love by establishing the material grounding by means of which love might be concretely investigated. Love, traditionally (or culturally) regarded as immaterial and psychological, can now be explained by reference to structures of the brain and its biochemical substances. Helen Fisher (1994), for example, contended that endorphins and peptides like oxytocin and vasopressin create and sustain feelings of attraction and love. This naturalistic reduction simplifies the phenomenon under investigation, transforming the immaterial, unobservable, and immeasurable phenomenon of love into an observable, measurable material reality. It also lends force to the attempts of evolutionary psychologists to establish genes as the substrate underlying all human activity.

Limitations

Despite the benefits the naturalistic framework provides social psychologists in their effort to scientifically investigate love, it offers significant drawbacks and creates obstacles to deeper understanding. Foremost, it does little to inform us of the meanings people attach to love and their experience in intimate relationships. When our understanding of love is limited to gene activity and the neuronal mechanisms, it is removed from the socially situated and relationally meaningful context in which we experience it. We love only because it is an adaptive psychological byproduct of our particular genetic makeup that functions according to the law of natural selection. Two people who make a decision to become long-term partners because they experience one another as unique and wonderful are merely identifying each other as satisfactory reproductive targets for their unconscious aims of genetic proliferation. From the perspective of naturalism, our psychological experience of choice and meaning in forming and maintaining intimate relationships is merely an epiphenomenon of a deeper material reality. This explanation of love tells us little of any real relevance about why we love those we do, in the myriad ways we do, and through the forms of expression unique to each relationship. It trivializes that which is among the most profound and transformative of human experiences.

It is also worth noting that framing love as a function of natural selection results in a social psychological account of love that is not social at all. Instead, it is biological and mechanistic, working at the level of DNA and neurotransmitters in the body. We noted earlier the limitations of studying any social phenomena (e.g., speech accents) as individual properties. Vivien Burr (1995) made a similar point about love and intimacy, contending that we act "as if [these words] referred to entities existing within the person they describe, but once the person is removed from their relations with others the words become meaningless" (p. 27). Because love, like speech accents, is a unique property of a particular relationship, it is greater than and also different from the thoughts, feelings, and behaviors of the people in love. Like accents, love cannot be understood atomistically but must be examined within the relational context that gives the experience its character and meaning. This may be why we use terms like *falling in love* to describe intimate relationships; we say we *fall into it* because it is outside of us and between us. Moreover, what we call or recognize as love, and the particular forms by which it is expressed, vary not only between relationships but also with the conventions established by cultures. Love, like other social phenomena, can only be properly understood as a relational property of the life space that transcends individuals and their biological processes or their status as objects responding to natural laws.

Moreover, while it is clear that the experience of love is correlated with biological structures and chemicals, there is no evidence that those structures and chemicals *cause* the experience of love. In fact, the direction of causality might just as easily go the other way. That is, it is just as possible and perhaps more likely that the significant meaning we attach to a particular person gives rise to the biological responses associated with love. After all, our bodies do not just respond to every person aptly suited to genetic proliferation. Rather, the release of endorphins and increased production of peptides occur when we encounter a particular person who matters to us in a special way. It is also possible that some third factor, not yet identified, is causally responsible for both our subjective experience of love and the biological responses we exhibit when we have this experience. This problem of insufficiency extends to animal studies and ancestral research as well. One simply cannot determine from similar kinds of behavior among animals or from human cultures in various times and places that the source of that similarity is a common natural law like natural selection. Those kinds of correlative relationships always allow for the possibility of an infinite number of other variables that could explain a given behavior. This is an example of the old "correlation does not imply causation" adage that psychologists are inclined to forget.

A related problem is that while the correlations observed do not allow us to prove that natural selection is responsible for love, they also do not allow us to disprove it. Karl Popper (1935) famously identified falsifiability as a necessary component of any scientific theory. That is, it is not enough (not sufficient) to find evidence (e.g., correlation between bodily state and subjective experience) to support a given theory. Evidence alone does not verify or prove that theory scientifically. To be properly scientific, a theory must, at least in principle, offer the possibility of being refuted or *disconfirmed* with further evidence. If a theory cannot be refuted, it does not meet Popper's criterion for good scientific explanation.

Immunity from falsifiability has been a reason cited for the failure of psychoanalysis to attain the scientific status Freud wished for it: Any evidence that could be offered as disconfirmation of the preemptive force of unconscious motivation (e.g. "that's not my conscious experience of the situation") could be argued away with further references to unconscious processes ("you don't experience it that way because it's unconscious"; e.g., see Grunbaum, 1984). For many, the depth, richness, and clinical utility of psychoanalysis compensate for its questionable scientific foundation. Evolutionary psychology's account of love, on the other hand, fails to offer similar depth, richness, or clinical value while being no less problematic as a scientific theory. The evidence cited is chronically retrospective, and all findings are explained in terms of the theory. It would be impossible to find evidence that would disconfirm the theory, because the argument is always that this trait was naturally selected and that there must be a reason for it being so.

Thus, it is not simply the case that scientific evidence demands the naturalistic account of love. When we consider how the assumption of naturalism acts to negate the psychological and social experience of love as a meaningful, freely chosen relationship, the benefits of endorsing a naturalistic account of love seem far outweighed by the costs.

ISSUE NO. 3: HELPING OTHERS

Social psychologists have long been interested in the motivations behind our helping or not helping other people. Popular wisdom and common sense lead many to believe that people will usually come to the suffering person's aid in an emergency. However, when Kitty Genovese was assaulted and murdered outside of her own apartment building in 1964 while her neighbors came to their windows and watched but did not help or call for help, social psychologists began to suspect that people's motives might not be so pure. In fact, after conducting several empirical studies of helping behavior, researchers began to identify a tendency toward bystander apathy among potential helpers (see Latané & Darley, 1970, for a review).

A more recent instance of bystander behavior reported by the CNN correspondent Ed Garsten (1995) seems to indicate bystander amusement as much as apathy in the face of another's suffering. When three men chased Deletha Word onto a crowded bridge outside of Detroit, Michigan on a hot summer night in 1995, forced her from her car, and began beating her and tearing off her clothes, several onlookers got out of their cars, not to help, but to stand, look, and cheer on the attack that took place during an otherwise boring traffic jam. Even as the three men chased her to the side of the bridge, where she was either pushed or jumped into the icy water below, the crowd did nothing but continued laughing. Only one man in that large crowd of people saw what happened and tried to help by jumping into the water after her. Unfortunately, his efforts to save her failed, and she drowned that night in the river. Given these anecdotal examples and a large body of empirical research supporting them, social psychologists are not especially optimistic about human helpfulness.

The Assumption

There is a significant, often unacknowledged reason for the pessimism about human helping behavior that stems from a particular bias of the Western philosophical tradition that pervasively informs psychological theorizing and practice. It is the assumption of egoism, the idea that human beings are selfish, either because it is in their nature to be so or because it is in the best interest of the individual and humankind as a whole for each person to pursue his or her own ends. Egoism's philosophical roots run as far back as ancient Greece, but it was perhaps most explicitly articulated by utilitarian philosophers in the 17th and 18th centuries like Thomas Hobbes, Jeremy Bentham, and John Stuart Mill who claimed not only that we *are* selfish but that we *ought* to be. In fact, to their thinking, all motivation springs from an instinct or drive to maximize pleasure and minimize pain. The satisfaction of these selfish desires and motives leads to happy, healthy, and fulfilling lives. Selfishness, from this perspective, not only brings happiness but promotes productivity, contributing to the overall good of the community and human race. Other people, according to this view, are either in competition with the self and must be viewed as a threat to the self and the self's possessions and happiness, or they are a means by which to accomplish selfish ends, a tool the self can use to maximize its benefit. To complete the reification of egoism as a fundamental motivation of human being, sociobiologists and evolutionary psychologists naturalized egoism by making it part of our physical makeup, so that some social psychologists now speak of a selfish gene that inclines us toward egoistic behavior (see Gantt & Reber, 1999, for a review).

Given this tradition, many social psychologists consider human beings essentially selfish, and social psychological theories about helping behavior are by and large egoistic in orientation. For many social psychologists, people are thought to be inherently motivated to maximize their own pleasure and minimize their own pain (see Batson, 1998, for a review). Hence, we might help others to increase or maintain a good mood that is pleasurable (Wegner & Petty, 1994) or to escape a bad mood that is painful (Cialdini, Darby, & Vincent, 1973). The assumption is that in doing so, we ultimately act for the sake of our own well-being rather than for the benefit of others. We act prosocially and help others only to the extent that we will ultimately get something out of it for ourselves, something that will contribute to our avoidance of pain and maximize our pleasure.

Advantages

The assumption of egoism has several advantages for social psychological research and theorizing on helping behavior. First, it does help to explain some behaviors that might seem puzzling or appalling. People often do not get involved, it seems, because they do not want to put themselves at risk. After all, if Kitty Genovese's neighbors went out on the street to help her, they might also have been attacked. Or, if the attacker discovered that it was they who called the police, he might come after them as well. Any number of unpleasant consequences might have resulted from attempting to help Kitty. Also, there are clear cases in which people help others to attain some egoistic reward. A dramatic example is the off-duty auto mechanic the first author of this chapter came across outside of Las Vegas who drives the freeways looking for people who are stranded and in need of help. He pulls up behind them as if he were just passing by, offers them assistance, and then charges them outrageous amounts of money in exchange for his service.

At other times people help because they do not want to feel the painful guilt that might result from not helping (Carlsmith & Gross, 1969). Sometimes they help in the hope that someone will do the same for them if they are ever in the same situation (Gouldner, 1960). Sometimes they do so because they want to gain or maintain a positive mood (Berkowitz, 1987). The list of egoistic reasons for helping or not helping is endless and has been well documented by hundreds of social psychological studies (see Batson, 1998, for a review). Batson's (1987) review of helping behavior research shows how egoistic theories of helping behavior have generated hundreds of empirical studies (i.e., studies of helping behavior that use scientific method and allow for causal inference). A study conducted by Regan, Williams, and Sparling in 1972, for example, manipulated a situation so that participants would help a person in need to relieve their own guilt. A confederate of the study asked passers-by to take her picture with her camera. The camera was rigged to break when the person took the picture to induce feelings of guilt. When those people who now felt badly about breaking the camera encountered another confederate carrying a shopping bag with candy spilling out, they were more likely to alert the confederate to the spillage than were people for whom the camera did not break. The only difference between the two conditions was the breaking of the camera. The interpretation given for the difference in actions was that guilt is painful and can be reduced by helping somebody in need.

Because egoism can be so universally applied to a variety of behaviors and situations, social psychologists can better predict whether, when, and where we will help a person in need. Indeed, with the assumption of selfishness firmly in place, social psychologists can assume that if they control extraneous variables and manipulate certain conditions the egoism of the helper will always shine through. For this reason, egoism also supports social psychology's standing as a social science.

Limitations

While the assumption of egoism has the advantage of explaining human helping behavior in many situations, its explanatory range does seem limited. For example, while egoism seems appropriate to explain the behavior of Kitty Genovese's neighbors and the crowd gathered on the bridge in Michigan, it is not necessarily the best explanation of the behavior of the one man on the bridge who jumped over the bridge in attempt to save Deletha Word that night. In fact, when reporters asked him why he jumped over the bridge to help her, he simply replied, as many helpers do, that it looked like she needed help, which is hardly indicative of a selfish motivation. A similarly nonegoistic explanation was often given by rescuers of Jews in Nazi-occupied countries during the Second World War. Unlike most of their neighbors and friends, these people were willing to put their own lives and even the lives of their loved ones at risk for complete strangers over an extended period of time. One rescuer described her experience this way:

> We knew what could happen. If they caught us, we would have been taken away. The children would have been taken away. We absolutely knew this. But when they're standing at the door, and their life is threatened, what should you do in this situation? You could never do that [turn them away]. (Monroe, 1996, p. 156)

Finally, egoism seems inadequate to explain the behavior of the many participants in a research study (Batson, Duncan, Ackerman, Buckley, & Birch, 1981) who were willing to trade places with another person suffering electrical shocks rather than quit the study or escape the situation in some other way.

Such seemingly altruistic counterincidents, or exceptions to the egoistic rule, raise a number of interesting questions. Why, if we are ultimately selfish, do we experience ourselves and others acting selflessly, albeit occasionally? Why do we even have the word *altruism* in our vocabulary if we are determined to pursue our own pleasure and avoid our own pain? Perhaps most paradoxically of all, why do we applaud and praise people who sacrifice their own well-being for others and deride and disapprove of people who behave selfishly? If we are naturally motivated to pursue our own pleasure and avoid pain, we should neither expect nor value altruistic behavior. Yet we do just that. We respect and appreciate the man who tried to save Deletha Word while we are angry and upset with the people who laughed at the attack. We respect and sometimes worship role models like Mother Theresa, Gandhi, and Jesus Christ as saints, heroes, and saviors because they sacrificed themselves for others, while on the other hand we detest the selfish thief, the unhelpful bystander, or the uncharitable Scrooge.

The egoistic response to these apparent exceptions is to suggest some less obvious, but still fundamentally selfish motivation for these behaviors. In the case of the man who tried to rescue Deletha Word, he may have been seeking the attention and praise of the media or he may have found the guilt of letting her drown without trying to help her unbearable. Mother Theresa might have helped the poor and sick in India for a greater reward in heaven or to rid herself of the sorrow she felt at the sight of their suffering. Indeed an egoistic explanation could be given for any helping behavior.

The possibility of thinking up a possible selfish motivation for a behavior, however, hardly proves that the behavior is egoistic. Altruistic motivations could be just as easily assigned to the act. Indeed, in the absence of compelling evidence one way or the other, perhaps some behaviors ought simply to be taken at face value according to the meaning that helpers and those receiving help assign to them. If the person says, "I helped because the person needed help," that might just be the reason for their assistance. There certainly is no compelling reason to accept egoistic explanations to the contrary. Nevertheless, that is exactly what the assumption of egoism forces social psychologists to do. To the extent that egoism is granted the status of a fundamentally natural human motivation for helping behavior, it must be invoked as *the* explanation of all our service activities.

As with naturalistic explanations of love, egoistic explanations of helping behavior drain the meaning we assign to our actions out of the experience. We are left with a course of action that could not have been otherwise, but was fully determined by egoistic motivations beyond our control. Thus, although Mother Theresa might have thought that she chose to give her time, money, and energy to relieving others' suffering, even until her last breath, she is actually only fulfilling the inescapable demands of her natural instinct to maximize her own pleasure and minimize pain, albeit in a complex and nonobvious way.

CONCLUSION

This examination of social psychological theorizing and research reveals numerous advantages to assumptions of atomism, naturalism, and egoism that underlie much of the research produced. Generally speaking, these assumptions facilitate the application of the scientific method to the investigation of social phenomena and strengthen social psychology's position as a proper subdiscipline of psychology. Moreover, because these assumptions are grounded in a natural, lawful, and therefore scientific worldview, they offer the promise of satisfying the demands of social science for universal applicability, predictability, control, and explanation. All of this has contributed to a fruitful program of research lasting over 100 years and yielding numerous theories and empirical results that have helped us understand our sociality.

At the same time, these assumptions limit social psychological understanding of human sociality in a variety of significant ways. Foremost, they hinder a properly *social* study of social phenomena by overemphasizing the individual and deemphasizing the relationship and the social context wherein the social phenomena occur and have their meaning. These assumptions also naturalize our social experiences, making them the necessary effect of natural laws acting on us in a fully determined manner rather than the meaningful, freely chosen, and fully human social phenomena we experience them to be. The consequence of these limitations is empirical or quasi-empirical studies of individuals in controlled laboratory or laboratorylike natural settings in which manipulation and measurement of variables supercede the meaningful experience of people in relationships and social contexts. By averting focus from the meaning and sociality of human experience, complex human actions and subjective experience are too easily reduced to biological mechanisms whose properties are fully self-contained and determined. In light of the limitations and advantages of the traditional assumptions discussed in this chapter and of the alternative assumptions described in the following chapter, the ultimate question is which assumptions more accurately and deeply facilitate our understanding of human sociality in its myriad forms, meanings, and practices.

REFERENCES

Allport, G. W. (1954). *The nature of prejudice.* Cambridge, MA: Addison-Wesley.

Aronson, E. (1999). *The social animal* (8th ed.). New York: Worth.

Aronson, E., Wilson, T. D., & Akert, R. M. (2002). *Social psychology* (4th ed.). Upper Saddle River, NJ: Prentice Hall.

Batson, C. D. (1987). Prosocial motivation: Is it ever truly altruistic? *Advances in Experimental Social Psychology, 20,* 65–122.

Batson, C. D. (1998). Altruism and prosocial behavior. In D. Gilbert, S. Fiske, & G. Lindsey (Eds.), *Handbook of social psychology* (4th ed., pp. 282–316). New York: McGraw-Hill.

Batson, C. D., Duncan, B. D., Ackerman, P., Buckley, T., & Birch, K. (1981). Is empathic emotion a source of altruistic motivation? *Journal of Personality and Social Psychology, 40,* 290–302.

Berkowitz, L. (1987). Mood, self-awareness, and willingness to help. *Journal of Personality and Social Psychology, 52,* 721–729.

Blair, I. V., & Banaji, M. (1996). Automatic and controlled processes in stereotype priming. *Journal of Personality and Social Psychology, 70,* 1142–1163.

Brehm, S. S., Kassin, S. M., & Fein, S. (2002). *Social psychology* (5th ed.). Boston: Houghton Mifflin.

Burr, V. (1995). *An introduction to social constructionism.* London: Routledge.

Buss, D. M. (1994). *The evolution of desire: Strategies of human mating.* New York: Basic Books.

Buss, D. M. (1995). Evolutionary psychology: A new paradigm for psychological science. *Psychological Inquiry, 6,* 1–30.

Carlsmith, J. M., & Gross, A. E. (1969). Some effects of guilt on compliance. *Journal of Personality and Social Psychology, 11,* 232–239.

Cialdini, R. B., Darby, B. L., & Vincent, J. E. (1973). Transgression and altruism: A case for hedonism. *Journal of Experimental Social Psychology, 9,* 502–516.

Feldman, R. S. (2001). *Social psychology* (3rd ed.). Upper Saddle River, NJ: Prentice Hall.

Fisher, H. (1994). The nature of romantic love. *The Journal of NIH Research, 6,* 59–64.

Franzoi, S. L. (2000). *Social psychology* (2nd ed.). New York: McGraw-Hill.

Gantt, E. E., & Reber, J. S. (1999). Sociobiological and social constructionist accounts of altruism: A phenomenological critique. *Journal of Phenomenological Psychology, 30*(2), 14–38.

Garsten, E. (1995). *Suspect charged with murder in Detroit bridge death.* Retrieved July 1, 2004, from http://edition.cnn.com/US/9508/bridge_death/

Gouldner, A. W. (1960). The norm of reciprocity: A preliminary statement. *American Sociological Review, 25,* 161–178.

Griffin, D. R. (2000). *Religion and scientific naturalism.* Albany, NY: SUNY Press.

Grunbaum, A. (1984). *Foundations of psychoanalysis: A philosophical critique.* Berkeley: University of California Press.

Homans, G. C. (1958). Social behavior as exchange. *American Journal of Sociology, 63,* 597–606.

Hutchins, E. (1995). *Cognition in the wild.* Cambridge, MA: MIT Press.

Koch, S., & Leary, D. (1992). *A century of psychology as science.* Washington, DC: American Psychological Association.

Latané, B., & Darley, J. M. (1970). *The unresponsive bystander: Why doesn't he help?* New York: Apple-Century-Crofts.

Lewin, K. (1951). *Field theory in social science: Selected theoretical papers.* New York: HarperCollins.

Milgram, S. (1965). Some conditions of obedience and disobedience to authority. *Human Relations, 18,* 57–76.

Monroe, K. R. (1996). *The heart of altruism: Perceptions of a common humanity.* Princeton, NJ: Princeton University Press.

Popper, K. (1935). *The logic of scientific discovery.* New York: Basic Books.

Regan, D. T., Williams, M., & Sparling, S. (1972). Voluntary expiation of guilt: A field experiment. *Journal of Personality and Social Psychology, 24,* 42–45.

Sherif, M. (1966). *In common predicament: Social psychology of intergroup conflict and cooperation.* Boston: Houghton Mifflin.

Slife, B. D., & Williams, R. N. (1995). *What's behind the research? Discovering hidden assumptions in the behavioral sciences.* Thousand Oaks, CA: Sage.

Smith, E. R., & DeCoster, J. (1998). Knowledge acquisition, accessibility, and use in person perception and stereotyping: Simulation with a recurrent connectionist network. *Journal of Personality and Social Psychology, 74,* 21–35.

Sternberg, R. J., & Barnes, M. L. (1988). *The psychology of love.* New Haven, CT: Yale University Press.

Taylor, S. E., Peplau, L. A., & Sears, D. O. (2003). *Social psychology* (11th ed.). Upper Saddle River, NJ: Prentice Hall.

Thibaut, J. W., & Kelley, H. H. (1959). *The social psychology of groups.* New York: Wiley.

Trafimow, D., Triandis, H. C., & Goto, S. G. (1991). Some tests of the distinction between the private self and the collective self. *Journal of Personality and Social Psychology, 60,* 649–655.

Triplett, N. (1898). The dynamogenic factors in pacemaking and competition. *American Journal of Psychology, 9,* 507–533.

Valsiner, J., & van der Veer, R. (2000). *Social mind: Construction of the idea.* Cambridge, England: Cambridge University Press.

Wegner, D. T., & Petty, R. E. (1994). Mood management across affective states: The hedonic contingency hypothesis. *Journal of Personality and Social Psychology, 66,* 1034–1048.

Zimbardo, P. G., Weber, A. L., & Johnson, R. L. (2003). *Psychology* (4th ed.). Boston: Allyn & Bacon.

4

SOCIAL PSYCHOLOGY: EXPLORING ALTERNATIVE CONCEPTUAL FOUNDATIONS

EDWIN E. GANTT

In this chapter, I take a brief look at some possible alternatives to the problematic philosophical assumptions discussed in the previous chapter that are present in so much of mainstream social psychological thought. In so doing, I not only examine some alternative conceptions of human social existence but also discuss some alternative means of investigating that social existence. In particular, I will be taking a look at some of the basic ideas behind three alternative approaches to the study of human social life: social constructionism, hermeneutics, and the ethical phenomenology of Emmanuel Levinas. The assumptions underlying these alternative approaches differ significantly from those more mainstream experimental approaches to social psychology that have tended to embrace and advocate the philosophies of naturalism, atomism, determinism, and egoism. The alternative conceptual foundations I explore in this chapter are most noteworthy for their assumptions regarding holism, agency, and the inescapably moral foundations of the self and social relationships. By comparing these alternative assumptions to the more mainstream ones, it will be possible to more critically evaluate the conceptual landscape of the modern psychological study of human social life.

SOCIAL CONSTRUCTIONISM AND THE RELATIONAL SELF

Drawing its inspiration from a wide variety of philosophical, sociological, and cultural sources, social constructionism is a broad and diverse intellectual movement that seeks to offer a radical reconceptualization of the fundamental nature and purpose of social scientific investigation. Social constructionism rejects the atomism that is so much a part of contemporary social psychological theory and research. In contrast to most mainstream theorizing, the social constructionist contends that all human action, and, indeed, individual identity itself, arises and takes place within an intricate historical web of culturally, politically, and socially constructed and mediated relationships (e.g., Burr, 1995; Gergen, 1987, 1994; Harré, 1993, 1998; Shotter, 1980, 1993). In other words, our social contexts, our relationships with others, and our meaningful understanding of those relationships play the primary role in making our actions what they are and in defining us as who we are. "One way of looking at this," said social constructionist Vivian Burr (1995), "is to think of personality (the kind of person you are) as existing not within people but between them" (pp. 26–27). Granting that this is not easy to conceptualize at first, Burr (1995) suggested the following exercise:

> Take some of the personality-type words we use to describe people: for example, friendly, caring, shy, self-conscious, charming, bad-tempered, thoughtless. If you like, make your own list of words you could use to describe people you know. I would predict that most of them will be words which would completely lose their meaning if the person described were living alone on a desert island. Without the presence of other people, i.e. a social environment, can a person be said to be "friendly", "shy" or "caring"? The point is that we use these words as if they referred to entities existing within the person they describe, but once the person is removed from their relations with others the words become meaningless. They refer to our behavior towards other people. The friendliness, shyness or caring exists not inside people, but in the relation between them. (p. 27)

In this sense, the spirit of contemporary social constructionist thought has much in common with that of the Gestalt social psychologist Kurt Lewin, whose work was briefly discussed in the previous chapter.

A central concept in many social constructionist accounts of human behavior is the notion of *joint action* (Shotter, 1980, 1993), or what Gergen (1987) called the *relational self*. Put simply, this is the idea that the fundamental human reality is best characterized as conversation or dialogue, an inherently social and cultural event that occurs only between people in particular situations and for particular reasons. For the social constructionist, the individual personality or mind is not the ultimate unit of explanation or focus of social psychological study. As Gergen (1994) argued, "For the constructionist, relatedness precedes individuality" (p. 214). Social constructionism places the fundamental reality of human nature not in the individual psyche or in some set of component parts that constitute the psyche (e.g., personality traits, attitudes, information-processing systems, cognitive schemas, needs) but in the vast ebb and flow of daily cultural and social life. Indeed, as the name of the movement indicates, people are social constructions, unique creations of the complex social relationships and shared traditions of the societies and groups in which they find themselves. Our identities as individuals and our motives for being who we are and for doing what we do are, therefore, ultimately tied to the particular network of social interactions and commitments that both shape us and are shaped by us. Burr (1995) described it this way:

> When people interact, it is rather like a dance in which they are constantly moving together, subtly responding to each other's rhythm and posture. The dance is constructed between them and cannot be seen as the result of either person's prior [mental] intentions. Likewise, when we interact, our talk and behavior is a joint effort, not the product of internal forces. (p. 28)

In contrast to more traditional atomistic accounts of human social behavior, the social constructionist argues that the reality of human life is not located somewhere *inside* the individual in the form of self-contained personality characteristics, psychological attitudes, mental schemas, or genetic predispositions governed by natural laws. Rather, the reality of human social existence and identity occurs *between* people in a complex and intricate relational dialogue that both creates them and is created by them. Thus, who we are and how we act are the socially negotiated outcomes of both the cultural discourse and interpersonal relationships in which we find ourselves and the particular desires and goals that we happen to take upon ourselves.

For the social constructionist, if modern social psychology is to shed genuine light on the nature of human social action, it must devote more serious attention to several areas of inquiry that have traditionally been neglected or marginalized by the discipline. For example, many social constructionists have argued that social psychology should encourage more "evaluative analyses of the culture generally" (Gergen, 1994, p. 133). That is, social psychologists should take a more active role in the cultural dialogue on values, ideologies, policies, and social goals not only by encouraging new ways of thinking and doing social research but also by challenging traditional assumptions and finding ways to bring more attention to typically neglected or marginalized cultural perspectives and understandings. For example, social psychologists might examine the nature of marital expectations and divorce in terms of their deeply embedded cultural assumptions about gender, gender roles, and individual rights. Further, many social constructionists would argue that social psychology should be more prepared to identify the social shortcomings and cultural blemishes of contemporary Western society and consider possible alternatives. This could be done, they might suggest, by identifying the "individualized forms of understanding common across Western institutions and point[ing] to their ill effects on organizational life, politics, education, and gender relationships" (Gergen, 1994, p. 133). In short, many social constructionist thinkers feel that social psychology should be more directly involved in ongoing discussions about the cultural good by stepping out of the insular confines of the experimental laboratory and into the broader culture as they challenge its often taken-for-granted views of human nature and identity.

In light of their thoroughgoing commitment to nonreductive approaches to the investigation and explanation of social behavior and interpersonal life, it is not surprising that most social constructionists reject the idea that knowledge and truth (scientific, religious, or otherwise) are best thought of as objective representations of an external reality that is in some fundamental way independent of human subjectivity and experience. Rather, for the social constructionist, what we take to be scientific or religious truth or knowledge is really just the culturally and historically constructed product of particular social and political interactions taking place between individuals and communities. Thus, as Gergen (1987) suggested, what is taken to be real and true is "derivative from the ongoing process of negotiation and conflict among persons," and, therefore, "understanding community is prior to and establishes the grounds from which psychological [scientific] construals are achieved" (p. 61). One result of this approach to knowledge is, in the words of Kvale (1994), a move away from "knowledge as abstract, universal and objective to socially useful, local knowledge" (p. 12). According to social constructionism, then, what we take to be knowledge is a product of the concrete social situations and particular cultural contexts in which we happen to find ourselves. Truth and knowledge are, in this approach, the products of the social negotiation and consensus building that are constantly taking place between people and cultures. Thus, what is taken to be true in one culture or community (even the scientific one) need not be taken to be true in another culture or community. Rather, what sorts of statements are accepted as true or false are seen to depend entirely on the utility such statements have in particular social relationships. For example, the concepts of the atom and a fundamentally material universe are likely to be very useful if you are a physicist in a community of scientists conducting experiments on fission, whereas the concepts of God and the eternal human soul may be vital to your spiritual life and practical self-understanding in a religious community. However, as Gergen (1999) would argue, "The existence of atoms is no more or less true than the existence of souls in any universal sense; each exists within a particular form of life" (p. 37).

It is clear that such ideas are bound to have profound implications for how one understands the ultimate goals and practices of any sort of scientific investigation, and most especially so when the principal focus of that investigation is human social life itself. One of the first casualties of this sort of thinking would be the traditional assumption that there is or could be a unified subject matter or methodology for social psychology. Rather, the comparative nature of constructionist analysis favors a "sharing of resources across cultures, and a broad enrichment of theories, methods, and practices" (Gergen, 1994, p. 138). Further, social constructionist thinking brings into question the common belief that modern science has a privileged means of access to and understanding of the human world and social life. Science, the social constructionist contends, is but one among many possible and plausible ways in which knowledge and reality are constructed for and by us. As such, then, it does not possess any methods of investigation or analytic practices that are inherently superior to those that might be found in other cultures or at other times in history. Granted, scientific investigations and understandings have much to teach us about ourselves and our world, but that does not mean that the modern scientific worldview is the only—or even the most—valid or informative one that is available to us.

The relativism of this position is, of course, one that many scholars have found to be more than a little difficult to accept. Critics of the social constructionist perspective often charge that, while it is certainly important to engage in critical self-reflection and cultural self-analysis, one need not embrace epistemological, cultural, or moral relativism as either inevitable or desirable (e.g., Capaldi & Proctor, 1999; Halling & Lawrence, 1999). Social constructionism, such critics argue, seems willing to tolerate any and all claims to truth, no matter how bizarre or unconventional, while itself standing for nothing and discouraging commitment to any set of values or ideals. Indeed, more than a few scholars have pointed out that the sort of relativism championed by many social constructionists is an inherently self-refuting philosophical position (e.g., Capaldi & Proctor, 1999). That is to say, the claim that "all truth is relative" is not itself a relative claim but rather an absolute one—thought by the social constructionist to be universally valid for all contexts and across all cultures. Further, the idea that we should always refrain from passing moral judgment on not only a given person's individual actions but also a particular culture's practices or beliefs is itself a universalized moral judgment, and one that comes with a number of problematic implications and conceptual costs. While various attempts have been made to respond to these and other such criticisms (see, e.g., Gergen, 1994, pp. 64–92), the issue of relativism remains a highly contentious one in the ongoing scholarly dialogue about the relationship between social constructionism and contemporary social psychology.

HERMENEUTICS AND RELATIONAL AGENCY

Although differing in some important respects, social constructionism and hermeneutics (also discussed in chap. 12, this volume) share a common aversion to the atomism and determinism that have come to characterize so much of contemporary social psychology. Like their social constructionist colleagues, hermeneutic thinkers do not accept the notion that human beings are best understood as individual selves, isolated minds, or internal and private personality characteristics or attributes. Further, hermeneutic psychologists argue that human behavior is not determined by "empirical laws, rational principles, or environmental causes that operate independently of the human being" (Slife & Williams, 1995, p. 83). Neither are human beings just another type of object (albeit a complex one) in a world of physical objects governed by impersonal natural laws and principles. Hermeneuticists reject outright this philosophy of naturalism and its underlying assumptions of atomism and necessary determinism and propose by contrast approaches to social psychology that emphasize embodied human agency, practical understanding, and meaningful social relatedness.

Hermeneutics is a disciplined form of study whose central goal is to "discover what is common to all modes of understanding," and, as such, it is concerned with "all human experience of the world and human living" (Gadamer, 1960/1975, pp. xviii–xix). It is a theoretical and reflective inquiry primarily concerned with "our entire understanding of the world and . . . all the various forms in which this understanding manifests itself" (Gadamer, 1976, p. 18). Hermeneutics is, therefore, concerned with "all forms of meaningful human activity, from the production of texts, in the narrow sense of the term, to the generation and maintenance of cultural forms of life" (Madison, 1997, p. 351). Indeed, the proper focus of all hermeneutic investigation is *meaning*. However, "meaning never exists in isolation but always in a life world context of other meanings and always for someone who has some interest in the matter; the chair in its context of other furniture, for example, and as something to sit on" (Fuller, 1990, p. 29). From a hermeneutic perspective, human beings are fundamentally actively self-interpreting beings whose identity, motives, and defining characteristics unfold in and through their participatory relationships with others in a world of meaning.

The task of a hermeneutic or interpretive social psychology is to articulate the meaning of human social action as it functions at various levels, from the individual to the cultural. Hermeneutic analysis is undertaken always with the central aim of laying bare the implicit and explicit meanings of a given social act, both for those particular agents involved in the act and for the cultural and social context within which the act takes place and from which it derives its meaning. Indeed, as Richardson, Fowers, and Guignon (1999) put it,

> because our intentions, desires, and beliefs are made possible and given concrete form by the background of self-interpretations and self-assessments circulating in a historical culture, a crucial part of understanding others will involve seeing where they stand in relation to the public meanings and projects of their community. (p. 236)

In other words, the hermeneutic task in social psychology is always to answer the questions: What does this human act mean *and* how has it come to mean this? In regard to this latter question, hermeneutic social psychology seeks to articulate the practical origins and contributing historical contexts out of which human social behavior arises. For example, what meaningful purpose does this behavior have? What sorts of reasons does this person have for behaving in this way? What sense does this behavior make given the unique historical, cultural, and interpersonal context in which it took place? How does this behavior flow out of and express this person's interpersonal relationships and the meaning of those relationships? Hermeneutic social psychology is, in essence, a science dedicated to *understanding* human behavior in its everyday context rather than to *explaining* behavior in terms of the natural forces or causal conditions thought to produce it. This means that hermeneutic psychologists are primarily interested in articulating the contextual and historical meanings within which human behavior makes sense and derives its purpose. Thus, they are concerned not only with accounting for the many ways in which culture and tradition provide the inescapably moral frameworks for all meaningful human activity but also in examining how everyday practical human activities and relationships give rise to those frameworks.

EXPERIMENTAL AND HERMENEUTIC SOCIAL PSYCHOLOGY IN CONTRAST

The foregoing introduction to hermeneutics as it is applied to social psychology suggests that within a general enterprise of social psychology, there are several points at which mainstream social psychology, particularly experimental social psychology, and a hermeneutic social psychology will diverge in important ways. Perhaps the first of these is their respective ontologies—their presumptive understandings of the fundamental nature of human beings. Much of contemporary social psychology begins with the assumption that the person, as Stanley Milgram (1992) suggested, is adequately understood as "the reactive individual, the recipient of forces and pressures emanating from outside oneself" (p. xix). That is to say, human beings are governed by forces and influences that not only originate from outside their control but do not even require any active or willful participation. As Milgram (1992) also said,

> the creative claim of social psychology lies in its capacity to reconstruct varied types of social experience in an experimental format, to clarify and make visible the operation of obscure social forces so that they may be explored in terms of the language of cause and effect. (p. xix)

Human beings are, in this regard, much like any other natural object found in the world. Indeed, as Heiman (2001) concluded, "in the same way that the 'law of gravity' governs the behavior of planets or the 'laws of aero-dynamics' govern the behavior of airplanes, psychologists assume there are laws of nature that govern the behavior of living organisms" (p. 7). Ultimately, from such a perspective, the only real thing that distinguishes us as human beings from all the other objects or organisms in the natural world is the degree of our complexity in comparison with those other things.

A hermeneutic social psychology, in contrast, begins with the assumption that human beings are fundamentally active meaning-making beings, not merely reactive organisms, and therefore are not adequately reducible to natural substances or processes. As such, at their root, human acts are always the result of some degree of active assent and participation, and always take place within a meaningful world of genuinely social relationships. This is to say, human beings are fundamentally the sorts of beings for whom their own actions, the actions of others, and the shared history and relationships among people necessarily mean something. What these actions and relationships mean, in turn, arises out of the entire communal and expressive social network within which individuals are born, live, and become who they are. Thus, from the point of view of hermeneutic analysis, meanings are neither simply subjective products of individual minds nor the experiential byproducts of impersonal biochemical or genetic processes. Rather meanings are made by people within historically situated communities with particular languages, expectations, and traditions. Romantic love, for example, has come to have its particular contemporary meaning for individuals in Western society in light of their agentive meaning making within a particular cultural tradition that embraces romance, intimacy, and commitment. Essential to understanding human beings from a hermeneutic perspective is the assumption that at whatever point we may undertake to study them, humans are already meaning-making agents, involved in the active, constructive interpretation of their selves and their social situations. A hermeneutic social psychology seeks to make clear these meanings, because in those meanings we will find the best, most adequate, and predictive explanations and understandings of human social behavior.

This point about hermeneutic social psychology leads directly to another important point of contrast. Much of mainstream social psychology assumes, and attempts to demonstrate, that the regularities one readily observes in the social world, including the social world "within the head" of individual persons, can and should be attributed to external lawlike forces and structures. These forces and structures, in their essence as well as their operation, are very much like the laws and structures presumed to operate in the natural world. The uncovering of these laws and structures is the affirmed goal of almost all mainstream approaches to social psychology. Humans, as social beings, are mere mediums of impersonal social forces, and their lives, the grounds on which these forces play themselves out. For example, Robert Wright (1998), adopting an evolutionary perspective on marital relationships, argued:

> Beneath the thoughts and feelings and temperamental differences marriage counselors spend their time sensitively assessing are the stratagems of the genes—cold hard equations composed of simple variables: social status, age of spouse, number of children, their ages, outside romantic opportunities, and so on. (p. 75)

Here, one can see clearly the claim that the social derives from the essentially nonsocial. If this sort of thinking is true, however, social psychology might not be all that social after all.

None of this should be taken to mean that hermeneutic thinking denies that there are patterns and regularities in human experience and social life. A hermeneutic social psychology shares with experimental social psychology the goal of understanding the regularity in social life, as well as the goal of formulating general knowledge having predictive power. However, the origins, as well as the nature of the regularity, along with the processes and justifications underlying generalizations and their predictive efficacy, are markedly different. Hermeneutic social psychology will always proceed on the basis of careful analysis of the meanings of human social life resident in languages and other symbolic and practical expressions. It will seek confirmation of its explanations and understandings that are present in actual discourse and social expressions, rather than proceeding in an objective fashion rooted to traditional practices of operationalization and measurement, control and prediction. These practices, which form the heart of experimental social psychology, distance the psychologist from the social phenomena in ways that a hermeneutic approach seeks to overcome by accepting at face value the data of social life and people's own understandings of their lives and meanings (see, e.g., Pollio, Henley, & Thompson, 1997). Consequently, when hermeneutic social psychologists study human behavior, they do so from a holistic perspective that values and attends carefully to the lived experiences of actual people engaged in meaningful activities in a concrete social world. It is typical of such psychologists that they use various forms of qualitative research methods (e.g., participant observation, ethnography, discourse analysis, grounded theory, case study) to carry out such inquiry (see Cresswell, 1998; Crabtree & Miller, 1999, for more detailed examinations of some of these methods).

Like social constructionism, hermeneutics has occasionally been criticized for encouraging relativism because it rejects the notion that there are universal laws governing the world of human affairs and that there is ultimately only one valid or reliable method (i.e., the scientific method) for discovering these laws (see, e.g., Capaldi & Proctor, 1999). However, unlike many social constructionists who seem to openly embrace the relativistic implications of their approach, most hermeneuticists argue that their philosophical approach neither requires nor implies relativism. Indeed, many hermeneutic thinkers have devoted a great deal of time and energy to addressing the questions of truth, knowledge, and morality and to articulating responses to traditional criticisms (e.g., Gadamer, 1960/1975; Guignon, 1983). Be that as it may, there remain for some critics substantial concerns about how exactly hermeneutic philosophy proposes to address and resolve these important issues.

Another concern that some scholars have expressed concerning the possibility of a hermeneutic social psychology has had to do with its advocacy of qualitative methods of investigation. Some common objections are that the qualitative methods used by hermeneutic researchers are not appropriate to psychology because they are not sufficiently objective, do not allow for generalization, do not involve rigorous hypothesis testing, reflect only commonsense understandings or folk wisdom, and rely too heavily on leading questions and individual researcher interpretations (see Kvale, 1994, for a review). Critics often argue that because qualitative methods do not involve controlled experimental conditions and rigorous statistical forms of analysis, they reflect a primitive and unsystematic approach to the study of behavior, and, thus, any findings generated by such methods are inherently unreliable. The principle assumption behind such objections seems to be that any program of research that does not rely primarily on the logic of experimentation and quantitative analysis is by definition an unscientific program of research. Of course, defenders of the hermeneutic perspective argue that this resistance to qualitative methods of research in social psychology is traceable to "a positivist philosophy of science, which, while philosophically obsolete, still survives in many social-science departments" (Kvale, 1994, p. 148; see also Slife & Gantt, 1999). In other words, the limitations of the hermeneutic alternative in social psychology, and of the qualitative research methods it espouses, are only limitations if viewed from a conceptually flawed and outdated understanding of what genuine scientific inquiry really means. It is likely that, at least in the foreseeable future, the debate over the philosophical validity of the hermeneutic perspective and over the scientific relevance of qualitative methods of investigation will continue to be the focus of a great deal of scholarly attention.

ETHICAL PHENOMENOLOGY AND THE MORAL FOUNDATIONS OF THE SELF

Although the work of Emmanuel Levinas (1961/1969, 1985) is not yet well known among social psychologists, many of those familiar with his work believe that it provides a viable alternative to the egoism and determinism that underlies so much of contemporary psychological theory and research (see, e.g., Kunz, 1998; Williams, 2002). Levinas manages to do this in a way that preserves individuality as essential to morality and meaningful relationships, while not falling into any sort of egoism that would destroy those very things. Although a philosopher and not a social psychologist, Levinas offers an account of human life that is more than just an exercise in armchair speculation. Rather, its foundation is an attentive and carefully descriptive account of our concrete lived experience as social and moral beings, and, as such, it has much to offer us as social psychologists.

The alternative offered by Levinas (1961/1969, 1985) begins with an analysis of human existence founded not on the self-same private minds, individual cognitive systems, DNA codes, personality types, and so on, but on the alterity (lit., "otherness") of the other person that provides the grounds for individual identity and experience. Levinas suggests that our very being human, our identity as unique persons, emerges only in the concrete, face-to-face relation with other people. That is to say, our life comes to have meaning and take on a particular character in that we are first and foremost relational beings; we are who we are because we are with others. Furthermore, our relationships are immediately and primordially relationships of intense moral obligation and responsibility. Indeed, for Levinas (1985), responsibility is "the essential, primary and fundamental structure of subjectivity" (p. 95). In other words, we are the sort of beings who are inescapably and fundamentally responsible to and for one another, and it is this very responsibility that makes us most uniquely human in the first place. To be human, then, is to sense—at the very core or our being—an obligation to account for ourselves, to answer for our choices and actions in the face of another person's needs or suffering, and to care about the welfare of our fellow beings in ways that go far beyond mere matters of personal like or dislike.

What is most significant, perhaps, is that Levinas does not ground this sense of obligation in any sophisticated cognitive functioning or abstract process of socialization that would allow us to "see" and "understand" or "internalize" such obligation. To do so would be to make morality ultimately derivative of whatever nonhuman social structures or egoistic psychological functions happened to be in place to produce such cognitions in the first place, and, thereby, destroy any possibility for real moral force that such a sense of obligation may have originally had. Rather, Levinas places our sense of obligation to one another prior to such impersonal psychological processes, locating it at the very beginning point of our being human. To be a human being at all is to exist in obligation to others, and no complex cognitive capacity, developed egoistic rationality, or biogenic capacity for recognizing genetic kinship is responsible or necessary for our awareness of this obligation. We find this obligation, this inescapable responsibility for each other, Levinas says, in the face-to-face reality of our daily social lives. We find in the face of the other person—whether that of our closest friend, a beloved family member, a crying infant, or the homeless stranger on a busy sidewalk asking us for something to eat—a demand that requires our deepest moral attention and response. This experiential reality, Levinas argues, is the essence of human social life.

By rejecting the all-too-common assumption of fundamental egoism, the Levinasian view provides the real conceptual possibility of living out of concern for an-other rather than out of concern for oneself, and, thereby, allows for genuine altruism in human action. From the Levinasian perspective, human action fundamentally flows out of a moral obligation to tend to the needs of those around us, not to fulfill their expectations and thereby gain their endorsement as some egoistically minded social psychologists would suggest, but to satisfy the moral demand of our mutual humanity. Certainly, the possibility exists that we may betray our obligation to others with whom we are in relation and act as if their needs were of secondary importance to our own drive to obtain social approval. The evening news broadcasts are replete with a multitude of examples of just this sort of behavior. But, conversely, the possibility exists that we may completely forgo the quest for social advantage (i.e., egoism) by simply responding openly and honestly to others, taking no thought as to what the relative risks or benefits to ourselves might be. Clearly, the courageous and selfless acts of those who rescued Jews in Nazi Europe provide a powerful lesson in the very real possibilities of doing just that. However, we need not look only to the heroic acts of a notable few for reasons to believe in the fundamental reality of moral concern; we can see it evidenced in the myriad encounters of daily living. It is there as we hold open the elevator door for a moment longer so that a harried young man late for an appointment can get in. It is there as we excuse ourselves from an important cell phone conversation to help a pregnant mother, whose hands are full with a rambunctious toddler, unload her groceries into the car. It is there as we find ourselves called out of our own worries by the frightened eyes of a ragged homeless woman and offer to buy her lunch and listen to her story. As we yield to the moral obligation we have to one another, we can act without falsifying artifice, self-consciousness, or guile, and, thereby, we can begin to lose ourselves in the business of the moment, the business of genuinely caring for one another.

If sociality and morality are connected in the way that Levinas argues, then a social psychology grounded in a genuine sociality would be a genuinely ethical discipline. It would be a social psychology that would seek to articulate the fundamentally moral character of our relations and social exchanges with one another, opening a discourse within which the parameters of moral life would emerge as the primary subject matter. Because Levinas's understanding of our sociality begins in a prereflective moral obligation, a social psychology faithful to that understanding would not privilege egoism or calculative rationality in accounting for the influence of other beings in our social responses. At the same time, this understanding would erase the barriers that have long insulated the individual ego from others. A social psychology thus grounded would not begin with the thesis that individuality must be overcome to establish intimacy but that the false consciousness of individualism must be overcome so that intimacy may reveal itself.

In this light, altruism in its meaningful form becomes not merely possible at times of extreme duress or environmental emergency, but it becomes the essential prototype of human social interaction. This turns the tables on contemporary social psychology. Under the regime of current theorizing, the question has been how to understand and arrange the conditions under which altruism is likely to emerge. Or, more generally, how can altruism exist in the context of theories that presuppose a fundamental selfishness and a universe of social variables acting on us at the level of this very nature (see, e.g., Gantt & Williams, 2002). Altruism, for these reasons, is a problem. Given a new grounding in the ethical phenomenology of Emmanuel Levinas, however, altruism is the expected response to the call of the other, a call which predates our own sense of self *as self*. The problem, then, for a social psychology grounded in ethical phenomenology is understanding how people come to be oblivious to the ethical obligation to act in the interest of others and how the elaborate social and personal machinations by which the sense of obligation is extinguished have come about. Put in its harshest terms, for contemporary social psychology, the problem is how to explain empathy and altruism. For a social psychology informed by Levinas, however, the problem is explaining selfishness, aggression, and murder.

If there is one thing on which both admirers and critics of Levinas agree, it is that his work represents a radical and provocative challenge to much conventional thinking in the social sciences. This is, perhaps, most particularly evident in the way in which his work stands as an unrelenting indictment of many of contemporary social science's most basic assumptions about the nature of human nature and the ultimate sources of human motivation. Not only does Levinas's work call for an extensive reexamination of our common understanding of the nature of motivation, but it also requires a critical reevaluation of the traditional belief that genuinely scientific work addresses only what *is* (facts) and avoids at all costs speculation about what *ought* to be (values). Such a reexamination, however, strikes at the very heart of what, for many, has always distinguished science from religion and moral philosophy.

In grounding the *is* of human social life in the *ought* of altruism and compassion, Levinas does much to blur the distinction between objective scientific description of the human world and religious or moral reflection about that world. In response, many contemporary social psychologists might argue that because it is grounded in the value-neutral methods of science, experimental research on human empathy and altruism reveals only what happens to be the case (i.e., fundamental egoism) in our world, and it does so regardless of how much the individual researcher might wish for things to be otherwise (see, e.g., Cialdini & Kenrick, 1976; Hoffman, 2000). Further, these psychologists would argue, only when social science restricts itself to providing objective descriptions of the world of facts is it possible to make reliable knowledge claims about the nature of human social life (see, e.g., Heiman, 2001; Stanovich, 2004). And, more importantly, only by maintaining a stance of strict value neutrality in scientific investigation will it be possible to protect science from becoming just one more tool in the service of various political or religious ends.

CONCLUSION

It is clear that each of the three alternative approaches that have been briefly discussed in this chapter reflects different visions of the nature, methods, and goals of social psychological inquiry. Each in its own way seeks to turn much of contemporary social psychological thinking on its head by questioning many of social psychology's most cherished assumptions about the nature of human nature. Because the philosophical criticisms embedded in each of these alternatives strike at the very conceptual heart of the discipline, adopting any one of these alternative perspectives will necessarily require that social psychology give up some things that have traditionally been felt to be vital to the entire disciplinary project. For example, it would have to rethink its emphasis on atomistic or individualistic forms of explanation in favor of more holistic and culturally sensitive ones. Likewise, social psychologists would need to carefully reexamine their commitment to determinism and causal explanation, as well as their commitment to the traditional scientific goals of prediction and control. Finally, social psychology would be called on to articulate the genuinely moral nature of human social relations in ways that avoid dissolving those relations into fundamentally nonsocial exchanges between inescapably self-interested and law-governed objects.

REFERENCES

Burr, V. (1995). *An introduction to social constructionism*. London: Routledge.

Capaldi, E. J., & Proctor, R. W. (1999). *Contextualism in psychological research? A critical review*. Thousand Oaks, CA: Sage.

Cialdini, R. B., & Kenrick, D. T. (1976). Altruism as hedonism: A social development perspective on the relationship of negative mood state and helping. *Journal of Personality and Social Psychology, 34*, 907–914.

Crabtree, B. F., & Miller, W. L. (Eds.). (1999). *Doing qualitative research* (2nd ed.). Thousand Oaks, CA: Sage.

Cresswell, J. W. (1998). *Qualitative inquiry and research design: Choosing among five traditions*. Thousand Oaks, CA: Sage.

Fuller, A. R. (1990). *Insight into value: An exploration of the premises of a phenomenological psychology*. Albany: State University of New York Press.

Gadamer, H.-G. (1975). *Truth and method* (G. Barden & J. Cumming, Trans.). New York: Seabury Press. (Original work published in 1960)

Gadamer, H.-G. (1976). On the scope and function of hermeneutical reflection. In H.-G. Gadamer (Ed.) (D. E. Linge, Ed. & Trans.), *Philosophical hermeneutics* (pp. 18–43). Berkeley: University of California Press.

Gantt, E. E., & Williams, R. N. (2002). Seeking social grounds for social psychology. *Theory and Science, 3*(2). Retrieved July 1, 2004, from http://theoryandscience. icaap.org/content/vol003.002/gantt.html

Gergen, K. J. (1987). Towards self as relationship. In K. Yardley & T. Honess (Eds.), *Self and identity: Psychosocial perspectives* (pp. 53–63). New York: Wiley.

Gergen, K. J. (1994). *Realities and relationships: Soundings in social construction*. Cambridge, MA: Harvard University Press.

Gergen, K. J. (1999). *An invitation to social construction*. Thousand Oaks, CA: Sage.

Guignon, C. B. (1983). *Heidegger and the problem of knowledge*. Indianapolis, IN: Hackett.

Halling, S., & Lawrence, C. (1999). Social constructionism: Homogenizing the world, negating embodied experience. *Journal of Theoretical and Philosophical Psychology, 19*(1), 78–89.

Harré, R. (1993). *Social being* (2nd ed.). Oxford, England: Blackwell.

Harré, R. (1998). *The singular self: An introduction to the psychology of personhood*. London: Sage.

Heiman, G. W. (2001). *Understanding research methods and statistics: An integrated introduction for psychology* (2nd ed.). Boston: Houghton Mifflin.

Hoffman, M. L. (2000). *Empathy and moral development: Implications for caring and justice*. Cambridge, England: Cambridge University Press.

Kunz, G. (1998). *The paradox of power and weakness: Levinas and an alternative paradigm for psychology*. Albany: State University of New York Press.

Kvale, S. (1994). Ten standard objections to qualitative research interviews. *Journal of Phenomenological Psychology, 25,* 147–173.

Levinas, E. (1969). *Totality and infinity* (A. Lingis, Trans.). Pittsburgh, PA: Duquesne University Press. (Original work published 1961)

Levinas, E. (1985). *Ethics and infinity*. Pittsburgh, PA: Duquesne University Press.

Madison, G. B. (1997). Hermeneutics' claim to universality. In L. E. Hahn (Ed.), *The philosophy of Hans-Georg Gadamer* (pp. 349–365). Chicago: Open Court.

Milgram, S. (1992). *The individual in a social world* (2nd ed.). New York: McGraw-Hill.

Pollio, H. R., Henley, T., & Thompson, C. B. (Eds.). (1997). *The phenomenology of everyday life*. New York: Cambridge University Press.

Richardson, F. C., Fowers, B. J., & Guignon, C. B. (1999). *Re-envisioning psychology: Moral dimensions of theory and practice*. San Francisco: Jossey-Bass.

Shotter, J. (1980). Action, joint action, and intentionality. In M. Brenner (Ed.), *The structure of action* (pp. 19–43). Oxford, England: Blackwell.

Shotter, J. (1993). *Conversational realities: Constructing life through language.* London: Sage.

Slife, B. D., & Gantt, E. E. (1999). Methodological pluralism: A framework for psychotherapy research. *Journal of Clinical Psychology, 55,* 1453–1465.

Slife, B. D., & Williams, R. N. (1995). *What's behind the research? Discovering hidden assumptions in the behavioral sciences.* Thousand Oaks, CA: Sage.

Stanovich, K. E. (2004). *How to think straight about psychology* (7th ed.). Boston: Allyn & Bacon.

Williams, R. N. (2002). On being for the other: Freedom as investiture. In E. E. Gantt & R. N. Williams (Eds.), *Psychology for the other: Levinas, ethics, and the practice of psychology* (pp. 143–159). Pittsburgh, PA: Duquesne University Press.

Wright, R. (1998). Our cheating hearts. In B. D. Slife (Ed.), *Taking sides: Clashing views on controversial psychological issues* (10th ed., pp. 68–78). Guilford, CT: Dushkin/McGraw-Hill.

III

NEUROSCIENCE AND EXPERIMENTAL PSYCHOLOGY

5

THE ASSUMPTIONS AND IMPLICATIONS OF THE NEUROBIOLOGICAL APPROACH TO DEPRESSION

DAWSON HEDGES AND COLIN BURCHFIELD

Ideologies and dogmas are the jailers.
—Jean-Pierre Changeux (Changeux & Ricoeur, 2000, p. 173)

In a move away from solely psychological explanations of normal and disordered behavior, the disciplines of biological psychiatry and biological psychology attempt to discover the ultimate causes of behavior in terms of neurobiology. Drawing from research in a number of related fields such as molecular genetics, neurobiology, neuropharmacology, and molecular biology, biological psychiatry and biological psychology categorize and explain behavior on the basis of neuroscientific underpinnings (Rudnick, 2002). Many reports, for example, attempt to correlate depression with multiple neuroanatomical, neuroendocrine, and neurotrophic abnormalities (e.g., Nestler et al., 2002), challenging the conception of depression as coming solely from a disordered mind and suggesting instead that the etiology of depression may be disordered neurobiological functioning. Both a result and crucial component of biological psychiatry (Rudnick, 2002), psychopharmacology specifically posits that medications, however imperfect they may be currently, are important aspects in the treatment of a vast array of mental disorders, including depression. Because of their neurobiological effects, the drugs used in psychopharmacology also form an integral aspect of the theory of biological psychiatry (Rudnick, 2002).

Many recent observers (e.g., Fisher, 1997; Gazzaniga, 1995; Slife, 2004; Williams, 2001) have called attention to the increasing explanation and treatment of psychological phenomena in solely biological terms. Psychologists, for example, find themselves weighing the merits of prescription privileges—a traditionally biological intervention—and viewing what were once distinctly psychological diagnoses as fundamentally biological in nature. Also, relatively new specialties, such as evolutionary psychology and cognitive neuroscience, have been developed and appear to have found a firm explanatory ground in their essentially biological explanations of traditionally psychological phenomena. Given space constraints, this chapter focuses on depression as an exemplar of the current trend toward neurobiological explanations of behavior, thought, and mind in the fields of psychology and psychiatry. Through this focus, this chapter presents a critical evaluation of the history, literature, assumptions, and implications of neuroscientific research and explores the underlying philosophy framing the research and its interpretation, particularly as it pertains to depression.

DEPRESSION AND MATERIALISM

A common mental disorder, depression has a lifetime prevalence of approximately 16% (Kessler et al., 2003) and is part of the growing pantheon of traditionally psychological phenomena that are explained and treated in the context of neurobiology. Furthermore, antidepressants are among the most frequently prescribed classes of medication (Antonuccio, Danton, & McClanahan, 2003), underscoring the importance of putative neurobiological factors in depression. Although the focus in this chapter is on depression, the research methods and techniques, as well as the underlying assumptions, apply to many other mental disorders as well. Current research into the etiology of all major mental disorders, for example, including affective disorders (Nestler et al., 2002; Post, Speer, Hough, & Xing, 2003), substance abuse (Chao & Nestler, 2004), schizophrenia (Heinz, Romero, Gallinat, Juckel, & Weinberger, 2003), and anxiety disorders (Den Boer, Slaap, & Bosker, 2001), involves investigations into the underlying neurobiology of these disorders. Psychopharmacological probes also form an integral component of neuroscientific research (Rudnick, 2002).

Although this methodology approaches mental illnesses from multiple levels (e.g., anatomical, physiological, and genetic), it converges on a molecular level of explanation and treatment (Rudnick, 2002). This convergence is a cogent indication of the assumption that, once all of the relevant work has been done, biological explanations will be able to fully account for these disorders. Known as *materialism*, this assumption postulates that biological explanations will at some point be able to fully account for and explain, among other things, psychological phenomena, including depression (see chap. 6, this volume, for related definition).

Though this materialism may appear as an indication of growing agreement in the field as to the causes of depression and other psychological disorders, questions and limitations remain. Due to the very nature of these questions and limitations, however, it is unlikely that they can be addressed solely through the systematic accumulation of research data. Instead, the assumptions that guide the generation and interpretation of these data require explication. Furthermore, the implications of these assumptions require careful consideration. In fact, the convergence of understanding into the neurobiological causes of depression may be due to a shared interpretation of the research findings. That is, a common philosophical framework—in this case the philosophy of materialism—might be at work, not only shaping the evaluation of neuroscientific findings but also, quite possibly, driving the very questions that are posed in the course of contemporary investigation of mental conditions. Similarly, as Gadamer (1960/1989) suggested, if materialistic assumptions guide the investigation, it is to be expected that materialistic answers will be produced.

In this vein, the goal of this chapter is to elucidate the role of assumptions—assumptions that are very often implicit, unacknowledged, and covert—in the generation and interpretation of data gleaned from research on depression and its treatment, as well as how these assumptions guide the manner in which research questions are framed. To do this, the epidemiology and history of depression are succinctly discussed with emphasis on depression's philosophical and neurobiological contexts. With this background in place, materialistic explanations of the neurobiology of depression and its treatment are reviewed, followed by a focus on the assumptions and implications of this viewpoint. The chapter then concludes with an overview of it salient points concerning the neurobiological conceptualization of depression.

PLACING DEPRESSION IN CONTEXT: EPIDEMIOLOGY AND HISTORY

Along with anxiety disorders and substance abuse, depressive disorders are some of the most prevalent of all psychological and psychiatric conditions (Nestler et al., 2002). Depression affects all age groups and according to the National Comorbidity Survey Replication, has a lifetime prevalence of approximately 16% in the United States (Kessler et al., 2003). Furthermore, depression is associated with substantial morbidity worldwide (Blazer, 2000) and confers a high risk of suicide, with approximately 15% of people suffering from major depression eventually committing suicide (Guze & Robins, 1970). Projected to become the second most common illness worldwide by the year 2020 (Murray & Lopez, 1996), depression appears to affect women approximately twice as frequently as it does men (Nestler et al., 2002). Although the causes of this inequality remain poorly understood, biological and cultural sources have been offered (Sloan & Kornstein, 2003). For example, in the United States, particularly, cultural norms may make it more permissible for women to express greater levels of sadness than men (Newmann, 1984).

Furthermore, David Healy has suggested that there may be even more cultural and contextual issues at play in the diagnosis of depression. In fact, Healy (1997) suggested that there was a relative scarcity in the diagnosis of depression prior to the introduction of the first antidepressants in the late 1950s. Consistent with this observation are the findings that, in an ethnically stable Welsh population, psychiatric admissions were significantly higher in 1996 than in 1896 in all diagnostic groups, including a sharp increase in admissions for depression (Healy, Savage, & Michael, 2001), despite the increased availability of antidepressant medication. Perhaps this is an indication that with ready availability of biological explanations of psychological disorder, diagnosis and treatment increase. Still the question of social construction of diagnosis remains (Gergen, 1985). That is, the question persists as to whether the increase in diagnosis legitimately indicates a greater prevalence of mental disorder or whether the increase reflects the social construction of the "reality" of a biological disorder, in this case depression. In either case, the point is that apart from neurobiology alone, social convention and culture may be important factors that contribute to the diagnosis of depression.

Focusing on internal psychological conflict in addition to social and biological factors, Sigmund Freud explored another avenue to account for depression. By the mid-20th century, Freudian psychoanalytic theory had become a prominent means of explaining psychiatric and psychological disorder. Because of its broad influence on a generation of psychiatrists and psychologists, as well as its persistent penetration into popular culture, particularly in the United States, Freudian theory is a good exemplar of psychiatric and psychological explanation.

A broad conceptualization of personality, Freudian theory provided many cogent explanations of seemingly unexplainable phenomena. For example, Freud (1911) observed that a series of unconscious processes, much like those he believed were set in motion by the death of a loved one, resulted in depression. Two types of people, Freud suggested, were particularly likely to become depressed in the face of loss: those whose parents failed to nurture them and meet their needs during the oral stage of psychosexual development and those whose parents gratified those needs excessively. These two types of individuals, according to Freud, either are overly dependent on others or find the oral stage so gratifying that they resist moving on to subsequent stages. In the face of the loss of a loved one, these individuals feel alone and abandoned—what Freud believed to be the essential features of depression. This loss, Freud believed, could also be symbolic or imagined, in which other sorts of events are equated with the loss of a loved one and, thusly, lead to depression.

Unfortunately, many philosophical problems plague Freudian explanations of depression and other mental disorders. Many of these philosophical problems result from Freudian theory relying so heavily on and containing the logical inconsistencies of Cartesian dualism (e.g., the dualism that the philosopher Rene Descartes believed existed). That is, observable, conscious, somatic, and deterministic terminology is used to explain one domain of life—the body—while unobservable, unconscious, psychic, and agentic (e.g., free will, choice) terminology was used to explain another domain—the mind (Rychlak, 1981; Viney & King, 1998). How these two domains interact, given the body's deterministic and materialistic characteristics and the mind's agentic and seemingly immaterial characteristics, in both Cartesian dualism and psychoanalytic theory, is unclear (see chap. 6, this volume). However, because the mind was taken to be responsible for the body's actions, an interaction between mind and body was assumed (Griffin, 2000).

Furthermore, it is unclear how behavior can be understood if a large part of mental reality remains unconscious, agentic, and, thus, unobservable and seemingly unpredictable. An additional problem confronting Freudian theory is controversy over the validity of the evidence used in its support (Grunbaum, 1984). These factors have contributed to a relative devaluation of Freudian psychoanalytic theory and practice. In the process, a vacuum was created, into which other approaches to explaining and treating mental illness quickly penetrated.

Though much more complex than can be detailed here, psychiatry, well before Freud, had begun to borrow heavily from the already burgeoning medical model in its search for a more justifiable and scientific perspective on psychological phenomena. Great progress, for example, was being made in determining, through biological research, the causes and cures of many disorders, including polio, smallpox, and even the behavioral disturbances associated with neurosyphilis. In this context, Phillipe Pinel (1806), considered to be one of the founders of modern psychiatry, articulated in his *Treatise on Insanity* what he assumed to be the correct application of scientific method to the study of mental disturbances:

> I therefore resolved to adopt that method of investigation which has invariably succeeded in all the departments of natural history, viz. to notice successively every fact, without any other object other than that of collecting materials for future use; and to endeavor, as far as possible, to divest myself of the influence, both of my own repossessions and the authority of others. (p. 2)

Pinel, here, demonstrates nicely how the epistemology of science (what we can know and, thus, "invariably succeed" in) led historically to the materialistic ontology of neuroscience (what is real). Furthermore, Pinel suggests the historical reason why early neuroscientists abandoned the immaterial half of Descartes' dualism: They simply could not conceive of a way to investigate it.

As the nascent science of psychiatry developed, the debates no longer centered on the legitimacy of material and immaterial explanations. Instead, they focused on which *material* explanations proved to be closer to the truth. In other words, these researchers simply focused on one side of the dualism and left the immaterial side unattended (or for others to deal with). One such pivotal debate developed as to the basic nature of the brain: Was the brain a single homogeneous mass of tissue without subdivision or was the brain composed of individual building blocks? By demonstration and careful argument, the neuroanatomist Santiago Ramón y Cajal showed that the brain was, in fact, composed of individual cells, ushering in the so-called neuron doctrine (Swanson, Lufkin, & Colman, 1999). Implicit in the newly acquired ability to gaze into what seemed the very matter of thought was the promise of understanding mental aberrations, and even the mind, in terms of biological explanation.

Now that individual neurons could be visualized, the possibility and assumption existed that the hitherto elusive mind itself could be understood in terms of the brain's individual components. That is, concomitant with the ability to visualize individual neurons, localization of specific functions to specific neurons also became possible—a goal, as Slife and Hopkins (see chap. 6, this volume) show, is implied by materialism. Or as Emil Kraepelin, a founder of modern psychiatry, wrote in 1899, the emphasis in understanding schizophrenia, and by extension other mental disorders, was with "a palpable pathological process in the brain" (Kraepelin, 1899/1990, p. 154). This goal continues to drive much of neuroscience, including current investigations into the neurobiology of depression.

Hence, with the apparent demise of Freudian theory and the rapid advances in other areas of medicine, including biochemistry, molecular biology, and neuropharmacology, conditions were set for the biological revolution in psychiatry and later in psychology. The medical model of mental disorder, with materialistic and biological explanations at its foundation, appeared to provide a genuinely scientific prospect to psychiatry. An essential, if implicit, feature of the emphasis on biological explanation of mental disorder is materialism—the notion that what matters, is valued, and is investigated is observable matter (Slife & Williams, 1995; see also chap. 6, this volume). That is, the assumption of materialism—that the important things are tangible, visible, substantial, and perhaps most importantly, measurable and thus quantifiable—was an implicit but essential component of the neurobiological model of mental disorders. The emphasis on the presumed empirical, material underpinnings of mental disorders has led to an emerging neurobiology of depression.

NEUROBIOLOGICAL FINDINGS ASSOCIATED WITH DEPRESSION

Although no firm understanding of the neurobiology of depression exists (Wong & Licinio, 2001), several neurobiological findings have been associated with depression. For instance, elevations in the hormone cortisol are found in some people who have depression (Wong & Licinio, 2001). In fact, abnormalities in the hypothalamic–pituitary–adrenal axis (Donati & Rasenick, 2003), which regulates cortisol and corticotropin-releasing hormone, are associated with depression (Wong & Licinio, 2001), and drugs that block the action of corticotropin-releasing hormone have been investigated for the treatment of depression (Wong & Licinio, 2001). Similar to findings implicating cortisol and corticotropin-releasing hormone in the etiology of depression is research that suggests that numerous biochemical abnormalities may be associated with depression (Wong & Licinio, 2001).

A highly influential theory of the biochemical basis of depression is the monoamine hypothesis (Hindmarch, 2001), which implicates abnormalities in the function of the monoamine neurotransmitters serotonin and norepinephrine as being important in the etiology and treatment of depression (Bymaster, McNamara, & Tran, 2003). Several lines of evidence support the notion that serotonin and norepinephrine are associated with depression, including putative mechanisms of action of many antidepressant medications themselves (Bymaster et al., 2003; Nutt, 2002). It has been suggested that an understanding of the neurobiological actions of antidepressant medications may be an important element in unraveling the biology of depression (Wong & Licinio, 2001), a notion that links the biology of depression with the pharmacology of antidepressant medication.

Antidepressant drug development is closely linked to the monoamine hypothesis of depression. In the 1950s, for example, the drug imipramine was reported to improve the mood of people with depression (Kuhn, 1958). Later, it was learned that imipramine affected the synaptic concentrations of the serotonin and norepinephrine (Nutt, 2002). Most clinically available antidepressants, in fact, appear to affect serotonin, norepinephrine, or both in one way or another (Nutt, 2002), although antidepressants also appear to affect multiple other neuronal processes, including intracellular signaling mechanisms (Donati & Rasenick, 2003). Other evidence too supports the monoamine hypothesis of depression. By lowering levels of norepinephrine and serotonin in some but not all people treated with antidepressant medication, a depressed mood can be induced (Nutt, 2002).

Despite the powerful association between the monoamine hypothesis of depression and the mechanism of action of antidepressant drugs, several factors limit the explanatory power of the monoamine hypothesis (Wong & Licinio, 2001). Most antidepressants affect norepinephrine and serotonin soon after they are first given; however, clinical response may take up to weeks of antidepressant treatment (Wong & Licinio, 2001), suggesting that additional neurobiological processes are involved. In fact, Valenstein (1998) noted that the numerous neurobiological changes associated with antidepressant use impede an evaluation of exactly what drug effects are associated with affective changes. Animal data, however, outline a process of antidepressant-induced serotonin-mediated neurogenesis in the hippocampus that appears necessary for behavioral changes in the animal to occur that predict antidepressant response in humans (Santarelli et al., 2003), suggesting a mechanism by which antidepressants can affect monoamines and still require several weeks for treatment effects to occur.

Despite the evidence supporting the monoamine hypothesis, epidemiological approaches urge caution when evaluating the monoamine hypothesis of depression by examining large-scale effects of antidepressants. The precipitous increase in antidepressant use, for instance, may not have met with any decrease in societal depression (Moncrieff, 2001). Commenting on findings of increased psychiatric admissions over the last century in relation to the presence of more treatments for these disorders, Healy et al. (2001) suggested that the "effects of modern treatments on the index conditions are more complex than has hitherto been accepted" (p. 787).

MATERIALISM INHERENT IN NEUROBIOLOGICAL
EXPLANATIONS OF DEPRESSION

The neurobiological model of depression possesses qualities of the natural sciences that had formally and at least traditionally assumed that only material phenomena are knowable (Changeux & Ricoeur, 2000; Griffin, 2000; Slife, 2004). Materialism is crucially linked to the primary epistemology of science—empiricism—which involves the search for knowledge in observable phenomena. Therefore, according to the coupling of materialism and empiricism, the focus of research should be on what is material (biological) because that is what can be empirically (sensorily) demonstrated. Materialism, then, is explanation solely in terms of matter, with all other possible explanations, by definition, not considered investigatable and thus not relevant (what Slife & Hopkins, chap. 6, this volume, call *sufficiency*). Furthermore, materialism, including neurobiological explanations of depression, implies the fundamental assumption that the world is "wholly made up of realities [defined] in terms of physics, chemistry, and biology—a world that is already scientifically organized" (Changeux & Ricoeur, 2000, p. 119).

Embedded in this assumption is the presupposition that "the mind is reducible to matter, meaning that the necessary and sufficient conditions for all psychological properties are contained in physiological processes" (Griffin, 2000, p. 31). Following from these assumptions, then, is the notion that the mind is dependent on the function of the matter forming the brain. An additional pivotal assumption underlying materialism, particularly as it applies to the neurobiology of depression, is the idea of a "closed system of *material* causes" (Griffin, 2000, p. 35). Moreover, as is shown later in this chapter, the epistemology (empiricism) in neuroscience is often confounded with the ontology (materialism) of the discipline: What is thought to be knowable (epistemological) has often led to what is thought to be real (ontological).

Following from this, one major reason for the appeal of materialism is that it appears to respond to the questions leveled against Cartesian dualism. Because the assumption of materialism assumes that the immaterial does not matter, at least for science, the dualistic problem of the interaction between the material and immaterial is apparently resolved: The immaterial and, by association, the agentic simply do not matter in this context. It seems then that attention can be focused on observable, empirical, and predictable phenomena in the material and biological realm, solely, and any immaterial phenomena can simply be ignored. In this way, the body, with its concomitant deterministic and, supposedly, scientific and predictable qualities, has supreme importance, whereas the mind, with its concomitant agentic and, supposedly, unscientific and chaotic qualities, only has importance as it relates to the body. Clearly stating the importance of materialism to biological psychiatry, Nancy Andreasen (Andreasen & Black, 1991) wrote:

> Ultimately, the drive of modern psychiatry is to develop a comprehensive understanding of normal brain function at levels that range from mind to molecule, and to determine how aberrations in these normal functions . . . lead to the development of symptoms of mental illness. (pp. 13–14)

With the problems of Cartesian dualism presumably over, a new biological monism is believed to be created, integrating brain and mind into one distinctly biological package. Unfortunately, however, this monistic goal is not, in fact, achieved by means of materialism. Instead, as we argue below, what can properly be labeled a *one-sided dualism* was created, wherein one aspect of the dualism (the immaterial) is ignored in the explanation of psychological phenomena but remains very much a part of the methods for investigating them (see also chap. 6, this volume).

How does this discussion of assumptions relate to depression? The short response is that the assumptions inherent in the shift from the dualism of both the mental and the material to the material alone drive much of the research on depression, as well as the interpretation of this research.

MATERIALISTIC ASSUMPTIONS IMPLICIT TO NEUROBIOLOGICAL RESEARCH

It is undeniable that there have been many advances due to materialistic investigations of depression. Treatment techniques such as antidepressant medications with complex physiological actions (Donati & Rasenick, 2003) have been developed essentially because of the materialistic focus of this research. Yet, the neurobiological basis of depression remains both elusive and inconclusive. Perhaps an understanding of the assumptions, and their implications, that underlie the materialistic treatments and investigatory methods of depression, as well as the interpretation of the research data, will help clarify why neurobiological explanations have been so readily accepted. Still, these treatment techniques, investigatory methods, and the interpretation of the data gleaned from such investigations possess other assumptions associated with materialism, with various important implications. Some of these other assumptions of materialism are material causal determinism, atomism, and objectivism. Therefore, the remainder of this chapter is focused on a different kind of research project than that most often set upon in neurobiology. It is a theoretical instead of empirical investigation, with the hope that this form of investigation can reveal assumptions inherent to the neurobiological investigation of depression that might contribute to the elusive and inconclusive nature of the research.

Material Causal Determinism

The first underlying assumption of materialism is *material causal determinism*, which reflects laws or principles of causation (Slife & Williams, 1995). These laws or principles of causation supposedly constitute the fundamental and invariant reality that provides the basis for the complex and changing world of humans and their behaviors. In deterministic fashion, then, these laws are fundamental, and there is always some force that can be found to cause behavior. According to this assumption, once the causal factors are elucidated, there will be sufficient neurobiological knowledge to explain and predict depression.

Under a materialistic ontology, material causal determinism is implied. This form of determinism—one of four that Aristotle (1999) proposed—is the assumption that matter is ultimately responsible for everything. As applied to human beings, the materialistic position assumes that some biological (material) force—a force over which the person ultimately has no control—determines behavior. Like molecules in a chemical reaction, an individual with depression has no choice either to become depressed or to change this behavior. Just as the molecules in the chemical reaction require some causal force acting upon them to begin their reaction, so must an individual's normal psychological state require a change in serotonin, cortisol function, and so on, for example, to begin a movement toward depression. Furthermore, just as some other force is required to stop the chemical reaction, once the change in the neurobiology has initiated the individual's movement toward depression, the individual continues to be depressed until some other causal force, such as an antidepressant, stops the depression. Analogous to the chemical reaction, any change in the psychological state of the individual also requires some causal force. The chemical reaction cannot agentically change its own course; only a causal force can. The individual with depression, analogously, cannot change his or her own depression; only the medication (or some other material causal force) can. The materialistic form of treatment for depression can also be seen to imply a material causal deterministic framework. Similar to the chemical reaction being controlled by some force that the reaction itself cannot control, the prescribed treatment (e.g., medication) reflects the perhaps implicit belief that the individual is determined by some force—such as abnormal serotonin function—over which the individual has no control.

Although not arguments against materialism, the assumptions of materialism have important implications. For example, material causal determinism assumes that biology alone is responsible for human behavior: Biological factors, not human agency or the self or the Cartesian mind, are responsible for behavior (Slife, Burchfield, & Hedges, 2002). Far from a purely academic issue, the assumption of biological determinism includes important *societal* implications. The assertion that depression is inherently biological contains the assumption that the treatment is pharmacological. Responsibility, then, is shifted from the person as agent to the medication as agent for well-being. This carries with it a consequent devaluation of relationships, accomplishment, and meaning of any kind. In other words, the assumption of material causal determinism, wherein solely biological factors are considered to cause changes in mood, affect, and personality, implies that other factors such as choice, free will, perception, and relational issues are not important considerations when evaluating the presentation of depression. One particular consequence of this is that problematic relationships, such as an abusive marriage, are not addressed nor are existential questions such as death, isolation, and accountability considered as relevant factors in a depressed and hopeless mood. The focus, instead, is on the individual and his or her own biochemistry as the causal factor.

Despite an impressive array of findings, the neurobiological research into depression has not resolved the problem of the "huge gap" (Valenstein, 1998, p. 96) between neurochemistry, such as serotonin physiology, and the subjective experience of depression. Even when a specific neurobiological finding is correlated with a certain subjective perception, it remains unexplained how the actual feeling of depression relates to the associated neurobiology. The nature of the relationship between objective, materialistic neurobiological findings associated with depression and the subjective, immaterial feeling of depression is simply unknown. It may be tempting to suppose that even though all of the details of the relationship between neurobiology and subjective feelings are not known, they soon will be, as material causal determinism unravels the relationship between neurobiology and subjective experiences, such as depression or consciousness. However, the belief that neurobiology will eventually provide a complete answer to how the subjective feeling of depression is generated also remains an assumption inherent to material causal determinism. The philosopher Colin McGinn (1999) argued, in fact, that despite an increasing understanding of neurobiology, humans may never be able to understand consciousness. As at least part of the phenomenon of depression is the conscious awareness of being depressed, McGinn's arguments also can extend to depression in that the gap between neurobiology and the subjective, conscious awareness of depression may not be able to be understood.

Atomism

Atomism reflects the notion demonstrated by Cajal that objects (such as the brain or even humans) are composed of individual, self-contained cells or atoms (Swanson et al., 1999). As related to the human experience, atomism reflects the assumptions that the properties and qualities of individuals are contained within each individual (see chaps. 3 and 7, this volume). One such type of atomism is the assumption that the *individual's* own neurobiology is responsible for the depression. The implication is that the individual diagnosed with depression is first and foremost an independent, self-contained entity with depression, who must then cross time and space to interact with others.

In other words, the assumption of atomism implies that the qualities of each individual with depression originate from within the individual (or atom), not from the interactions he or she has with other individuals (or even himself or herself), completely discounting any relational accounts (Bednar & Peterson, 1995; DeBerry, 1993; Frankl, 1984) of depression before any data have been gathered. The atomistic assumptions of materialism imply the devaluation of experiential (e.g., phenomenal or relational) factors that may be relevant in understanding the genesis of the depression. According to the assumptions of atomism, individuals with a disorder such as depression are considered to be self-contained, and empirical research into depression focuses on the unique factors or treatment techniques that will effect change *within* this type of individual, as well as on the neurochemistry that each individual with depression carries with himself or herself from situation to situation. The investigation, therefore, is aimed at an objective analysis of the biochemical determinants (determinism) of psychological disorder (materialism) in the atom within which it is contained (atomism; i.e., the individual with the disorder) without recognition of an individual's agency and the emotional and social context.

In accordance with the assumptions of atomistic reductionism, investigators of depression and its treatment assume that they are studying and finding in their results a self-contained phenomenon (depression), the unique "variables" of change (techniques or treatment modality), and disorder (individuals with depression, their neuroanatomy, their neurochemicals, their genes, etc.). At the very least, these neurochemical factors exist by themselves first and then interact with other "subjective" factors, rather than the other factors constituting the very nature of the neurochemical. These variables are considered to be separable from and independent of other variables, each with unique and self-contained characteristics. Hence, materialism (and its assumption of atomism) implies that investigators can isolate variables, such as individual techniques or individuals with a particular disorder, from all other variables.

Suggesting caution against an uncritical or unacknowledged acceptance of the assumption of atomism, significant research indicates an important relationship between the early social environment and depression in adulthood (Gutman & Nemeroff, 2003). Such an integrationist approach shows the importance of including social interactions in the investigation of depression. The social environment of childhood in abusive circumstances, in fact, appears to alter the physiology of corticotropin-releasing hormone, an altered physiology that may affect how a person responds to subsequent stress (Gutman & Nemeroff, 2003). However, although social factors such as an abusive early environment may be considered alternatives that avoid the assumptions of atomism altogether, these conceptions frequently are little more than aggregations of materialistic variables. Nonmaterial factors still may be rarely acknowledged, with variables such as social and cultural factors defined and objectified in materialistic or "naturalistic" (see Slife, 2004) terms (e.g., environment). As DeBerry (1993) suggested, such conceptions may reduce to a deterministic interaction of materialistic factors and remain fundamentally atomistic in nature.

Objectivism

The final assumption addressed is *objectivism*, defined here as the assumption that carefully delineated materialistic methods for investigating materialistic phenomena will eventually provide observable, transparent truth, without regard to the assumptions that are embedded in the research methods themselves. Limitations of the research methods themselves and the problems of underdeterminism are two important difficulties that argue against a simple acceptance of the assumption of objectivism.

Research Limitations

Some methodological issues in research regarding antidepressant efficacy can suggest potential limitations of objectivism and underscore the need for a critical evaluation of research methodology when interpreting findings concerning the neurobiology of mental disorders. If the research that underlies a particular conclusion has unevaluated and unacknowledged assumptions, it follows that the conclusion itself may have limitations, thus undermining the core assumption of objectivism that materialistic research methodologies eventually provide observable truth.

As previously noted, research on antidepressant drugs was one of the driving forces for the development of the monoamine hypothesis of depression. Also, the use of antidepressants for the treatment of depression has escalated considerably since the introduction of selective serotonin reuptake inhibitor drugs (Moncrieff, 2001). The statistics show that antidepressant medications are now in the United Kingdom, as Moncrieff (2001) reported, "the most commonly prescribed class of psychotropic drug and by far the most costly" (p. 288). However, just as there are methodological and conceptual limitations with the monoamine hypothesis of depression, so are there such limitations with the research on antidepressant medication, illustrating the need to carefully examine the methodology that produces the research results.

Double-blind, randomized clinical trials, for example, are the "gold standard" of antidepressant research. Through the use of placebos, such studies attempt to "blind" both the participant and investigator as to a participant's true medication status. Unfortunately, studies concerning the maintenance of this "double-blind" indicate that this standard is hardly ever reached (Moncrieff, 2001). In fact, Slife et al. (2002) summarized how several limitations affect the simple interpretation of findings from randomized, double-blind clinical trials. Some of the methodological limitations of these trials include the following:

- *Unblinding*—the potential for active drugs to produce unintended physiological and psychological experiences (e.g., side effects) can unmask the blinding because the side effects may reveal to both participants and investigators which participants received which medication (Moncrieff, 2001; Montcrieff, Wessely, & Hardy, 1998).
- *Wash out*—the finding that a placebo whose side effects resemble those of the active drug may not significantly separate from the active drug (Antonuccio, Danton, DeNelsky, Greenberg, & Gordon, 1999; Greenberg, Bornstein, Greenberg, & Fisher, 1992; Kirsch & Sapirstein, 1998).
- *Early subject withdrawal*—which may include the exclusion of individuals who withdraw early from treatment from analysis and results in higher effects sizes for antidepressants (Bollini, Pampallona, Tibaldi, Kupelnick, & Munniza, 1999; Colditz, Miller, & Mosteller, 1989; O'Sullivan, Noshivani, Marks,

Monteiro, & Leiliot, 1991; Schultz, Grimes, Altman, & Hayes, 1996).

- *Withdrawal symptoms*—discontinuing antidepressant treatment may result in a set of withdrawal symptoms that can be mistaken for relapse, thus depressing the outcome of the placebo group (Moncrieff, 2001).
- *The nonspecificity antidepressant response*—that many non-antidepressant medications can be used to effectively treat depression, including some antipsychotics, barbiturates, benzodiazepines, and buspirone (Moncrieff, 2001; Thase & Kupfer, 1996).
- *Sponsorship effects*—the finding that the study sponsor is the strongest predictor of antidepressant efficacy (Freemantle, Anderson, & Young, 2000; Friedberg, Saffran, Stinson, Nelson, & Bennett, 1999).

These methodological limitations appear to indicate that the double-blind, randomized clinical trials of antidepressants may be less than ideal and, as suggested by Moncrieff (2001), "that depression is susceptible to a variety of non-disease specific pharmacological actions, such as sedation or psychostimulation, as well as the effects of suggestion" (p. 292).

Furthermore, the argument for the monoamine hypothesis based on the action of antidepressants amounts to a *post hoc ergo propter hoc* argument (Williams, 2001). That is, the logic is that when we administer the antidepressant, the synaptic concentrations of monoamines are increased, and the depression is lessened; therefore, the lowered content of monoamines was the cause of depression. This is akin, as Williams (2001) noted, to saying that flu is due to a lack of aspirin in the bloodstream, given the finding that aspirin lessens flu symptoms. It also assumes that altered neurobiology and subjective experience are identical (Changeux & Ricoeur, 2000), when no theory or empirical formulation has ever explained how this is possible, let alone presumable. Just how does pathological neuronal function produce subjective feelings of depression? As Valenstein (1998) pointed out, the monoamine hypothesis amounts to a description of the chemical processes for alleviating symptoms of depression, not an explanation of how these chemical processes might produce the depression. As observed by Ricoeur, "human experimentation is limited. . . . The correlation between neuroscience and the world of experience becomes problematic" (Changeux & Ricoeur, 2000, pp. 66–67). That is, despite intense neurobiological research, ontological questions remain about the relation between body and mind.

Underdeterminism

In addition to the methodological issues, it must be noted that the data of materialistic (and empirical) studies are, like all studies, underdetermined. Underdeterminism is the notion that data from such research can be used to support several interpretations, and they cannot point to material causation and determinism solely. Popper (1959) and Rychlak (1980), for example, noted that the inferential leap from empirical investigation to a claim of validation stems from the common logical error in empirical investigation of affirming the consequent—the belief that the theory is true because it predicted the data. As Scottish philosopher and historian David Hume noted, however, the data arraying as predicted—even experimental data—does not by itself allow such inferences about causality (Popper, 1959; Rychlak, 1980; Slife & Williams, 1995).

Hume instead demonstrated that we infer causality subjectively. According to Hume, we do not have any direct knowledge of the reality of the causal chain. Instead, all causal reality is interpreted reality, meaning that causation, even in experimental studies, is always inferred and never observed. This is the often neglected fourth component of Hume's theory necessary for determining causality: necessary conjunction. Even after one has established the antecedence, contiguity, and constant conjunction of events,[1] one still is left with the problem of establishing necessary conjunction—ruling out all other possible causal interpretations. Furthermore, any interpretation of reality depends on the explanatory and interpretive framework one uses. Correlational and even experimental data, supportive of many types of explanation, quickly can become proof of materialism when investigators have an unacknowledged materialistic philosophical framework. In short, the interpretation of data depends on the implicit and explicit philosophy investigators bring to bear on the investigation.

ONE-SIDED DUALISM

With regard to the etiology and treatment of depression, the assumptions and research methodologies of materialism have produced a tentative and preliminary but potentially powerful neurobiology of depression with numerous implications about what it means to be human and even the meaning of joy and suffering themselves. Just as importantly, this early neurobiology of depression also confronts directly any dualistic notion of mind and brain and argues instead for the monism that mind is dependent solely on brain. In part because of the implications of such a notion, the assumptions that underlie this postulated monism require careful evaluation. Because materialism is a reaction against dualism, an essential assumption regards the

---

[1]According to the empiricist David Hume, to determine causation, four requirements need to be met: antecedence, contiguity, constant conjunction, and necessary conjunction. *Antecedence* refers to conditions of priority in which the cause must *precede* the effect in temporal sequence. *Contiguity* refers to conditions of nearness in space (e.g., the cause must be in close proximity to that which it is acting upon in spatial terms). *Constant conjunction* means that the cause and effect must have a correlation of 1.0. That is, the effect must always occur in relation to the cause. Finally, *necessary conjunction* means that we must be able to rule out all other possible causes of a given effect. Hume, however, believed that necessary conjunction was, theoretically, impossible (Slife & Williams, 1995).

question of whether materialistic explanations by themselves truly circumvent the problems inherent in dualism—that is, do they indeed form a true monism—or whether they are simply a one-sided dualism, ignoring instead those aspects of psychological phenomena that are not readily studied by materialistic methodology.

By focusing on the material, neurobiological part of the Cartesian duality to explain aspects of the subjective experience of depression, the nonmaterial aspect of Cartesian dualism is implied. In other words, the assumption that psychological disorders such as depression can be explained by biology itself assumes that psychological phenomena are valid to begin with (Slife & Williams, 1995), an assumption that keeps the immaterial aspects of mental function very much a part of the investigation. For example, in determining whether depression is the result of biochemical actions in the brain, there is first the assumption that the *experience*—which requires the subjective recognition of the feeling—of depression is itself valid. Despite their impressive discovery of neurobiological findings associated with depression and other mental phenomena, materialistic studies, then, imply a one-sided dualism and not a true monism, wherein both sides of the duality are used in the methods, but only one dimension of the duality—the material—is used in the explanatory theory (see chap. 6, this volume). This in not to say that neurobiological processes are not important (neuroscience clearly demonstrates the importance of pathophysiological processes in depression [e.g., see Wong & Licinio, 2001]) but rather that they do not explain the whole phenomenon of depression, omitting nonmaterial factors, such as agency (see chap. 6, this volume) from consideration. In short, if neuroscience is a one-sided dualism, as we argue, it has not resolved the problems inherent in Cartesian dualism (e.g., how a material realm interacts with a nonmaterial realm and how agency interacts with a material brain), necessitating the search for other alternatives in addition to Kraepelin's (1899/1990) "palpable pathological process" that could provide a true monism that resolves the problems of Cartesian dualism (see chap. 6, this volume).

In addition, such a one-sided dualism necessarily restricts the methodology that can be applied to the phenomenon under question. An emphasis on only materialistic methodology precludes all other potentially relevant methodologies. That the stance of excluding nonmaterialistic methodologies may violate the essence of science itself is suggested by the physicist Bridgman (1955), who wrote that "the scientific method insofar as it may be considered to be a method consists in doing one's damnedest with one's mind, no holds barred" (p. 535).

CONCLUSION

An analogy, borrowed from a commonly used metaphorical story, may help to pull together the conclusion to this chapter. Late at night, a young man was walking home on a dark street when he came across another man frantically searching for something underneath a street light. The young man stopped and asked the other man what he was looking for. The other man stopped his search and said, "I'm looking for my keys." To this, the young man replied, "Did you lose them under the lamp?" The other man responded, "No, but this is where the light is."

This story serves our conclusion by illustrating that natural scientific method—the light—drove neuroscience to materialism—looking under the lamp. However, such a focus may constrict our interpretations or even deter us from finding alternative explanations of given phenomena. In this chapter, we have explained depression with various hypotheses, including prominent hypotheses that are highly based on neurobiological findings associated with depression. However, such neurobiological hypotheses involve various assumptions (e.g., materialism, determinism, and atomism) and implications (e.g., ignoring of the "immaterial" aspects of depression, societal responsibility, agency, and contextual issues). Perhaps most significant, however, is that materialism, a reaction against Cartesian dualism and supposedly a monistic bastion of psychological explanation, is itself reduced to a one-sided dualism. Although neuroscience points to a fascinating intersection (Changeux & Ricoeur, 2000) between neurobiological processes and the subjective experience of mental phenomena, such as depression, the nature of the relationship—the interaction of the material with the immaterial—remains as elusive as ever. The following chapter offers some alternatives to the assumptions discussed here.

REFERENCES

Andreasen, N. C., & Black, D. W. (1991). *Introductory textbook of psychiatry*. Washington, DC: American Psychiatric Press.

Antonuccio, D. O., Danton, W. G., DeNelsky, G. Y., Greenberg, R. P., & Gordon, J. S. (1999). Raising questions about antidepressants. *Psychotherapy and Psychosomatics, 68*, 3–14.

Antonuccio, D. O., Danton, W. G., & McClanahan, T. M. (2003). Psychology in the prescription era: Building a firewall between marketing and science. *American Psychologist, 58*, 1028–1042.

Aristotle. (1999). *Physics* (R. Waterfield & D. Bostock, Trans.). London: Oxford University Press.

Bednar, R. L., & Peterson, S. R. (1995). *Self esteem: Paradoxes and innovations in clinical theory and practice*. Washington, DC: American Psychological Association.

Blazer, D. G. (2000). Mood disorders: Epidemiology. In B. J. Sadock & V. A. Sadock (Eds.), *Comprehensive textbook of psychiatry* (pp. 1298–1308). New York: Lippincott Williams & Wilkins.

Bollini, P., Pampallona, S., Tibaldi, G., Kupelnick, B., & Munniza, C. (1999). Effectiveness of antidepressants: Meta-analysis of dose–effect relationships in randomized clinical trials. *British Journal of Psychiatry, 174*, 297–303.

Bridgman, P. (1955). *Reflections of a physicist.* New York: Philosophical Library.

Bymaster, F. P., McNamara, R. K., & Tran, P. V. (2003). New approaches to developing antidepressants by enhancing monoaminergic neurotransmission. *Expert Opinion on Investigational Drugs, 12*, 531–543.

Changeux, J. P., & Ricoeur, P. (2000). *What makes us think? A neuroscientist and philosopher argue about ethics, humans nature, and the brain.* Princeton, NJ: Princeton University Press.

Chao, J., & Nestler, E. J. (2004). Molecular neurobiology of drug addiction. *Annual Review of Medicine, 55*, 113–132.

Colditz, G. A., Miller, J. N., & Mosteller, F. (1989). How study design affects outcomes in comparisons of therapy: I. Medical. *Statistical Medicine, 8*, 441–454.

DeBerry, S. T. (1993). *Quantum psychology: Steps to a postmodern ecology of being.* Westport, CT: Praeger Publishers.

Den Boer, J.-A., Slaap, B. R., & Bosker, F. J. (2001). Biological aspects of anxiety disorders and depression. In S. A. Montgomery & J. A. den Boer (Eds.), *Perspectives in psychiatry: Vol. 7. SSRIs in depression and anxiety* (2nd ed., pp. 25–85). West Sussex, England: Wiley.

Donati, R. J., & Rasenick, M. M. (2003). G protein signaling and the molecular basis of antidepressant action. *Life Sciences, 73*, 1–17.

Fisher, A. M. (1997). Modern manifestations of materialism: A legacy of the enlightenment discourse. *Journal of Theoretical and Philosophical Psychology, 17*, 45–55.

Frankl, V. E. (1984). *Man's search for meaning.* New York: Washington Square Press.

Freemantle, N., Anderson, I. M., & Young, P. (2000). Predictive value of pharmacological activity for the relative efficacy of antidepressant drugs: Meta-regression analysis. *British Journal of Psychiatry, 177*, 292–302.

Freud, S. (1911). Mourning and melancholia. In W. Gaylin (Ed.), *The meaning of despair: Psychoanalytic contributions to the understanding of depression.* New York: Science House.

Friedberg, M., Saffran, B., Stinson, T. J., Nelson, W., & Bennett, C. L. (1999). Evaluation of conflict of interest in economic analyses of new drugs used in oncology. *Journal of the American Medical Association, 282*, 1453–1457.

Gadamer, H.-G. (1989). *Truth and method* (2nd ed., rev.) (J. Weinsheimer & D. G. Marshall, Trans.). New York: Continuum. (Original work published 1960)

Gazzaniga, M. S. (Ed.). (1995). *The cognitive neurosciences.* Cambridge, MA: MIT Press.

Gergen, K. J. (1985). The social constructionist movement in modern psychology. *American Psychologist, 40*, 266–275.

Greenberg, R. P., Bornstein, R. F., Greenberg, M. D., & Fisher, S. (1992). A meta-analysis of antidepressant outcome under "blinder" conditions. *Journal of Consulting and Clinical Psychology, 60*, 664–669.

Griffin, D. R. (2000). *Religion and scientific naturalism: Overcoming the conflicts.* Albany, New York: SUNY Press.

Grunbaum, A. (1984). *The foundations of psychoanalysis: A philosophical critique.* Berkeley: University of California Press.

Gutman, D. A., & Nemeroff, C. B. (2003). Persistent central nervous system effects of an adverse early environment: Clinical and preclinical studies. *Physiology & Behavior, 79,* 471–478.

Guze, S. B., & Robins, E. (1970). Suicide and primary affective disorder. *British Journal of Psychiatry, 117,* 437–438.

Healy, D. (1997). *The antidepressant era.* Cambridge, MA: Harvard University Press.

Healy, D., Savage, M., & Michael, P. (2001). Psychiatric service utilization: 1896 and 1996 compared. *Psychological Medicine, 31,* 779–790.

Heinz, A., Romero, B., Gallinat, J., Juckel, G., & Weinberger, D. R. (2003). Molecular brain imaging and the neurobiology and genetics of schizophrenia. *Pharmacopsychiatry, 36*(Suppl. 3), S152–S157.

Hindmarch, I. (2001). Expanding the horizons of depression: Beyond the monoamine hypothesis. *Human Psychopharmacology, 16,* 203–218.

Kessler, R. C., Berglund, P., Demler, O., Jin, R., Koretz, D., Merikangas, K. R., et al. (2003). The epidemiology of major depressive disorder: Results from the National Comorbidity Survey Replications (NCS-R). *Journal of the American Medical Association, 289*(23), 3095–3105.

Kirsch, L., & Sapirstein, G. (1998). Listening to Prozac but hearing placebo: A meta-analysis of antidepressant medication. *Prevention & Treatment, 1,* Article 0002a. Retrieved September 14, 2004, from http://www.journals.apa.org/prevention/Volume1/pre0010002a.html

Kraepelin, E. (1990). *Psychiatry: A textbook for students and physicians* (6th ed.). Caton, MA: Science History. (Original work published 1899)

Kuhn, R. (1958). The treatment of depressive states with G-22355 (imipramine hydrochloride). *American Journal of Psychiatry, 115,* 459–464.

McGinn, C. (1999). *The mysterious flame: Conscious minds in a material world.* New York: Basic Books.

Moncrieff, J. (2001). Are antidepressants overrated? A review of methodological problems in antidepressant trials. *Journal of Nervous and Mental Disease, 189,* 288–295.

Moncrieff, J., Wessely, S., & Hardy, R. (1998). Meta-analysis of trials comparing antidepressants with active placebos. *British Journal of Psychiatry, 172,* 227–231.

Murray, C. J., & Lopez, A. D. (1996). Evidence-based health policy: Lessons from the Global Burden of Disease Study. *Science, 274,* 1593–1594.

Nestler, E. J., Barrot, M., Dileone, R. J., Eisch, A. J., Gold, S. J., & Monteggia, L. M. (2002). Neurobiology of depression. *Neuron, 34,* 13–25.

Newmann, J. (1984). Sex differences in symptoms of depression: Clinical disorder or normal distress? *Journal of Health and Social Behavior, 25,* 136–159.

Nutt, D. J. (2002). The neuropharmacology of serotonin and noradrenaline in depression. *International Clinical Psychopharmacology, 17*(Suppl. 1), S1–S12.

O'Sullivan, G., Noshivani, H., Marks, I., Monteiro, W., & Leiliot, P. (1991). Six year follow up after exposure and clomipramine therapy for obsessive–compulsive disorder. *Journal of Clinical Psychiatry, 52*, 150–155.

Pinel, P. (1806). *A treatise on insanity*. London: Cadell & Davies.

Popper, K. (1959). *The logic of scientific discovery*. New York: Basic Books.

Post, R. M., Speer, A. M., Hough, C. J., & Xing, G. (2003). Neurobiology of bipolar illness: Implications for future study and therapeutics. *Annals of Clinical Psychiatry, 15*, 85–94.

Rudnick, A. (2002). The molecular turn in psychiatry: A philosophical analysis. *Journal of Medicine and Philosophy, 27*, 287–296.

Rychlak, J. F. (1980). The false promise of falsification. *Journal of Mind and Behavior, 1*, 183–195.

Rychlak, J. F. (1981). *Introduction to personality and psychotherapy: A theory-construction approach* (2nd ed.). Boston: Houghton Mifflin.

Santarelli, L., Saxe, M., Gross, C., Surget, A., Battaglia, F., Dulawa, S., et al. (2003). Requirement of hippocampal neurogenesis for the behavioral effects of antidepressants. *Science, 301*, 805–809.

Schultz, K. F., Grimes, D. A., Altman, D. G., & Hayes, R. H. (1996). Blinding and exclusions after allocation in randomized clinical trials: Survey of published parallel group trials in obstetrics and gynaecology. *British Medical Journal, 312*, 742–744.

Slife, B. D. (2004). Theoretical challenges to therapy practice and research: The constraint of naturalism. In M. Lambert (Ed.), *Handbook of psychotherapy and behavior change* (pp. 44–83). New York: Wiley.

Slife, B. D., Burchfield, C. M., & Hedges, D. W. (2002, April). *Hook line and sinker: Psychology's uncritical acceptance of biological explanation*. Invited address to the meeting of the Rocky Mountain Psychological Association, Park City, UT.

Slife, B. D., & Williams, R. N. (1995). *What's behind the research? Discovering hidden assumptions in the behavioral sciences*. Thousand Oaks, CA: Sage.

Sloan, D. M., & Kornstein, S. G. (2003). Gender differences in depression and response to antidepressant treatment. *Psychiatric Clinics of North America, 26*, 581–594.

Swanson, L. W., Lufkin, T., & Colman, D. R. (1999). Organization of nervous systems. In M. J. Zigmond, F. E. Bloom, S. C. Landis, J. L. Roberts, & L. R. Squire (Eds.), *Fundamental neuroscience* (pp. 9–37). San Diego, CA: Academic Press.

Thase, M. E., & Kupfer, D. J. (1996). Recent developments in the pharmacotherapy of mood disorders. *Journal of Consulting and Clinical Psychology, 64*, 646–659.

Valenstein, E. S. (1998). *Blaming the brain: The truth about drugs and mental health*. New York: Free Press.

Viney, A. W., & King, D. B. (1998). *A history of psychology: Ideas and context* (2nd ed.). Boston: Allyn & Bacon.

Williams, R. N. (2001). The biologization of psychotherapy: Understanding the nature of influence. In B. D. Slife, R. N. Williams, & S. Barlow (Eds.), *Critical issues in psychotherapy: Translating new ideas into practice* (pp. 51–67). Thousand Oaks, CA: Sage.

Wong, M. L., & Licinio, J. (2001). Research and treatment approaches to depression. *Nature Reviews Neuroscience, 2,* 343–351.

6

ALTERNATIVE ASSUMPTIONS FOR NEUROSCIENCE: FORMULATING A TRUE MONISM

BRENT D. SLIFE AND RAMONA O. HOPKINS

The field of experimental psychology, especially neuroscience, is exploding with important advances in research and medical technology as well as significant findings in brain–behavior relationships. As Hedges and Burchfield have shown in the previous chapter (chap. 5, this volume), the history of neuroscience research on depression is filled with noteworthy developments. For this reason, the current assumptions and overall view of neuroscience research appear to have served this field well. Why, then, explore alternatives? Why describe in this chapter a different set of presuppositions for neuroscience inquiry?

The answer is at least twofold. First, presuppositions are notoriously difficult to critically examine and test. They occur at such a basic and often unrealized level that testing them scientifically is difficult, if not impossible. In fact, we argue in this chapter that the current assumptions of neuroscience have *not* been empirically tested. Second, there is reason to believe that some of the main assumptions of neuroscience, at least as understood by many, are somewhat constricted and often misleading. We try to show in this chapter that a better approach might be possible, one that is more consistent with current neuroscience research and more stimulating for future investigations.

Our alternative is a particular kind of *monism*, or oneness of mind and body, that we believe is more in keeping with the original pioneers and spirit of neuroscience. Indeed, we hold that many neuroscientists already assume this type of monism informally. Our job is to articulate it more fully for possible use in experimental research and practical application. Consequently, we outline some of the implications of this alternative conception for neuroscience, using research on children who are diagnosed with attention-deficit hyperactivity disorder (ADHD) as an example of how this alternative view of inquiry might make a significant and positive contribution.

CURRENT ASSUMPTIONS

Perhaps the central presupposition of neuroscience is that the mechanisms of biology are sufficient to explain the human mind and behaviors. In other words, many neuroscience researchers assume that they can explain their findings exclusively in terms of biological mechanisms. Consider the research on children diagnosed with ADHD. Kirley et al. (2002) and Hawi et al. (2002), for example, indicated that abnormalities in the dopamine and serotonin systems of the prefrontal cortex and related subcortical systems explain (or are responsible for) the distractibility of ADHD children. Although these researchers placed several qualifications on their conclusions, it is clear they considered biological factors in the brain to be responsible for the behavioral effects that occurred in the individuals of their study who were diagnosed with ADHD. No other factors than biological were identified as having this responsibility, even partially. The biology of the body alone was assumed to be sufficient to explain and account for their research findings.[1]

This presupposition or assumption is known generally as *materialism*— the *sufficiency* of the material of the body (biology) alone for explaining our minds and behaviors (chap. 5, this volume; Churchland, 1986; Dupre, 1993; Fisher, 1997; Muse, 1997). This assumption is so common in neuroscience that it is rarely made explicit or formalized. Indeed, few neuroscientists specifically argue for it, and many neuroscientists may not formally intend to make this assumption. They are merely using the traditional explanations and methods of their discipline, which allows them to garner research funding and publish their findings. Yet, this lack of explicit intention does not mean that this presupposition is not assumed. As noted neuroscientist Elliot S. Valenstein (1998) observed,

---

[1]We acknowledge that some studies have demonstrated the effectiveness of biological interventions, such as drugs, for some behaviors associated with ADHD. However, we are not challenging the importance of biology, but the sufficiency of biology.

It was not so very long ago that the cause of mental disorders was thought to be rooted in early experiences within the family, but now it is widely believed by most authorities and the public alike that the cause is a chemical imbalance in the brain. . . . Brain chemistry is believed to be not only the cause of mental disorders, but also the explanation of the normal variations in personality and behavior. (p. 1)

Two features of materialism will help clarify *how* materialism is assumed in neuroscience. First, materialism does not mean here merely the importance of the body. As we will show, our alternative to this assumption also involves the importance of biology and the body. Materialism (and sufficiency) here means exclusive reliance on mechanisms of the body for explanation, whereby other, nonmaterial and nonbiological factors are viewed as less than fundamental or unimportant (see chap. 5, this volume). Materialism in this sense does not mean the nonexistence of the nonbiological factors; it means their lack of importance. Only the matter matters. If nonbiological factors were fundamental or important, they would be involved in this research at the outset or described as distinctly missing for full understanding and explanation.

The second feature of this materialist assumption is that it only pertains to the explanations or interpretations made of neuroscience data, not to the data themselves. For example, the data of Kirley et al. (2002) and Hawi et al. (2002) may clearly indicate the involvement of neurotransmitter abnormalities in the distractibility of those diagnosed with ADHD. However, it is the assumption of materialism—not the data—that leads these researchers to make the additional inference that only biological factors are involved in their findings. These researchers do not state this inference explicitly, but they interpret and explain their findings as though nonbiological factors are irrelevant to their data. The problem with this interpretation is that no data in their studies support it. Indeed, as we will show, it would be a very rare piece of research that *could* make the additional inference that nonbiological factors (e.g., culture, spirit) can be ruled out as important in interpreting the results. This interpretation is typically made because of a usually unexamined theoretical assumption—the assumption that the biological is sufficient for such explanations.

Even when nonbiological factors have demonstrated involvement in a psychological disorder, neuroscience research is primarily interpreted as if biological factors are sufficient (Churchland, 1986). In ADHD research, for example, there is considerable evidence that environmental factors, such as family environment (Biederman et al., 1995), play an important role. Still, few neuroscience researchers assess both the biological and environmental factors involved in ADHD. Common research practices, especially, lead these researchers to assume that they can conduct their studies and explain their findings without reference to nonbiological realities. Researchers may assume they can limit a specific study to the biological only, with some other investigator studying the nonbiological facets of the topic of interest. However, this assumption is still materialistic because it assumes that the biological can be studied without the nonbiological, or, to put it another way, that the nonbiological is not needed to make sense of the biological.

Many neuroscientists also couch their explanations in qualified terms, such as "is implicated in," "plays a role in," and "contributes to"—as in "serotonin systems *play a role* in ADHD distractibility." This terminology implies that other factors could be involved—play a role—in the object of inquiry (e.g., ADHD distractibility). We support this qualification, as our own alternative will show. Still, such qualifications do not violate the assumption of materialism unless *non*biological factors are the "other factors" to which these qualifications refer. A quick review of neuroscience articles, however, shows that this qualifying terminology refers primarily, if not exclusively, to *other* biological factors. Nonbiological factors are seldom implied, let alone explicitly noted in this regard, leaving the assumed sufficiency of the biological (materialism) intact.

Again, we recognize that materialism is so common in neuroscience that it is rarely made explicit or formalized. Few neuroscientists specifically argue for it, and many may not formally intend to make this assumption at all. They are merely following the traditional explanations and methods of their discipline. However, our point here is that this lack of explicit intention does not prevent the assumption of materialism from being influential to those who read and consume neuroscience articles—such as students, physicians, the lay public, drug company executives, and psychologists—thus having potentially significant practical implications.

IMPLICATIONS OF CURRENT ASSUMPTIONS

Let us take a look at some of these implications, especially as neuroscience research is interpreted by psychologists, students, and the general public. We will see that the assumption of materialism, however unintended, is a potent force in psychology, neuroscience, medicine, and society. The power of the pharmaceutical industry is perhaps one of the primary and continuing impetuses for this materialist interpretation (Relman & Angell, 2002). If a person's biology (e.g., brain electrophysiology) is solely responsible for his or her emotion and behavior (e.g., ADHD, depression), then drugs are an effective and easy treatment for changing emotion and behavior, which benefits the pharmaceutical industry. If, however, nonbiological factors are also important to mood and behavior, then these drugs could be perceived as less effective, resulting in decreased pharmaceutical revenues. In other words, there are significant economic forces that support the assumption that nonbiological factors are unimportant.

What types of nonbiological factors might there be? Many scholars have suggested, for example, that culture is an important consideration in understanding and accounting for human behavior (Geertz, 1973; Ratner, 1997; Richardson, Fowers, & Guignon, 1999; Shweder, 1991). If culture is not a biological factor, as many scholars presume (see Pinker, 2002, for an alternative view), then materialism would imply that the researchers do not need culture to explain their findings. In this sense, explaining the distractibility of ADHD children requires only brain mechanisms and not cultural factors. After all, Kirley et al. (2002) and Hawi et al. (2002), discussed earlier, did not present their findings as if they were incomplete and required cultural factors to make full sense of their data. Their explanations make clear that they believed the biological mechanisms cited in their articles were alone responsible for their findings.

By contrast, the importance of nonbiological factors has long been widely recognized in psychology and psychiatry, as evidenced by the number of compound-word models—"bio-psycho-socio-etc."—that are proposed as alternatives to materialism in psychology (e.g., Paris, 1998; Sarafino, 2001; Whitbourne, 2000).[2] These models show how many scientists sense the incompleteness of materialist explanations and postulate a number of other factors, such as culture (the "socio"), to make them complete.[3] We support these efforts. However, these compound-word alternatives rarely serve as true alternatives to current neuroscience assumptions. As we will see, many compound-word conceptions retain assumptions associated with materialism and overlook the most difficult issue of materialism—the issue of human agency.

Agency

Human agency is the notion that humans have free will, choices, or possibilities. Whatever humans do—however they think and behave—the notion of agency says that they could have acted or thought otherwise (J. F. Rychlak, 1988; Slife & Fisher, 2000). Human agency is rarely mentioned in neuroscience research. As chapter 5 (this volume) explains, the assumption of materialism—the custom of explaining things as though the biological were sufficient in itself—has led neuroscientists to present their findings as if they were complete without human agency. This is not to say that some neuroscientists do not assume informally that something like agency, such as top-down causation, is occurring in the human mind, with some assuming it more formally (e.g., Brown, Murphy, & Maloney, 1998). Nevertheless, most neuroscientists make no mention at all of agentic factors in their research reports. They, instead, explain their findings using conventional understand-

---

[2]We recognize that some neuroscientists would hold that the most fundamental elements of the "psycho" or the "socio" in compound-word models are the biological representation of the psycho and socio. In other words, they would contend that these models are really bio-bio-bio-etc. models and do not entail nonbiological entities at all.
[3]Research shows that genes are not the sole determinant of brain anatomy and behavior; environmental factors not only can modify gene expression but also can influence brain anatomy (Valenstein, 1998).

ings of biology, such as natural laws. The clear implication to the lay con-sumers of this research is that these neuroscientists consider biological mecha-nisms to be solely responsible for their findings.

If biological mechanisms are solely responsible—sufficient in themselves to explain human behaviors, thoughts, and values—the implication is that agentic factors, such as a person's decisions, cannot be responsible, even par-tially. Some neuroscientists might say these decisions are themselves taking place in the brain (and, as we later describe, there is an important sense in which we agree). Still, it is one thing to assume that decisions take place in the brain and quite another to assume that the mechanisms of biology are solely responsible for these "decisions." In other words, the issue here is not the importance of biology per se; the issue here is the adequacy of the mecha-nistic interpretation of biology. By *mechanistic*, we mean that biology is fre-quently understood to be governed and controlled by natural laws (causal necessity), much as machines are considered to be controlled by natural laws, hence the label *mechanistic*.

With this interpretation, human action, and thus brain action, are no different from any other natural event. The natural event of a boulder rolling down a mountain is not considered to be agentically responsible for the di-rection it rolls. The boulder cannot do otherwise than what natural physical laws—the mechanisms of nature—dictate. The boulder has no self-directed possibilities and thus no agency. It might seem silly to talk about boulders in this manner—analogizing boulder actions to human actions—but we use this analogy to raise the natural law question: If our brains are governed by natu-ral laws, why expect our brains, and thus our minds, to be different in kind from the boulder rolling down a mountain?

We should be clear that we, like many neuroscientists, consider our brains to be quite different from boulders. The boulder analogy is only meant to help us begin to understand the reason for this difference. Or put another way, this analogy is intended to help us understand how the brain and the boulder *have* to be different: They both cannot be governed by natural laws in the same sense. Otherwise, our actions are no more purposeful and mean-ingful than those of the boulder.

We recognize that some people may contend that the boulder analogy is too simple—that biochemical processes are far more complex than a boul-der rolling down a mountain. Some may even hold that such processes are so complicated that they emerge into a different form altogether, with different qualities and properties (e.g., Brown, 2002; Brown et al., 1998). However, the question here is, Do these emergent processes transcend the determi-nants of natural law? In other words, these processes could have quite differ-ent properties from those they emerged from, without these properties escap-ing the control and determinism of natural laws.

Complicating our boulder analogy might help illustrate this issue. We could enlist millions of boulders for our analogy, rolling down complex mountains and hitting one another in complicated ways. There is no doubt that we would have a fascinating system of boulders interacting in patterned and perhaps even "emergent" ways. However, there is also no doubt that most people would view this system of complex boulder interactions as still controlled and ultimately determined by natural laws. Neuroscientists may suspect that biochemical processes are different from even complex boulder systems, but the natural law question is again pertinent: Do these differences include the escape of natural law determinism? Maybe the reason the boulder analogy seems oversimplified is agency itself. That is, our brains have a kind of agency and are not merely complex systems of natural laws.

Mixing Agency and Natural Law

Can we put agency and natural law together in the same explanation? Let us return to our boulder analogy for help. If the boulder was to roll into a hiker, we would likely not hold the boulder agentically responsible for the hiker's injuries, because the boulder could not have done otherwise than it did. If humans (or human brains) were understood from this same mechanistic, natural law governed point of view, they would have no possibilities in this agentic sense and could not be held agentically responsible for their actions (J. F. Rychlak, 1988; Slife & Williams, 1995). The good deeds of humans could not be praised and their criminal actions could not be blamed, because the people involved in these behaviors were not ultimately responsible for them (Honderich, 1988, 1993; Pereboom, 2001). Even a person's desires, intentions, and preferences would be totally determined by natural laws and thus determined by the causal necessity of the relevant neurochemical processes.[4]

The responsibility issue has led some neuroscientists to recognize the importance of agency in the brain. Pinker (2002), for example, straightforwardly acknowledged its importance in this passage: "The experience of choosing is not a fiction regardless of how the brain works. It is a real neural process, with the obvious function of selecting behavior according to its foreseeable consequences" (p. 174). The problem is that free will (choosing) and determinism (mechanistic processes) are typically viewed as incompatible with one another (J. F. Rychlak, 1981; Slife & Fisher, 2000). How, then, can agency be a "real neural process" and thus allow for personal and agentic responsibility?

First, there is an important sense in which materialism allows a type of responsibility. After all, when the boulder hits the hiker, there is a real sense in which the boulder is responsible for the hiker's injuries. Similarly, there is a sense in which people acting criminally—whether or not they are controlled by external means such as natural laws—are responsible for their actions (Slife, Yanchar, & Williams, 1999). However, this is not the type of

---

[4]We include "desires, intentions, and preferences" here to indicate that there is no room here for what philosophers call the compatibilist's view of free will/determinism (Richardson & Bishop, 2002).

responsibility in question here. The issue in question is whether the boulder and human criminals could have directed themselves to act otherwise than they did. In this chapter, we have consistently referred to this issue as *agentic responsibility*. Without agentic responsibility, the boulder and criminal have to act the way they do because the natural laws and principles that supposedly govern all natural events, including their biology, determine them.

A major problem with this deterministic feature of biological materialism is that many people believe that humans have agency, and thus some agentic responsibility for their actions. This belief might be easily discounted if it were merely the belief of naïve lay persons. However, many prominent scholars and researchers of many disciplines have contended that agency is a basic characteristic of humanity (Van Inwagen, 1983). The law, for instance, presumes that humans have agency until proven otherwise (R. J. Rychlak & Rychlak, 1998), and ethicists assume that moral actions require specifically *agentic* responsibility (see Richardson, Fowers, & Guignon, 1999). In addition, many psychologists and neuroscientists hold that humans are agentically responsible and thus self-determined in this same sense (Brown, 2002; Howard, 1994a; Pinker, 2002; J. F. Rychlak, 1988).

Although the amount of self-determination may be in question, humans are frequently thought to make decisions and choices that are reflected in their behavior and attitudes. Unlike boulders, and even complex interactions among millions of boulders, humans are thought to act purposefully, choosing one possibility from among others and implying that there are reasons or meanings involved in the particular possibility chosen. In this sense, a good deed from a human being is meaningful because the person could have acted otherwise. A "good deed" from a computer, on the other hand, is not meaningful in the same sense because it could not have acted otherwise than what the mechanisms of its hardware and software specify. Thus, many scholars and researchers believe that possibility—the "otherwise"—is necessary for meaning as well as agentic responsibility. In other words, neither meaning nor agentic responsibility is conceivable if biological mechanisms are the only factors responsible for our behaviors and thus are sufficient for explanation. Humans would not be different, in this sense, from a computer in its lack of agentic responsibility—another type of mechanism.

Materialism as a One-Sided Dualism

This problem of agency is the reason that some have cast the assumption of materialism as a one-sided dualism (chap. 5, this volume; Muse, 1997). Conventional (two-sided) dualism is the notion that humans have two (dual) separate realities: the immaterial mind and the material body. The philosopher Rene Descartes is noted for believing that two such realities are necessary to truly understand humans (Descartes, 1641/1952). In fact, the problem of agency is one of the main reasons he felt it necessary to postulate two separate realities (Griffin, 2000; Toulmin, 1990). Although Descartes would have agreed with today's neuroscientists that the body is best understood as a predictable reality, governed by natural laws (mechanism), he realized that such entities are rarely considered agentic. As we have discussed, mechanisms such as computers cannot do other than what they are told through their hardware and software, so Descartes formulated a second, nonmechanistic reality to house agency: the mind.[5]

Few neuroscientists have followed Descartes' lead in endorsing this second reality. Indeed, many neuroscientists have argued that they are monists (with only one reality) because their explanations assume that *only* the body is responsible for behavior, including what might be considered "agentic" or decision-making behavior. If this is true, then they are materialists in the sense we have defined it here, because this type of monism would imply the sufficiency of the body and the biological for their explanations. However, as chapter 5 describes, this materialist position can also be understood as a one-sided dualism. That is, neuroscientists could merely be focusing on the body side of Descartes' dualism, ignoring what Descartes considered the mind, and keeping all the other assumptions of Descartes intact.

The obvious problem with this understanding is that neuroscience is, in an important sense, all about the mind. This discipline investigates and delves into memory, intelligence, decision making, and a host of other topics involving the mind—the "neuro" of neuroscience denoting this fact. Still, it is also clear that many neuroscientists view the mind as a mechanism of the body or the brain. Just as they have assumed that the material of the body is sufficient to explain the body, they have assumed that the material of the body is sufficient to explain the mind, another form of materialism.

If, however, the material of the body works mechanistically, then the agency that Descartes housed in the mind either remains to be explained or does not occur. The brain would work like any other natural object—bound by natural laws like the boulder or the computer—and disallow true choices and decisions, meaning and personal responsibility. We say *true* choices and decisions because choices and decisions that are controlled ultimately by external entities, such as natural laws, are not truly the choices and decisions of the people supposedly making them; they are the "decisions" of the natural laws that control them. It is this sense in which many neuroscientists can be said to be one-sided dualists. The assumption of materialism prevents them from understanding or accounting for the qualities of the Cartesian mind, especially its agentic qualities, so they do not focus on such qualities in their research. They focus instead on the mechanisms of the body. This does not

---

[5]As Stephen Toulmin (1990) observed,

> At the base of Descartes' epistemology lay the distinction between *rational freedom* of moral or intellectual decision in the human world of thought and action, and the *causal necessity* of mechanical processes in the natural world of physical phenomena. This distinction cut so deep that, in Descartes' eyes, it justified separating the two "substances" of mind and matter. (p. 107)

mean that the body is not vitally involved in decision-making and choosing, but it does mean that decisions and choices, and thus the mind in Descartes' sense, cannot be explained through a mechanistic view of the body.

As chapter 5 argues, there is also considerable evidence that this one-sided dualism (materialism) is method-driven. The original move of neuroscience to the body was not the result of neuroscience data. Early scientists moved toward the bodily and material side of Descartes' dualism because the methods that had worked so well in the natural sciences were specifically formulated for material and nonagentic objects. These scientists had no methods to study the Cartesian mind, even if they had wanted to. The Cartesian mind was immaterial and filled with, presumably, an unpredictable free will. Understandably, they ignored study of this notion of the mind and focused instead on the body, with its mechanistic predictability.

The point is that there is an important sense in which neuroscience explanations are dualistic, because they have not—under the assumption of materialism—accounted for important, agentic qualities of the mind or body. We will say more about this implicit dualism in the next section. At this point, it is important to note that some scholars may believe they have evidence that agentic qualities do not exist. They might argue that neuroscience data indicate the elimination or nonexistence of agentic qualities because biological mechanisms are sufficient in themselves (Churchland, 1986; cf. Pinker, 2002; Valenstein, 1998). However, as we have discussed above, the sufficiency of the mechanistic and the elimination of the agentic are the result of inferences beyond what the data can truly support. In other words, assumptions have been made in the interpretation of the data, such as materialism, without the data requiring these assumptions (see "Current Assumptions" section above). If this is true, then there is no evidence against agency; there are only interpretations made about the data that omit agency as a consideration rather than eliminate it as a reality, leaving a one-sided dualism.

This creates an interesting dilemma, which is a modern variation of the ancient mind–body problem. Materialism presumes that the mechanisms of the body are sufficient and thus operate like any other natural process, whereas agency presumes that at least some qualities of the mind are not mechanistic in this sense and cannot be controlled by natural (biological) laws. Either humans have a predictable mind that is controlled mechanistically by the body (its neurobiology) and thus cannot have meaning and agentic responsibility, or humans have an unpredictable mind that is controlled agentically by its choices and thus has little scientific merit and conflicts with the predictability of many neuroscience findings.

THE ALTERNATIVE: HOLISTIC MONISM

In this section, we explore the possibility of resolving this dilemma in a way that is consistent with neuroscience findings. Specifically, we advocate a particular monism that postulates the oneness or unity of mind and body and avoids both one-sided and two-sided dualism. However, to conceive of a monism, we have to know its requirements, so we begin by attempting to clarify what these might be. This clarification also helps us to know when conventional approaches to the mind–body problem are dualistic.

Requirements of Monism

Two requirements are needed to formulate a true monism, as opposed to a two-sided or a one-sided dualism:

1. A monism cannot postulate two completely different realities (or ontologies), such as a material reality and an immaterial reality. A monism requires, by definition, only one postulated reality or ontological framework.
2. A monism must account for the basic qualities of both mind and body, including, but not necessarily limited to, agentic responsibility and biological predictability. In other words, a monism cannot be attained by arbitrarily ignoring, deleting, or destroying one aspect of these qualities.

We assume that Requirement 1 is noncontroversial because a monism, by definition, is the postulation of one basic reality, though this reality may have many qualities or "aspects." Requirement 2 is also straightforward, but some readers may need further justification. Basically, there are two reasons why a monism cannot be based on the arbitrary elimination of the qualities of one side of a conventional dualism. First, a monism is not a monism just because someone says it is. In other words, the *arbitrary* elimination of one side's qualities, such as agency, implies that this elimination occurs without appropriate evidence or rationale. Agentic qualities are not so much eliminated as left unaccounted for or ignored. As mentioned, there are some neuroscientists who would argue that research has demonstrated the nonexistence of agentic qualities (e.g., Churchland, 1986). However, as described above ("Current Assumptions" section), these arguments stem from theories or interpretations, not data (see also "Causation and Method" section below). There is no neuroscience evidence against agency; there are only assumptions and interpretations made about the data, such as materialism, that omit agency as a consideration rather than eliminate it as a mode of explanation.

This omission of agency hints at the second reason for Requirement 2. Even if one side of a conventional dualism is appropriately eliminated from consideration (the first reason), this elimination does not necessarily imply that the general framework associated with dualism is itself eliminated. For example, the notion of "eliminating one side" itself assumes that the two sides operate independently of one another to some degree.[6] In other words,

---

[6]Other examples of an implicit dualism include scientists who believe they need agency to conduct their research purposely and responsibly (Primus, 2002), and many research programs requiring

it assumes that the two sides are not so interconnected that the elimination of one side also eliminates the other side. This assumption of self-containment and independence is itself a defining assumption of dualism (see chap. 5, this volume, on "atomism"; Richardson et al., 1999; Slife, 2004). Consequently, if Requirement 2 is not met, dualism may be implicit.

Let us now apply Requirements 1 and 2 to conceptions of the mind and body in psychology. Conventional dualisms, such as Freud's theory (chap. 5, this volume; J. F. Rychlak, 1981), violate the first requirement because they postulate two completely different realities: the immaterial mind and the material body. However, one-sided dualisms are just as problematic. As mentioned, many neuroscientists have contended that materialism—the sufficiency of the body—is itself a monism (Churchland, 1994). The problem is that this sufficiency eliminates rather than accounts for the basic agentic qualities of the mind, such as meaning and responsibility, violating Requirement 2 (see Agency section above). A similar problem occurs with another type of one-sidedness, the sufficiency of the mind, sometimes considered the monism of idealism. Here, for example, agency alone (e.g., free will) is sometimes thought to explain or account for human behavior (see Slife & Fisher, 2000). Yet, this one-sidedness cannot be a monism because it omits the import and qualities of the biological, also violating Requirement 2.

The point is that the notion of sufficiency, either from the body or the mind, is incompatible with monism. Giving special reality status to one side of a dualism—particularly through theoretical assumption rather than empirical evidence—does not account for the qualities of the other side. Indeed, the heart of the mind–body problem is that the qualities of each side of the dualism cannot account for, or be reduced to, the qualities of the other side. As described in the section above, the mechanistic body does not appear to account for the agentic mind, and the agentic mind does not seem to account for the predictability and automaticity of a healthy body, at least as conventionally conceived (Bargh & Chartrand, 1999; Park, 1999). Somehow, both properties of the mind and the body must be fully included in a true monism (Requirement 2).

Our proposal in this light is a deceptively simple one: We propose that the mind and the body are *necessary* rather than *sufficient* conditions for understanding and explaining human behavior. No one condition can be sufficient in itself for explanation and understanding. However, each condition plays an irreducibly necessary role in understanding human behavior in the same way that each part plays an irreducibly necessary role in a whole (Gazzaniga, Irvy, & Mangun, 2002; Gehring & Knight, 2000). Indeed, our notion of necessary condition here is best viewed as analogous to a part of a metaphoric whole (Bohm, 1980). Each individual part has a distinct role in

---

(ultimately) measures of a subjective, nonmaterial feeling (e.g., depression; Hedges & Burchfield, chap. 5, this volume; Slife & Williams, 1995).

the whole, yet each of these roles is united in a mutually constitutive arrangement of parts—the whole. In other words, each part has a unique and unduplicated function in the whole, but each part plays a pivotal role in the qualities of the other parts, and thus how this uniqueness is expressed. To make this clear, we pause briefly from the mind and body here to explicate the qualities of a whole.

Holism

First, let us see how the qualities of a whole meet the requirements of a monism above. Beginning with Requirement 2, how does a whole allow each part to have its own qualities or role without other parts dictating those qualities or reducing them to their own qualities (i.e., sufficiency)? The key is that each part of a whole is unique and irreducible, meaning that each part cannot be reduced to or explained by the other parts. This irreducibility is evidenced by two commonsensical qualities of any whole. First, a part's very existence within a whole depends on its being uniquely differentiated and identified *as* a part. Second, and perhaps more importantly, each part is a necessary condition for the whole. Each part has a distinct and necessary status because deleting any one part destroys or changes the identity of the whole.

Consider a simple stick figure. Removing its legs changes the whole from a stick figure to a symbol for a female. Also, simultaneous with this change in the whole is a change in meaning of each part. The "circle" at the top of the stick figure, for instance, loses its headness in this change. Consider also the explanation for a tragic plane crash many years ago ("Debacle of the DC-10," 1979; Slife & Lanyon, 1991). All the conditions that caused the crash—the wind sheer, the weight of the fuel, the design of the plane, the tensile strength of the rivets—were simultaneous and necessary. If any one condition were absent, no crash would have occurred. The point with both of these wholes—the stick figure and the cause of the plane crash—is that all elements or parts are irreducibly necessary conditions for the whole to be the particular whole it is. Each part is distinctly and uniquely needed because its elimination is the elimination of the unique qualities of the whole itself. This irreducibility satisfies the second requirement of a monism because holism preserves the basic qualities of each part.

Does holism satisfy Requirement 1? That is, does a whole also imply one basic reality for all its unique and necessary parts? This requirement might seem contradictory to Requirement 2, because the second requirement demands separability, whereas Requirement 1 demands inseparability—hence, the age-old difficulty in resolving the mind–body problem. However, the qualities of a whole involve this type of dialectic. The parts of a whole are inseparable as a unit, and the same parts cannot be reduced to one another (and must be valued for what they uniquely bring to the whole). They are the classical definition of a dialectical relationship: They are one and they are many, simultaneously (Gunton, 1992; J. F. Rychlak, 1976).

Requirement 1 is satisfied because each part is inextricably dependent on all the other parts for its very nature and qualities. All parts have a shared being and thus one reality because they mutually constitute one another. The head of the stick figure, for instance, gets its qualities of headness not only from its circular shape, and thus its irreducible uniqueness, but also from its relation to the other parts—the figure's trunk and legs. Another way to put this is that the qualities of each individual part stems, at least to some extent, from its relation to the other parts. Studying the parts individually will miss not only vital qualities of the whole but also vital qualities of each part, because each part derives its very nature and meaning from its relations to the other parts. In this sense, any substantive change in one part changes the whole and thus the meaning of each part.

If all things, including biological things, are wholes in this basic sense, then all the properties of wholes just described apply to them. In medicine, for instance, the insufficiency of a single biological factor is well recognized. The pathogen of disease, for example, is rarely considered a sufficient cause for the disease itself. Other conditions of the body are also necessary, such as immune system problems, for this entity to become a pathogen. Many pathogens, such as bacteria, are often already present in the body or its environment, waiting for other conditions to change. Indeed, whether a factor is considered a pathogen at all—its very nature—depends on a multiplicity of other factors. In this sense, these other factors *constitute* pathogens. Pathogens also cannot be sufficient conditions for a disease; pathogens are only necessary conditions, among many other necessary conditions.

As perhaps a more relevant example to neuroscience and psychology, consider the phenomenon of depression. Hedges and Burchfield (chap. 5, this volume) argue that depression is better understood through necessary rather than sufficient causes. Although monoamines were once considered to be the sufficient cause of depression, many researchers now argue that this theory is, at best, overly simplistic. Many other biological mechanisms appear to be involved (e.g., "cascading effects"; Valenstein, 1998). Moreover, Hedges and Burchfield (chap. 5, this volume), along with Healy (1997), have noted the intimate involvement of nonbiological factors, such as culture, in the diagnosis and manifestation of depression. The point is that single biological factors are insufficient in themselves to produce particular cognitive and behavioral effects such as depression.

Causation and Method

These holistic explanations challenge important understandings of scientific research, including causation and the scientific method. The notion of *cause*, for instance, is frequently understood as a factor that is sufficient for the effect that follows (Bunge, 1959; J. F. Rychlak, 1988). That is, no other factor is necessary for the effect to occur; otherwise, it is not the cause. This understanding of causal sufficiency is the reason that certain variables are considered to be *independent variables* in experimental designs. These variables are thought to be independent of, and thus causally sufficient for, the effect that follows—the *dependent variable*.

The problem is that this understanding of cause and effect would mean that pathogens are sufficient alone to cause disease. It would also imply that pathogens are pathogenic by nature and thus inherently sufficient causes of disease, when pathogens only make sense in conjunction with other necessary (and simultaneous) factors. Pathogens, in this sense, are not sufficient causes; they are necessary causes. This distinction also better explains the claim that smoking causes cancer. Smoking is a necessary and not a sufficient cause of some cancers, because some people who smoke never even get lung cancer. Thus, holism better explains the causality of pathogens and other medical phenomena, because a holistic cause only makes sense in relation to other simultaneous causes. Just as parts derive their very qualities from their relationship to other parts, variables considered as causes derive their specific nature and qualities from other simultaneous variables or causes. Many causes, in this sense, are only necessary and not sufficient conditions.

Current scientific methods make it impossible to determine anything more than necessary conditions. That is, no data can indicate the sufficiency of *any* factor. All data are gathered under conditions that include other conditions than the specific factor being studied. This situation is obviously true for correlational data. Correlation, as the research aphorism goes, never yields causation in the sense of sufficiency. In other words, the factors under study are never measured in a way that excludes the influence of other factors that are holistically related to the factors studied. However, the "gold standard" of neuroscience is experimental design in the formal sense of randomized, controlled, and double-blind studies (Moncrieff, 2001). According to method texts, these designs involve the independent variables mentioned above, and thus should theoretically provide causally sufficient conditions—conditions that are independent of other conditions—for the dependent variables or effects that follow.

However, these experimental designs rarely seem to be interpreted as causally sufficient data. Reports of neuroscience studies, regardless of their experimental nature, rarely use causally sufficient terms, such as "produces," "causes," or "stimulates," to describe their findings. As mentioned above, researchers frequently use terms associated with necessary conditions, such as "is implicated in" or "plays a role in," as in "neurofibrillary tangles *play a role in* Alzheimer's disease." We believe there are two reasons for this necessary-condition terminology. First, neuroscientists recognize the distinct possibility that other, perhaps unrealized necessary conditions may also "play a role" in their findings, in the best tradition of medical research (e.g., pathogens). As explained earlier, this recognition does not necessarily mean that they have given up materialistic sufficiency, because they may assume that the other necessary conditions are exclusively biological.

Second, neuroscientists intuitively understand the frequently unacknowledged limits of scientific method. Even the most highly controlled of experimental studies—a truly experimental design—contains factors other than the independent variables that contribute to the study's outcome. These factors may be controlled or equated across experimental groups or conditions, but they are never eliminated. Their influence is present and still necessary to whatever effect occurs. For instance, the influence of gravity in most earthbound experiments may be taken for granted and even measured as equal across experimental conditions. However, this control and this equality do not mean that gravity is not a necessary condition for whatever occurs, or that the loss of gravity would not change the outcome of whatever occurs.

These understandings of causation and scientific method have significant import for neuroscience. Taken together, they imply that evidence of causal sufficiency is not possible with current research. Inherent method limitations mean that inferences about causal sufficiency are always overinferences; researchers have evidence of necessary and not sufficient conditions. Consequently, a necessary-condition framework, such as holism, better fits neuroscience findings than a sufficient-condition framework, such as materialism. As we will also see, a necessary-condition approach better accounts for the mind and the body, not to mention the relation between the two.

MIND AND BODY AS HOLISTIC MONISM

A holistic monism means that the qualities of mind and body are necessary rather than sufficient conditions. Both sets of qualities are vital, even pivotal, to understanding the behaviors of a person, yet neither set is sufficient to explain either itself or the person as a whole. Agency is not present in a nonfunctional body, and biology is not meaningfully human without human agency. Still, agency and biology are not identical or reducible to each other. Our biology is not solely a product of our will, and our will is not solely a product of our biology.

In this sense, mind and body can each be understood as having *causal* import—if we understand causation in the holistic way described above. Causation from this perspective cannot be a sufficient condition for an effect. A cause is only a cause in its relation to other conditions (e.g., the pathogen). A decision or a choice, in this sense, is only a mental cause in relation to its constitutive biological causes. Indeed, these necessary causal conditions are all our methods can ever tell us about mind and body, because our methods do not exclude all other conditions. Agentic conditions are not excluded in research on the body, nor are biological conditions excluded in research on agency. (For examples of empirical research on agency, see J. F. Rychlak, 1988; Howard, 1994a.) Indeed, if monistic holism is correct, neither set of qualities could be excluded because humans are *embodied agents*.

Embodied Agency

Embodied agency means that agency occurs in and through the context of the body, or the body occurs in and through the context of the agent (see Brown, Murphy, & Maloney, 1998). That is, agency is manifested in, and is not separate from, the body. However, this one basic reality—this monism— of two distinct qualities may seem contradictory to many readers. After all, the body has traditionally been associated with mechanistic predictability, whereas agency has traditionally been associated with an unpredictable, "free," and thus independent will. Fortunately, however, both these traditional associations are just that—associations. Viewing the body as a mechanism is an *interpretation* of its predictability, not a *fact* of its predictability. The predictability of the body can be understood in other ways, with other interpretations, as we shall see.

Likewise, viewing agency as completely unpredictable is also an interpretation. In fact, this view is likely to be a *mis*interpretation, because agentic theorists rarely, if ever, see agency as completely unpredictable (Howard, 1994b; Howard & Conway, 1986; J. F. Rychlak, 1988; Slife & Fisher, 2000). Many agentic theorists, for example, consider a person's agency—their choices, meanings, and so on—to be aligned with a person's goals and purposes, so that any assessment of goals, reasons, and purposes is a good predictor of agency. Similarly, a person's behavioral history is an indicator of prior choices, goals, and meanings—all, in this sense, potential predictors of a person's future behavior.[7]

The notion that agency is unpredictable stems from a common but false dichotomy—that natural events are either determinate or indeterminate. Neuroscientist Pinker (2002) exemplified this false dichotomy when he alluded to David Hume's fork: "Either our actions are determined, in which case we are not responsible for them, or they are the result of random events, in which case we are not responsible for them" (p. 178). Either events are "caused," and thus determined by and related to other events, or events are uncaused or chance, and thus undetermined and unrelated to other events.

To understand how this either/or dichotomy is false, we need to provide a little background. Most scientists have rightly assumed that the world consists of many related events. Otherwise, there is little reason to do sci-

---

[7]Awareness of goal or purpose is not a requirement of agency (Slife & Williams, 1995). Goals may be agentically selected (e.g., avoiding speeding trucks) without a full awareness that the behaviors that follow from these goals (e.g., walking on the sidewalk rather than the street) are connected to them. In this sense, a lack of full awareness of predictable bodily processes does not imply a lack of agency.

ence. If the world consists only of unrelated events and there is no order, then the world is chaotic or even random, with no scientific knowledge available. The problem is that if agency and free will are not determined, as we have described, then agency fits better the indeterminate side of this dichotomy and becomes the enemy of science and knowledge. In a leading methods text in psychology, for example, Heiman (1995) assumed not only that free will is essentially unpredictable or random in this indeterminate sense, but also that free will is fundamentally unrelated to anything else—otherwise, it is not "free" and independent.

This misconception of agency is significant because it has led many scientists to assume that agentic explanations cannot account, even in part, for their findings of predictability. Similarly, it has led many to assume that any reasonable level of predictability is an indication of deterministic results. For example, the behaviors of most college students are fairly predictable at the end of class—they leave. The dichotomy of determinate and indeterminate events would lead us to presume that this predictable behavior was necessarily determinate in the causally sufficient sense; the students had no real choice but to leave. Yet, there is nothing about this predictability that prohibits the students' own self-generated goals and choices—their agency—from being a necessary condition in this behavior. Their predictable behaviors could stem from consistent choices and overall goals, which are themselves freely chosen. The predictability of the body and behavior, from this perspective, occurs *as a consequence of* agency, not in spite of it (Howard & Conway, 1986; J. F. Rychlak, 1988; Slife & Fisher, 2000).

Consider, for example, how agentic factors contribute to the neuroscience and predictable findings of Baxter et al. (1992) and Schwartz, Stoessel, Baxter, Martin, and Phelps (1996). In investigating the neurological effects of certain therapeutic processes, these researchers demonstrated that consciously and willfully withholding obsessive–compulsive behavior had the same eventual effect on distributions of neural activity—measured by positron-emission tomography (PET scans)—as the recommended drug (clomipramine) for obsessive–compulsive disorder. In other words, these findings indicated that agentic factors, such as exerting one's will to consciously withhold certain behaviors, can be just as effective as biological factors, such as drugs, in predicting even the neurological outcome of treatment for obsessive–compulsive disorder.

Mind–Body System

An embodied agentic explanation also moves us away from the spatial and self-containment metaphors of the dualist Descartes. With Descartes, the mind and body reside in separate "spatial" locations, with the qualities of each considered to occur in self-contained and relatively independent entities. However, with the holism of embodied agency, mind and body are viewed as parts of a larger system in which mind and body mutually constitute one another. They are not, in this sense, independent or self-contained. Moreover, mutual constitution is not mutual interaction. When psychologists discuss interactions, whether between people or between variables, they typically mean the interaction of self-contained and thus localized entities, with the nature of each entity *self*-constituted *before* interaction.

Mutual constitution, on the other hand, means that *other* entities contribute to the very nature of the entity. Mind and body have a shared existence, with neither being entirely separable or localizable in the traditional sense. Interestingly, this holistic and systemic sense of the body has been supported by recent neuroscience research. Materialist assumptions have traditionally led neuroscientists to localize mental functions in separate spatial locations of the brain (see chap. 5, this volume). Indeed, holism would support this tradition to some degree and predict a unique contribution from distinct parts of the brain (Requirement 2). Still, holism would also predict that these unique parts receive at least some of their unique qualities from their relationship to other parts of the brain (Requirement 1). No one part of the brain, and thus no one spatial location, is sufficient in itself to produce the effect in question.

Consider Broca's and Wernicke's areas, for example. Until the last decade or so, these locations in the brain were understood to be responsible or sufficient for language and speaking (Damasio & Damasio, 2000). However, recent research has indicated that this materialistic understanding—both of brain function and of language—is, at best, simplistic. Language is far more complex a phenomenon, involving semantic and syntactical structures that are not material and thus not observable. Also, neuroscience research has demonstrated that language requires more than Broca's or even Wernicke's area of the brain, including many neural sites linked as systems and working in concert (Damasio & Damasio, 2000). Broca's area may be a necessary condition for language, but an act of language entails an entire system of brain functions and location (not to mention cultural factors). Damaging any one region—any one necessary condition—affects language. People might continue in some manner without the damaged region, but their linguistic expressions are greatly affected.

Widening the System

From this holistic perspective, there is no need to stop with the mind–body system. Holistic monists would also include the wider system of which the embodied agent is part—its *context*, including its environment, culture, and history (see chap. 5, this volume). Because holism does not limit its parts or its wholes to their locality, there is no reason to assume that an embodied agency is solely within an individual, bounded by our skin. This wider system does not mean, via Requirement 2, that we are not separable blobs of protoplasm or locatable in this sense. It merely means that we are not fully explained or understood without this wider system (Richardson et al., 1999).

As neuroscientist Valenstein (1998) noted, "it is impossible to understand consciousness and thought without considering the psychosocial context that not only shapes the content of thought, but also the physical structure of the brain" (p. 140). Indeed, modern physics has itself questioned the traditional localization of material entities (Wolf, 1981). Increasingly, context is viewed as a necessary condition for understanding the material events of physics, such as Einstein's inertial frame of reference being necessary to measure motion and time (see chap. 5, this volume; Slife, 1993). We propose a similar move, in which an embodied agent's context is also an irreducibly necessary condition for full understanding and explanation.

Consider, for example, the good deed. We would argue that all three sets of necessary conditions—mind, body, and context—are required to account for or explain this deed. First, and perhaps least controversial, at least among neuroscientists, a good deed requires a relatively sound body. Good deeds simply cannot be performed without the biological properties of a relatively healthy body. Second, the meaning of "good deed" requires human agency. As we described above, few would consider a boulder that just happens to roll past a hiker to have done a good deed in avoiding the hiker, because boulders are determined and cannot have done otherwise. Agency, then, is pivotal for a human to be purposefully and meaningfully responsible for a good deed.

However, we are still missing a vital element in the good deed. We are missing the moral or cultural context that allows the behavior to be considered good. That is, if we are concerned at all about human meaning, and we must be if we are to account for the humanity of humans, then we need context as well as agency in accounting for it. Deeds are not inherently good, nor are deeds inherently "deeds," *without* the cultural and moral contexts in which they occur. In the same sense that a word or sentence gets its meaning from a paragraph or chapter, an action or behavioral pattern (personality) gets its meaning from a cultural context. Healy (1997, 1999) showed, for example, how depression gets its meaning, indeed its very existence, from the context of its culture.

Consequently, there are *at least* three "parts" or three general categories of necessary conditions required for a complete explanation of any human behavior: its context (the deed is good), the mind (the purposefulness of the deed-doer), and the body (the biological properties to perform the purpose). We emphasize "at least" these three conditions because we do not rule out the possibility of more necessary conditions. One of the many virtues of a holistic monism is that it allows the data to indicate what the necessary conditions are and where they begin and end. In other words, the holist has no preinvestigation restrictions about the number and quality of conditions that are truly necessary to explain human behavior. Indeed, our own postulation of three sets of necessary conditions is itself subject to test and verification.

Our point here is that holistic monism is scientifically open to whatever investigations yield on this issue. Conventional explanatory frameworks, such as materialism (body only), idealism (ideas only), and dualism (two categories only), ultimately restrict the conditions open to investigation *before* investigation begins. That is, these conventional frameworks are ultimately philosophical rather than scientific in nature. Holistic monism, by contrast, carries no such preinvestigatory, philosophical restrictions concerning conditions. It is, in principle, open to several creative possibilities. For example, several leading neuroscientists have argued that research indicates a fourth necessary condition: spirituality (e.g., Eccles & Robinson, 1984; Popper & Eccles, 1977; Sperry, 1988, 1995). We do not mean to argue for a fourth condition here. We merely wish to note the heuristic openness of holistic monism for scientific investigation.

RESEARCH IMPLICATIONS

For several reasons related to research, holistic monism is a better framework for neuroscience. First, it takes into account the inferential limits of current methods—namely, that traditional scientific methods can yield only necessary, rather than sufficient, conditions. Second, a holistic monism is more amenable to being data-driven—more open to other empirical possibilities and necessary conditions—than other frameworks. The problem is that conventional quantitative methods have not themselves been open to other empirical possibilities, favoring, as they have, the bodily and the biological at the expense of the agentic and the contextual (see chap. 5, this volume). That is, traditional scientific methods were originally formulated to investigate the observable and material conditions of natural science events. Even studies of the "operationalized" manifestations of nonobservable factors (e.g., attitudes) do not mean we are studying the nonobservable factor itself (Slife, 2004; Slife, Wiggins, & Graham, in press). Recall that this was the initial historical impetus for neuroscientists focusing on the mechanistic qualities of the body rather than the agentic qualities of the mind.

If holism is correct, however, then all categories of qualities require investigation. Agentic and contextual conditions are just as necessary and important as biological and neurological conditions. Perhaps more significantly, no category of necessary conditions can be understood fully without the other categories. Research methods are needed not only to investigate less conventional agentic conditions, such as meaning and choices, but also to *complement* in the holistic sense the traditional, quantitative methods of biology. Space limitations prohibit a complete discussion of this issue here. However, several authors have proposed a *methodological pluralism* in which different methods, with many differing conceptual targets and philosophical bases, complement rather than conflict with one another (Roth, 1987; Slife & Gantt, 1999).

As an example, remember how the restriction to materialism and conventional quantitative methods has limited our understanding of children diagnosed with ADHD (or depression in chap. 5). Conventional methods have focused on the effectiveness of certain drugs in treating observable symptoms—an obviously important issue. However, these methods generally attempt to establish effectiveness by controlling and excluding, through the sterility of laboratories and the determinism of experimental design, both context and agency—two conditions necessary to understanding the meaning of ADHD and thus the *experiential* effects of these drugs. Only recently have methods been formulated that specifically include context and agency in understanding meaning and experience. Often labeled *qualitative methods*, to distinguish them from quantitative methods, these methods target the meanings of humans in their lived experiences of the world—their understandings, interpretations, and perceptions.

A preliminary study of children diagnosed with ADHD (Burchfield & Slife, 2004) illustrates not only the usefulness of qualitative methods in this regard but also the conceptual influence of materialism and determinism in the lives of these children and their parents. Preliminary results of this qualitative study show what taking drugs for ADHD behaviors means to these children. Foremost perhaps, the results show that many of these children view themselves as not agentically responsible for their behaviors associated with ADHD. Although they might consider themselves agentically responsible for other behaviors, they view their biology, not their personal agency, as responsible for their "hyper" or "bad" behaviors. Parents, too, receive similar materialistic meanings. Drug taking means to them that they are not bad parents—that their children's "bad" (ADHD) behaviors have nothing to do with their parenting. Their children's biology is viewed as solely responsible or sufficient for these behaviors, so there is no point in even trying to parent them for these behaviors.

Qualitative research of this sort is important in many ways. First, it complements the quantitative research already being conducted. Information from qualitative investigations could be significant in providing complete care to ADHD children and their parents, not just treatment for their physical symptoms. Second, it seems vital that we know the specific human meanings associated with the diagnosis and treatment of ADHD. Do we want these children taking less responsibility for their ADHD behaviors? Do we want parents taking less responsibility for parenting their children? Third, qualitative research gives visibility to relatively overlooked necessary conditions in medicine and psychology—contextual and agentic conditions. This visibility cannot only spur more research, in new and less known areas, but also help professionals to view their clients in more comprehensive, beneficial, and human ways.

CONCLUSION

Like many assumptions, materialism is rarely discussed and even more rarely advocated, at least explicitly in neuroscience research. Nevertheless, as the results of the qualitative study (above) reveal, this lack of explicit discussion does not mean that materialism is not highly influential in people's practical lives. Many children and their parents may orient much of their behavior and attitudes to this assumption, mostly without awareness. Indeed, there is little doubt that the considerable power of the pharmaceutical industry is being brought to bear in promoting materialism at this practical level (Relman & Angell, 2002). The problem with this promotion is, as we have shown, there is no empirical evidence for the assumption of materialism. Neuroscience has clearly demonstrated the importance, even the necessity, of the biological and the physical. Still, no research has shown—indeed, no research *can* show—that biological factors are the only factors of importance. Nonbiological factors must also be considered seriously, even in neuroscience research.

We believe that our proposal of holistic monism will best facilitate this research because it does not arbitrarily rule out agentic and contextual factors before investigation has occurred. We are aware that valuing nonbiological and biological factors may itself seem dualistic. However, holistic monism differs from dualism in three important respects. First, it deals only with explanations and interpretations of data, not the data themselves. For this reason, we are not postulating different "realities" with these factors; we are postulating different aspects of our interpretive framework for understanding and making sense of neuroscience data and related everyday experiences. Second, the various necessary conditions of our explanatory framework are inseparable, as in any whole. Unlike Cartesian dualism, in which the different realities operate relatively independently, the necessary conditions of our interpretive monism are mutually constitutive, and thus inextricably united and monistic. Third, these necessary conditions do not contradict the predictability of neuroscience research. The agency of the human body preserves the purposefulness of humans and their biologies, without construing them as inherently chaotic and unpredictable.

The key to making this shift from materialism to holism, we believe, lies in distinguishing data from data interpretation. Neuroscience findings are always data interpretations, not the data themselves, so there is always more than one way to interpret these data. The alternative interpretive framework we offer here—holistic monism—takes into account both biological and nonbiological necessary conditions and encourages new and creative ways of interpreting data and doing research. Moreover, holistic monism acknowledges the limits of current research methods, which yield only necessary and not sufficient conditions. Thus, we believe it provides a more adequate and comprehensive understanding of meaningful human action, while helping to resolve many of the controversies surrounding today's neuroscience and psychology.

REFERENCES

Bargh, J. A., & Chartrand, T. L. (1999). The unbearable automaticity of being. *American Psychologist, 54,* 462–479.

Baxter, L. R., Schwartz, J. M., Bergman, K. S., Szuba, M. P., Guze, B. H., Mazziotta, J. C., et al. (1992). Caudate glucose metabolic rate changes with both drug and behavior therapy for obsessive–compulsive disorder. *Archives of General Psychiatry, 49,* 681–689.

Biederman, J., Milberger, S., Faraone, S. V., Kiely, K., Guite, J., Mick, E., et al. (1995). Family-environment risk factors for attention-deficit hyperactivity disorder: A test of Rutter's indicators of adversity. *Archives of General Psychiatry, 52,* 464–470.

Bohm, D. (1980). *Wholeness and the implicate order.* London: Routledge & Kegan Paul.

Brown, W. S. (2002). Nonreductive physicalism and soul: Finding resonance between theology and neuroscience. *American Behavioral Scientist, 45,* 1812–1821.

Brown, W. S., Murphy, N., & Maloney, H. N. (Eds.). (1998). *Whatever happened to the soul? Scientific and theological portraits of human nature.* Minneapolis, MN: Fortress Press.

Bunge, M. (1959). *Causality.* Cambridge, MA: Harvard University Press.

Burchfield, C., & Slife, B. D. (2004). *The meaning of being diagnosed and prescribed medication for ADHD.* Unpublished manuscript.

Churchland, P. S. (1986). *Neurophilosophy: Toward a unified science of mind–brain.* Cambridge, MA: MIT Press.

Churchland, P. S. (1994). Can neurobiology teach us anything about consciousness? In H. Morowitz & J. Singer (Eds.), *The mind, the brain, and complex adaptive systems: Santa Fe Institute studies in the sciences of complexity* (Vol. 22, pp. 99–121). Reading, MA: Addison-Wesley Longman.

Damasio, A. R., & Damasio, H. (2000). Aphasia and the neural basis of language. In M. M. Mesulam (Ed.), *Principles of behavioral and cognitive neurology* (2nd ed., pp. 294–315). New York: Oxford University Press.

Debacle of the DC-10. (1979, June 18). *Time,* 14–16.

Descartes, R. (1952). Meditations on first philosophy. In *Great books of the Western world.* Chicago: Encyclopedia Brittanica. (Original work published 1641)

Dupre, J. (1993). *The disorder of things: Metaphysical foundations of the disunity of science.* Cambridge, MA: Harvard University Press.

Eccles, J., & Robinson, D. N. (1984). *The wonder of being human: Our brain and our mind.* New York: Free Press.

Fisher, A. M. (1997). Modern manifestations of materialism: A legacy of the enlightenment discourse. *Journal of Theoretical and Philosophical Psychology, 17*(1), 45–55.

Gazzaniga, M. S., Irvy, R. B., & Mangun, G. R. (2002). *Cognitive neuroscience: The biology of the mind* (2nd ed.). New York: Norton.

Geertz, C. (1973). *The interpretation of cultures.* New York: Basic Books.

Gehring, W. J., & Knight, R. T. (2000). Prefrontal–cingulate interactions in action monitoring. *Nature Neuroscience, 3,* 516–520.

Griffin, D. R. (2000). *Religion and scientific naturalism: Overcoming the conflicts.* Albany, NY: SUNY Press.

Gunton, C. (1992). *The one, the three and the many: God, creation and the culture of modernity.* Cambridge, England: Cambridge University Press.

Hawi, Z., Dring, M., Kirley, A., Foley, D., Kent, L., Craddock, N., et al. (2002). Serotonergic system and attention deficit hyperactivity disorder (ADHD): A potential susceptibility locus at the 5-HT (1B) receptor gene in 273 nuclear families from a multi-centre sample. *Molecular Psychiatry, 7,* 718–725.

Healy, D. (1997). *The antidepressant era.* Cambridge, MA: Harvard University Press.

Healy, D. (1999). The three faces of the antidepressants: A critical commentary on the clinical–economic context of diagnoses. *Journal of Nervous and Mental Disorder, 187,* 174–180.

Heiman, G. W. (1995). *Research methods in psychology.* Boston: Houghton Mifflin.

Honderich, T. (1988). *A theory of determinism.* Oxford, England: Clarendon Press.

Honderich, T. (1993). *How free are you?* Oxford, England: Oxford University Press.

Howard, G. S. (1994a). (Ed.). Free will in psychology [Special issue]. *Journal of Theoretical and Philosophical Psychology, 14*(1).

Howard, G. S. (1994b). Some varieties of free will worth practicing. *Journal of Theoretical and Philosophical Psychology, 14*(1), 50–61.

Howard, G. S., & Conway, C. G. (1986). Can there be an empirical science of volitional action? *American Psychologist, 41,* 1241–1251.

Kirley, A., Hawi, Z., Daly, G., McCarron, M., Mullins, C., Millar, N., et al. (2002). Dopaminergic system genes in ADHD: Toward a biological hypothesis. *Neuropsychopharmacology, 27,* 607–619.

Libet, B. (1985). Unconscious cerebral initiative and the role of conscious will in voluntary action. *The Behavioral and Brain Sciences, 8,* 529–566.

Moncrieff, J. (2001). Are antidepressants overrated? A review of methodological problems in antidepressants trials. *Journal of Nervous and Mental Disease, 189,* 288–295.

Muse, M. J. (1997). The implicit dualism in eliminative materialism: What the Churchlands aren't telling you. *Journal of Theoretical and Philosophical Psychology, 17*(1), 56–66.

Paris, J. (1998). Significance of biological research for a biopsychosocial model of personality disorders. In K. R. Silk (Ed.), *Biology of personality disorders* (pp. 129–148). Washington, DC: American Psychiatric Press.

Park, D. C. (1999). Acts of will? *American Psychologist, 54*, 451–461.

Pereboom, D. (2001). *Living without free will.* Cambridge, MA: Cambridge University Press.

Pinker, S. (2002). *The blank slate: The modern denial of human nature.* New York: Viking Penguin.

Popper, K., & Eccles, J. C. (1977). *The self and its brain.* New York: Springer-Verlag.

Primus, H. (2001). Hidden determinism, probability, and time's arrow. In H. Atmanspacher & R. Bishop (Eds.), *Between chance and choice* (pp. 425–446). Thorverton, England: Imprint Academic.

Ratner, C. (1997). *Cultural psychology and cultural methodology: Theoretical and empirical considerations.* New York: Plenum Press.

Relman, A. S., & Angell, M. (2002, December 16). How the drug industry distorts medicine and politics: America's other drug problem. *The New Republic,* 27–41.

Richardson, F. C., & Bishop, R. (2002). Rethinking determinism in social science. In H. Atmanspacher & R. Bishop (Eds.), *Between chance and choice* (pp. 425–446). Thorverton, UK: Imprint Academic.

Richardson, F. C., Fowers, B. J., & Guignon, C. B. (1999). *Re-envisioning psychology: Moral dimensions of theory and practice.* San Francisco: Jossey-Bass.

Roth, P. A. (1987). *Meaning and method in the social sciences: A case for methodological pluralism.* Ithaca, NY: Cornell University Press.

Rychlak, J. F. (1976). *Dialectic: Humanistic rationale for behavior and development.* Basel, Switzerland: Karger.

Rychlak, J. F. (1981). *Introduction to personality and psychotherapy: A theory-construction approach* (2nd ed.). Boston: Houghton Mifflin.

Rychlak, J. F. (1988). *The psychology of rigorous humanism* (2nd ed.). New York: New York University Press.

Rychlak, R. J., & Rychlak, J. F. (1998). Mental health experts on trial: Free will and determinism in the courtroom. *University of West Virginia Law Review, 100,* 193–242.

Sarafino, E. P. (2001). *Health psychology: Biopsychosocial interactions.* San Francisco: Jossey-Bass.

Schwartz, J. M., Stoessel, P. W., Baxter, L. R., Martin, K. M., & Phelps, M. E. (1996). Systematic changes in cerebral glucose metabolic rate after successful behavior modification treatment of obsessive–compulsive disorder. *Archives of General Psychiatry, 53,* 109–113.

Shweder, R. (1991). *Thinking through cultures: Expeditions in cultural psychology.* Cambridge, MA: Harvard University Press.

Slife, B. D. (1993). *Time and psychological explanation.* Albany: SUNY Press.

Slife, B. D. (2004). Theoretical challenges to therapy practice and research: The constraint of naturalism. In M. J. Lambert (Ed.), *The handbook of psychotherapy and behavior change* (pp. 44–83). New York: Wiley.

Slife, B. D., & Fisher, A. M. (2000). Modern and postmodern approaches to the free will/determinism dilemma in psychology. *Journal of Humanistic Psychology, 40*(1), 80–108.

Slife, B. D., & Gantt, E. E. (1999). Methodological pluralism: A framework for psychotherapy research. *Journal of Clinical Psychology, 55*(12), 1–13.

Slife, B. D., & Lanyon, J. (1991). Accounting for the power of the here-and-now: A theoretical revolution. *International Journal of Group Psychotherapy, 41*, 145–167.

Slife, B. D., Wiggins, B. J., & Graham, J. T. (in press). Avoiding an EST monopoly: Toward a pluralism of methods and philosophies. *Journal of Contemporary Psychotherapy.*

Slife, B. D., & Williams, R. N. (1995). *What's behind the research? Discovering hidden assumptions in the behavioral sciences.* Thousand Oaks, CA: Sage.

Slife, B. D., Yanchar, S., & Williams, B. (1999). Conceptions of determinism in radical behaviorism: A taxonomy. *Behavior & Philosophy, 27*, 75–96.

Sperry, R. W. (1988). Psychology's mentalist paradigm and the religion/science tension. *American Psychologist, 43*, 607–613.

Sperry, R. W. (1995). The riddle of consciousness and the changing scientific worldview. *Journal of Humanistic Psychology, 35*, 7–33.

Toulmin, S. (1990). *Cosmopolis: The hidden agenda of modernity.* Chicago: University of Chicago Press.

Valenstein, E. S. (1998). *Blaming the brain.* New York: Free Press.

Van Inwagen, P. (1983). *An essay on free will.* Oxford, England: Clarendon Press.

Whitbourne, S. K. (2000). *Adult development and aging: Biopsychosocial perspectives.* San Francisco: Jossey-Bass.

Wolf, F. A. (1981). *Taking the quantum leap.* New York: HarperCollins.

IV

COGNITIVE PSYCHOLOGY

7

COGNITIVE PSYCHOLOGY: HIDDEN ASSUMPTIONS

ROBERT C. BISHOP

Psychology has sometimes been characterized as the scientific study of the mind and human behavior, and perhaps cognitive psychology, as usually conceived, comes as close to fulfilling this characterization as any branch in psychology. This penchant for scientific status comes across, for example, in typical textbook histories of cognitive psychology, beginning with the pioneering work of Wilhelm Wundt and Edward Titchener, through the behaviorist revolution to the so-called cognitive revolution inspired by the advent of the digital computer (e.g., Ashcraft, 1998, pp. 14–23). The computer as information processor did more than any other development to inspire a model of the human mind, indeed to, as Jerome Bruner put it, bring mind back into the human sciences after a long cold winter of behaviorism (Bruner, 1990, pp. 1–4). Mental processes became the focus of the new way called cognitive psychology.

Broadly speaking, cognitive psychology is the study of cognition and its attendant mechanisms (memory, perception, attention, learning, etc.). This is consistent with its most fundamental assumption as discussed in textbooks:

The research for this chapter was carried out while the author was at the Abteilung für Theorie und Datenanalyse, Institut für Grenzgebiete der Psychologie, Freiburg, Germany.

Mental processes exist and can be studied scientifically (e.g., Aschcraft, 1998, chap. 1; Sternberg, 1999, chap. 1). Cognitive psychology is embedded within a larger approach to human thought and agency, called cognitive science, and takes the computer as the central model shaping its theoretical and experimental practice. In brief, this model can be characterized as follows. The mind is conceived to operate along an input–processing–output scheme, in which the rules and structures of this scheme and the nature of the information input (environmental stimuli) into the system govern all mental processes (e.g., Ashcraft, 1998; Izawa, 1989; Sternberg & Ben-Zeev, 2001). Consider a word processor. The hardware fixes the basic possibilities for processing while the software provides instructions for the particular types of processing the hardware will carry out. But the information I type (information input) is crucial to the response of the system. For example, if I misspell a word, the program may automatically correct it or place a red line under it, indicating a problem.

Cognitive psychology exemplifies this model, relying on the crucial role information input and processing play in explaining cognition. Information enters through the senses from the environment, is taken up by the various components of the cognitive system, and is processed, yielding some output (behavior). This information-processing view can be quite sophisticated, including many modes of memory storage and retrieval, multi- or parallel processing, feedback loops among various levels of processing, mediation in which cognitive processes select and modify information at each stage of processing, and so on. This approach to conceiving mind and behavior, whether one uses the computer as literal model or as metaphor, allows cognitive psychologists to understand some of the ways in which the mind organizes sensory input, memory, past experience, thinking, and so forth. Indeed, it presents a picture of an active mind in contrast with behaviorism's passive view of mind acting merely as a conduit for stimuli and responses (e.g., Bandura, 1977; Sternberg & Ben-Zeev, 2001).

For example, motives, intentions, desires, thoughts, and so on are reduced to information input and cognitive processing units (Sternberg & Ben-Zeev, 2001). Consider a father who never expresses love or praise, thereby causing his son to grow up with a set of perfectionist behavior patterns always striving to win the approval of potential father/authority figures. These early childhood dynamics can be viewed as "programming" or "software" providing instructions for how various cognitive units ("hardware") are to process new information derived from the son's social interactions with peers and authority figures along with information stored in memory. In this way, cognitive psychology seeks to make such behaviors understandable, quantifiable, and measurable.

These latter kinds of characteristics are just what a science of the mental appears to need and represent part of the promise and appeal of cognitive psychology. So it is no wonder this subdiscipline and its perspective have become very influential in psychology. Furthermore, its emphasis on processing units has allowed cognitive psychology to connect its concerns with that of cognitive neuroscience, studying the activity of various centers of activity in the brain (chaps. 5 and 6, this volume). Nevertheless, I want to suggest that the appeal of cognitive psychology is due at least as much to a number of underlying, largely unexamined, hidden assumptions regarding moral ideals and human capacities. These assumptions surreptitiously shape much of cognitive psychology. As such, highlighting them is a first step in understanding cognitive psychology's promise and limitations, as well as for proposing modifications and alternatives.

HIDDEN ASSUMPTIONS

The idea of hidden assumptions is that a theory or approach has some number of assumptions crucially shaping it, though some of these assumptions may be implicit or concealed below view when the theory or approach is discussed and applied. Just because these hidden assumptions go undetected, however, does not mean their influence is negligible; rather, their influence is substantial precisely because practitioners are unaware of them.[1] In this section, I develop some of the hidden assumptions underlying cognitive psychology to make clearer what is going on in this influential field as well as to explain, at least to some degree, why this approach is so appealing. I focus on four assumptions almost exclusively ignored in the mainstream literature: efficient causation, instrumental reason, individualism, and atomism. Whether the mind is conceived of more narrowly as a computer or more generally as an information processor, these assumptions are at work, shaping the typical understandings of cognitive psychology.

Efficient Causation

The mainstream cognitive psychologist's picture of the world, like most behavioral scientists, is that of a realm composed of efficient causal chains, providing both a target for scientific inquiry and an arena for effective action (Bishop, 2003; Slife & Williams, 1995; Taylor, 1985). Efficient causation is the most widely acknowledged form of causation in the sciences. The two key features characterizing efficient causation are (a) a transference of energy, momentum, or some other physical quantity and (b) an antecedent relationship between cause and effect. This antecedence could be logical (i.e., the cause precedes its effect in logical order) or temporal (i.e., the cause precedes its effect in time). The temporal notion of antecedence has come to

---

[1]See Slife and Williams (1995) and Richardson, Fowers, and Guigon (1999) for good examples of analysis of some hidden assumptions at work in psychology as well as the behavioral sciences.

dominate the use of efficient causation in the sciences. The standard example is that of a moving cue ball striking a stationary eight ball, transferring energy and momentum, and sending the latter in motion.

The information-processing approach of cognitive science focuses on pathways of efficient causation in which information input triggers processing units, whose outputs, in turn, determine behaviors. For example, the kinds of cognitive mechanisms studied as well as the research methods used—with the possible exception of some sparsely used self-reporting and ecological approaches—presuppose efficient causation as the only causal channel of influence (e.g., Ashcraft, 1998; Izawa, 1989; Sternberg, 1999). All questions about human behaviors are reduced to questions about the internal transfer of information in and the nature of the information input into the cognitive system. One only has to view the cover of Mark Ashcraft's (1998) *Fundamentals of Cognition*, with its sprockets and gears, to get a palpable sense for the sequential, machinelike workings of cognitive systems in mainstream cognitive approaches.

On the computer model analysis, for example, a spouse's loving behavior is reduced to information input, representation, and cognitive computation. On this analysis, each partner in a marriage will have a mental representation of the other, including not just physical form but also personality traits, desires, and so forth. The couple constantly receives information input from each other through conversations and actions. Cognitive units process this input and generate responses. Perhaps the representation undergoes a change, for example, learning something new about a partner's interests. Or perhaps a conflict arises with one partner building up resentment as a response to the frequent negative stimuli received from a particular annoying habit exhibited by the other. At some level, pros and cons of staying in the relationship are weighted based on the information received, the processing performed, and the outputs generated that compose the relationship.

Loving appears, then, to be constituted by information input and processing, taking on a machinelike or computational character rather than being constituted by the meanings we often take it to have. This information-processing characterization of loving contrasts strongly with our experience of loving, which is relational in character in that it is constituted by a relationship between people. And it is within the context of this relationship that any "information" passed between two partners is interpreted and given significance. The actions and feelings of loving are what we experience, and they are indelibly relational, requiring people to be in particular kinds of relationships with each other (e.g., marriage). Loving is very much constituted by context and cannot simply be a matter of information input and processing.[2] Indeed, this reliance on information processing has led some

---

[2]For more on the role of context, see the following Atomism section and chapter 8, this volume.

critics within cognitive psychology to argue that this approach has gained "its technical successes at the price of dehumanizing the very concept of mind it had sought to reestablish" (Bruner, 1990, p. 1) by reducing the making and remaking of important human meanings and ideals—such as loving—to a much narrower kind of "information processing" as described above.

Still, focusing on efficient causation allows cognitive psychologists to attempt to design controlled experiments to test relationships among environmental causes from the past, current input, and information storage in observed human behavior. And if the contributions of these various elements turn out to be measurable and predictable, then there is the possibility of using this knowledge for human betterment in the form of improvements in therapies, management techniques, learning strategies, organizational structures, and so forth. Furthermore, this emphasis on efficient causation looks well suited for achieving an integration between cognitive psychology and cognitive neuropsychology.

However, there are other types of causation, formal causation for example, that look to be important in understanding human activity. A formal cause (Aristotle *Metaphysics Book V, Part II* (1933/1989); Slife & Williams, 1995, chap. 4) is the form or structure of a process or event relating parts and wholes, or constraining how parts can function in a whole (as in a blueprint for the construction of a house). Furthermore, this kind of constraining or regulation of parts takes place simultaneously in time, whereas, by contrast, efficient causation takes place sequentially through time (see, e.g., chap. 8, this volume). For example, cognitive psychology commonly appeals to past events as efficient causes, in the form of information, acting across time to understanding present behavior (Izawa, 1989). But current circumstances also act simultaneously, forming a *context* in which past influences come to expression as well as limiting the range of possibilities for those past influences. Indeed, it may be impossible to understand influences from the past apart from the context of present circumstances as formal causes, constraining or activating past influences and shaping possible responses to the current situation.

By way of clarification, consider the contrast between cognitive psychology's brute reliance on sequential information input and mechanistic models of information processing (the computer model) with the more holistic—and, thus, more formally causal—narrative character of everyday living (Bishop, 2002; also chap. 8, this volume). Human action always takes place against a backdrop of explicit or implicit assumptions, values, commitments, and practices deriving from our cultural–historical situation—cultural traditions, family upbringing, past experiences, and so forth—which cannot always be articulated and often remain unclarified (Polanyi, 1962; Taylor, 1985, 1993), somewhat like the assumptions described here. Our actions are always simultaneously channeled by this background (formal causation) as well as simultaneously shaped by our vision and understanding of our own future (final causation[3]). Furthermore, this narrative structure is also dynamic: As we engage in the daily activities of life, the meanings this background and our vision of the future have for us are always changing.

From this holistic perspective, the past (memory) and the future (as presently envisioned by us) are simultaneous with our present, influencing our interpretation of the present, whereas the present colors our interpretation of our past and future. The story of our lives has the character of an unfinished novel, but it is also reinterpreted and adapted in the light of new, often surprising realities. And while it is true that these events occur sequentially (just as they do in a novel), the narrative structure constituted by the simultaneous presence of past, present, and future acts as a context (formal causation) for interpretations of and responses to these new events. For example, a student's understanding of her past and future typically changes markedly from entering college to graduation, due in part to the friends she meets, courses she takes (including those not her first choice!), and the new community she moves to during her studies. She starts out with a current set of various expectations about her future (to become a nurse) and a current understanding of her past (as someone always quick to aid someone in need). But through the unpredictable twists and turns of college life she emerges with new expectations (to become an inner-city school teacher) and a changed vision of her past (as someone who has always wanted to make a difference in the lives of those who are less fortunate than her). In this holistic sense, the present changes the past as much as the past—from the efficient causal perspective—changes the present.

Many would claim that our lived experience is more holistic in character, with a past, present, and future that co-constitute a current context in this formal causal sense (e.g., chap. 8, this volume). They would argue that a strict reliance on efficient causation leaves out crucial features of human interactions and behaviors—such as how our current vision of the future reshapes our interpretations of the past—about which we surely want to understand more.

Many cognitive psychologists might object that they do take into account formal causation, in terms of scheme and cognitive structure, as well as final causation, in terms of goals and wishes. Unfortunately, cognitive psychology typically understands scheme and cognitive structures in terms of information stored in memory and the coordination of processing units (e.g., Izawa, 1989, chap. 10; Sternberg & Ben-Zeev, 2001, chaps. 3 and 4), the latter coordination arising from "software" (previously learned instructions) and "hardware" (neurophysiology). So whatever they take to stand in for formal causation is deeply colored by the computer metaphor and is driven almost entirely by the efficient causal effects of past input. Similarly, the goals

---

[3]*Final causation* is not only the influence our goals and purposes (e.g., to get a university degree) have on our current behavior (e.g., studying diligently) but also includes the vision of the kind of person we want to become (e.g., a person of integrity).

and desires taken to stand for final causation are also viewed as the products of past information input and processing. Hence, what passes for formal and final causation in the information-processing view really amounts to efficient causation. However, if cognitive psychologists limit themselves to researching efficient causal channels only, they end up restricting themselves to the study of a possibly narrow range of human actions (Bishop, 2003).

These possible limitations of cognitive psychology's efficient causal approach to understanding humans are closely linked to its retaining a rigid deterministic viewpoint on human action. Its commitment to an input–processing–output model of cognitive functioning characterizes human activity as a flow, albeit at the level of cognition or mental events, of law-governed efficient causes and their effects (Taylor, 1985). Behaviors may not be seen as determined by the underlying physical or chemical "hardware" of the body or brain or by environmental stimuli or reinforcements—as in behaviorism—but more by the information input and innate or acquired "software." On the information-processing view, the past is viewed as fixed, determining our responses to current circumstances. Indeed, the metaphor of a deterministic computer has led to many scientific advances, including important conceptions of learning and memory as well as enabling cognitive psychology to ally itself more easily with deterministic understandings of the brain (e.g., cognitive neuroscience). Hence, many cognitivists believe that any denial of this deterministic picture in order to endorse some capacities for human freedom implies stepping outside of the domain of science altogether (e.g., Bandura, 1977, 1986).

One might initially think that the presence of mediation and complex feedback loops loosen up this deterministic picture. But even these more complicated and subtle forms of information processing are portrayed as determined, in an efficient causal way, by prior environmental input and innate capacities. For example, compare the word processor and the approval-seeking son. What would be necessary, on the information-processor view, for the son to have the possibility to behave differently given the same past and current circumstances? How would this sort of agency (possibility) disrupt the flow and predictability of many mainstream cognitive models? In contrast, from the holistic view, emphasizing the formal and final causal structure of narrative, although past events are fixed, our interpretations of the past can change, affording new opportunities and options for acting in current circumstances. The basic approach of cognitive psychology presupposes a machinelike, deterministic picture aiming for complete scientific predictability but is inconsistent with such agency (Richardson & Bishop, 2002).

Instrumental Reason

The reliance on efficient causation and mechanism in cognitive psychology also derives some plausibility from the *instrumental* view of reason presupposed by the cognitive approach. On the instrumental view, agents are fully immersed in the efficient causal flow of events and processes, while, at the same time, are somehow able to turn onto this causal flow and manipulate it to determine the future course of such events and processes according to their preferences. On the information-processing paradigm, these preferences are formed by information input and processing and, in turn, play an important role in that processing, forming a basis on which "computations" might be carried out to determine how to steer the course of events.

This form of reason appears to fit well within a physical world of efficient causal interactions and, in part, explains why cognitive scientists, along with most other behavioral scientists, feel so comfortable with their mechanistic/deterministic pictures of the world and action. Agents, operating through efficient causation acting on a world conceived of as an interconnected web of efficient causes, present a strongly compelling picture of action in the world amenable to scientific study. Instrumental reason fits within such a scheme very nicely indeed, but there is a tension here. At the same time agents are manipulating the causal flow of the world around them, they are pictured as subject to a rather hard determinism due to the very same channels of efficient causation flowing through them. In other words, there is an implicit assumption of some kind of freedom *and* a picture of agents that leaves no room for such freedom. This tension is left largely unaddressed in mainstream cognitive psychology, as well as in mainstream behavioral science generally (Bishop, 2003; Richardson & Bishop, 2002).

Viewing reason as instrumental gains some plausibility by presupposing worthwhile, meaningful ends directing human action (e.g., finding the most effective means for boosting education performance in service of the goal of producing a better educated citizenry). I want to suggest, however, that the unexamined assumptions regarding moral ideals and human capacities associated with this instrumental view of reason have consequences for cognitive psychology. The critical theorists of the Frankfurt School (e.g., Habermas, 1973, 1991; Horkheimer, 1947/1974) have developed a famous "critique of instrumental reason" going to the heart of the problems with this conception. Apparently, thinkers in cognitive psychology have not consulted this critique, perhaps because the perceived fit between instrumental reason and efficient causation does not suggest that there might be any serious problems with this conception of reason (hence no felt need to look to other perspectives for insight on this matter).

The core idea of this critique is that modern Western culture is built largely on a damaging confusion of culturally meaningful activities (e.g., voting or religious rituals) and shared meanings (e.g., notions of patriotism or dignity), on the one hand, with means–ends reasoning and technical know-how on the other (focusing almost exclusively on knowledge and techniques for bringing about desired ends). This results in society's tendency to collapse activities, such as voting, and moral dimensions of life, such as equality and justice, into merely technical and instrumental considerations. In the realm of psychology, for example, we imagine applying theory chiefly as a matter of right technique—applying universal principles uncovered by empirical science as instruments—to produce desired results. For example, if we understood the laws governing cognitive processing, one might think it plausible that we could adjust environmental influences to better facilitate learning and help people lead more effective lives, or more effectively help people adopt healthier cognitive schemes.

This heavy emphasis on instrumental reason both reflects and encourages modern Western society's emphasis on gaining control over natural and social processes to enhance human welfare, dignity, and other worthwhile goals. Doubtless this increased capacity for control is often beneficial. But a key shortcoming of this elevation of technical know-how and control over culturally meaningful activity and shared meanings is that, even as we grow in instrumental prowess, we progressively lose our ability to evaluate the worth of ends on any basis other than personal preference or sheer desire (e.g., choosing a career solely because it will make me a lot of money or because I merely want to help people). As a result, too many spheres of life have become dominated by a calculating, instrumental viewpoint, discerning means–ends relationships, performing cost–benefit analyses, and seeking to maximize, as an end in itself, mastery and control over events at the expense of analyzing whether the goals in sight are really worthwhile (e.g., focusing on techniques for raising self-esteem to improve test scores with no sense for the real worthiness of either higher self-esteem or improved grades).

Think again of the computer model view of loving in a marriage. Positive and negative stimuli are supposedly being received by both partners. The benefits of staying in the marriage are weighed against each spouse's preferences and goals: Are the latter being met adequately? At what cost? This is, essentially, a model treating marriage partners as strategic calculators seeking to maximize their self-gratification.[4] From this perspective, intentions, thoughts, wishes, and meanings all turn out to be the results of information input, representation, and cognitive computation. Each partner is constantly processing the information input from the relationship relative to the stored goals and objectives for the relationship, weighing the merits of various options (maintain the status quo, make minor or major adjustments, break the relationship, etc.). Marriage then becomes a means toward maximizing gratification or toward self-actualization. However, this view turns marriage into an instrument, focusing on what is considered best or beneficial for the spouse rather than on any deeper meaning of love or sacrifice.[5]

---

[4]That much mainstream marriage research and therapy presupposes this kind of calculating view has been forcefully demonstrated by Richardson et al. (1999, chap. 7).
[5]While it is true that in the cognitive picture we can tell stories about deeper meanings regarding our relationships, these stories turn out to also be instrumental as well in that they are convenient fictions covering up the underlying, mostly unconscious calculations.

That this commitment to instrumental reason is pervasive in cognitive psychology can be seen in the representational treatment of knowledge typical of textbooks (e.g., Sternberg, 1999, chaps. 7 and 8). According to the computer model, all knowledge or information—including meanings and values—is representational; that is, mental structures (images, propositions, etc.) stand for what we know and think about the world outside our minds (e.g., our marriage partner, the structure of the relationship). This knowledge is typically either declarative (facts like your date of birth) or procedural (steps that can be implemented like adding a column of numbers or starting a car) and is the target for manipulation and computation by various processing units. Nobody denies that there is representational knowledge that we use instrumentally on a daily basis (e.g., determining the most efficient route for a trip). Indeed, it seems that we must encode some knowledge in terms of representations as a means for efficiently coping with a number of ordinary tasks like those involving spatial reasoning or imaging (e.g., getting to the right classroom on a regular basis or explaining to someone how to get to the nearest post office). And here cognitive psychology's exploration in spatial and imaging tasks has shed some light on the role representational knowledge plays in these cases. This work, in turn, has clarified much about the nature of mental imagery and problem solving (e.g., Sternberg & Ben-Zeev, 2001).

However, cognitive psychology tends to take these latter cases as paradigms for all knowledge and reasoning. The force of the critique of instrumental reason is that this is not all there is to knowledge and rationality and mind in general. In particular, we also use other forms of knowledge and understanding that are clearly not representational, such as understanding how to comfort a small child or knowing when and how to show deference. Our responses in such situations are played out in social contexts that simultaneously shape our options and actions, operate on subtle cues taking place in interaction with others, and take embodied forms (a hug or showing deference to my wiser companion). On the mainstream cognitive analysis, the response of something like deference is the result of information input and processing based on representations (e.g., shaped objects, measures of distance) so that "getting deference right" is more a matter of right technique and appropriate calculation. The response is then a matter of going from one representation (e.g., shaking hands at half arms length) based on an appropriate set of rules to another representation (e.g., standing a half step further back) based on past and present information (e.g., Sternberg & Ben-Zeev, 2001, chap. 4).

But showing deference is not a matter of applying rules and representations. Deference is an action constituted by my sense for what ought to be done given a feeling of humility. My feeling of humility when in the presence of a wiser person has to do with my sense of how we are related socially, as well as with the traditions and expectations of my society regarding how a person of her status is to be appropriately treated (Bourdieu, 1972/1977). These traditions and expectations are not completely internalized but are defined in relation to constantly changing social contexts; hence they do not function as rules (e.g., Dreyfus & Dreyfus, 1986/1988). My understanding and appraisal of this feeling of humility is due to the meaning things have for me, involving my values and ideals, what I take to be important concerns for me, my current understandings of my social surroundings, and the subtle influences of these surroundings taking place simultaneously, many of which are largely unnoticed by me but are tacit rather than explicit in contributing to my sense of the situation. Actions such as showing deference are mostly matters of prudence, insight, moral judgment, and wisdom, not mere matters of correct procedure applied to representations as suggested by the instrumental view of reason.

Individualism

The instrumental view of reason, in cognitive psychology, as in the behavioral sciences more generally, certainly gains some measure of plausibility from our scientific/technological worldview. For many cognitive psychologists, the flow of events as sequences of efficient causes and effects seems to mesh well with a conception of human reason as mainly concerned with an individual's manipulation of those causes to produce desired results. But this worldview is not the only source of plausibility for an instrumental conception of reason. It is important to note here that agents' purposes in this view usually are portrayed as ideally deriving from inbuilt inclinations or personal choices of the individual, not from some wider cultural, moral, or spiritual community to which the individual belongs or with which she identifies (e.g., chap. 1, this volume). For example, instead of seeing a student's choice to become an inner-city school teacher as being partly constituted by the religious community, cultural surroundings, and influential persons shaping her beliefs, desires, and vision of herself as she grows and develops as a person, an individualist view treats her decision as if her beliefs, desires, and vision of herself are fashioned by her with no influence from her social–cultural surroundings other than that they offer her opportunities (information input) to consider in relationship to her self-made character and ideals. This concept of self-determination presupposes that people draw their desires and purposes out of themselves, often seeing wider social–cultural influences as possible threats, perhaps oppressively subordinating people's desires and purposes. In this sense, instrumental reason incorporates a profound aspiration to individuality and separateness that Charles Taylor argued presupposes a "punctual self"—a self viewed as free and rational to the extent it has fully distinguished itself from the natural and social worlds and is able to treat these worlds instrumentally for the goal of securing the welfare of itself and others (see Taylor, 1995, p. 7).

This view of the self is closely connected to the *Cartesian split*, in which there is a sharp distinction between self and world (chaps. 5 and 6, this volume). In this view, knowledge and understanding are not derived from authority, custom, tradition, or a sense of place in the world. Rather, knowledge and understanding consist of correct inner representations of an outer reality composed of independent objects, both physical and social. And this split is the driving factor behind the dominant way of conceiving knowledge and cognition since Descartes. Furthermore, this split between mind and world motivates a purely representational view of knowledge (e.g., your using a mental map that corresponds to the layout of the city as you explain to someone how to get to the nearest post office). In turn, this representational approach to knowledge often has seemed to support and be supported by the successes of natural science, in which we are taken to be value-neutral observers of an external world described by value-free theories.

However, that is no longer the case. Observation is considered to be dependent to some degree on theory, and the confirmation or rejection of theories is to some degree conventional and influenced by particular values (Bernstein, 1983; Kuhn, 1970; Polanyi, 1962), so that even natural science does not proceed by value-free representations of the world (chap. 1, this volume). Still, the representational view seems to have done little damage in the past to deter progress in natural science, and its picture of the scientist as a separated, neutral, individual observer mapping an independent and objective order of fact continues to shape the outlook of cognitive psychology.

But powerful as the affinity with science and technology is in cognitive psychology, there is also a deep ethical commitment at work as well, for the aspiration to individuality exhibited by the Cartesian split is as much a *moral* ideal as of knowledge or science. It reflects and is reinforced by the intense liberationist or antiauthoritarian temper of modern Western culture, which dictates that any overlap between self and world will compromise the individual's integrity and dignity. For example, from this perspective, allowing a religious community or influential people to significantly shape the student's choice to become an inner-city school teacher runs the risk of subordinating her desires to some authority outside herself. The strong individualist streak in modern Western culture seeks to liberate people from potentially bad authorities and make individuals the captains of their own souls, so to speak. Hence, the instrumental conception of reason in cognitive psychology is deeply reinforced by, and in turn reinforces, a powerful set of cultural and moral ideals regarding dignity, integrity, liberty, and autonomy, among others, reflecting a strongly individualist cast. So, if our student's desire to become a teacher is not due totally to her internal cognition, then, on the individualist view, her autonomy, dignity, liberty, and so on are threatened. This adherence to individualism helps explain why mainstream social science typically advocates strictly value-neutral explanations or descriptions of human dynamics and has insisted on treating cultural and moral values as purely subjective (Slife & Williams, 1995, p. 195; Richardson, Rogers, & McCarroll, 1998). The motivation for this approach is, in part, that important meanings and values "must be kept at a considerable distance or they will compromise our autonomy and integrity in a domineering manner" (Richardson et al., 1998, p. 499).

Cognitive psychology reflects the punctual conception of the self and the Cartesian split in its one-sided focus on internal content as generated by information processing of cognitive units and knowledge as representational (e.g., Ashcraft, 1998; Izawa, 1989; Sternberg & Ben-Zeev, 2001). Analyses of human behavior are carried out totally in individualist terms, emphasizing how various cognitive mechanisms process information. This approach seemingly allows cognitive psychologists to study individuals in a somewhat controlled and isolated fashion. Unfortunately, wider social influences on the self are left out of the picture except to the extent that they provide external information input. And no matter how much one tries to enrich this basic picture, it fundamentally amounts to individual information processors "bumping into" each other, making it difficult to understand wider notions like community, social ties, and culture on these individualist terms.[6]

This is in contrast to the narrative character of life mentioned above, where social and cultural influences play a crucial role in constituting human behavior. On this latter picture, our everyday experience takes place in a lifeworld, where sights, sounds, smells, tastes, contexts, interruptions, surprises, and so forth are integrated in a holistic and dynamic unity tied together primarily by meanings rather than mechanisms (this does not imply mechanisms are absent; see chap. 8, this volume). One cannot neatly distinguish between the self and the physical, cultural, historical, and social lifeworld shaping that self; even the meanings and concerns of individuals are largely shaped by this lifeworld (e.g., a student's choice to become a teacher is partly constituted by these larger influences). Hence, some would consider the punctual self and Cartesian split inadequate conceptions from which to make sense of beings who are largely socially constituted and whose "individual" projects are always "joint" projects, so to speak, carried out in dependence on other people and the meanings such people give to the activities of life.

Atomism

The strong notion of individualism coloring cognitive psychology also lends support to another key assumption, namely an atomistic view of agents. In general, *atomism* is the idea that the fundamental elements—the atoms—are independent of each other though they may be combined in complicated ways (chaps. 3 and 5, this volume). The atomistic view of agents in cognitive

---

[6]Taylor (1985) argued that cognition and sociality are mutually constitutive of one another and, therefore, cannot be understood independently of the other (see the following chapter).

psychology takes two forms: social atomism and information atomism. The first, social atomism, is the idea that society is composed of self-contained individuals, each seeking his or her own purposes (Taylor, 1985; also chap. 8, this volume). It flows directly out of the punctual self and the Cartesian split as indicated above and is reinforced by the general liberationist/individualist society so pervasive in Western cultures. Social atomism is deeply tied up with notions of autonomy and freedom (e.g., Richardson & Bishop, 2002). Furthermore, this form of atomism might be one reason cognitive psychology does not view minds as at least partially constituted by the social–historical context in which they are embedded (as in the lifeworld mentioned above and in the following chapter). Social atomism assumes that people are basically hermetically sealed agents interacting within the world. This picture of agents fits nicely with assumptions such as strict adherence to efficient causation, instrumental reason, and individualism, and it colors much of cognitive psychology.

The second form, information atomism, is certainly consistent with social atomism, but is, perhaps, more directly the result of cognitive psychology's reliance on the information-processing model. Here reliance on efficient causation also provides some motivation for viewing agents as acting causally. Typically, efficient causation is viewed as channels of cause–effect sequences. A cause at Time 1 gives rise to an effect at Time 2. Just as in computers, causal processes in the mind are viewed as running sequentially, processing isolated bits of information, where each bit is independent of all others (atomism). The mind receives information in bits from the environment and is taken to process these bits in turn (e.g., see the discussion of attentional processes in Aschcraft, 1998, chaps. 1 and 2), perhaps assembling the atoms of information into a representation of a car coming the wrong way down a one-way street. Indeed one can tell a quite compelling story of limits on cognitive function in terms of information overload, processing limitations, and so on for all kinds of mental processes, like perception, memory, and reasoning, following this line of thought (e.g., Ashcraft, 1998; Sternberg, 1999). Just think of how tired you would feel if you tried to read this entire book through in one sitting, processing all the supposedly independent bits of information! Furthermore, this picture of the mind seems consistent with the overall determinist picture yielded by the machinelike approach: Past events causally influence present behaviors along efficient causal channels (Bishop, 2003).

Social Atomism

So the assumption of atomism—in either social or information form—finds a very congenial home in the typical cognitive psychologist's picture of agents. However, atomism on either level is quite problematic. At the social level, it seems to presuppose an individualist picture of agents as punctual selves, contrasting sharply with the more holistic lifeworld mentioned earlier, which is rich with meanings, values, hopes, fears, dependencies, and struggles, all of which take shape for us against the backdrop of our view of our past and future (e.g., apart from the religious community, significant persons, and other social experiences within her culture forming such a backdrop, our student would not have formed the desires and vision of herself leading to her becoming a teacher). Furthermore, such qualities also take shape for us against the social–cultural–historical matrix in which we live, move, and have our being. To consider the psychological subject as somehow standing apart from these constitutive influences, as the punctual self and Cartesian split imply, is to literally view the subject as disengaged from the complex nature of life.

No doubt cognitive psychologists see themselves as attempting to understand agents as acting in the everyday world so that to attribute a disengaged flavor to their approach seems terribly unfair. But here we have to clearly distinguish two different conceptions of engagement. The first conception of engagement is characterized by the way efficient causes impinge on us due to our embodiment, that is, due to the constraints our bodies place on the causal channels for information input. For example, at this moment I cannot see the wall behind me because the light refracted off its surface cannot reach my retina. My physical disposition—embodiment—and the physical properties of light are currently juxtaposed such that, in the main, channels of efficient causation shape my perception and, hence, my world and my engagement with it. Call this a *weak sense* of engagement, in which the characteristic feature is how my surroundings are externally related to my body in terms of efficient causation.

The second conception of engagement—I refer to it as the *strong sense*—is qualitatively different. Consider an example from Taylor (1993):

> As I sit here and take in the scene before me, this has a complex structure. It is oriented vertically, some things are "up," others are "down"; and also in depth, some are "near," others "far." Some objects "lie to hand," others are "out of reach"; some constitute "unsurmountable obstacles" to movement, others are "easily displaced." My present position doesn't give me a "good purchase" on the scene; for that I would have to shift farther to the left. And so on. (p. 318)

To say that we are engaged in this strong sense means that understanding such an experience necessarily draws upon concepts only making sense against the background of the particular type of bodies we have. That is to say, the kinds of bodies we have—along with their specific bodily capacities—constitute many of the experiences we as humans can have. So all the terms in quotes in the Taylor passage are understood only from the perspective of an embodied agent with our capacities. For instance, to understand what it is to "lie to hand" requires being an agent with our bodily capacities. This is to say, that the very nature of experiencing things in the world as human beings is primarily constituted by our *particular* form of embodiment and not in the main by efficient causal relations or sequential information processing. For example, to see a small child crying over the loss of a favorite toy certainly makes use of efficient causation in the sense that photons refracting off the child reach my retina and sound waves from the child's crying reach membranes in my ear. However, to interpret what has happened to the child and its significance for her, as well as to know how to comfort her in this situation, derives from my embodied experience as a person feeling what is happening to her. To comfort the child requires my embodiment with the particular capacities of a human being (e.g., warm hug, soft and soothing speech, confident and encouraging manner). Furthermore, my knowing how to comfort her draws heavily on a social–historical–cultural background that both activates and limits the range of interpretations I can have of the scene before me, deeply colors the kinds of concerns I bring to bear regarding her predicament, and guides the forms of action and response available to me. In short, the strong sense of world-shaping amounts to deep engagement with the child embedded within a lifeworld and particular bodily capacities enabling me to understand and respond, where formal and final forms of causation, rather than efficient causation, are the major factors constituting the experience.

To the extent that the agents conceived of in cognitive psychology are engaged, they can only be considered so in the weak sense of engagement, colored almost exclusively by channels of efficient causation. For example, historical and cultural realities have to be represented somehow in stored memory as the results of efficient causal inputs from our past. But viewed in this way, it is very problematic to understand how the historical and cultural influences constituting deference can be meaningful (see the next page). However, many would argue it is the strong sense of engagement that is characteristic of humans, setting them apart from other things like rocks, ameba, and computers, which all "engage" their surroundings only through efficient causal relations. Cognitive psychology's picture of the subject is a disengaged one, restricted to probing only those channels of efficient causation deemed relevant to the appropriate cognitive processing units. In contrast, the strong sense of engagement requires formal and final notions of causation as well as a more holistic conception of the lifeworld inhabited by human beings to make sense of human activity in all its involvements (e.g., chaps. 2 and 8, this volume).

Assuming social atomism allows cognitive psychologists to pursue studying participants in an isolated fashion, paralleling the kinds of controlled, reproducible experiments that are the hallmark of so much of the natural sciences. However, because this assumption represents a limited view of living beings, adopting such an approach means cognitive psychologists are effectively settling for studying a subject limited with respect to the full range of social connections and human capacities with which we are interested.

Information Atomism

The assumption of information atomism—assuming that cognitive units process information as isolated bits—is also problematic. This assumption does allow cognitive psychologists to focus on the function of individual processing units in the brain, and thereby establish contact with cognitive neuroscience. Moreover, on a parallel processing view, interconnections and dependencies among various processing units may be conceived and studied. Unfortunately, assuming information atomism leads to the loss of meaning because the meaning of a spoken sentence, say, is partly derived from the whole of the sentence and partly derived from the context in which the sentence is uttered. For example, if I tell you "Please follow me," this carries a very different meaning if I am leading you down a hall for a potentially painful medical procedure than if I am escorting you to a table in a fine restaurant.

If cognitive function is purely information processing, then whether it is performed bit by bit or performed on many bits in parallel, the holism of the context crucial for understanding the message is lost because the information bits moving through the cognitive system are still treated as independent (e.g., Rumelhart, 1989), even though there are dependencies among the various processing units themselves.[7] Taken in isolation, the sentence "Please follow me" can take on a wide range of meanings even if it could be processed as a unit. This is because the sentence underdetermines the meaning, whereas the different contexts are formal causes, delimiting the range of possible meanings for this sentence. These contexts are holistic; their meanings cannot be derived from processing the "parts" that supposedly make up the whole. This is to say that these contexts are not information being fed into an information processor bit by bit. Rather, they structure and give significance to the possible information contained in the sentence. And it is our embeddedness or involvement within such social and historical contexts that provides the meaningfulness of cultural and historical influences (e.g., constituting what deference is as well as when and how it is practiced in a given cultural context). Hence, such influences cannot be treated adequately as information stored in memory as indicated above.

CONCLUSION

Psychology as a discipline inquires into the most intimate and personal sphere of life. Ironically, the same strength that appears to offer cognitive science such promise—its dispassionate approach to efficient causes and "objective" analyses of processing units—seems to distance it from the intimate

---

[7]Focusing on "conceptually driven processing" (e.g., Ashcraft, 1998) seems helpful here as conceptual schemes could play a role in the organization and interpretation of information bits. However, it is not clear how these conceptual schemes are to be accounted for on computer models.

nature of its intended subject matter. Of course, one might argue that cognitive psychology has to make the kinds of assumptions I have discussed to have an *empirically accessible* form of behavior to study *scientifically*. To abandon the resulting view of agents would supposedly render its subjects of study beyond the reach of scientific investigation. But this would mean that to "scientifically study" behavior, we must reduce it to some manageable minimum ultimately bearing limited resemblance to everyday human action embedded in a rich social–cultural context. Why grant the restricted notion of empiricism lying behind this line of argument, hence dooming cognitive psychology to the consciously restricted study of a subdomain of human behavior painfully limited with respect to our full range of activities, capacities, ways of knowing, interests, and concerns? This restricted notion of empiricism cannot, itself, be the result of scientific investigation. Rather, it can only be imposed on other grounds, and I suggest the kinds of assumptions I have described here *are* some of the major grounds. The resulting conception of empiricism is limited to measurable, quantifiable magnitudes, whereas, from a broader empirical perspective, we observe every day that human agency is clearly more than quantified elements of behavior.

There are several reasons why cognitive psychology has been so long in coming to grips with the assumptions I have elaborated here. First, as I have indicated, efficient causation, instrumental reason, individualism, and atomism are wonderfully mutually reinforcing. Second, even with these assumptions in place, cognitive psychology has produced small, but often helpful, islands of insight, and such successes tend to make us forget our failures and keep us ever hopeful that our approach is basically on the right track. Third, as I have suggested, these assumptions are literally hidden from view. They lie beneath the surface of our practices and are intimately tied up with larger cultural assumptions about human nature and its capacities, leading us to never think of questioning such assumptions.

Learning to think critically about a discipline means digging beneath the surface, questioning the underlying practices and the assumptions. And for cognitive psychology to become more self-critical as a discipline, the kinds of assumptions I have discussed here will need to be thoroughly sifted and questioned. No doubt such a searching process of self-examination will likely lead to reshaping the practices and goals of cognitive psychology, as proposed in the following chapter, which discusses a contextualist alternative to cognitive psychology. Exploring such an alternative in the light of these hidden assumptions holds great promise for leading cognitive psychology beyond its current limitations. But the discipline will be better for the undertaking.

REFERENCES

Aristotle. (1989). *XVII, Metaphysics, I–IX*. (H. Tredennick, Trans.). Cambridge, MA: Harvard University Press. (Original work published 1933)

Ashcraft, M. H. (1998). *Fundamentals of cognition*. New York: Prentice Hall.

Bandura, A. (1977). *Social learning theory*. Englewood Cliffs, NJ: Prentice Hall.

Bandura, A. (1986). *Social foundations of thought and action: A social cognitive theory*. Englewood Cliffs, NJ: Prentice Hall.

Bernstein, R. (1983). *Beyond objectivism and relativism: Science, hermeneutics and praxis*. Philadelphia: University of Pennsylvania Press.

Bishop, R. C. (2002). Deterministic and indeterministic descriptions. In H. Atamanspacher & R. Bishop (Eds.), *Between chance and choice: Interdisciplinary perspectives on determinism* (pp. 5–31). Thorverton, England: Imprint Academic.

Bishop, R. C. (2003). *Crisis in the behavioral sciences*. Manuscript submitted for publication.

Bourdieu, P. (1977). *Outline of a theory of practice*. Cambridge, England: Cambridge University Press. (Original work published 1972)

Bruner, J. (1990). *Acts of meaning*. Cambridge, MA: Harvard University Press.

Dreyfus, H., & Dreyfus, S. (1988). *Mind over machine: The power of human intuition and expertise in the era of the computer*. New York: Free Press. (Original work published 1986)

Habermas, J. (1973). *Theory and practice*. Boston: Beacon Press.

Habermas, J. (1991). *The philosophical discourse of modernity*. Cambridge, MA: MIT Press.

Horkheimer, M. (1974). *Eclipse of reason*. New York: Continuum. (Original work published 1947)

Izawa, C. (Ed.). (1989). *Current issues in cognitive processes: The Tulane Flowerree Symposium on Cognition*. Hillsdale, NJ: Erlbaum.

Kuhn, T. (1970). *The structure of scientific revolutions* (2nd ed.). Chicago: University of Chicago Press.

Polanyi, M. (1962). *Personal knowledge*. Chicago: University of Chicago Press.

Richardson, F. C., & Bishop, R. C. (2002). Rethinking determinism in social science. In H. Atmanspacher & R. Bishop (Eds.), *Between chance and choice: Interdisciplinary perspectives on determinism* (pp. 425–445). Thorverton, England: Imprint Academic.

Richardson, F. C., Fowers, B. J., & Guignon, C. (1999). *Re-envisioning psychology: Moral dimensions of theory and practice*. San Francisco: Jossey-Bass.

Richardson, F. C., Rogers, A., & McCarroll, J. (1998). Toward a dialogical self. *American Behavioral Scientist, 41*, 496–515.

Rumelhart, D. E. (1989). Toward a microstructural account of human reasoning. In S. Vosinadou & A. Ortony (Eds.), *Similarity and analogical reasoning* (pp. 298–311). New York: Cambridge University Press.

Slife, B., & Williams, R. N. (1995). *What's behind the research? Discovering hidden assumptions in the behavioral sciences*. Thousand Oaks, CA: Sage.

Sternberg, R. J. (1999). *Cognitive psychology* (2nd ed.). Fort Worth, TX: Harcourt College.

Sternberg, R. J., & Ben-Zeev, T. (2001). *Complex cognition: The psychology of human thought.* New York: Oxford University Press.

Taylor, C. (1985). *Human agency and language: Philosophical papers I.* Cambridge, England: Cambridge University Press.

Taylor, C. (1993). Engaged agency and background in Heidegger. In C. Guignon (Ed.), *The Cambridge companion to Heidegger* (pp. 317–336). Cambridge, England: Cambridge University Press.

Taylor, C. (1995). *Philosophical arguments.* Cambridge, MA: Harvard University Press.

8

A CONTEXTUALIST ALTERNATIVE
TO COGNITIVE PSYCHOLOGY

STEPHEN C. YANCHAR

Imagine a small child running across a field in the spring. With little to care about aside from the green expanse that lies ahead, he runs, jumps, and laughs, first chasing a bird and then running from a parent who has joined the fun. The child takes delight in the open space and the unlimited freedom it seems to offer. Although this situation is not particularly unique, it is a good example of how even common experiences are richly meaningful for the people involved. How would contemporary psychologists account for such a meaningful experience? Although many theoretical perspectives are possible, the previous chapter has shown that most contemporary psychologists are likely to view the child's activity from the perspective of cognitive theory. As suggested in the previous chapter, the assumptions of mainstream cognitive psychology—from early information-processing models (e.g., Atkinson & Shiffrin, 1968) to contemporary parallel-distributed processing (Rumelhart, 1989) and connectionist approaches (e.g., Bowers, 2002; O'Brien & Opie, 2002)—suggest something distinct about a child running across a field: that the inner realm of his mind organizes sensory stimuli that have been inputted from an external reality; that the contents of his mind are representations, mediated through an elaborate process of encoding, processing, storage, retrieval, and manipulation; and that to function in the world—that is, to generate output—he manipulates the representations stored in his cognitive system.

The aim of this chapter is to present an alternative conception of human mental life and functioning that is not based on the assumptions of mainstream cognitive theory. The alternative presented—referred to as *contextualism*—is drawn from several related sources, including Gestalt Psychology (e.g., Kohler, 1947; Lewin, 1936; Wertheimer, 1959), Pepper's (1942/1961) contextualism, and the hermeneutic–phenomenological tradition of philosophy (e.g., Dreyfus, 1994; Gurwitsch, 1966; Heidegger, 1962; Husserl, 1962; Kockelmans, 1967). Contemporary theorists within psychology, such as Fuller (1990), Gillespie (1992), Sarbin (1986), and Slife (1995), have also advanced this alternative. Stated briefly and broadly, contextualism implies that the meanings or qualities of any individual, part, or element are not self-contained or inherent *in* the part, individual, or element, but derive instead from its relationship to other parts or elements and the larger whole (or context) within which it is situated. In the case of human mentation, this suggests that the mind and the world are co-constituting parts of a greater meaning or whole, and thus share their very natures (or being) with one another. Context (and changing contexts) becomes all-important because nothing can be understood apart from the context with which it shares its being and from which it derives its qualities.

This theoretical position will differ from that of mainstream cognitive psychology in many respects. It will not respond precisely to all of the questions that cognitive psychology has traditionally addressed, because from the perspective of contextualism, many of these questions do not arise in the first place. Instead, this chapter suggests that contextualism provides an account of human mentation that is theoretically rich and evocative in its own right. To illustrate the differences between these two perspectives, this chapter presents three underlying assumptions of contextualism and compares them with those of mainstream cognitive psychology. It will also demonstrate some of the implications that contextualism holds for psychological investigation and explain how contextualism accounts for, and indeed predicts, many unexpected findings of cognitive research.

ASSUMPTION 1: HOLISM

As suggested in the previous chapter, traditional cognitive models are based on the reception, encoding, and movement of bits of information through fixed stages of processing in serial fashion (e.g., Ashcraft, 1998). Although people might experience the world holistically, traditional models hold that perception and mental activity are accomplished through the decontextualization and decomposition of that holistic experience into independent elements for processing (Dreyfus, 1994, pp. 206–224; Slife, 1993, pp. 20, 132–133). For example, when the child described earlier perceives and processes an object such as a stone, his cognitive system must decompose the stone into bits of information pertaining to features such as color, shape, size, texture, weight, functionality, and so on and process those features as independent bits of information. Once the features have been independently processed, the cognitive system is theorized to recombine them into a coherent informational whole—that is, back into a mental representation of a stone—that can be categorized, stored, and accessed from memory at a later time. This decontextualization and decomposition occurs also in parallel-distributed processing (PDP) models, which process large amounts of data simultaneously through the independent (multiple) processors of a single processing system (see, e.g., Rumelhart, 1989). Despite the simultaneous and rapid flow of information through the multiple processors, PDP systems also deal with independent bits of information that, once decomposed, are inputted into the cognitive apparatus and processed separately (albeit in parallel).

Mainstream cognitive models that postulate this decomposition have been criticized on the grounds that they do not satisfactorily account for the *reconstruction* of the whole after decomposition has occurred (e.g., Slife, 1995). Because the information flow is comprised of independent bits of information that move through the cognitive system one at a time, there can be no relation among those bits as they are processed. A similar problem arises for PDP models. Their postulation that information moves through the separate processors of the PDP system (e.g., Rumelhart, 1989) precludes the possibility that the meaningful relationship among the bits can be maintained. In other words, there can be no processing of the whole context in which the bits were originally embedded (e.g., a stone) because the meaningful contextual relation that existed originally among the bits is lost through decomposition (see Slife, 1995).

In responding to the question of how inputted information is reorganized into meaningful patterns such as letters, words, and objects after decomposition has occurred, cognitive theorists may appeal to constructs such as data-driven processing, conceptually driven processing, and scripts (e.g., Ashcraft, 1998, pp. 43–56, 206–210; Bishop, chap. 7, this volume; Slife, 1993, pp. 116–117). But this kind of explanation raises logical questions about how basic patterns (e.g., the letter "A," the feature "/," or a stone) and scripts (e.g., ordering in a restaurant) are formed in the first place (Slife, 1993, pp. 119–121). For example, given that scripts are necessary for organizing serially processed bits of information, it is not clear how these scripts—which organize inputted information—are themselves organized out of decontextualized, serially processed bits of information. Are they organized by previously existing scripts? And if so, how were those previously existing scripts organized? This kind of explanation creates an infinite regress of prior scripts that cannot account for how the original scripts were developed.

From the perspective of contextualism, on the other hand, holistic experience is not decomposed into individual bits of information, and so no processing and reconstruction of individual bits into a coherent whole is required. Gestalt psychologists (e.g., Wertheimer, 1959) were perhaps the most well-known theorists within psychology to make this holistic assumption, although other psychologists have also recognized its importance (e.g., Fuller, 1990; Slife, 1995). According to these psychologists, humans experience the world in terms of whole patterns or "gestalten" (Kohler, 1947, p. 160) rather than individual elements of experience. The nature of any gestalten is not determined by individual elements; rather the nature or meaning of the individual elements is determined by how they fit into the broader whole or context (Kohler, 1947; Wertheimer, 1959). Stated slightly differently, the whole is a system of interrelated pieces that constitutes an organized form different from that of the independent pieces merely added together. As Fuller (1990, pp. 87–88) put it: "A gestalt's sensible characteristics, rather than following strictly from its parts viewed in isolation, have an emergent character. . . . Something happens with the whole that is neither to be found in its parts individually nor to be predicted from them."

According to the contextualist assumption of holism, then, there are no "sensory impressions" or representations—as independent bits of information—traveling across time and space to be received by the cognitive system and organized into a meaningful pattern. Rather, humans, such as a young child running across a field, are in direct contact with the world of their experience—that is, they are in direct contact with objects and people that already exist as organized patterns and that together form the whole context surrounding the experience. A stone, then, is not a processed and reconstructed representation of sensory impressions, but a whole pattern meaningfully situated within a broader context. As Slife (1995, p. 545) stated: "No informational flow is necessary because the two parts communicate by virtue of their relation as parts of a superordinate gestalt."

To some readers it may sound counterintuitive to suggest that no informational flow is needed to describe human experience of the world. This reaction is likely to result from the familiar, though often implicit, assumption that there exists a fundamental distinction between the perceiving subject and the external object to be perceived (see Bishop, chap. 7, this volume). From this traditional subject–object distinction, some "communication"—such as information flow and sensory perception—is necessitated; otherwise, the subject and object would never "communicate" with one another; they would be fundamentally isolated. However, the need to overcome this isolation is not a by-product (or implication) of reality itself; rather, it is a by-product (or implication) of a conceptual interpretation of reality—the assumption of a subject–object split. Put more concisely, the theoretical need for "communication" between subject and object arises only when the hard distinction between them is already assumed.

When the distinction between subject and object is dropped, as contextualism would suggest, the need for informational flow that "connects" object with subject disappears. Although parts of a whole (such as subject and object) might still need to "communicate" or "connect" with one another in some sense, the nature of that "communication" or "connection" is different under contextualism. Whereas mainstream cognitive theories assume that information (or meaning) must be transmitted across time and space from one part to another, contextualism assumes that the parts are already connected and meaningful because of their shared existence within the whole context, in which the meaning of one part is codetermined or mutually constituted by the other parts. That is, contextualism assumes that the shared existence of parts within a context gives them their meaning in the first place; without the shared context, none of the parts would make sense. Because this is so, the removal or alteration of any part would simultaneously change the nature of the whole context. Subject and object, then, are integral parts of a whole context that require one another for their meaning; they "communicate" immediately—that is, without mediation or informational flow across time and space—by virtue of their codetermination within the whole.

ASSUMPTION 2: THE LIFEWORLD IS FUNDAMENTAL

As suggested in the preceding chapter, many theorists in the Western tradition have tried to explain human mental life by postulating a fundamental separation between the inner realm of the experiencing mind (subject) and the external world of sensory stimuli (objects; e.g., Descartes, 1637/1968). Mainstream cognitive psychology has become the contemporary heir of this tradition by having posited that "it is not the *world as it is* that determines action but one's *cognition of the world*" (Gergen, 1994, p. 120). This separation of mind and world has long been a topic of critical debate, and as the previous chapter has suggested, creates substantial problems. The principal challenge to this inner–outer distinction lies in accounting for the relationship or interaction between these two realms: How do representations of external reality get into the mind? How does the mind imbue sensory stimuli with meaning? How does the immaterial mind interact with material reality? Considering the example of a running child, one might ask how the surrounding world "gets into" his cognitive system and how the rich meaning of this experience is possible.

In the contextualist view, the question of how outer and inner interact does not arise because contextualism does not recognize a fundamental split between an outer reality of sensory stimuli and a private, inner world of meaningful organization. Rather, the contextualist account begins theoretically with what may be termed the "lifeworld" (Fuller, 1990, p. 24), or the world of meaningful human activity as experienced prior to detached contemplation and scientific analysis. Within the lifeworld, the mind has direct or unmediated access to objects and people. Humans experience themselves as fully part of the world around them, engaging it in a seamless and direct way rather than processing and manipulating representations of objects and people that are "out there" in the external reality. Indeed, from the contextualist perspective, the experiencing human is "outside" in the external reality with other objects and people (Slife, 1995, p. 546). As she participates directly with the world, she is tacitly involved with tools and other objects that become practical extensions of herself, such as a hammer becoming a practical extension of her fist or a bicycle becoming a practical extension of her arms and legs. For the contextualist, the objects of the lifeworld and the mind thus constitute a total context or an uninterrupted unity.

Furthermore, the meaning of objects in the lifeworld does not inhere in the objects themselves as if they were self-contained and self-defining (often implied by terms such as *stimulus* or *information bit*) but emerges from the relationship of one object to one another within a broader context. This can be seen in the very meaning, form, and function of objects. As an example, consider a tool such as a hammer. Hammers are not composed of self-contained or self-defining information bits; rather, the meaning of hammers derives from their function within the overall context of carpentry and their relationship with other objects such as nails, wood, and hands. In other words, from the contextualist perspective, the process of carpentry provides a meaningful context for hammers. Thus, it is not mere coincidence that hammers exist, look a particular way, and are made out of certain materials; the very nature of hammers derives from, or is defined by, how they fit into the broader process context of pounding and pulling objects such as nails.

Of course, hammers can be used for other purposes as well, such as throwing in a sporting event or holding down papers in a breeze. In these cases, the meaning of the hammer is once again derived from its simultaneous relationship to the rest of its context—that is, it is *not* "first" processed and "then" linked to its present or past context. Although the meaning of the hammer has, in a sense, changed, it is still meaningful by virtue of its relation to other objects and processes. In this sense, the meaning of the hammer and its context are inseparable. Indeed, from the contextualist perspective, it can be generally said that although artificial distinctions are often used to describe reality (e.g., the internal subject and the external object), they are not suggested by immediate experience and they are not fundamental to it. As useful as these distinctions may sometimes be, they are nonetheless abstract or intellectualized interpretations that become possible only in a world that is already known holistically.

A concrete example may help clarify the difference between the lifeworld of contextualism and the subject–object split of mainstream cognitive psychology. Think again of the child running across a field. From the mainstream cognitive perspective, the mind of this child is a private, inner realm that receives sensory stimuli of a detached world, transmitted across space and time. The inputted sensory information then is organized, integrated, and endowed with meaning at an almost unimaginably fast rate as it is encoded, processed, stored, retrieved, and manipulated. The child comes to have mental representations (i.e., scripts or networks) of the external reality stored in his cognitive system that he manipulates to function in the world. When he picks up a stone, the stone is nothing more than sensory stimuli—a self-contained mass of physical energy—that he endows with meaning and manipulates through the retrieval of stored information and the accompanying coordination of his body's movement. Thus, despite the smooth, quick, and meaningful manner in which he runs and plays, his consciousness is separated from external reality, locked inside a private, inner realm that knows the external reality only as processed representations.

From the contextualist perspective, on the other hand, the child's mind and the world of his experience form a unity. He is in direct (unmediated) contact with the world. The meaning of what he confronts is not attached later by perception, encoding, and related processes but comes from his direct relationship to the objects of the world. He is, in a sense, out there among the objects and people rather than merely accessing and manipulating representations of them from inside his cognitive apparatus. He is able to act smoothly, quickly, and meaningfully in his surroundings because he is in immediate contact with them; together, he and they form a single context. If he hits a tree trunk with a stick, the stick becomes part of who he is, an experienced extension of him and his practical involvement in the world. Although an observer could theorize that the child, the tree, and the stick are merely separate objects juxtaposed, such an account would be an abstraction that becomes possible only after the whole context and its elements are experienced holistically.

ASSUMPTION 3: NARRATIVE STRUCTURE

As the previous chapter has clarified, mainstream cognitive approaches draw a metaphorical relationship between humans and machines, utilizing concepts such as hardware, networks, feedback loops, and central processing units to describe the flow and processing of information. To be sure, this mechanistic approach has provided many insights and understandings that were not possible under behaviorism—for example, clarifying the nature of memory, knowledge representation, and related cognitive phenomena. However, the machine metaphor is also limited, as all metaphors are limited, and forecloses on some avenues of theorizing and research just as it raises the possibility of others.

As the previous chapter demonstrated, one important area of theorizing and research that is closed off by the machine metaphor has to do with human agency (sometimes referred to as free will), which is commonly defined as the ability to have acted otherwise, all other factors remaining equal (e.g., Slife & Fisher, 2000). As a glance into cognitive textbooks and the primary literature reveals, human agency is not typically considered a theoretical possibility within mainstream cognitive models. This is because these models—and the scientific tradition from which they arise—assume an inherent machinelike determinism in the thought and behavior of human beings, with hardware (biological and cognitive structures) and programming (e.g., scripts) determining present behavior (e.g., Rychlak, 1991). Just as machines operate in accordance with hardware and past programming, according to mainstream cognitive models, so do human beings. This conclusion may seem surprising to some, given that cognitive models have long been considered a way of studying the *active mind*, in contrast to the passive mind of behaviorism (e.g., Matlin, 1998, p. 20). Nonetheless, as the previous chapter has pointed out (see also Rychlak, 1991), mainstream cognitive models are based on underlying assumptions such as efficient causation and mechanism that rule out the possibility of agency.

Contextualism opens certain possibilities not available under the mainstream cognitive approaches because it is based on the assumption of *narrative structure* rather than mechanism. The assumption of narrative structure suggests that people experience their lives in a sort of meaningful sequence, much like a narrative. The narrative structure underlying human experience is clarified in the following quote:

> [H]uman beings think, perceive, imagine, and make moral choices according to narrative structures. Present two or three pictures, or descriptive phrases, to a person and he or she will connect them to form a story, an account that relates the pictures or the meanings of the phrases in some patterned way. On reflection, we discover that the pictures or meanings are held together by the implicit or explicit use of plot. When the stimulus material depicts people, the story will reflect recognizable human sentiments, goals, purposes, valuations, and judgments. (Sarbin, 1986, p. 8)

An interesting implication of the shift from mechanism to narrative involves the agency/determinism issue. Whereas mainstream cognitive models assume that human behavior is determined by hardware and programming (as described above), narrative accounts assume that people have the ability to have done otherwise, all other factors remaining equal. A narrative account of the important concept of memory, for example, holds that a person's past experience and activity can be viewed as an unfolding story in which one event or situation provides a meaningful context for another, as in a novel in which one event or scene flows into the next and they together form coherent prose. On such a view, the relation among the past events of one's life is *not* one of necessity and linearity, in which past informational inputs and scripts (i.e., memories) determine present behavior in a mechanistic way. Rather than viewing the past (e.g., prior informational inputs) as locked away in memory and fundamentally separate from the present, it views past memories and present experience as parts of a simultaneous whole or gestalt. Thus, for the contextualist, memory *is* the meaning of the past in the present. After all, our memories do not exist in the past; they exist in the present. The simultaneity of memory and present experience becomes apparent to people when they realize that present experiences are meaningful and intelligible only in relation to their memories of the past, as they exist in the present. Slife and Fisher (2000, p. 97) described the relationship between memory and present experience in the following way:

> How one interprets events and renders judgments depends on one's memories and prior information. Memories and information from the past exist completely in the "now." Indeed, this is the reason memories are subject to the vagaries of present moods and circumstances . . . they occur in the present to be influenced by the present.

Given that memory *is* the meaning of the past in the present, it is often the case that present experience also provides a meaningful context for memory. This can be seen when people reinterpret the meaning of past memories in the present. For example, consider a person who views an earlier incident, such as being harshly reprimanded by a boss, as important to his adult sense of work ethic and integrity. Although the experience seemed unfair and unpleasant at the time, he is now grateful for the invaluable lesson it taught him about the world of work. Such an experience suggests that the meaning of a past event—that is, a memory—can be reinterpreted in light of present circumstances and take on a decidedly different tone. From the contextualist perspective, this is possible because memories and present experience are parts of a narrative, existing in simultaneous relation to one another and comprising a *temporal gestalt* wherein life's activity is played out. In this sense, the parts of time—past, present, and future—are co-constituting elements of a whole, just as mind and world are co-constituting elements of a whole, and cannot be meaningfully separated. This temporal gestalt—which differs from the linear sequence of memory representations strictly determining the course of present activity—makes a sort of agency possible, in which the past does not reside in a separate spatial region, like storage in the brain, mechanistically determining our "processing" and behavior in the present, but rather provides a meaningful context for present action that can unfold in a variety of ways.

RESEARCH FROM THE CONTEXTUALIST PERSPECTIVE

The three assumptions of contextualism discussed above—holism, the lifeworld, and narrative structure—differ markedly from those underlying mainstream cognitive psychology and offer a unique conceptualization of the thinking human as a unit of analysis in research. However, as unique as the contextualist perspective may be in psychology, it is neither new nor untested. Indeed, contextualist researchers have already generated a large body of research findings that are interesting and informative in their own right. This can be seen perhaps most obviously in the learning and problem-solving research of gestalt psychologists such as Wertheimer (1959) and Kohler (1947), as well as in the personality research of Kurt Lewin (1936). More recently, movements within the broad field of cognitive psychology—including *situated cognition* (e.g., Kirshner & Whitson, 1997) and *ecological cognition* (e.g., Gibson, 1966; McCabe & Balzano, 1986)—have emphasized the functional interdependency of organisms (as parts) and their environment (as context). In their own way, these movements have recognized the contextualist notion that organism and environment cannot be meaningfully divided into artificial distinctions such as subject and object.

Also in a contextualist vein, hermeneutic–phenomenological psychologists have sought to understand the rich meaning and holistic nature of people's lived experience rather than isolated variables (e.g., Packer & Addison, 1989), using qualitative methods such as case studies, ethnographies, phenomenological studies, and other related forms of investigation (see Cresswell, 1998, for more on these methods). Qualitative research in psychology has shed light on many human experiences, ranging from those more or less cognitive in nature, such as the tip-of-the-tongue phenomenon (Schwartz, 2002) and memories of childhood abuse (Dale & Allen, 1998), to those concerned with fundamental moral (Giorgi, 1992) and spiritual (Adams, 1996) issues.

ACCOUNTING FOR MAINSTREAM COGNITIVE RESEARCH RESULTS

Although contextualism provides an alternative perspective from which to study human mentation and activity, a legitimate question concerns how this approach responds to the vast assemblage of data that mainstream cognitive research has generated. No doubt, the empirical basis of mainstream cognitive psychology has been an important factor in its success over the past 50 years, with research generating important insights into memory, problem solving, decision making, imagery, and related phenomena. Thus, any alternative to mainstream cognitive approaches must theoretically account for, or explain away, these findings.

In responding to the empirical basis of mainstream cognitive research, it is important to note that there are always many ways to interpret research data (Rychlak, 1980) and that contextualism, like mainstream cognitive psychology, can theoretically account for much of what cognitive researchers have already observed in their laboratories. Despite contextualism's emphasis on lived experience and the felt qualities of human mentation, then, it is interesting to consider how many findings of traditional cognitive research fit easily within the contextualist perspective. The following examples illustrate contextualist interpretations of well-known findings from cognitive research.

Reconstructive memory. Consider first the vast body of memory research demonstrating that past information is not stored in a pristine form, as originally experienced, but rather is reconstructed or reinterpreted over time (e.g., Ashcraft, 1998, pp. 199–223). Such a finding, though provocative from the mainstream cognitive perspective, is entirely understandable from the perspective of contextualism. As stated previously, contextualism holds that memories and present experience share a holistic relationship and, in that sense, occur simultaneously. This means that the past is always understood and reinterpreted in light of present experience, just as the present is interpreted in light of past experience (Slife, 1995). The dynamic nature of memory, then, including the manner in which present experience and past memories interact, is precisely what contextualist theorists would predict.

Encoding specificity. Evidence for contextualism is also found in the related notion of encoding specificity, which holds that "retrieval is better if the retrieval context is like the encoding context" (Matlin, 1998, p. 140), and, in the specific case of word learning, "one learns more than just one word. One learns the word together with its context. In this case, the context would include what one thinks and understands about the world" (Reisberg, 1997, p. 178). Contextualist theorists would predict these findings in memory and learning studies because they would assume that the material to be learned and the broader context surrounding the learning are experienced and remembered as parts of a single context.

Mood congruence. A similar pattern of findings has been reported in regard to the mood congruence phenomenon, in which researchers have found that "memory is better when the material to be learned is congruent with a person's current mood" (Matlin, 1998, p. 144). Such research has demonstrated not only that remembering varies depending on the broader context but also that the broader context, in this case, mood, affects *how* memories are viewed (Slife, Miura, Thompson, Shapiro, & Gallagher, 1984). Such research strongly suggests that mental acts like remembering and the surrounding context form an experiential gestalt.

Problem solving. Consider next the contextual nature of problem solving. Although gestalt psychologists studied the holistic ways in which people attempt to solve problems in general (Murray, 1995), contemporary researchers have searched for evidence that people mentally dissect problems into smaller parts and then focus on those parts that are essential to generating a solution (e.g., Reeves & Weisberg, 1994). However, empirical findings have shown that people experience and interpret these problems as whole contexts and rarely dissect them without some explicit hint or instruction (Reeves & Weisberg, 1994). Although people's holistic experience of a problem may hinder their ability to generate viable solutions, this state of affairs is precisely what would be predicted by contextualist theorists who argue that a problem is experienced as an uninterrupted whole. Although people can be trained to differentiate between various parts of a problem, this differentiation is possible only after the problem is experienced holistically.

Decision making. Just as problem solving can be understood contextually, so can decision making. As contextualist theorists would predict, research has suggested that people's decision making is often less than optimal because people are influenced by the entire context of the situation rather than just the information that would lead to a purely logical choice. In the case of framing effects, for instance, people are not able to separate the "background context" and "wording of a question" from the central message being conveyed (Matlin, 1998, p. 420). This was seen in classic research by Tversky and Kahneman (1981), who found that framing a decision in terms of what might be gained resulted in a different pattern of responding than framing a decision in terms of what might be lost. Research participants experienced the entire context of the decision-making situation (including the psychological experience associated with it) rather than specific decontextualized elements.

Mental imagery. As a final example of how contextualism can account for cognitive findings, consider mental imagery. Many researchers in this area have equated imagery ability with the vividness of a person's mental images and assumed that vividness varies across people but is consistent within a single person (Ahsen, 1985). Moreover, these imagery researchers have assumed that images are somehow stored in the cognitive system, although the precise nature of this storage has long been debated (e.g., Kosslyn & Koenig, 1992; Pylyshyn, 1984). Ahsen's research (e.g., 1985), on the contrary, has suggested that imaging ability is not stable within a person but varies depending on the context surrounding the imaging experience. For example, he demonstrated that imagery vividness, as measured by standard imagery tests, varies substantially depending on what participants were asked to keep in mind as they performed various imagery tasks (Ahsen, 1985). Such findings, which fit nicely within the contextualist perspective, have suggested that the general context of a person's mental activity—for example, what they might be thinking about, emotionally experiencing, and so forth—plays a vital role in the process of imaging and in imagery test results. As Ahsen (1986) concluded,

> The emphasis on context—why a person sees a vivid or unvivid image—rather than on the so-called general ability to image vividly appears to

be important. . . . Most of the subjects who show lack of "imagery ability" can be shown to possess the same in a different context. (p. 5)

CONCLUSION

Contextualism offers a different kind of account than mainstream cognitive psychology—it does not seek to explain human mentation by postulating the processes of encoding, processing, storage, and retrieval, and it is not constrained to view human beings as determined, machinelike organisms (see Bishop, chap. 7, this volume). Rather, it is based on an admittedly perspectival description of how people experience the world around them, with its assumptions stemming from this lived experience. Moreover, it rests on assumptions that allow it to overcome some of the problems of mainstream cognitive psychology, such as those created by the inner–outer split, yet it can still account for traditional cognitive phenomena and much of the extant data generated by mainstream cognitive research.

Contextualism does not deny that elements and parts exist in some sense—as parts of a whole context—or that they can be useful abstractions; it only suggests that these elements and parts are experienced as parts of whole contexts, and that these whole contexts—that is, these relations among parts—are fundamental to meaning. For this reason, a contextualist theorist might say that the *meaning* of a stone or a stick, as an individual element of a young child's life, derives from the total context of which they are a part. They must be known relationally before they can be known individually. Contextualism's privileging of context allows the child in the field to be a child truly in the field, rather than a cluster of information bits or an isolated information processor, because it views the child as situated in a meaningful context first and foremost (see also Slife, 1995).

Finally, the concepts of agency and narrative structure open many possibilities for future research and applications. Although agency is a controversial topic with a rich and variegated literature (Sappington, 1990), it has been suggested by some contextualist theorists to be a viable way of understanding human action (e.g., Slife & Fisher, 2000). It is possible to study contextualist themes such as agency using both traditional empirical-quantitative and qualitative approaches, although it is clear that qualitative methods are particularly sensitive to the lived experience of human beings. Moreover, concepts such as agency have usefully informed counseling and psychotherapy, as seen in movements toward humanistic, phenomenological, and existential systems. Contextualism is thus an intellectual *and* practical alternative to traditional cognitive accounts. For these reasons, it is useful for psychologists to consider contextualism's contributions and limitations, along with those of mainstream cognitive psychology, to deepen their understanding of both.

REFERENCES

Adams, W. (1996). Discovering the sacred in everyday life: An empirical phenomenological study. *The Humanistic Psychologist, 24*, 28–54.

Ahsen, A. (1985). Unvividness paradox. *Journal of Mental Imagery, 9*, 1–18.

Ahsen, A. (1986). Prologue to unvividness paradox. *Journal of Mental Imagery, 10*, 1–8.

Ashcraft, M. H. (1998). *Fundamentals of cognition.* New York: Prentice Hall.

Atkinson, R. C., & Shiffrin, R. M. (1968). Human memory: A proposed system and its control processes. In W. K. Spence & J. T. Spence (Eds.), *The psychology of learning and motivation: Advances in research and theory* (Vol. 2, pp. 89–195). New York: Academic Press.

Bowers, J. S. (2002). Challenging the widespread assumption that connectionism and distributed representations go hand-in-hand. *Cognitive Psychology, 45*, 413–445.

Cresswell, J. W. (1998). *Qualitative inquiry and research design: Choosing among five traditions.* Thousand Oaks, CA: Sage.

Dale, P., & Allen, J. (1998). On memories of childhood abuse: A phenomenological study. *Child Abuse and Neglect, 22*, 799–812.

Descartes, R. (1968). *Discourse on method and the meditations.* New York: Penguin Classics. (Original work published 1637)

Dreyfus, H. L. (1994). *What computers still can't do: A critique of artificial reason.* Cambridge, MA: MIT Press.

Fuller, A. R. (1990). *Insight into value: An exploration of the premises of a phenomenological psychology.* Albany, NY: SUNY Press.

Gergen, K. J. (1994). *Realities and relationships: Soundings in social constructionism.* Cambridge, MA: Harvard University Press.

Gibson, J. J. (1966). *The senses considered as perceptual systems.* Boston: Houghton Mifflin.

Gillespie, D. (1992). *The mind's we: Contextualism in psychology.* Carbondale: Southern Illinois University Press.

Giorgi, A. (1992). An exploratory phenomenological psychological approach to the experience of the moral sense. *Journal of Phenomenological Psychology, 23*, 50–86.

Gurwitsch, A. (1966). *Studies in phenomenology and psychology.* Evanston, IL: Northwestern University Press.

Heidegger, M. (1962). *Being and time.* New York: HarperCollins.

Husserl, E. (1962). *Ideas toward a pure phenomenology and phenomenological psychology.* New York: Macmillan.

Kirshner, D., & Whitson, J. A. (Eds.). (1997). *Situated cognition: Social, semiotic, and psychological perspectives.* Mahwah, NJ: Erlbaum.

Kockelmans, J. J. (1967). *Phenomenology: The philosophy of Edmund Husserl and its interpretation.* Garden City: NY: Doubleday Anchor.

Kohler, W. (1947). *Gestalt psychology*. New York: Liveright.

Kosslyn, S. M., & Koenig, O. (1992). *Wet mind: The new cognitive neuroscience*. New York: Free Press.

Lewin, K. (1936). *Principles of topological psychology*. New York: McGraw-Hill.

Matlin, M. W. (1998). *Cognition* (4th ed.). Ft. Worth, TX: Harcourt Brace.

McCabe, V., & Balzano, G. J. (Eds.). (1986). *Event cognition: An ecological perspective*. Hillsdale, NJ: Erlbaum.

Murray, D. J. (1995). *Gestalt psychology and the cognitive revolution*. New York: Harvester/Wheatsheaf.

O'Brien, G., & Opie, J. (2002). Radical connectionism: Thinking with (not in) language. *Language and Communication, 22*, 313–329.

Packer, M. J., & Addison, R. B. (1989). Introduction. In M. J. Packer & R. B. Addison (Eds.), *Entering the circle: Hermeneutic investigation in psychology* (pp. 13–36). Albany, NY: SUNY Press.

Pepper, S. (1961). *World hypotheses: A study in evidence*. Berkeley: University of California Press. (Original work published 1942)

Pylyshyn, Z. W. (1984). *Computation and cognition*. Cambridge, MA: MIT Press.

Reeves, L. M., & Weisberg, R. W. (1994). The role of content and abstract information in analogical transfer. *Psychological Bulletin, 115*, 381–400.

Reisberg, D. (1997). *Cognition: Exploring the science of the mind*. New York: Norton.

Rumelhart, D. E. (1989). Toward a microstructural account of human reasoning. In S. Vosniadou & A. Ortony (Eds.), *Similarity and analogical reasoning* (pp. 298–312). New York: Cambridge University Press.

Rychlak, J. F. (1980). The false promise of falsification. *Journal of Mind and Behavior, 1*, 183–195.

Rychlak, J. F. (1991). *Artificial intelligence and human reason: A teleological critique*. New York: Columbia University Press.

Sappington, A. A. (1990). Recent psychological approaches to the free will versus determinism issue. *Psychological Bulletin, 108*, 19–29.

Sarbin, T. R. (1986). The narrative as a root metaphor for psychology. In T. R. Sarbin (Ed.), *Narrative psychology: The storied nature of human conduct* (pp. 3–21). New York: Praeger Publishers.

Schwartz, B. L. (2002). The phenomenology of naturally-occurring tip-of-the-tongue states: A diary study. In S. P. Shohov (Ed.), *Advances in psychology research* (Vol. 8, pp. 73–84). Huntington, NY: Nova Science.

Slife, B. D. (1993). *Time and psychological explanation*. Albany, NY: SUNY Press.

Slife, B. D. (1995). Information and time. *Theory & Psychology, 5*, 533–550.

Slife, B. D., & Fisher, A. M. (2000). Modern and postmodern approaches to the free will/determinism dilemma in psychotherapy. *Journal of Humanistic Psychology, 40*, 80–107.

Slife, B. D., Miura, S., Thompson, L. W., Shapiro, J. L., & Gallagher, D. (1984). Differential recall as a function of mood disorder in clinically depressed patients: Between- and within-subjects differences. *Journal of Abnormal Psychology, 93,* 391–400.

Tversky, A., & Kahneman, D. (1981). The framing of decisions and the psychology of choice. *Science, 211,* 453–458.

Wertheimer, M. (1959). *Productive thinking.* New York: HarperCollins.

V

DEVELOPMENTAL PSYCHOLOGY

9

DEVELOPMENTAL PSYCHOLOGY
AND THE DEATH OF GOD

BRIAN VANDENBERG AND SHAWN P. O'CONNOR

"God is dead." So said Nietzsche in 1882, almost the very hour the field of psychology was born. This is not coincidental. Nietzsche's (1882/1974) pronouncement signaled that the Judeo-Christian religious tradition, which had anchored Western thought for nearly two millennia, was losing its authority. A primary reason for the erosion of authority was the success of science in explaining the physical world. Darwin's *On the Origins of Species* appeared in 1859, changing the conception of humans from angels to apes. His theory followed earlier scientific discoveries that revealed that the earth is not the center of the cosmos, but instead is a changing planet of immense age within a dynamic universe. These discoveries contradicted, and undercut, biblical interpretation.

The first psychological laboratory was founded in 1879 by Wilhelm Wundt, who brought the methods of science to the study of psychology. The hope was that this approach would transform our understanding of the human psyche just as it had altered our knowledge of the physical world; that objective facts would replace religious dogma. Psychological theory has been shaped by the historical tension between religion and science in ways neither straightforward nor obvious. This is especially true of the idea of development, which not only is integral to many psychological theories, but also has become a subdiscipline in its own right.

The aim of this chapter is to demonstrate how historical understanding can aid critical thinking about contemporary psychological theories. Specifically, this chapter argues that foundational assumptions about human development derive from the historical tension between religion and science, and that appreciation of these origins enables us to recognize shortcomings and problems in the manner in which development is often conceptualized. We begin with an overview of Jean Piaget, who is used as an exemplar of contemporary theories. His theory is the most far-reaching, systematic, and thorough appraisal of human development, and while it has come under critical scrutiny, it has yet to be replaced by a more comprehensive approach (Lourenco, 2000). Furthermore, despite research that has identified empirical inaccuracies and conceptual limitations with Piaget's theory, its fundamental assumptions are shared by almost all contemporary developmental approaches: that human life is dynamic and changing, and that it is governed by adaptive forces immanent in the organism that progressively move toward more complex, adaptive organizational structures.

It may seem obvious that humans are developing organisms that must continually adapt, acquiring ever more complex skills and behaviors necessary for success in a changing environment. In fact, however, this perspective presumes a scientific worldview that differs, radically, from the prior, dominant, theological cosmology: The term "*organisms*" identifies humans as fundamentally organic (not divine) entities whose nature is best understood through more general biological (not biblical) laws that apply to a range of species, humans being but one (who are not special, not made in God's image); "*development*" presumes causes immanent in (not apart from) the material world, moving toward higher (not "fallen") states of organization; "*adapt*" suggests, again, the central role of biological and evolutionary (not sacred or eschatological) factors that influence the fate of human life; "*skills*" (not the condition of one's soul) and "*behavior*" (not one's conduct) are essential for "success" (not salvation) in a "changing" (not foreordained) "environment" (not moral universe). We humans have, indeed, been transformed by remaking our own images of ourselves and our world. The second section of this chapter examines how this shift, from sacred to secular, from religious to scientific, occurred.

The chapter concludes with a discussion of issues and problems that arise from these assumptions. The scientific study of human development presumes that individuals are epistemic subjects, and focuses on how we change and adapt, learn and grow, acquire information and develop skills. Overlooked are existential issues, issues addressed by religion, that haunt humankind: How do we explore the randomness and wonder of finding ourselves alive? Why are we here? How are we to understand our impending death? (Vandenberg, 1991). Furthermore, the shift from a moral to an epistemological worldview carries with it, implicitly, the ethics of science, which posits an objective world that is ascertained by separating fact from value, *is* from *ought*. The study of human psychological life and development, however, cannot meet this demand. It cannot separate is from ought; it cannot offer value-free appraisals that do not, themselves, make assumptions about the nature of the good (Vandenberg, 1999). Piaget attempted to address both of these issues, indirectly and unsuccessfully. A more complete understanding of development requires that we address, directly, these most pressing and important issues in human life.

PIAGET

Piaget is one of the geniuses of the 20th century. He was born in 1896 in Switzerland and published his first scientific paper at the age of 10. By the time he received his PhD in biology at the age of 22, he had published nearly two dozen papers on mollusks and related zoological topics. He was widely read in philosophy, psychology, religion, and sociology, and after receiving his degree, he decided to apply his biological training to the study of the development of human intelligence.

This may seem an unusual career path for a biologist, but Piaget saw human intelligence as biological adaptation to the environment not unlike the modifications in other species over time. Therefore, he assumed that processes analogous to those governing biological functioning and adaptation must also apply to psychological functioning. Furthermore, applying the methods and perspectives of biology to psychology and, in particular, to the development of intelligence, provides the opportunity to scientifically address important philosophical questions about the origins and nature of human knowledge. Indeed, this was Piaget's primary goal. He referred to himself not as a child psychologist but as a genetic epistemologist (Piaget, 1970/ 1971). *Genetic* here means "developmental," not "genes" (but does imply a biological process of some sort), and *epistemology* refers to his fundamental concern with philosophical issues to be answered scientifically.

Piaget argued that assimilation and accommodation, which are essential biological functions that enable the organism to adapt to challenges posed by the environment, also operate in mental adaptation. These functions enable the organism to incorporate the world into its existing structures (assimilation) and also to adjust its structures to the environment (accommodation). Every act of apprehension involves both assimilation and accommodation, and the tension between the organism's existing structures and environmental demands results in the development of increasingly adaptive mental structures. Earlier stages of development, which are unstable and inflexible, give way to progressively more complex and sophisticated structures leading, ultimately, to a stable, dynamic equilibrium with the environment (Piaget, 1983).

Piaget undertook very detailed and highly original studies of infants' and children's understanding of the basic properties of the physical world, such as space, time, and causality, as well as the development of moral reasoning. He argued that development progresses through four major stages, beginning with the *sensorimotor* intelligence of infancy, which is succeeded by the *preoperational* understanding of preschoolers, followed by the *concrete operational* thought of middle childhood, and culminating in the *formal operational* thought of adolescence. Earlier, less stable stages transform into later, more adaptive stages, each with its own qualitatively distinct universe of understanding (Piaget, 1983). Hence, young children's animism and magical thinking about the physical world is supplanted by logical thinking and scientific understanding, and belief in moral absolutes and justice tied to overt consequences is replaced by the morality of cooperation and justice tied to subjective intentions (Piaget, 1927/1970, 1932/1965). Thus, thinking about how the world is and how one ought to behave becomes more complex and adaptive with development.

Key assumptions of Piaget's theory include the following:

1. Human life is dynamic and changing. This may seem obvious, but for centuries, prior to the onset of science, stasis was considered the most perfect, natural state and change was viewed as a corruption.
2. Change results from material (biologically derived) forces immanent in the system, not from transcendental acts of God outside the system. The separation of scientific and religious spheres of explanation and understanding was a hard-earned achievement and is manifest in Piaget's theory.
3. Humans are biological organisms subject to the same evolutionary demands as other species: that they successfully adapt to the environment, which is a physical presence that requires appropriate adaptive responses for physical (not spiritual) survival.
4. Early, primitive, less developed states are replaced by ever more sophisticated, stable, and adaptive stages. Change has direction; it is *inherently progressive*. This remarkable belief has a complex history and has also led to troubling, often unappreciated difficulties in the conceptualization of human development.

SCIENCE, RELIGION, AND DEVELOPMENT

We now turn to a brief historical overview of how stasis was replaced by change, how biblical interpretation was supplanted by material cause, how the universe became disenchanted of moral purpose, and how progressive development emerged as an explanation for change in both the physical world and in human history. In the physical sciences, these transformations first occurred in cosmology, which in turn contributed to similar developments in the study of the earth and the nature of life. So, we begin with cosmology.

Cosmology

Biblical scripture has been the basis of thought about the universe for most of Western history. A core belief has been that an omnipotent Being created the cosmos around 4000 B.C.E., which has endured in precisely the same form since. The earth is thought to be the center of the universe, around which the sun and stars revolve in circular motion; circular because that is the most perfect form, with no beginning or end, a recurrent harmony. There could be no change in this God-given order (except by divine intervention), as this would imply that the cosmos was not perfectly created by God, that He had somehow miscalculated, which, of course, was impossible. According to this view, how the world actually *is*, empirically, is congruent with what scriptural interpretation says it *ought* to be. Thus, the physical workings of the cosmos conform to the moral order revealed in the bible (Cassirer, 1979; Vandenberg, 1995).

Yet, this cohesion began to dissolve in the 17th century, which is generally considered one of the most revolutionary eras in Western thought (Cassier, 1979; Hazard, 1935/1963). Modern science emerged in full, robust form in this century, with the cosmological discoveries of Johannes Kepler, Galileo Galilei, and Isaac Newton. They sought to understand the natural laws governing the cosmos, laws given by God, the supreme lawgiver, who has provided the world with reasoned order. They were pious believers who sought to fathom God's design; ironically, their discoveries challenged Church teachings and scriptural interpretation.

Kepler was guided by the assumption that humans can gain access to God's design through the divinely inspired faculty of reason. An important difference between Kepler and most of his predecessors is that he based his conclusions on detailed observations, not a priori deduction from scripture. This distinction freed Kepler from biblically based assumptions about how the world *ought* to be, giving him the ability to see the world as it *is* (Randall, 1976).

Utilizing extensive and precise observations of the planet Mars, Kepler discovered that it traverses an ellipse, not a circle. On the basis of these results, he postulated general laws of planetary motion, presuming that a God-given rationality would guarantee that regularities found for Mars would also hold for other planets. Thus, while religious considerations led Kepler to assume a universal rational order, his conclusions, derived from empirical evidence, revealed how the world *is*, which was not how biblical interpretation suggested it *ought* to be.

Galileo also used this approach, and his discoveries proved even more troublesome for the Church. His observations through the newly invented telescope revealed that there are more than seven heavenly bodies, contradicting Church teaching that there must be *only* seven (as seven is a perfect number). His observations also indicated that the earth was not the center of the universe but rotated around the sun. Furthermore, his work provided the first scientific understanding of the dynamic properties of matter, which he asserted was more fundamental than stasis. Galileo concluded that biblical text can instruct how to go to heaven but does not reveal how the heavens go (Randall, 1976). For that, empirical observation and fact are required. His views were heretical, suggesting that the domain of ethics, salvation, and scripture is unrelated to the workings of the physical world; that *is* and *ought* must be separated.

Newton, building on the work of Kepler and Galileo, discovered universal laws of motion that could be mathematically described and applied to a wide array of phenomena, from planetary motion to projectiles and collisions. The universe is a vast, lawful machine, or clock, which God set in motion at the beginning of creation. Key assumptions of the modern idea of development are contained in Newton's work: The universe is dynamic and conforms to material laws immanent in the physical system. Furthermore, Newton also disenchanted matter, replacing a theologically infused cosmos with a disinterested material universe, giving rise to the contemporary understanding of "environment," which is integral to Piaget's theory.

There were, however, two problems with Newton's theory that had a bearing on subsequent ideas about development. First, Newton hypothesized that matter is inert, yet he argued that matter exerts gravitational force. Whence this force, if not matter? Second, some planets deviated from their expected orbits, suggesting that the solar system was not perfectly balanced and that eventually it would collapse. Newton argued that God must periodically intervene to readjust planetary trajectories to keep this from happening (Vandenberg, 1995).

Gottfried Wilhelm Leibniz offered an alternative solution. Drawing on a theological tradition stressing that God is not a transcendental being but immanent in nature, Leibniz argued that matter is inherently active and that the *solar system is evolving*. It was not given in its present state at creation but is developing in accordance with laws and principles that are immanent in the material system itself. This was one of the first developmental hypotheses within a modern scientific framework, and was based on both empirical and theological considerations (Funkenstein, 1986).

The problems with Newtonian mechanics were subsequently resolved by Pierre-Simon Laplace, who had the benefit of much more detailed observations and more sophisticated mathematics (Hahn, 1986). Laplace provided a material explanation similar to that of Leibniz but without recourse to theology. He argued that gravity and other attractive forces (e.g., magnetism) were inherent properties of matter. Furthermore, evidence from other star systems indicated that the solar system evolved from gaseous nebula, a process characterized by the physical transformation of simple, diffuse, and unstable processes to complex, organized, and stable states of equilibrium (Merleau-Ponty, 1977). The universe is continually developing, driven by inherent material forces that evolve toward increasingly stable dynamic structures. Theology played no role in Laplace's theory. Indeed, he said of God, "I have no need for that hypothesis" (Hahn, 1986, p. 256). Scientific investigation now focuses on how the world *is*, not how it *ought* to be. Fact is distinct from value, and existential questions about the meaning of human existence and ethical concerns about the nature of the good are no longer relevant to the scientific study of the cosmos. The material, mathematical description of celestial phenomena, sans theology, provided a model for other emerging sciences. Geology and biology had formative influence on the modern idea of development, and the histories of both are marked by materialistic explanations replacing theological presumptions.

Geology

A similar historical sequence subsequently occurred in the study of the earth. Prior to the 16th century, the earth was viewed as an unchanging stage, created by God around 4000 B.C.E., on which the crucial human drama of salvation is enacted. Questions arose, however, in the 17th century as newly discovered fossils were recognized as the remains of plants and animals that no longer existed, suggesting that oceans once existed where there is now dry land and that there were forms of life that are now extinct (Toulmin & Goodfield, 1965). These conclusions challenged biblical scripture. Subsequent discoveries proved even more problematic. It was discovered that some mountains are the result of volcanoes and that the formation of these mountains required much more time than biblical chronology allows. Furthermore, new fossil discoveries revealed qualitatively distinct epochs, suggesting that entire worlds, much different from our own, have been created and destroyed. In addition, the evidence indicated that once life appeared on the planet, it became increasingly more complex and diverse in each succeeding strata (Rudwick, 1986).

Two main arguments were offered to reconcile these empirical discoveries with biblical text. One approach argued that mechanical, material forces were organized in a lawful, self-regulating, developing system that progressively moved toward more complex forms, culminating in the terrestrial home for humanity. The earth was formed over a longer period than the Bible suggests, but the mechanical perfection of the system was evidence of God's design, which established the earth as a suitable habitat for the drama of human salvation. The second approach challenged this explanation, asking: "If the formation of the earth was a continuous mechanical process, then how can these cataclysmic changes be explained?" This approach argued that the radical changes and the progressive development of the earth could only be explained by divine intervention in the earth's history (Vandenberg, 1995).

This debate raised important developmental issues. The observations from the earth's strata provided one of the first instances in the physical sciences documenting that change can be directional and progressive. It also was one of the earliest scientific attempts to address the problem of how continuous, uniform forces result in the development of qualitatively distinct stages. The issue was resolved with the accumulation of new evidence that revealed the magnitude of tectonic and volcanic forces shaping the world and the enormous time period involved (Lawrence, 1977). The qualitative changes did, indeed, result from the continuous effects of material forces, and the earth is an evolutionary system that has progressively become more complex and diverse. Theological explanations, again, were no longer necessary or appropriate. And this issue is echoed in Piaget's theory, which postulates the emergence of qualitative stages resulting from the continuous action of assimilation and accommodation.

Biology

The emergence of the field of biology followed a path similar to those of cosmology and geology. Once again, biblical scripture influenced early theories about the origins of life. It was believed that life is a divine gift, and that all species were created in their current form by God at the beginning of time. Species cannot change, and living forms constitute a great chain of Being, an invariant hierarchy, with humans, who are made in God's image, at the pinnacle. Yet, the evidence from the earth's strata revealed a multiplicity of life forms that no longer exist. Where did they come from? Where did they go? Furthermore, the fact that these forms appeared to become progressively more diverse and complex over time could not be explained by biblical interpretation (Bowler, 1984; Mayr, 1982).

Darwin drew on the discoveries in earth science that demonstrated how incremental changes over a long period of time could result in dramatic, qualitative changes. It was this evidence—minute amounts of variation across immense amounts of time—that enabled Darwin to explain the evolution of species. His theory is similar to those in cosmology and geology. Species are not forever fixed but are part of a dynamic, changing universe that results from immanent, material forces. Humans evolved from more primitive forms, and their survival depends on successful adaptation to changing demands of the environment. Darwin's theory replaces the view that humans are divinely created beings, placed at the center of the cosmos, on an earth specifically designed for the enactment of the moral drama of salvation. Rather, humans are biological organisms that, like all others, must adapt to a material environment on an indifferent planet—or perish. Theology may tell us how to go to heaven, but biblical description of the heavens, the earth, and the origins of life are supplanted by material, scientific explanations. And these scientific explanations serve as the assumptive ground for Piaget's theory.

There is one crucial difference, however, between Darwin's theory of evolution and the early scientific theories in cosmology and geology: It is not progressive. Darwin argued that species adapt to their environment. When the environment changes, species must adapt or risk extinction. What is critical is the fit between environment and organism, and there is no necessary reason why environmental changes, and species' adaptation (and extinction), should trace a progressive trajectory (Gould, 1989). The adaptations of organisms do not indicate advancement toward a "higher" stage of development, but rather, reflect changes in the external environment; changes that had already become understood as natural phenomena in the long life of an earth in flux. Nevertheless, evolutionary theory often has been misinterpreted as progressive, as if the changes observed in species over time reflect improvement toward a predetermined end. This is particularly true for theories about human history and culture, which utilized Darwinian theory, in its bastardized progressive form, to conclude that since change is progressively adaptive, then current social practices and social forms are inherently superior to earlier ones (Toulmin, 1972).

Why was Darwin's theory misread and inappropriately applied? The prior discoveries in cosmology and geology certainly played a role. Equally important, however, were the efforts in historiography prior to Darwin. Indeed, the relatively quick acceptance of evolutionary theory was the result of the pervasive belief in the modern idea of development that was already a crucial component of the major theories of human history (Toulmin, 1972). A central assumption was that change is progressive, which was inaccurately imputed to Darwin's theory. This assumption plays a subtle but important role in Piaget's theory—a biological theory applied to psychological development with stages analogous to earlier theories of human history. Understanding the history of historiography, then, is essential for appreciating the implication of key assumptions in contemporary theories of human development.

Historiography

The study of human history, for most of the Middle Ages, was dichotomized into *sacred history*, which was revealed in the Bible, and *profane history*, which consisted of the flux of events in the mundane world. Sacred history addressed the origins and fate of all of God's creation, reflecting the universality of the biblical message. This history has a beginning, at Creation, and an end, at the Day of Judgment. Profane history, in contrast, has no inherent direction or significance. What matters in profane history is not factual accuracy, but the moral lessons to be learned about the rewards of virtue and the pitfalls of evil (Breisach, 1983).

There were two problems with the biblical text that changed understanding of profane history. First, animal sacrifice was practiced in the Old Testament, sometimes at God's command, yet it was no longer a part of Church liturgy. Are the later practices, then, incorrect? Second, the prophecies of the Old and New Testament were not identical, nor was the relationship between God and humanity the same. These discrepancies were explained by the doctrine of divine accommodation, which argued that God incrementally reveals His intentions to humankind, resulting in increased understanding of Divine will. God does not change, but He is continually accommodating his revelations to the current level of human understanding. Hence, Old Testament prophecies and practices, including animal sacrifice, are superseded by new revelations that reflect a more developed relationship with God. Profane human history is, thus, progressive (Breisach, 1983; Funkenstein, 1986).

Profane history also became more factual. This was prompted by the discovery of classical texts, which resulted in efforts to free the texts of the errors and additions of translators. Philologists became quite sophisticated in identifying anachronisms in texts, which reflected an understanding that periods of human history have their own unique, organic unity that distinguishes them from other periods. This marked the beginning of an appreciation that human history may consist of distinct stages (Breisach, 1983; Funkenstein, 1986; Toulmin & Goodfield, 1965). Thus, two essential features of contemporary developmental theory were integral to historical understanding prior to the 17th century: Human history is progressive and consists of qualitatively distinct periods.

A series of challenges to sacred history that appeared in the 17th century contributed to the decline in authority of biblical accounts of the past. The discovery of Egyptian and Chinese cultures, with their written histories predating 4000 B.C.E., raised doubt about biblical chronology. In addition, the discovery of races and cultures in the New World, not accounted for in biblical history, also posed problems. Furthermore, critical textual analysis, which had unearthed anachronisms in classical documents, was applied to the Bible. It was discovered that numerous authors contributed to the Bible, that it had been rewritten and altered many times, and that there were a number of chronological inconsistencies and inaccuracies. The factual challenges to sacred history eroded the political authority of the Church.

Indeed, the power and force of these critiques helped shift the locus of authority for understanding our human past from sacred (biblical) to profane (factual) historiography (Vandenberg, 1993a). Drawing on the success of Newtonian mechanics, historiography now sought to understand the natural laws governing human affairs through observation and reason. Comparative analyses of cultures and customs were undertaken, and the quest for universal principles replaced aspirations for a universal sacred history. Causal explanations for the course of human history focused on immanent, material factors, such as environmental conditions, economic considerations, and political practices, rather than divine intervention (Cassirer, 1979). Thus did a radically new approach emerge in the 18th century that replaced biblical, sacred history with an empirical, material one.

But while history became secular, it still retained important features of the prior, sacred historiography; that an "invisible hand" moves human affairs toward progressively more advanced stages of development. The "hand" was no longer connected to God but to material factors in human life. These later, more scientific approaches to history reflect a secularization of Christian eschatology (Blumenberg, 1983). God was replaced by Nature in the physical sciences and by History in human affairs.

A number of important approaches to human history emerged in the 18th and 19th century, but the approaches of two theorists, Giambattista Vico and Auguste Comte, are particularly important for our discussion. Vico was an 18th-century theorist who is sometimes considered to be the progenitor of the human sciences (Pompa, 1990). Vico's comparative analysis of various societies led him to conclude that societies progress through three stages: the age of gods, which is characterized by communities that rely on myths, divinely given laws, and magical thinking; the age of heroes, consisting of a political state governed by a militaristic aristocracy whose laws are still tied to religion; and the age of men, whose society is governed by cooperative civic responsibility and whose thinking is dominated by reason, logic, and science (Vandenberg, 1992).

Vico's conclusions are echoed in a number of subsequent approaches, including that of Comte, a 19th-century theorist who is often considered to be the founder of the discipline of sociology. Comte also argued that there are three qualitatively distinct stages of human history. The first, the theological stage, is characterized by beliefs in supernatural deities, magical thinking, and animism. This is succeeded by the metaphysical stage, in which belief in deities is replaced by metaphysical and philosophical speculation. The final stage is scientific or positivistic, and is marked by reason, logic, and epistemological concerns (Vandenberg, 1992).

Ironically, the secularization of Christian eschatology found in progressive historiography led to conclusions that theological concerns are a vestige of an earlier, less developed era. A further irony is that this historiography gave impetus to progressive theologies that challenged traditional approaches advocating literal interpretation of biblical text and a transcendental God. Progressive theologies view God as immanent in the material world, whose features are revealed by science. The debate between traditional and progressive theologies galvanized 19th-century theology and continues to this day (Gilkey, 1969; Marty, 1982). These issues are also integral to Piaget's theory.

EXISTENTIAL ISSUES AND THE NATURE OF THE GOOD

Religious doctrine and biblical text, which provided the spiritual and ethical foundation for life in the West for over a millennium, have been undercut by science. The shift from sacred to secular has resulted in greater empirical knowledge and certainty at the expense of increased moral and existential confusion. Science addresses how the world is, but cannot answer how we ought to live. Nor can it address basic existential questions about the meaning of life and death. Science attempts to explain *how* the world is but cannot explain *that* the world is (Wittgenstein, 1921/1961, p. 149). Nietzsche's famous remark, and the thrust of his philosophy, make precisely this point: The biblical framework that has held things together for so long has lost its authority, and we must now confront basic existential and ethical issues without a theological safety net.

Progressive Development

Progressive development has been used in attempts to bridge the divide between the empirical certainty of science and the uncertainty of existential and ethical issues. Because development is assumed to be progressive, later stages are considered in some way superior to earlier ones. Thus, there is an implicit value expressed in the natural order of things. According to White (1983)

> The story of developmental histories is largely the story of people trying to divine what the good and the providential is in human affairs through an analysis of the systematics of human history. If providential history will reveal its principles to you, then you have made science and scholarship and evidence tell you what the good is. You do not need religion. You have found a source of values that is stronger than faith. (p. 73)

But this is a misapplication of science. As Toulmin (1972) pointed out, "if a conception, however scientific in birth or ancestry, is used in practice only as a way of dealing with nonscientific questions—whether ethical, philosophical, or theological—then it . . . has ceased to itself be a scientific term at all" (pp. 24–25).

This error has plagued the study of human development. Indeed, the founders of developmental psychology, who were working at the end of the 19th and early 20th centuries, were not simply concerned with the study of children but were attempting to empirically establish the universal laws of progress that applied to individual development, and in so doing, address moral and religious questions about the nature of God and the good (Karier, 1986; Kessen, 1990). This gave rise to the pervasive use of biological metaphors in studying children, for "the child as developing organism" situates the psychological study of children within a biological (progressive) evolutionary framework, thereby affording a measure of security for inferences about the ethical nature of human life (Morss, 1990). And, indeed, this is precisely what Piaget did.

Piaget Reconsidered

Piaget was very concerned with reconciling science and religion through the empirical investigation of progressive evolution and development (Chapman, 1988). The biological perspective adopted by Piaget, which he emphasized in both his biological and psychological research, was in harmony with the assumption that change is progressive, rather than with the Darwinian approach (Morss, 1990; Vidal, Buscaglia, & Voneche, 1983). Early in his career, Piaget was quite explicit in using a progressive evolutionary perspective to address the questions about God and the good, publishing a quasi-autobiographical novel that addressed theological questions, as well as essays on the relation between religion and science (Piaget, 1914, 1916, 1918). Piaget was a defender of liberal Protestant theology, arguing that God is immanent, not transcendental, and that answers to questions about God and the good were to be found in empirical investigation, not in biblical exegesis (Piaget, 1930).

A critical question that Piaget sought to answer early in his career was "From what point of view can we say that one religious experience is superior to another?" (Vidal, 1987, p. 271). Piaget sought to address this question through the study of the development of human thought. His research indicated that beliefs that characterized traditional religious thought, such as animism and magical thinking, are found in an earlier, more primitive stage of intelligence. This stage is superseded by a more advanced stage marked by logic, reason, and scientific analysis (Piaget, 1927/1970, 1983). The study of moral development yields similar results: An early stage of development, in which morality is tied to coercion and obedience to externally imposed norms, is replaced with morality based on social contract and reciprocity among equals (Piaget, 1932/1965).

Thus, Piaget argues, the natural ordering evinced in the progressive stages of human development reveals that traditional religious beliefs and morality are less adaptive and developmentally inferior to those associated with theology. Furthermore, Piaget's stages mirror those posited by Comte for the development of human cultures. Indeed, Piaget (1927/1970) asserted that this parallel is the result of general evolutionary laws governing both ontogeny and human history. That is, the natural ordering revealed in individuals' intellectual development—from animism, magical thinking, and a morality based on obedience, logic, reason, and a morality of social reciprocity—necessarily parallels that found in the history of human cultures. Piaget stopped writing about the relation of his work to religious issues after 1930.

The reasons are unclear, but it is likely that his work continued to be guided by these concerns (Chapman, 1988; Vidal, 1987).

Piaget's efforts to ground religion and ethics in research on human development are problematic. His belief in the ubiquitous influence of progressive evolution is in keeping with the historical emergence of the modern idea of development in both the physical and social sciences. From an empirical standpoint, however, the progressive nature of change has been overturned by subsequent discoveries in both cosmology and geology, and the random nature of evolution is fully appreciated in biology. In historiography, the belief in human progress has become problematic in the face of two world wars, nuclear brinkmanship, and the collapse of the Marxist state, which was founded on a messianic, progressive historiography. Furthermore, the theoretical basis for this belief has been challenged by critics who argue that progressive histories are metanarratives that serve to legitimize the values of the author by making them appear universal (Lyotard, 1979/1984). Thus, depending on the author, progressive histories have asserted the "natural" supremacy of European civilization, capitalism, communism, science, progressive theology, reason, and Christianity (among others).

Piaget's discovery of a "natural ordering," from magical thinking, animism, and moral coercion to logic, reason, and moral reciprocity, is also problematic. The religious beliefs and practices of many adults, not only in European-American, Western societies but also other, non-Western cultures, involve types of thinking that Piaget would label "immature" (Lillard, 1998; Vandenberg, 1991). But if the judgment of what is most "mature," or better, is based on what is more developmentally advanced, and if a large proportion of adults, perhaps even a majority, evince beliefs that could be classified as magical, then how can these be judged developmentally inferior? Have these adults "regressed"? But who is to say that it is a regression and not a new, more mature form of "advancement"? Perhaps it is more accurate to simply acknowledge that individuals differ in how they make sense of basic existential and ethical issues in their lives and that there is no "natural", "more advanced" solution to these issues that can be derived from the study of human development.

Piaget approaches human development as a scientist, using a biological metaphor to understand human functioning. He provides empirically based explanations for how the world is, how humans came to reason about the world. Explanations that explicitly recognize the central importance of existential issues, which spring from the mystery that the world is, are avoided. Nevertheless, Piaget used his findings to address fundamental existential issues about humanity's place in the cosmos. Indeed, Piaget's work is considered to be one of the most important efforts in the 20th century to address these concerns (Chapman, 1988). Yet these issues, so central to Piaget's aims, so essential to the evaluation of the ultimate significance of his work, are not included in his theory. Genetic epistemology is used to indirectly address religious questions about the cosmic meaning of human life, but the source and significance of these concerns are unacknowledged by the theory itself (Vandenberg, 1991, 1993a, 1993b).

LIMITATIONS, FUTURE DIRECTIONS

This paradox, as well as the exclusion of existential issues from developmental theory, is a legacy of the historical relation between religion and science. However, the erosion of authority of biblical text has not eliminated the importance of ontological, existential, and theological concerns. Indeed, the loss of significance of sacred myths, as Nietzsche points out, has sharpened these concerns. A science of psychology that does justice to the full range of human experience must provide understanding of these central human issues (James, 1961; Vandenberg, 1992). This does not mean that psychological theories must incorporate religious beliefs or explanations. Quite the contrary. What is required are robust psychological theories that provide understanding of the meaning of these issues in human life and development; approaches that not only examine how we come to know about the world but also the implications of intuiting the mystery that there is a world at all, that there is something rather than nothing (Vandenberg, 1991).

Furthermore, fact and value, *is* and *ought*, cannot be separated, even for scientists, and especially for those investigating others. The history of science is one of explanation being freed from theology, a recognition that the physical world does not conform to a biblical moral order. *Is* is distinct from theological *ought*. However, scientific inquiry is not value free, not an objectivity devoid of ethical implications. The choice of what to ask, and what to ignore, and the assumption that scientific investigation is a valuable social–cultural enterprise, all entail decisions, judgments, values, and ethical interpretations. This is further complicated when inquiry is directed toward others. In this case, the experimental context is a social, interpersonal encounter of asymmetric authoritative inquiry that is necessarily ethical; so, too, are the conclusions (Vandenberg, 1999).

Scientific analysis of human life can, and should, provide explanations free of theological *oughts*, but it cannot offer evidence that is free of moral values and ethical implications. Indeed, scientific inquiry, itself, underscores that ethics does not simply arise from episodic "moral dilemmas" that force difficult decisions, and that moral choices are not somehow distinct and infrequent occurrences that leap out of a flat epistemic landscape at moments of crisis. Rather, human life is fundamentally ethical, and every action is a decision about how to comport ourselves in the face of ethical demands engendered by being with others (Taylor, 1989; Vandenberg, 1999).

The historical emergence of the modern idea of development came to fruition at the end of the 19th and early 20th centuries, precisely the time when Piaget began his work. He is an offspring of this era, and his theory of human development reflects its influence. He presumes that development is natural, resulting from immanent material forces that progressively reveal an inherent, hierarchical ordering. He assumes this natural ordering can be determined through objective inquiry that separates *is* from *ought*, and the results can be used to address questions about religious–existential issues and the nature of the good. His efforts yielded brilliant insights. The limitations of his theory, which can only be fully appreciated by understanding the historical context of his work, are revealed in the paradoxical difference between how the theory depicts others (as biologically structured, epistemic subjects seeking adaptation to the demands of the physical world) and his own use of the results of his findings (to address existential and ethical issues that are not presumed to play an important role in the development of those he studied).

These limitations suggest that future approaches to human development address a twofold need: (a) recognition of the importance of existential issues, which give rise to the centrality of religious beliefs, spiritual concerns, and theological questions in peoples lives; and (b) appreciation that human life is inescapably ethical, that there is a plurality of moral frameworks, and deciding among competing goods cannot be adjudicated by science. The following chapter addresses this second need.

REFERENCES

Blumenberg, H. (1983). *The legitimacy of the modern age*. Cambridge, MA: MIT Press.

Bowler, P. J. (1984). *Evolution*. Berkeley: University of California Press.

Breisach, E. (1983). *Historiography*. Chicago: University of Chicago Press.

Cassirer, E. (1979). *The philosophy of the Enlightenment* (F. C. A. Koelln & J. P. Pettegrove, Trans.). Princeton, NJ: Princeton University Press.

Chapman, M. (1988). *Constructive evolution*. Cambridge, England: Cambridge University Press.

Funkenstein, A. (1986). *Theology and the scientific imagination*. Princeton, NJ: Princeton University Press.

Gilkey, L. B. (1969). *Naming the whirlwind: The renewal of God language*. Bloomington: Indiana University Press.

Gould, S. J. (1989). *Wonderful life: The Burgess Shale and nature of history*. New York: Norton.

Hahn, R. (1986). Laplace and the mechanistic universe. In D. C. Lindberg & R. I. Numbers (Eds.), *God and nature* (pp. 256–276). Berkeley: University of California Press.

Hazard, P. (1963). *The European mind (1680–1715)*. Cleveland, OH: World. (Original work published 1935)

James, W. (1961). *The varieties of religious experience*. New York: Collier-Macmillan.

Karier, C. J. (1986). *Scientists of the mind: Intellectual founders of modern psychology*. Urbana: University of Illinois Press.

Kessen, W. (1990). *The rise and fall of development*. Worcester, MA: Clark University Press.

Lawrence, P. (1977). Heaven and earth: The relation of the nebular hypothesis to geology. In W. Yourgrau & A. D. Breck (Eds.), *Cosmology, history and theology* (pp. 253–282). New York: Plenum Press.

Lillard, A. (1998). Ethnopsychologies: Cultural variation in theories of mind. *Psychological Bulletin, 123*, 3–32.

Lourenco, O. (2000). Conceptual development: A plea for grand theories. *Contemporary Psychology, 45*, 662–664.

Lyotard, F. (1984). *The postmodern condition: A report on knowledge*. (G. Bennington & B. Massumi, Trans.). Minneapolis: University of Minnesota Press. (Original work published 1979)

Marty, M. M. (1982). The idea of progress in twentieth-century theology. In G. A. Almond, M. Chodorow, & R. H. Pearce (Eds.), *Progress and its discontents* (pp. 482–500). Berkeley: University of California Press.

Mayr, E. (1982). *The growth of biological thought: Diversity, evolution, and inheritance*. Cambridge, MA: Belknap Press.

Merleau-Ponty, M. (1977). *Aventures de la Dialectique* [Dialectic Adventures]. Paris: Gallimard.

Morss, J. R. (1990). *The biologising of childhood: Developmental psychology and the Darwinian myth*. Hove, England: Erlbaum.

Nietzsche, F. W. (1974). *The gay science* (W. Kaufmann, Trans.). New York: Vintage. (Original work published 1882)

Piaget, J. (1914). Bergson et Sabatier [Bergson and Sabatier]. *Revue Chretienne, 61*, 192–200.

Piaget, J. (1916). *La mission de l'idee* [The mission of the idea]. Lausanne, Switzerland: La Concorde.

Piaget, J. (1918). *Recherche* [Search]. Lausanne, Switzerland: La Concorde.

Piaget, J. (1930). *Immanenitisme et foi religieuse* [Immanentism of religious faith]. Geneva: Groupe romand des Anciens Membres de l'Association Chretienne d'Etudiants.

Piaget, J. (1965). *The moral judgment of the child* (M. Gabain, Trans.). London: Routledge & Kegan Paul. (Original work published 1932)

Piaget, J. (1970). *The child's conception of physical causality* (M. Gabain, Trans.). London: Routledge & Kegan Paul. (Original work published 1927)

Piaget, J. (1971). *Psychology and epistemology* (A. Rosin, Trans.). New York: Viking Press. (Original work published 1970)

Piaget, J. (1983). Piaget's theory. In W. Kessen (Ed.), *Handbook of child psychology: Vol. I. History, theory, and methods* (pp. 103–128). New York: Wiley.

Pompa, L. (1990). *Human nature and historical knowledge: Hume, Hegel, Vico.* Cambridge, England: Cambridge University Press.

Randall, J. H. (1976). *The making of the modern mind.* New York: Houghton Mifflin.

Rudwick, M. J. S. (1986). The shape and meaning of earth history. In D. C. Lindberg & R. L. Numbers (Eds.), *God and nature* (pp. 296–321). Berkeley: University of California Press.

Taylor, C. (1989). *Sources of the self.* Cambridge, MA: Harvard University Press.

Toulmin, S. (1972). *Human understanding.* Princeton, NJ: Princeton University Press.

Toulmin, S., & Goodfield, J. (1965). *The discovery of time.* Chicago: University of Chicago Press.

Vandenberg, B. (1991). Is epistemology enough? *American Psychologist, 46,* 1278–1286.

Vandenberg, B. (1992). Sacred text, secular history and human development. *Family Perspective, 26,* 405–421.

Vandenberg, B. (1993a). Developmental psychology, God, and the good. *Theory and Psychology, 3,* 191–206.

Vandenberg, B. (1993b). Existentialism and development. *American Psychologist, 48,* 296–297.

Vandenberg, B. (1995). Ripples of Newtonian mechanics: Science, theology, and the emergence of the idea of development. *Journal of Mind and Behavior, 16,* 21–34.

Vandenberg, B. (1999). Levinas and the ethical context of human development. *Human Development, 42,* 31–44.

Vidal, F. (1987). Jean Piaget and the liberal Protestant tradition. In M. G. Ash & W. R. Woodward (Eds.), *Psychology in twentieth-century thought and society* (pp. 271–294). Cambridge, England: Cambridge University Press.

Vidal, F., Buscaglia, M., & Voneche, J. J. (1983). Darwinism and developmental psychology. *Journal of the History of the Behavioral Sciences, 19,* 81–94.

White, S. H. (1983). The idea of development in developmental psychology. In R. M. Lerner (Ed.), *Developmental psychology: Historical and philosophical perspectives* (pp. 55–78). Hillsdale, NJ: Erlbaum.

Wittgenstein, L. (1961). *Tractatus logico-philosophicus* (D. F. Pears & B. F. McGuinnes, Trans.). London: Routledge & Kegan Paul. (Original work published 1921)

10

MORAL VISIONS OF DEVELOPMENTAL PSYCHOLOGY

JOHN CHAMBERS CHRISTOPHER

Researchers and theorists in the field of developmental psychology surely have unearthed a number of interesting and helpful findings and perspectives on the unfolding of a human life. However, this field seems to be hampered by many of the unexamined and perhaps faulty assumptions that have been discussed throughout this book. One symptom or sign of this problem is the fact that research and theory in this subdiscipline, like much of psychology, are greatly fragmented such that no cohesive and compelling perspective on human development has yet emerged. Another serious shortcoming of the field is that it has yet to become fully aware of its own cultural roots and develop an orientation that speaks to all cultural traditions.

Much of developmental psychology is centered around research programs consisting of lots of small studies of very circumscribed phenomena analyzed in the languages of diverse theoretical frameworks that do not mesh very well with one another. The common assumption within psychology has been that "Major issues such as moral development must be reduced to researchable pieces" (Eisenberg, 1996, p. 58). However, increasingly we have come to realize that findings from such small pieces of research do not by themselves add up to a convincing or useful understanding of human phenomena. (I recall a graduate school colleague of mine who had transferred from developmental psychology to another area of the field once remarked that she left partly because she was "afraid she would spend her entire academic career studying 'looking responses' in 4 year olds!") Particular findings only take on meaning in the light of some wider theory of human action or personality in much the way that most paragraphs in a novel only take on meaning in the light of the novel's story as a whole. Unfortunately, even when findings are linked to theory, we have to deal with the fact that different researchers and schools of thought, such as Piagetian thought, psychodynamic theory, learning theory, and a host of others, hold to different theoretical commitments that speak in different, often incommensurable terms about human behavior. A kind of relativism pervades psychology in which different schools of thought are recognized and tolerated but rarely challenged. Consequently, within developmental psychology, as in most other areas of psychology, schools, theories, models, and research traditions coexist in an uneasy truce, with surprisingly little engagement and cross-fertilization among them. This situation can be frustrating and discouraging to the thoughtful student and casts a shadow of doubt over the entire field.

The other main problem developmental psychology faces is that it has yet to effectively deal with the nature of culture and the fact that humans are deeply cultural beings (Cole, 1996; Jahoda, 1986, 2000; Valsiner & Lawrence, 1997). For example, Jerome Bruner (1990) argued that the tremendously influential "cognitive revolution" in psychology over the last half century has misfired in many ways because it views human life through the overly narrow lens of what is conventionally called *information processing*. By focusing on information rather than the richer phenomenon of cultural meaning, psychology, according to Bruner, precludes asking such questions as "How is the world organized in the mind of a Muslim fundamentalist?" or "How does the concept of Self differ in Homeric Greece and in the postindustrial world?" (p. 5). In Bruner's view, human behavior consists most basically of *acts of meaning*. Thus, human beings

> do not terminate at their own skins; they are expressions of culture. To treat the world as an indifferent flow of information to be processed by individuals each on his or her own terms is to lose sight of how individuals are formed and how they function. . . . Given that psychology is so immersed in culture, it must be organized around those meaning-making and meaning-using processes that connect man to culture. (Bruner, 1990, p. 12)

Like Bruner, Shweder (1990), and others, I suggest that developmental psychology needs to focus on acts of meaning. Only if we do so will we be able to discern and take responsibility for the cultural underpinnings—and cultural blind spots—of our theories of human development. Critics have argued that developmental psychology relies too heavily on unexamined assumptions and tacit values rooted in parts of the Western cultural heritage. In the previous chapter, Vandenberg and O'Connor (chap. 9, this volume) indicate how the notion of development has been linked with modern Western notions of *progress*. Others have pointed out that our conceptions of development appear to assume *individualistic* assumptions and values that shape what our theories designate as the desired endpoint of development (Cirillo & Wapner, 1986; Cushman, 1991; Harkness, Raeff, & Super, 2000; Kaplan, 1986; Kim & Choi, 1994; Kirschner, 1996; Riegel, 1972; Sampson, 1977; Shweder, 1998).

In the modern West, we tend to share commonsense, taken-for-granted understandings of ourselves as separate, autonomous, self-motivated agents. Geertz (1983) provided the classic description and this outlook when he wrote:

> The Western conception of the person as a bounded, unique, more or less integrated motivational and cognitive universe, a dynamic center of awareness, emotion, judgment, and action organized into a distinctive whole and set contrastively both against other such wholes and against a social and natural background is, however incorrigible it may seem to us, a rather peculiar idea within the context of the world's culture. (p. 59)

It is illuminating to compare this notion of the person with the one designated by the Japanese word for self, *jibun*, which literally means "self part," implying that the self by itself is not the basic unit of identity (Rosenberger, 1992). As Markus and Kitayama (1991) observed:

> [I]n some cultures, at least, on certain occasions, the individual, in the sense of a set of significant inner attributes of the person, may cease to be the primary unit of consciousness. Instead, the sense of belongingness to a social relation may become so strong that it makes better sense to think of the relation as the functional unit of conscious reflection. (p. 226)

A result, as discerned by Tobin, Wu, and Davidson (1989), is that for many Japanese, "a child's humanity is realized most fully not so much in his ability to be independent from the group as his ability to cooperate and feel part of the group" (p. 39).

In the field of psychology, the legacy of the great 17th-century philosopher René Descartes weighs heavily on us. Along with John Locke, Descartes authored what Charles Taylor (1989, pp. 159–176) called the modern *punctual self*, the self as an extensionless center of pure agency that, because it is unconstrained by prior bonds to the world, is capable of making and remaking its identity as it wishes. Taylor showed how this notion of a disengaged self crops up again and again in Western thought. The assumption of such a highly individualistic, punctual self poses at least two major problems for developmental psychology. First, it greatly obscures how very different kinds of selves or identities develop in different cultural eras or contexts. If we ignore that ours is just one way of being human, we risk a disrespectful and imperialistic attitude and approach. Second, it turns out to be very difficult to explain the development of such a separate, sovereign, highly autonomous self out of the dense nexus of dependencies and interdependencies that constitute childhood and cultural life generally. We might say that these theories have a hard time explaining how greater human capacities and maturity naturally grow out of the soil of social life rather than being wrested from life by the force of an individual will.

To its credit, developmental psychology has worked hard in recent years to become more culturally sensitive, in part by including individuals from other cultural groups and traditions in its research. But a more adequate overall theoretical or philosophical perspective on human development is needed if we truly are to avoid misinterpreting others from our cultural vantage point. Fashioning such a perspective will be a great challenge. On the one hand, there almost certainly are some fundamentals or universals of being human and developing over time into more capable and mature people. On the other hand, different cultures and different experiences within cultures shape very different kinds of people, with quite different characters or identities and quite different visions of the good life. I think it might now be possible to sort out these two sides of the story and do justice to both in a more plausible and cohesive picture of human development. Of course, I can only roughly sketch what might be some of the contours of such an approach. To this end, in the remainder of the chapter, I weave together insights from interactivism, an emerging school of thought developed by Mark Bickhard and his colleagues, and the hermeneutic philosophy of Martin Heidegger, Hans-Georg Gadamer, and Charles Taylor.

PROCEDURAL KNOWING AND BEING-IN-THE-WORLD

Building on the philosophy of pragmatism and formed in dialogue with Piagetian principles, the interactivist view (Bickhard, 1980, 1992a, 1992b, 2000; Bickhard & Christopher, 1994; Campbell & Bickhard, 1986; Campbell, Christopher, & Bickhard, 2002) considers development at its heart to be characterized by the ability to abstract from or transcend the patterns of interaction and thought that we are currently engaged in so that we can move to a "higher" level in which we can reflect on what we had previously taken for granted. Piaget (2000) referred to this ability as *reflective abstraction*. It can be defined as "the relationship between adjacent levels of knowing . . . in which properties resident in a given level, implicit in the organization or functioning of that level, are explicitly known at the next higher level" (Campbell & Bickhard, 1986, p. 85). If we begin with reflective abstraction as a basic developmental principle, then we need to describe what the "ground" of human development is, what is the first level on which such differentiation can begin to occur.

Interactivism refers to the ground of development—our most basic and developmentally earliest way of existing—as "Knowing Level 1." At this level, which occurs from infancy to about age 4, knowledge is constituted in the ability to interact with the world. Our earliest forms of knowing center around learning what procedures work in the world. Knowledge is initially a thoroughly procedural affair. Through trial and error, infants learn procedures for how to do or accomplish various things. At first, such procedures involve the beginnings of motor coordination, simply learning how to move limbs. Knowledge comes from learning in a sensorimotor way the consequences of moving different parts of the body at different times when in the proximity of different kinds of objects. An infant will learn, for instance, that kicking the side of the crib shakes a mobile. Infants also begin to develop procedures that have social and emotional considerations: They learn what impact crying or smiling has on their caretakers. Through the process of trial and error, or what interactivist theory terms a *variation and selection constructivism*, infants begin to develop increasingly more sophisticated patterns of interacting with their world, both of objects and of people. What is crucial about Knowing Level 1 is that *all* of the knowledge and learning that occurs does so in an unreflective, pre-self-conscious way. Prior to age 4 there is no self-aware, self-directed sense of personal agency that guides learning and development. Infants and young children know and learn without knowing that they know. It is with the subsequent level, Knowing Level 2, that children for the first time develop a sense of self that can know and reflect on the world and their experience of it.

Research on the development of memory corroborates the interactivist understanding of Knowing Level 1. The most fundamental form of memory seems to be procedural or enactive memory (Tulving, 1985). This is the memory of how to do things. Procedural memory stores the knowledge of how to turn a door knob or ride a bicycle. Episodic or event memory, the recollection of events that stand out from the flow of experience, develops considerably later. This is the type of memory that we most frequently associate with memory—for example, the memory of internal images of specific events, like a childhood birthday party. Event-based memory can contain images of ourselves interacting with others and can include the thoughts and feelings we had at the time. Procedural memory, in contrast, is more rudimentary, being mainly about what to do in concrete situations and lacking the capacity to store self-conscious occurrences.

The hermeneutic philosopher Martin Heidegger (1962) helps to broaden and deepen our understanding of this most basic kind of living and learning that interactivism calls Knowing Level 1. Heidegger was concerned with the way that much of Western culture splits the subject off from the object, the self from others, the mind from the body, and facts from values. Heidegger believed that this dualistic outlook distorts the fact that at the most fundamental level we are beings engaged in the world doing things, what he called *being-in-the-world.* His classic example of this is a craftsman in a workshop. Heidegger draws attention to the phenomenology or actual lived experience of the craftsman who is engaged in building something. For such a person who is hammering two things together, the hammer is not experienced as a separate and discrete object that the person is set over and against. The hammer is instead an extension of the person. Hammers, nails, wood, and the person are all caught up in and subsumed by the bigger project. Hammers, nails, wood, and the person are all different aspects of a more experientially primary activity, namely building something. In fact, "objects" only become recognized as separate objects when they no longer fit seamlessly into the current activity; when, for instance, we have a ball peen hammer in hand but we really need a sledge hammer.

In this way, Heidegger tries to describe the most fundamental and enduring way that humans exist in the world, one very different from what Descartes thought was most primary, namely the *cogito*, the *I* that thinks. Heidegger believes that we are not basically *detached knowers* of objective facts (including, sometimes, facts about ourselves) that we seek to manage, manipulate, or control for our purposes. Only occasionally do we approach the world that way as natural scientists or everyday problem solvers. Rather, we are fundamentally much less reflective and much less control-oriented *participants* in a meaningful lifeworld. Heidegger has a distinctive conception of that world or lifeworld in which we are immersed and participate. According to Richardson, Fowers, and Guignon (1999), Heidegger

> resists the temptation to see the meaningfulness of things as mere "projections" of human mental "coloring" onto intrinsically meaningless and valueless objects. Heidegger wants us to see that, in our initial, everyday, pre-reflective encounter with the world, things show up for us directly as already value-laden and as having significance. While it is certainly true that meanings cannot exist unless there are agents (humans) in the world, there is no reason to think that meanings exist only in our minds. Instead, they are as much a part of the furnishings of the world as mass, velocity and position. On this view, then, meanings and values do not exist in our heads; they are "out there" in the dynamic life-world we encounter in our day-to-day affairs. On this view, the subjectivization of meaning and value in modern naturalism is a high-level theoretical construct, the result of a sort of "breakdown" in our ordinary being-in-the-world, which gives us no insight into the true nature of reality as we actually encounter it. (p. 209)

Thus, hermeneutic writers stress that the mature human agent is not a "thinking substance," a la Descartes, a mind that ideally adopts an "outsider" viewpoint, gazing as objectively as possible on the world. Rather, this approach insists on holding fast to an "insider's" perspective as the

> source from which all reflection, including philosophy, ultimately originates. The awareness that we cannot escape the insider's perspective re-

sults from acknowledging our own "finitude"—our rootedness in a cultural, historical, and linguistic context we can never fully objectify or ground. (Guignon, 1991, pp. 96–97)

Heidegger shows us that the practical, procedural, largely un-self-conscious flow of living and learning that goes on at the first level of knowing continues as the basic reality and rhythm of a human life throughout its course. Heidegger's craftsman represents quite a advancement, of course, over an infant finding a way to make noise by banging his or her toy hammer on the side of the crib. But the former is an extension and refinement of the latter, not a leap to a qualitatively different kind of knowing and living. As an adult, the craftsman will have his moments of self-consciousness, explicit analysis, perhaps even formal theorizing, in the service of his aims. But these are temporary interruptions in the more practical, intuitive flow of living in which we apprehend and appreciate things more directly and immediately as "engaged agents" (Taylor, 1995, p. 21) who take for granted the folkways and mores of our community or culture.[1]

SOCIAL PRACTICES

Heidegger's craftsman working on a project is an example of a social practice, an activity that draws its meaning from a larger social context. The building of a bookshelf only makes sense within a society that is literate, values books, and most likely is relatively sedentary. Heidegger maintains we are born into and take over in a largely preconscious way an unending series of social traditions and practices. American children, for example, learn early on about "going shopping" and over time know how to navigate through malls on their own. In doing so, Heidegger would argue, they not only learn the various physical and social mechanics to shop; they are all participating in, taking over, and reinforcing the social meanings and values that give birth to shopping and malls in the first place. Similarly, the members of a traditional Japanese village learn the subtle art of deliberating together until a virtually unanimous consensus is achieved. How different is our way of life in which we decide many basic moral and social issues through elections

---

[1]None of this means that we cannot criticize the values and practices of our society or way of life. According to Richardson, Rogers, and McCarroll (1998),

> Thus, the practical flow of living is already defined for us by particular commitments and identifications taken for granted by our culture. They are our starting point. We can and often should criticize various of our norms and practices. But, in the hermeneutic view, we always critique them on the basis of other commitments or insights from our traditions that for the moment we take for granted. In this view, our various cultural and moral traditions are actually rich resources for such critique. The common view of them as stable, monolithic authorities is actually a narrow, prejudiced outgrowth of the Enlightenment. In fact, they seem essentially to be multivocal, interminably noisy debates rather than static pronouncements or sets of norms. (p. 507)

with secret ballots! In these worlds, values are not separated off from facts. Our behaviors reveal what Heidegger (1962) called *care*. What we do, where we focus our time and attention, indicates what we find meaningful, compelling, or of undeniable worth to us.

Recently social theorists, many influenced directly by Heidegger or, as with the Russian sociocultural school, by Marx and Hegel, have sought to draw out the implications of what it means to be engaged or immersed in social practices. Indeed, notice has been taken of a significant "practice turn" in much contemporary social theory (Schatzki, Knorr-Cetina, & Savigny, 2001). According to Pierre Bourdieu (1990), social practices are "actions that are repeated, shared with others in a social group, and invested with normative expectations, meaning, or significance that go beyond the immediate goals of the action" (p. 13). Miller and Goodnow (1995) stressed the importance of social practices as "contexts for development" and suggest that they have these five main features:

1. Practices provide a way of describing development-in-context, without separating child and context and without separating development into a variety of separate domains.
2. Practices reflect or instantiate a social and moral order.
3. Practices provide the route by which children come to participate in a culture, allowing the culture to be "reproduced" or "transformed."
4. Practices do not exist in isolation.
5. The nature of participation in practices has consequences. (pp. 8–13)

The social or cultural practices approach helps us to move beyond our conventional dualistic ways of thinking about life by pointing to the patterns of interactions that precede the separation of the world into subjects and objects, selves and others, facts and values, and minds and bodies. The social practice perspective also helps us to think more deeply about the nature of culture itself. Often, in psychology, attempts to take culture into account rely on Bronfenbrenner's (1977) ecological model of human development, or a similar view, in which concentric circles around a core are used to depict the self. Geertz (1973) described such models, which he called "stratigraphic models of the self," in this way:

> Strip off the motley forms of culture and one finds the structural and functional regularities of social organization. Peel these off in turn and one finds the underlying psychological factors—"basic needs" or what-have-you—that support and make them possible. Peel off psychological factors and one is left with biological foundations—anatomical, physiological, neurological—of the whole edifice of human life. (p. 37)

The downside of such attempts to factor culture into the equation of human development is that it reduces culture to a mere extraneous context. Models and theories that take this approach adopt and reinforce the supposition that the individual is ontologically prior to the social; that it somehow makes sense to think of the individual as a biological entity existing independently of society and culture. Different versions of this notion of the self have been much touted in modern times as a bulwark against violations of individual autonomy, rights, and integrity by the state or others. Unquestionably, it has served that worthy end. But that may turn out to be like cutting off one's foot to cure an infected toe—eliminating all or most of culture to get rid of bad culture, so to speak (Bellah, Madsen, Sullivan, Swidler, & Tipton, 1985; Cushman, 1990; Lasch, 1979; Putnam, 2000). In the end, it may encourage a destructive emotional isolation and erode the social ties and commitments that alone make freedom or autonomy meaningful.

Cole (1996), Shweder (1990), Kashima (2000), and Poortinga (1997), among others, offered trenchant critiques of the many approaches in which culture is treated, essentially, as a mere additional, independent variable in the explanation of behavior. What these approaches ignore is the degree to which culture precedes us. Culture, rather than consisting mainly of beliefs and values that become internalized, is implicit in the patterns of interaction the child learns from infancy onward. As mentioned in the previous chapter, Geertz (1973, p. 5) considered a human being to be "an animal suspended in webs of significance he himself has spun" and "culture to be those webs" of meaning that underlie all social functioning and give sense and coherence to our lives. These webs of significance permeate our lives so thoroughly that any attempt to separate human nature from culture is distorting and incoherent. In this spirit, Cole (1996) wrote, "An 'act in its context'" might be understood in terms of a "weaving metaphor" that requires a "relational interpretation of mind; objects and contexts arise together as part of a single bio-social-cultural process of human development" (p. 136). Thus, culture is more than a context; it is a ground of human being and inseparable from such being, which is why Bruner (1990) characterized us as "expressions of culture." The interactivist concept of *implicitness* can help to deepen our understanding of how culture is woven into the very marrow of our being.

IMPLICITNESS

Implicitness is a way of addressing how values, meanings, and assumptions are inherent or entailed in our thoughts, feelings, and behavior without them having to somehow be internalized or known by the person. One of the consequences of individualistic assumptions about the self is that they presuppose that the boundaries of the person are roughly at the surface of the skin, creating a divide between the internal and the external realms. This split brings with it the problem for developmental psychology of accounting for how external influences, like socialization agents, can affect the internal experience and subjectivity of the developing person (Bickhard & Christopher, 1994; Christopher & Bickhard, 1992). Typically, developmentalists assume that for something to have an influence on the child it must be internalized or in someway brought into or made present within the mind of the child. Different psychological mechanisms are posited to take what is outside and internalize or introject it so that it becomes a part of the developing child. For instance, attachment theory relies on a notion of internalization to create internal working models of primary caretakers. Theorists such as Piaget (1945/1962), Piaget and Inhelder (1966/1971), Vygotsky (1978), Valsiner and Lawrence, (1997), and Wertsch and Stone (1985) have used notions of internalization as a key element of their theories. And still other theories simply posit the existence of some internal belief or representational structure such as low self-esteem or unconscious self or object representations to account for the child's behavior. Among other problems, these approaches tend to attribute to the child cognitive capabilities that the child does not yet possess, making it difficult to account adequately for his or her behavior or growth (Bickhard & Christopher, 1994; Christopher, Bickhard, & Lambeth, 2001). Implicitness is a way of bypassing this issue by suggesting that these influences can occur without a sharp internal–external or objective–subjective divide needing somehow to be broached. From the interactivist perspective, the notion of such a divide is based on a faulty individualistic premise: namely, that the individual is sharply distinct from its context. The notion of implicitness allows us to conceive of how the environment can influence a person without requiring that the source of the influence be a kind of thing or force present within the person. In more formal terms, certain things can be functionally true of an entity in interaction with its environment without those things having to be necessarily present or existent anywhere within the entity.

A very simple example of implicitness at work is a thermostat. For a thermostat to do what we want it to do, a number of things must be presupposed in its basic design and functioning. A thermostat assumes that the temperature will not exceed a certain range and that changes in temperature are relatively gradual. These kinds of presuppositions are instantiated in the design of a thermostat but are not actually present—they are implicit.

The patterns of interaction that a child learns from infancy onward within the family constellation embody a number of implicit presuppositions or tacit meanings—the sort of meanings that hermeneutic thought, as we saw, views as being as much in the world "out there" as "in here" in the mind. For example, consider an infant raised in the 1950s in a responsible but stereotypically emotionally distant American Protestant family. Armed with the latest child-rearing manuals, the parents maintain strict, clock-based caretaking routines. Attempting to instill independence and emotional maturity, they insist on the infant learning to "cry it out" alone and sleep by herself. We can easily imagine that the infant would cry for food, attention, and emotional responsiveness in response to various basic needs and promptings. However, the infant soon would discover that such cries go largely unheeded and that crying only exacerbates her discomfort by causing additional physiological and emotional stress. Through trial and error, the infant happens on quietude and a degree of passivity much of the time as the best solution.

Any pattern of interaction and way of being like this has layers of presuppositions or tacit meanings. In this case, the lack of responsiveness to the infant per se presupposes that other things are more important than the infant's current emotional needs. It also implies that self-control, orderliness, tight schedules, and a healthy dose of self-denial should take precedence over emotional displays of dependency or need and spontaneous caring responses to them. It implies that the kind of more or less rigid autonomy that is built by this regimen is the cornerstone of the most dignified and decent kind of life, one that ought to be nurtured by one and all and that in some sense may be the most satisfying kind of life, the truly good life, over the long run. Thus, one very specific pattern of interaction like this can entail an extensive web of presuppositions or meanings concerning the nature of the self, others, and the whole of life. However, the interactivist notion of implicitness guards against prematurely attributing such presuppositions to specific cognitive elements (such as internal representations, beliefs, schemas, etc.) in the child's mind. Various presuppositions or tacit meanings may be implicitly present in the infant's way of being in the world even though the infant is not yet cognitively capable of having *any* of the explicit cognitions that would be necessary to conceive of such things as self-control, caring, indifference, or propriety as qualities and powerful determinants of her own or other people's way of life.

Meanings or presuppositions of this sort are not simply about the child. They also hold for the environment, for the whole world the child knows. They refer to patterns of interaction that undercut and transcend simple dichotomies of self and object. The infant and young child are cognitively incapable of making distinctions or differentiating the properties of the current environment from other possible environments. They also are incapable of differentiating who contributes what to any given interaction. Moreover, the child cannot cognitively differentiate a sense of self from the totality of his or her being. As a consequence, interactive patterns are not something children have or engage in as self-aware, choosing individuals. Rather, they are prereflective players in a game of life that is the only game or world they know. Such interactive patterns or social practices afford ways of being, but these ways of being are implicitly about the entire world, actual and potential, not just this part of it into which they have been born. Children are not able to differentiate the way of life that they have learned from other possible ways of life. "A *lack* of differentiation of this situation from others, of these caregivers from others, *implicitly presupposes* totality, again without any explicit cognitions or cognitive capabilities on the part of the infant" (Bickhard & Christopher, 1994, p. 244).

Implicitness affords developmental psychology a way to model how the social practices in which we are immersed influence us without our having to be aware at all of this influence. Implicitness addresses how it is that we live on the basis of meaningful self-interpretations and interpretations of life without our needing at any point to actually make such interpretations or even consciously know what these interpretations are. It is also a way of discussing culture that avoids treating culture as either external to the individual or located in the individual's mind. As such, the concept of implicitness helps to correct a tendency for the interpretive and narrative dimension of hermeneutic thought to be understood in an overly mentalistic or intellectual manner. Thus, interactivism may contribute something essential to explicating what Taylor (1993) seemed to mean by a "fully engaged agency."

HIGHER LEVELS OF KNOWING

So far, I have been discussing Knowing Level 1 and what is available to the child at that level. With cognitive maturation, the child develops the capacity for what interactivist thinkers call Knowing Level 2 (Campbell & Bickhard, 1986; Campbell et al., 2002). On the basis of reflective abstraction, the child develops the ability to differentiate from and represent what he or she was initially immersed in. The child begins to reflectively abstract from the patterns of interaction and social practices he or she has learned. At Knowing Level 1, the child cannot know himself or herself. At Knowing Level 2, the child can begin to explicitly know the self. Knowing Level 2 can potentially make aspects of Knowing Level 1 explicitly known and understood. Examples of Knowing Level 2 would be the kinds of self-beliefs and self-statements that can be spoken to others and ourselves. It requires Knowing Level 2 to be able to articulate (even in a rudimentary way) who we are, how we are different from other people, and what is important to us. At Knowing Level 1, these things are implicit.

At Knowing Level 1, the goals that guide a child's behavior and interactions are implicit; the child just lives out these goals. At the next knowing level, the child can consciously know what these goals are and begin to organize them around higher order goals. For instance, a child may develop a higher order goal of not upsetting her parents. Such a goal would help a child learn to subordinate or deselect certain Level 1 goals, like playing with her mother's office equipment, that experience has shown conflict with this higher order goal. Level 2 goals then can direct the formation and selection of goals at Level 1. Knowing Level 2 begins to develop at around 4 years of age. Evidence for Knowing Level 2 includes the development of metacognition

(Flavell, Green, & Flavell, 1986; Gopnik & Astington, 1988; Perner, 1991, 1992) and of autobiographical memory (Nelson, 1992, 1994).

The process of reflective abstraction is potentially unbounded. The knowing levels as a cognitive process are potentially infinite (Campbell & Bickhard, 1986). A third knowing level can emerge that is able to know aspects of the second; aspects of Level 3 can potentially be known by Level 4, and so on. At Level 3 the person can begin to engage in the process Erikson (1963) termed *identity formation*. While operating at Level 2, the child *is* an identity but would not be said to *have* an identity. At Level 3, however, the child can begin to *have* an identity. To have an identity means to know one's identity, to compare it with others, to explicitly evaluate it at times, and possibly to try to transform it. As Campbell and Bickhard (1986) described,

> The child at the first level, then, implicitly has a self, but cannot know that self. At the second level, the child knows that self, and thereby has an implicit representation of his or her self. At the third level, the child can know that self-representation, thereby making it explicit. Now the child can compare his or her self to a system of alternatives, judge it against values, and construct it in accordance with those judgments. (p. 119)

Level 3 is also the level at which we can form metavalues, or values about values. In terms of the self, at Level 3 people can form explicit judgments about what kind of a person they are and what kind of a person they ought to be. Research suggests that Level 3 begins to emerge from 9 to 11 years of age (Campbell & Bickhard, 1986).

The knowing levels complement the hermeneutic emphases on our situatedness in cultural practices and on narrative and dialogical understandings of identity by providing a developmental account of how both aspects of human being emerge. We are both situated in culture and capable, through the higher knowing levels, of attaining the kind of self-reflexiveness that we characteristically see as definitive of human agency. Thus, the account of knowing levels provides an expanded model of engaged agency.

Unlike some stage theories of development, like those of Piaget and Inhelder (1966/1969),[2] Kohlberg (1984), or Kegan (1982), the knowing levels are not global cognitive structures that require simultaneous or near simultaneous levels of development across all domains of the person's life. They are instead a capacity that may or may not be realized. Most often, higher levels of knowing come into play in some areas of our life and not in others. Knowing Level 1 is always operating; the other levels are in a sense incidental or supplemental to it.

---

[2]However, Chapman (1988) argued powerfully that psychology has often distorted Piaget's work by attributing to him the oversimplified claim that "cognitive stage development is inherently linked with age and that the concept of structure implies synchrony in development across different areas of content" (p. 2).

In the interactivist view, multiple meanings and goals are always at work with human beings. A variety of implicit meanings and goals exist at Level 1 in various states of conflict and convergence. With the development of higher knowing levels, additional meanings and goals emerge and interact with those of Level 1. Consequently, human beings consist of a variety of goals, values, and meanings that exist at different levels of knowing and in various states of tension and harmony. In this way interactivism is similar to Mikhail Bhaktin's (Morson & Emerson, 1990; Wertsch, 1991) view that human beings are constituted by a polyphony of voices. The interactivist contribution is to see these multiple voices existing at different levels of awareness; some exist implicitly in behavior and feeling, others are explicitly known in our thoughts and beliefs, and still others are implicit in what we are consciously aware of.

There is in interactivism an inborn conservatism with regard to how much of ourselves we can consciously know. In this sense interactivism is similar to the hermeneutic view that we are situated in our lives and can never be fully away of ourselves. In Heidegger's (1962) words, we are "proximally and for the most part" being-in-the-world; in the words of interactivism, Level 1 is always ontologically primary. Consequently, we can often best know ourselves "not by inward turning and introspection" in the manner of Descartes, "but by catching sight of ourselves as we are engaged and preoccupied in everyday contexts" (Guignon, 1984, p. 232). One implication of this is that who we are, in a sense, is distributed across the knowing levels. We are both the sense of self that is implicit in the behavioral choices we make on an ongoing basis and also who we consciously think we are and identify with. Thus, we might say that through the knowing levels mode, interactivism integrates, on the one hand, the emphasis of Marx, Heidegger, Vygotsky, and Luria on the situated and embedded aspect of human agency with, on the other, the revelations of Descartes regarding the *cogito*, the thinking subject.

MORAL VISIONS: THE BACKDROP OF DEVELOPMENT

Interactivism and hermeneutic thought agree that there is much about human existence that is implicit and cannot be fully known by us. A rich tapestry of assumptions and ideals undergirds patterns of interaction and social practices. These implicit assumptions and values link the individual and culture. Much of the story of human development has to do with how individual's lives and identities are shaped at the core by these assumptions and values, which they reinterpret and extend in different ways, to one extent or another, over the course of their living. Perhaps everyone puts their unique stamp on their culture's story concerning what life is all about at the same time that none of us are as unique as we sometimes think we are.

Geertz (1973) defined culture as having two basic dimensions: worldview (or *Weltanschauung*) and ethos. A culture's *worldview* is its more cognitively oriented maps of reality. Worldviews describe the nature of the universe or cosmos, its principles of causality, its understanding of time and space, and its theories about the inhabitants of the universe, including people. A culture's *ethos*, in contrast, refers to the more aesthetic and ethical dimensions of life. An ethos delineates what constitutes the good, beautiful, and desirable. The "webs of significance" that Geertz suggested comprise human culture roughly integrate the different aspects of a culture's worldview and ethos.

For example, infants and children in middle America are quickly initiated into the custom of taking baths. When children participate in bathing rituals and eventually come to adopt them on their own, they are participating in the elements of culture that are implicit in the activity. For instance, some of what is implicit in taking a bath are elements of worldview: To be able to take a hot bath requires a considerable amount of technological and scientific understanding regarding porcelain, metallurgy, hydrology, plumbing, water sanitation, and so on. We take for granted that turning the tap will give us clean hot water. However, for this tap-turning behavior to work, a wealth of background knowledge that is not actually present in material artifacts or in the minds of most of the people taking baths is required. Thus, much of this activity rests ultimately on the hard-won scientific worldview and technology cultivated by our civilization.

An ethos is also implicit in bathing. We bathe in the ways we typically do in American culture because of a variety of values concerning the significance of bathing. These values may include "Cleanliness is next to Godliness," the association of cleanliness with responsibility, health, success, and well-being, and the value of neutralizing much of the evidence of certain human bodily functions: sweat, odor, or skin and hair oils. Indeed, these presuppositions shape our view of maturity, wellness, and even mental health (one of the diagnostic criteria of schizophrenia has to do with neglecting one's hygiene). Bathing is also associated with nurturing ourselves: American culture has developed whole industries designed to pamper the self and buffer it from the perceived ravages of nature and harshness of the world of work—legacies of our Romantic heritage (Bellah et al., 1985; Taylor, 1985). However, none of these cultural values or assumptions need to be consciously recognized by the individual for culture to be propagated and reinforced through the practice of bathing.

What some writers call folk psychologies (Bruner, 1990) or indigenous psychologies (Heelas & Lock, 1981) may be thought of as subsets of cultural values and assumptions that pertain to human beings. A folk psychology is the popular, usually implicit, understanding of such things as motivation, emotion, deviance or psychopathology, well-being, morality, and the self. Folk psychologies provide a set of more or less connected, more or less normative descriptions about how human beings "tick," what our own and other minds are like, what one can expect situated actions to be like, what are possible modes of life, how one commits oneself to them, and so on. (Bruner, 1990, p. 35)

One basic dimension of a folk psychology defines what a person is and what his or her capabilities, resources, and characteristics are. In this way, a culture's worldview determines the ontology of the person or what and who we think we are. Another aspect of a folk psychology delineates norms, standards, or parameters for desirable ways of functioning and interacting. This part of the folk psychology that shapes notions of what a person ought to be is informed by a culture's ethos. Thus, worldviews lay out the nature of the person that will develop, whereas ethos guides the direction that development should take.

One implication of such a perspective is that all people, as Kaplan (1986) noted, are in a sense developmental psychologists. Each of us have some sense of what promotes and hinders growth and development. *Developmental* folk psychologies may be partially explicit but are more often implicit in the received customs and social practices surrounding child rearing and later developmental stages.

I use the term *moral visions* to acknowledge that implicit in our ways of being in the world and the social practices that collectively organize our existence are the answers to two fundamental existential questions: What is a person, and what should a person be or become? Moral visions refer to the constellations of cultural values and assumptions that constitute our understanding of the nature of the person and of the good life (Christopher, 1996, 2001). In much modern thought in general and academic psychology in particular, cultural and moral meanings and values are treated as subjective projections onto a neutral world of facts. But I have suggested that hermeneutic philosophy helps us appreciate anew that such meanings and values are no more "in our heads" as they are "out there," part of the very fabric of the dynamic lifeworld into which our lives are woven. From both hermeneutic and interactivist perspectives, values and goals inhere in all human activity. Implicitly or explicitly, moral visions inform us about what is deemed higher, deeper, or more worthy. Thus, they define what gives us strength, integration, wholeness, vitality, dignity, and goodness, and they direct us in how we can embody these ideals (Taylor, 1989). Conversely, our moral visions define what we should avoid, resist, or oppose, both internally and externally. Moral, in this sense, has less to do with rules concerning what is right or wrong as with our deepest understanding of what is good, worthy, and desirable (Brinton, 1987).

In line with this notion of moral vision, Taylor (1988) argued that human beings necessarily exist in an "inescapable" moral framework that he called a *moral topography* or *moral space*. To give a feel for this notion of moral space, Taylor (1988) noted that all people have a sense of what it means to be "out-of-joint":

This is conceptually expressed in a host of ways: as being lost, or condemned, or exiled, or unintegrated, or without meaning, or insubstantial, or empty, to name some categories. Corresponding to each of these descriptions of breakdown is some notion of what it would be to overcome it, to have integration, or full being, to be justified, or found, or whatever. But more, there is a notion of "where" this integration, fullness, etc., might come from, what might bring it about. . . . In other words, these different, often indefinite and tentative senses of what integration consists of incorporate notions of where it might be found, in the sense of where the strength lies, where the sources or resources are situated, which could bring integration, or fullness about. (pp. 300–301)

This perspective on moral visions recognizes that across cultures and over time human beings have formed quite different self-interpretations. These include different ways of defining the boundaries of the person or self (e.g., more or less individualistic or collectivistic ways) and different conceptions of the constituent elements of a person. Is the person composed of reason, will, and desire as Plato suggested; cognitions, emotions, and behavior as many contemporary psychologists believe; or the four siblings that exist on the astral plane as with the Balinese? Moral visions go further and prescribe what a person should be or become—the stance we should adopt toward aspects of ourselves, others, and the world. This aspect is well stated by Kaplan (1986), who observed that

different sociocultural groups may have different notions as to what constitutes ideal human development. They may also have different notions as to the "causes" that promote or preclude whatever they take to be ideal human development. And, finally, they may have different notions as to what has to be done to get individuals on the right track with regard to the approximation or attainment of ideal human development. (p. 92)

Sometimes moral visions or their components are explicitly known at higher knowing levels and therefore able to be communicated explicitly among people. Much of the time, however, they are implicit, operating at Knowing Level 1, and transmitted through the propagation of various social practices. Dunn (1988) provided compelling examples of how infants are inducted into the social world in this manner. Goodnow (1990) described how the kinds of messages, both verbal and nonverbal, that children receive from caretakers and other children contain "tacit messages" that draw them into the webs of meanings that encompass their community's way of life. Shweder, Mahapatra, and Miller's (1987) account of social communication captured the way the moral dimension is interwoven into human activity. They maintained that moral socialization rests on children's ability to "discern the moral order as it is dramatized and made salient in everyday practices" (p. 73).

In our conception of "social communication," morally relevant interpretations of events by local guardians of the moral order (e.g. parents) are typically presented and conveyed to young children in the context of routine family life and social practices. Those moral premises are carried by the messages and meanings implicit in the emotional reactions of others (anger or disappointment or "hurt feelings" over a transgression). They are carried by the verbal exchanges—commands, threats, sanction statements, accusations, explanations, justifications, excuses—necessary to maintain routine social practices. (Shweder et al., 1987, p. 73)

Bickhard (1989) argued that a valuing process is inherent in all human functioning, and Taylor (1989) contended that "Selfhood and the good, or in another way selfhood and morality, turn out to be inextricably intertwined themes" (p. 3). But this implicitness of moral visions in all social interactions has generally not been recognized by developmental psychology. To give just two examples, DeLoache and Gottlieb (2000), in conceptualizing the personal characteristics of the child, treated life skills as something quite separate from values and beliefs. In a similar vein, schools of research based around Kohlberg (1984), Turiel (Turiel, Killen, & Helwig, 1987), and Eisenberg (Eisenberg, Miller, Shell, McNalley, & Shea, 1991) all restrict the moral dimension of human life to other-regarding behavior and matters of justice and rights, thus obscuring the ways that moral visions concerning what it is fundamentally good to do or be imbue *all* our activities. Until this narrowness of vision is corrected, developmental psychology will continue to somewhat distort the reality of human development in our own society as well as fail to do justice to other cultural perspectives (Campbell & Christopher, 1996a, 1996b; Shweder et al., 1987). Also, it will fail to heed possible insights from other strains within Western culture, such as the "civic republican" ethical and political philosophy stemming from Aristotle that is experiencing a considerable revival at present.[3]

CONCLUSIONS AND IMPLICATIONS

What might developmental psychology look like if it were pursued within a perspective of the sort I have outlined in this chapter? First, developmental psychology would take a hard look at the question, "What is the developing self or agent that is the subject of developmental psychology?" The hermeneutic and interactivist ideas about human being and becoming I have dis-

---

[3]The following comments by the political philosopher Ronald Beiner (1992) illustrate well the tenor of this neo-Aristotelian, sometimes called *communitarian*, school of thought. Beiner suggested that the "central purpose of a society, understood as a moral community, is not the maximization of autonomy . . . but the cultivation of . . . a variety of excellences, moral and intellectual" (p. 14). Beiner also noted pithily that it is "not that liberal autonomy is a bad thing, but that without the 'thick' attachments provided by the kind of ethos that builds meaningful character, free choice . . . hardly seems worth the bother" (p. 37). My point is not to recommend these ideas—although I find them compelling—but to point out that they presuppose that what I have termed moral visions imbue all of social life, requiring us to reject the sharp dualism between fact and value that has been taken for granted by much modern social science theory and research.

cussed entail a profound critique of the individualistic cultural roots of much developmental psychology theory, research, and practice. This critique would point out that the familiar Western notion of the individual as (ideally) highly separate, autonomous, and self-reliant—if it does enshrine and advance moral ideals we rightly cherish—has serious flaws. It obscures that fact that we acquire this notion from one particular cultural tradition rather than discover it to be objectively and universally true through reason and science. Paradoxically, even though it was cultivated in the first place to oppose arbitrary authority, it has become rather imperialistic in its own right. And it deters meeting human needs for lasting social ties and loyalties and for any sort of deeper sense of purpose or meaning beyond being free from unjust interference and "doing one's own thing" (Schumaker, 2001).

Second, given the argument of this chapter, developmental psychology would continue to reflect on and refine its basic presuppositions or ontology of human existence, perhaps drawing on the hermeneutic and interactivist perspectives I have outlined. I have tried to suggest how these perspectives might allow us to identify certain universals or constants across people and cultures without obscuring or downplaying the fact that diverse traditions and cultures cultivate a splendid if sometimes bewildering variety of moral visions concerning human maturity and the good life.

Third, developmental psychology, using what might best be termed an interpretive social science approach (Hiley, Bohman, & Shusterman, 1991; Rabinow & Sullivan, 1979, 1987), would study what Taylor (1985) called the wide *diversity of goods* as they relate to human development that exist both within and across cultures. Developmental psychology would examine (with the help of other branches of psychology, other social sciences, and humanities) the moral visions of other cultural groups, including local or indigenous understandings of the person and accounts of the good life. It would try to understand why these accounts are often so compelling to those who embrace them. Moreover, it would recognize that understandings of the self and the good life exist for people at different levels of knowing. Some of these are implicit and embodied in the daily actions and practices that Heidegger described as *structures of care*. Others are the more consciously expressed and espoused goods that are more readily accessible to self-reports and interviews. Understanding the interplay and development of these notions of the self and the good life at different levels of knowing would become an important topic of research. Developmental psychology would consider both professional and scholarly accounts as well as lay accounts of these matters. It would consider developmental changes in the structure of self-interpretations and goods that animate people's lives, considering how they are influenced by and in turn influence social and economic forces. It would consider social practices and life forms as different "takes" on the meaning of life and be open to insights that might clarify them from history, philosophy, and cultural studies.

Finally, developmental psychology would become a more self-reflective discipline, including in a practical or ethical sense. Social inquiry understood as an interpretive process is not simply a method for understanding the goods that animate *others'* lives. It also applies to ourselves as theorists, researchers, and practitioners. We must recognize that such inquiry always represents (whether it knows it or not) one strand of the human search for understanding and wisdom about what constitutes a good and decent human life. In other words, social theory is always, in part, a "form of practice" (Richardson & Christopher, 1993). Social theory and social science, at their best, understand themselves to be part of the quest for understanding that Alasdair MacIntyre (1981) described as a "quest" that is "not at all . . . a search for something already adequately characterized . . . but always an education both as to the character of that which is sought and in self-knowledge" (p. 219). The sort of developmental social inquiry discussed in this and the previous chapter, I believe, could help us become more self-aware and could be a usefully critical endeavor. It could help us better understand and critically sift the goods that come from both the community and the particular background of the researcher, including challenging the implicit developmental folk psychology that already exists within Western psychology. Put another way, in the terms of this chapter, we must apply the knowing levels to ourselves as developmental psychologists to understand not only what we consciously espouse and maintain (higher knowing levels) but also what is implicit in our practices (Knowing Level 1).

Gaining more clarity about ourselves and our traditions allows us to discern the ways that we fall short of our own best ideals. Moreover, through openness to the insights of other traditions and cultures, we acquire the opportunity to learn from others and possibly integrate some of their wisdom into our ways of thinking and living. As Paolo Friere (1970) concluded, "It is not our role to speak to the people about our own view of the world, nor to attempt to impose that view on them, but rather to dialogue with the people about their view and ours" (p. 77).

REFERENCES

Beiner, R. (1992). *What's the matter with liberalism?* Berkeley: University of California Press.

Bellah, R. N., Madsen, R., Sullivan, W. M., Swidler, A., & Tipton, S. M. (1985). *Habits of the heart: Individualism and commitment in American life.* New York: HarperCollins.

Bickhard, M. H. (1980). A model of developmental and psychological processes. *Genetic Psychology Monographs, 102,* 61–116.

Bickhard, M. H. (1989). Ethical psychotherapy and psychotherapy as ethics: A response to Perez. *New Ideas in Psychology, 7,* 159–164.

Bickhard, M. H. (1992a). How does the environment affect the person? In L. T. Winegar & J. Valsiner (Eds.), *Children's development within social context: Vol. 1. Metatheory and theory* (pp. 63–92). Hillsdale, NJ: Erlbaum.

Bickhard, M. H. (1992b). Scaffolding and self-scaffolding: Central aspects of development. In L. T. Winegar & J. Valsiner (Eds.), *Children's development within social context: Vol. 2. Research and methodology* (pp. 33–52). Hillsdale, NJ: Erlbaum.

Bickhard, M. H. (2000). Motivation and emotion: An interactive process model. In R. D. Ellis & N. Newton (Eds.), *The caldron of consciousness: Motivation, affect and self-organization—An anthology* (pp. 161–178). Amsterdam: John Benjamins.

Bickhard, M. H., & Christopher, J. C. (1994). The influence of early experience on personality development. *New Ideas in Psychology, 12,* 229–252.

Bourdieu, P. (1990). *The logic of practice.* Stanford, CA: Stanford University Press.

Brinton, C. (1987). *A history of Western morals.* New York: Paragon House.

Bronfenbrenner, U. (1977). Toward an experimental ecology of human development. *American Psychologist, 32,* 513–531.

Bruner, J. (1990). *Acts of meaning.* Cambridge, MA: Harvard University Press.

Campbell, R. L., & Bickhard, M. H. (1986). *Knowing levels and developmental stages.* Basel, Switzerland: Karger.

Campbell, R. L., & Christopher, J. C. (1996a). Beyond formalism and altruism: The prospects for moral personality. *Developmental Review, 16,* 108–123.

Campbell, R. L., & Christopher, J. C. (1996b). Moral development theory: A critique of its Kantian presuppositions. *Developmental Review, 16,* 1–47.

Campbell, R. L., Christopher, J. C., & Bickhard, M. H. (2002). Self and values: An interactivist perspective for moral development. *Theory & Psychology, 12,* 489–517.

Chapman, M. (1988). *Constructive evolution: Origins and development of Piaget's thoughts.* New York: Cambridge University Press.

Christopher, J. C. (1996). Counseling's inescapable moral visions. *Journal of Counseling & Development, 75,* 17–25.

Christopher, J. C. (2001). Culture and psychotherapy: Toward a hermeneutic approach. *Psychotherapy: Theory, Research, Practice, and Training, 38,* 687–711.

Christopher, J. C., & Bickhard, M. H. (1992). Remodeling the "as if" in Adler's concept of the life-style. *Individual Psychology: Journal of Adlerian Theory, Research & Practice, 48,* 76–85.

Christopher, J. C., Bickhard, M. H., & Lambeth, G. S. (2001). Otto Kernberg's object relations theory: A metaphysical critique. *Theory & Psychology, 11,* 687–711.

Cirillo, L., & Wapner, S. (1986). *Value presuppositions in theories of human development.* Hillsdale, NJ: Erlbaum.

Cole, M. (1996). *Cultural psychology: A once and future discipline.* Cambridge, MA: Harvard University Press.

Cushman, P. (1990). Why the self is empty: Toward a historically situated psychology. *American Psychologist, 45*, 599–611.

Cushman, P. (1991). Ideology obscured: Political uses of the self in Daniel Stern's infant. *American Psychologist, 46*, 206–219.

DeLoache, J. S., & Gottlieb, A. (Eds.). (2000). *A world of babies: Imagined childcare guides for seven societies.* New York: Cambridge University Press.

Dunn, J. (1988). *The beginnings of social understanding.* Cambridge, MA: Harvard University Press.

Eisenberg, N. (1996). Caught in a narrow Kantian perception of prosocial development: Reactions to Campbell and Christopher's critique of moral development theory. *Developmental Review, 16*, 48–68.

Eisenberg, N., Miller, P. A., Shell, R., McNalley, S., & Shea, C. (1991). Prosocial development in adolescence: A longitudinal study. *Developmental Psychology, 27*, 849–857.

Erikson, E. H. (1963). *Childhood and society.* New York: Norton.

Flavell, J. H., Green, F. L., & Flavell, E. R. (1986). Development of knowledge about the appearance–reality distinction. *Monographs of the Society for Research in Child Development, 51*, 1–68.

Friere, P. (1970). *Pedagogy of the oppressed.* New York: Continuum.

Geertz, C. (1973). *The interpretation of cultures.* New York: Basic Books.

Geertz, C. (1983). *Local knowledge: Further essays in interpretive anthropology.* New York: Basic Books.

Goodnow, J. J. (1990). The socialization of cognition. In J. W. Stigler, R. A. Shweder, & G. Herdt (Eds.), *Cultural psychology: Essays on comparative human development* (pp. 259–286). New York: Cambridge University Press.

Gopnik, A., & Astington, J. W. (1988). Children's understanding of representational change and its relation to the understanding of false belief and the appearance–reality distinction. *Child Development, 59*, 26–37.

Guignon, C. (1984). Moods in Heidegger's being and time. In C. Calhoun & R. C. Solomon (Eds.), *What is an emotion?* (pp. 230–243). New York: Oxford University Press.

Guignon, C. B. (1991). Pragmatisim or hermeneutics? Epistemology after foundationalism. In J. Bohman, D. Hiley, & R. Schusterman (Eds.), *The interpretive turn* (pp. 81–101). Ithaca, NY: Cornell University Press.

Harkness, S., Raeff, C., & Super, C. M. (Eds.). (2000). *Variability in the social construction of the child.* San Francisco: Jossey-Bass.

Heelas, P., & Lock, A. (1981). *Indigenous psychologies: The anthropology of the self.* New York: Academic Press.

Heidegger, M. (1962). *Being and time* (J. Macquarrie & E. Robinson, Trans.). New York: Harper & Row.

Hiley, D. R., Bohman, J. F., & Shusterman, R. (Eds.). (1991). *The interpretive turn: Philosophy, science, culture.* Ithaca, NY: Cornell University Press.

Jahoda, G. (1986). A cross-cultural perspective on developmental psychology. *International Journal of Behavioral Development*, 9, 417–437.

Jahoda, G. (2000, July). *The shifting sands of culture.* Paper presented at the XIV International Congress of the International Association for Cross-Cultural Psychology, Pultusk, Poland.

Kaplan, B. (1986). Value presuppositions in theories of human development. In L. Cirillo & S. Wapner (Eds.), *Value presuppositions in theories of human development* (pp. 89–103). Hillsdale, NJ: Erlbaum.

Kashima, Y. (2000). Conceptions of culture and person for psychology. *Journal of Cross-Cultural Psychology, 31,* 14–32.

Kegan, R. (1982). *The evolving self: Problem and process in human development.* Cambridge, MA: Harvard University Press.

Kim, U., & Choi, S.-H. (1994). Individualism, collectivism, and child development: A Korean perspective. In P. M. Greenfield & R. R. Cocking (Eds.), *Cross-cultural roots of minority child development* (pp. 227–257). Hillsdale, NJ: Erlbaum.

Kirschner, S. R. (1996). *The religious and romantic origins of psychoanalysis.* New York: Cambridge University Press.

Kohlberg, L. (1984). *The psychology of moral development: The nature and validity of moral stages.* San Francisco: HarperCollins.

Lasch, C. (1979). *The culture of narcissism: American life in an age of diminishing expectations.* New York: Warner Books.

MacIntyre, A. C. (1981). *After virtue: A study in moral theory.* Notre Dame, IN: University of Notre Dame Press.

Markus, H. R., & Kitayama, S. (1991). Culture and the self: Implications for cognition, emotion, and motivation. *Psychological Review*, 98, 224–253.

Miller, P. J., & Goodnow, J. J. (1995). Cultural practices: Toward an integration of culture and development. In J. J. Goodnow, P. J. Miller, & F. Kessel (Eds.), *Cultural practices as contexts for development* (pp. 5–16). San Francisco: Jossey-Bass.

Morson, G. S., & Emerson, C. (1990). *Mikhail Bakhtin: Creation of a prosaics.* Stanford, CA: Stanford University Press.

Nelson, K. (1992). Emergence of autobiographical memory at age 4. *Human Development, 35,* 172–177.

Nelson, K. (1994). Long-term retention of memory for preverbal experience: Evidence and implications. *Memory, 2,* 467–475.

Perner, J. (1991). *Understanding the representational mind.* Cambridge, MA: MIT Press.

Perner, J. (1992). Grasping the concept of representation: Its impact on 4-year-olds' theory of mind and beyond. *Human Development, 35,* 146–155.

Piaget, J. (1962). *Play, dreams and imitation in childhood* (C. M. Gattegno & F. M. Hodgson, Trans.). New York: Norton. (Original work published 1945)

Piaget, J. (2000). *Studies in reflecting abstraction* (R. L. Campbell, Trans.). Hove, England: Psychology Press.

Piaget, J., & Inhelder, B. (1969). *The psychology of the child* (H. Weaver, Trans.). New York: Basic Books. (Original work published 1966)

Piaget, J., & Inhelder, B. (1971). *Mental imagery in the child: A study in the development of imaginal representation* (P. A. Chilton, Trans.). New York: Basic Books. (Original work published 1966)

Poortinga, Y. H. (1997). Towards convergence. In J. W. Berry, Y. H. Poortinga, & J. Pandey (Eds.), *Handbook of cross-cultural psychology: Vol. 1. Theory and method* (2nd ed., pp. 347–387). Needham Heights, MA: Allyn & Bacon.

Putnam, R. D. (2000). *Bowling alone: The collapse and revival of American community.* New York: Touchstone Books/Simon & Schuster.

Rabinow, P., & Sullivan, W. M. (1979). *Interpretive social science.* Berkeley: University of California Press.

Rabinow, P., & Sullivan, W. M. (1987). *Interpretive social science: A second look.* Berkeley: University of California Press.

Richardson, F. C., & Christopher, J. C. (1993). Social theory as practice: Metatheoretical options for social inquiry. *Theoretical & Philosophical Psychology, 13,* 137–153.

Richardson, F. C., Fowers, B. J., & Guignon, C. B. (1999). *Re-envisioning psychology: Moral dimensions of theory and practice.* San Francisco: Jossey-Bass.

Richardson, F. C., Rogers, A., & McCarroll, J. (1998). Toward a dialogical self. *American Behavioral Scientist, 41,* 496–515.

Riegel, K. F. (1972). Influence of economic and political ideologies on the development of developmental psychology. *Psychological Bulletin, 78,* 129–141.

Rosenberger, N. R. (1992). *Japanese sense of self.* New York: Cambridge University Press.

Sampson, E. E. (1977). Psychology and the American ideal. *Journal of Personality & Social Psychology, 35,* 767–782.

Schatzki, T. R., Knorr-Cetina, K., & von Savigny, E. (2001). *The practice turn in contemporary theory.* New York: Routledge.

Schumaker, J. F. (2001). *The age of insanity: Modernity and mental health.* Westport, CT: Praeger Publishers.

Shweder, R. A. (1990). Cultural psychology: What is it? In J. W. Stigeler, R. A. Shweder & G. Herdt (Eds.), *Cultural psychology: Essays on comparative human development* (pp. 1–43). New York: Cambridge University Press.

Shweder, R. A. (Ed.). (1998). *Welcome to middle age! (And other cultural fictions).* Chicago: University of Chicago Press.

Shweder, R. A., Mahapatra, M., & Miller, J. G. (1987). Culture and moral development. In J. Kagan & S. Lamb (Eds.), *The emergence of morality in young children* (pp. 1–83). Chicago: University of Chicago Press.

Taylor, C. (1985). *Philosophical papers: Vol. 2. Philosophy and the human sciences.* New York: Cambridge University Press.

Taylor, C. (1988). The moral topography of the self. In S. B. Messer, L. A. Sass, & R. L. Woolfolk (Eds.), *Hermeneutics and psychological theory: Interpretive perspec-*

tives on personality, psychotherapy, and psychopathology (pp. 298–320). New Brunswick, NJ: Rutgers University Press.

Taylor, C. (1989). *Sources of the self: The making of the modern identity.* Cambridge, MA: Harvard University Press.

Taylor, C. (1993). Engaged agency and background in Heidegger. In C. Guignon (Ed.), *The Cambridge companion to Heidegger* (pp. 317–336). New York: Cambridge University Press.

Taylor, C. (1995). *Philosophical arguments.* Cambridge, MA: Harvard University Press.

Tobin, J. J., Wu, D. Y. H., & Davidson, D. H. (1989). *Preschool in three cultures: Japan, China, and the United States.* New Haven, CT: Yale University Press.

Tulving, E. (1985). How many memory systems are there? *American Psychologist, 40,* 385–398.

Turiel, E., Killen, M., & Helwig, C. C. (1987). Morality: Its structure, functions, and vagaries. In J. Kagan & S. Lamb (Eds.), *The emergence of morality in young children* (pp. 155–243). Chicago: University of Chicago Press.

Valsiner, J., & Lawrence, J. A. (1997). Human development in culture across the life span. In J. W. Berry, P. R. Dasen, & T. S. Saraswathi (Eds.), *Basic processes and human development* (2nd ed., Vol. 2, pp. 69–106). Needham Heights, MA: Allyn & Bacon.

Vygotsky, L. S. (1978). *Mind in society: The development of higher psychological processes.* Cambridge, MA: Harvard University Press.

Wertsch, J. V. (1991). *Voices of the mind: A sociocultural approach to mediated action.* Cambridge, MA: Harvard University Press.

Wertsch, J. V., & Stone, C. A. (1985). The concept of internalization in Vygotsky's account of the genesis of higher mental functions. In J. V. Wertsch (Ed.), *Culture, communication, and cognition: Vygotskian perspectives* (pp. 162–182). New York: Cambridge University Press.

VI

METHODOLOGY IN PSYCHOLOGY

11

THE LANGUAGE AND METHODS OF SCIENCE: COMMON ASSUMPTIONS AND UNCOMMON CONCLUSIONS

RICHARD N. WILLIAMS

It is not uncommon in the common disciplinary and pedagogical discourse of psychology to refer to *science* as if the word had a single referent, clearly understood by all who use it. Notwithstanding the work of many notable intellects over several centuries (e.g., Plato) and renewed efforts within the last century among proponents of a unified science (e.g., the logical positivists), it remains unclear whether the word *science* has, or ought to have, a single referent or, indeed, just what any proper set of referents might be (see, e.g., Bohman, 1993). Nevertheless, the lack of closure on this issue has not prevented a common discourse about science from emerging and informing ideas about psychology and its knowledge claims. This common discourse and the assumptions on which it depends constitute the major topic of this chapter. A common defense of thinking about science in this way is that it is pragmatically useful to do so, allowing the work of the discipline to continue while lending prestige to psychology's truth claims, and unifying psychologists' discourse and approach. The counterassumption on which the present argument is based is that, because of the problematic nature of the fundamental assumptions underlying our common discourse about science, the perved advantages of psychology's being a science are largely illegitimate. In w of this, it would seem prudent to suspend most discourse that simply ....erts that psychology is or ought to be a science, pending a more adequate understanding of science and the nature of our confidence in it.

ASSUMPTIONS UNDERLYING SCIENTIFIC METHODS AND PSYCHOLOGY'S FAITH IN THEM

In our understanding of science, as in most other contemporary intellectual issues, we are indebted to the ancient Greeks. Science, as well as philosophy, was born in the confidence of the earliest pre-Socratics that a rational and serviceable account of the universe could be rendered relying on reason itself, without recourse to myth or tradition (Stumpf, 1977; Wheelwright, 1960). From these attempts grew our Western preoccupation with metaphysics and epistemology. Metaphysics points toward the discovery and explication of the most fundamental realities of the universe, those from which all others derive. Epistemology illuminates the necessity of defending the legitimacy of any and all truth claims regarding that reality. We can situate 21st-century psychology comfortably in these two 3rd-century B.C.E. projects. Contemporary psychology seeks to find and articulate the fundamental causes or sources of human behavior, and to do so using methods that lend legitimacy to the truth claims made by the theories and models that are built on these sources and causes. For example, behaviorism claims that virtually all human behavior arises out of a fundamental substrate of stimuli, responses, and contingencies (reinforcements). It relies on empirical demonstrations to justify its claims that this is indeed the case. Other psychological theories make parallel claims about the origins of behavior. Today, most rely on methods of empirical science borrowed from the natural sciences to justify the truth claims their theories and models make based on those origins.

Some would argue that this process is precisely what science is, and what it is for. The adoption of scientific methods and criteria sets modern psychology apart from the merely speculative philosophical meanderings of ancient Greece, and every other era prior to the beginnings of contemporary social science. What this perspective fails to acknowledge, however, is that modern scientific psychology (and modern science itself) is far from being an alternative to philosophy. Rather, it is a product of the larger and older philosophical traditions that it now rejects as being rather hopelessly speculative (see Slife & Williams, 1995, for a discussion of the theory-laden nature of science). The philosophical pedigree of modern science is impeccable. As much as contemporary psychology may wish to contrast itself with philosophy and other speculative disciplines (such as religion), the roots of psychology go deep into the soil of philosophy, and its theories and methods are reflections of the metaphysical and epistemological projects it inherited from its intellectual history. This is important because it teaches us that the methods of modern psychology are not prima facie valid; they are not guaranteed to be appropriate to questions of human behavior. Any belief that they are appropriate or valid is nothing more than a philosophical commitment (see Slife & Williams, 1995).

The philosophical origins of science are clearly seen in Aristotle's development of the principles of formal logic as a method for natural science. These principles continue to be the foundation for modern conceptions of logic at least as these are applied in psychology. This logic-based scientific method was well suited to the classificatory function of Aristotelian science for which it was chiefly developed. It is important to point out that the major purpose of the rational methods of this early science was to distinguish real scientific knowledge from speculation and other erroneous conclusions. Modern scientific methods have never evolved beyond this essential purpose nor beyond the essential rationality at their core. The chief purpose of scientific psychology today is the legitimation of some knowledge claims over others based, ultimately, on an appeal to rationality itself (see Slife & Williams, 1995).

Since the time of Aristotle, of course, formal logic has been refined in many ways, including the development of the propositional logic familiar to students and professionals in most disciplines. It is common, in recounting the history of philosophy, to point to a rather dramatic shift in emphasis that marked and largely defined the modern period. René Descartes (1596–1650) is often given credit for its earliest formal conceptual expression. The shift was away from metaphysical speculation about the realities of the universe to a concentration on the epistemological question—the question of certainty and the defensibility of truth claims (Descartes, 1641/1986). It is not coincidental that Descartes and others based their hopes of achieving trustworthy knowledge on the certainty obvious in mathematics. Epistemology began to parallel analytical geometry. Mathematics, it should be noted, was regarded as the best example of the purely rational reasoning originally incorporated in the formal logic of Aristotle. The idea that philosophical logic should reflect the same essential structure as mathematics, and the related idea that mathematics offers the best example of epistemological thinking, are common themes throughout the history of ideas. The fundamental principles of later scientific thought and method can be found in the work of Descartes and others who followed in the early modern period. For purposes of this chapter, I emphasize three prominent themes of this early modern epistemological work that underlie the project of scientific thinking in modern psychology.

Experimental Control, the Null Hypothesis, and the Skepticism of Radical Doubt

Descartes took the skepticism of previous centuries and turned it into an epistemological tool. The path to certainty began with radical doubt. One should trust only those things that could be defended, and any proper defense must show that it is unreasonable to doubt them. This skepticism is reflected today in our desire for methods that are rationally convincing. In contemporary empirical work in psychology, the convincing power that overcomes doubt is empirical demonstration under controlled conditions. The controlled conditions are simply those that one (or the body of scientific peers) finds rationally compelling. The importance of doubt is also seen today in the institutionalized determination to maintain an epistemological commitment to the null hypothesis—informally understood as the assumption that there is no significant effect in the experimental data—until presented with (at least temporarily) compelling evidence otherwise. Systematic doubt is the watchword of our experimental design as well as our statistical analyses.

Control and Manipulation of Variables, and the Criterion of Rational Certainty

As stated above, the goal of Cartesian analysis is, essentially, to arrive at ideas that are impossible to reasonably doubt. These ideas constitute reliable knowledge. Certainty was defined in terms of that which satisfied our rational capacity for analysis. Descartes' classical dictum, *Cogito ergo sum* (usually rendered, "I think, therefore, I am") is as much a rationally compelling necessity as it is an experiential one. It might well be rendered, "Because I can find no rational way to doubt the fact that I am thinking, I am left to conclude that I exist, since someone must be doing the thinking." In similar fashion, contemporary scientific methods incorporate in their design conditions of observation carefully and rationally selected to overcome doubt. Variables are selected, measured, and controlled in ways that rational analysis suggests should be important. Empirical observations attained under circumstance thus rationally prescribed take on an air of certainty because rational objections have been anticipated, addressed, and preempted in the design of the conditions under which the observations are made. Thus, empirical results appear more certain than other forms of knowledge for the very reasons we have always found rational arguments to be persuasive. But, note that the basis of the apparent certainty is nothing more nor less than human reason. Scientific methods are not alternatives to rational methods but examples of them (see Newton-Smith's 1981, analysis of the relationship of rationality to science).

Objectivity and the Search for a Privileged Perspective

If nothing else, Descartes' method of radical doubt afforded him, as he supposed, a privileged perspective from which to "observe" and, thus, from which to make valid knowledge claims. What he could reasonably hold to be true from the perspective of radical doubt of everything else was taken to be true, because such knowledge could be considered "pure" in the sense that it was not compromised by other ideas that were not themselves so pure and certain (Descartes, 1641/1986). Everything Descartes had assumed he knew before he achieved the perspective uninfluenced by possibly misleading factors was not trustworthy. Only what was known from the privileged perspective was certain, and other knowledge should be built from that essential substrate. In contemporary, perhaps folklorical, understandings of traditional scientific method, great stock is placed in objectivity as the essential element that assures that scientific knowledge is truly scientific (i.e., certain) because all potentially contaminating (noncertain) influences have been eliminated. Objectivity is thus the modern equivalent of the privileged perspective that has been the ideal of modern rationalism. (See, for example, Singleton, Straits, & Straits, 1993, pp. 31–32, for a more refined view of objectivity that nonetheless addresses this issue.)

The foregoing analysis is intended to illustrate the continuity between philosophy and science. It is not uncommon for psychologists to suggest that the emergence of psychology from the shadow of philosophy was its defining moment, and that it was "science" that allowed it to establish itself as an independent discipline able to make knowledge claims that surpass in some way those offered by philosophy (e.g., Brennan, 2003). The alternative position is that science is nothing more than a stylized manifestation of the traditional Western philosophical project rendered evermore impressive as recent, seemingly miraculous technological advances have enhanced tremendously our ability to focus our senses and to observe. Notwithstanding such awesome expansion of our sensory functions, the methods of contemporary science do not offer an alternative to "mere" rationalism but merely offer a technological instantiation of it. Regardless of the level of technological advance, empirical scientific studies are still persuasive because they incorporate, in their designs, the criteria called for by rational analysis.[1]

PSYCHOLOGY'S ASSUMPTION THAT METHOD UNCOVERS TRUTH

In the introduction of his *Meditations* (Descartes, 1641/1986), René Descartes was explicit that his epistemological approach held out the prom-

---

[1]The foregoing analysis applies most clearly to distinctly *empirical science*, or that science that takes empirical observation to be the foundation of method and of scientific knowledge. Other conceptions of science, such as that represented by theoretical physics, or that made possible by technologies, such as advances in microscopy that allow visual study of molecules, do not rely on observation and validation in the same way that most scientific psychology does. Theoretical physics, as indicated by its use of mathematical language, and the new approaches to science based on greatly enhanced observation, are distinct from the positivistic, hypothesis-testing empirical science characteristic of contemporary scientific psychology.

ise of putting knowledge on a firm (indubitable) ground. He also suggested that the method might be profitably adopted and applied by anyone given adequate native intelligence and sufficient training. Undoubtedly, this confidence in his method derived from an idea, an assumption that methods afford a privileged perspective that, once achieved, precludes influence by factors that would obscure or distort the facts. This same spirit pervades contemporary psychology's confidence in traditional empirical scientific methods. For this reason, scientific testability has emerged as one of the important dimensions on which theories of all types are judged. If a theory cannot be tested by the methods of empirical science, it is generally deemed to be of little value, because it is verification by method that lends credence to theories and moves them along the path to the status of truth claims. Psychology has found great appeal in the assumption that methods might guarantee to any practitioner real knowledge, given that minimal conditions of training and expertise are met and regardless of the presence of other factors such as the cultural, moral, and philosophical commitments of the practitioner himself or herself. It is assumed that methods as methods are immune from the influence of these things, or that they have built-in guarantees against such influences when properly applied.[2] In addition to reinforcing psychology's commitment to science in general, this assumption—that properly scientific methods properly applied *ipso facto* lead to truth or at least justifiable knowledge claims—has the additional effect of consolidating commitment to empirical natural scientific methods above all others. The resulting hegemony of empirical scientific method is well documented by even a cursory review of the literature of the discipline.

Because psychology's pronounced preference for empirical methods is fundamentally a philosophical position, based on rational arguments about what is and what is not justification for a truth claim, it is, or ought to be, open to examination and to comparisons with other positions regarding the nature and role of method in science. One important alternative has been derived from the work of the hermeneutic philosopher, Hans-Georg Gadamer (1982). To understand the position, it is important to remind ourselves that what we refer to as *scientific method* was derived from philosophical assumptions and from epistemological positions based on reason, and about reason itself. Scientific method is a human construction designed according to what its designers deemed important and convincing. Gadamer pointed out that it cannot be the case that methods lead inexorably to truth (even when applied correctly). Rather, reflection on the issue will reveal that methods them-

---

[2]It should be noted that many recent and contemporary works in the philosophy of science have taken issue with this assumption about the irrelevance of such social and cultural factors. Certainly, the work of Thomas Kuhn, first presented in his now classic essay on the structure of scientific revolutions (Kuhn, 1970), can rightly be read in this spirit. The reader is also referred to the work of Paul Feyerabend (1975) and to Donald Polkinghorne (1983) and Richard Bernstein (1983) for good summaries of this issue.

selves reflect prior assumptions and intellectual commitments about the nature of truth—and about the world those methods are designed to investigate. In other words, methods are developed by thoughtful people in such a way that they can be confident that the methods will be sensitive to the world and to truth as they—the developers—already understand it to be. Thus, methods do not necessarily produce truth; rather, preunderstandings of truth produce methods, and methods reflect back various aspects of those preunderstandings.

This principle can be seen in the design of measuring instruments. A barometer, for example, is designed as it is because of the way its designers conceptualized air pressure. The barometer is thus sensitive only to what it was designed to be sensitive to. It can thus only give back to its designers numerical indices reflecting something very close to what they originally understood. This is also true of methods. Any method, including the methods of science, can only reflect back to us something about truth as we already believed it to be. For this reason, it might be said, empirical science is best designed to answer "whether" questions. It might tell us *whether* some state of affairs is more consistent with one than another preconceived notion, but it is not designed to answer "what" questions regarding *what* really is the state of reality and *what* is not.

This issue seems to be less important for some of the natural sciences in which extremely impressive technology has successfully convinced us of the utility, if not the truth, of very many of our assumptions about the natural world. However, in the social sciences, the record of accomplishment, technological, intellectual, or moral, seems not to rise to that same level (e.g., the relative power to impress of Martian probes and microchips vs. the Minnesota Multiphasic Personality Inventory and token economies), leaving us justifiably wondering about the efficacy of our adopted methods in achieving understanding about the real sources of human behavior, and about the "knowledge" the methods reflect back to us from our own prior understandings. In light of this, we might profitably consider whether our current assumptions about the human world are the best ones. If they are not, then the methods we use because of our commitment to those assumptions will be unable to offer any corrective and will certainly fall short of verifying truth claims. We also might profitably consider whether alternative methods, reflecting alternative assumptions about our subject matter (human behavior), might not be more successful at revealing to us our own human nature.

ASSUMPTIONS ABOUT VERIFICATION, FALSIFICATION, AND CAUSATION

In order to understand more clearly just how it is that the methods of empirical science cannot justify the faith placed in them by contemporary psychology, we will examine the assumptions about such methods that lie at the heart of that faith. The essential issue is whether the methods of empirical science really have the power to verify and falsify theories or hypotheses and to support causal inferences in psychological explanations.

Verification in Psychology

Fundamental to the notion of science *as* science, and fundamental to the attraction social sciences feel toward science itself, is the assumption that the methods of science offer a privileged knowledge because they can provide validation of what would otherwise be mere theories or hypotheses. Such a promise is certainly at the heart of the logical positivism that was essential to the establishment of psychology as a science in the first place (see Koch, 1959, 1992). All claims of this sort can be included under the general term *verificationism*, which simply defined is the position that science can verify the truth value of its theories and hypotheses. Traditional scientific methods are designed to do just this. Confidence in verification operates on at least two levels. Most people will grant that an empirical demonstration, an observable event, is more convincing than a mere verbal statement, description, or prediction of an event. In this sense, confidence in scientific demonstration relative to speculation is well placed, and while not wholly unproblematic, is at least reasonable.

At a higher and more complex level, verificationist claims are much more problematic. To see the problematic nature of the claims, we need to be reminded that the persuasive power of science is logical argument. Empirical scientific studies instantiate to the greatest degree practicable the conditions of observation that might persuade us in favor or against the thesis that the empirical study is designed to verify. An example of this logical argument would be,

If Theory A is true then Observation A' will follow.

This provides a test of Theory A based on an observation. It is assumed because of the way the experiment is designed that the occurrence of Observation A' is due to Theory A and not to some number of other factors, due to the ability of the experimental design to eliminate or otherwise account for such alternative influences.

If the experiment is successfully carried out, then,

Observation A' occurs.
The conclusion then must be that:
Theory A' is true.

However, a closer examination of this logic reveals a logical fallacy known as *affirming the consequent*, or an argument of the form *modus ponens*.

It does not follow that the antecedent "Theory A" is true just because Observation A' occurred. There are potentially very many other factors that might have resulted in Observation A'. Without potentially infinite control over all such factors, no valid conclusion can be reached on the basis that Observation A' occurred (except, perhaps, that Observation A' occurred).

One might argue at this point that a reasonable person might conclude that Theory A is true on the basis of Observation A' even if the proof is not absolute. Indeed, a reasonable person might conclude that Theory A is true without Observation A', based on rational argument alone. Thus, science is placed on the same ground as reason, and we are left with the informal or "commonsense" belief in the power of observed events to bolster one's faith. However, we are a long ways from formal verification of the truth of a theory. This problem was introduced into the literature of psychology as early as 1937 in a brief article by Donald K. Adams. Although the logic is compelling, the argument has not significantly curtailed empirical scientific endeavors in the discipline. Its tempering influence survives in the common disclaimer that an experiment does not really prove a hypothesis true because there are, in theory, an infinite number of explanations for any given observation. The more important result of this line of reasoning is that, when viewed carefully, and in terms of their logical structure, the methods of empirical science cannot verify the truth of theories or explanations of states of affairs. This may call the thoughtful scientist to rethink his or her understanding of the nature and task of empirical science, as well as the status of empirically derived knowledge.

Falsification in Psychology

Many scholars within psychology and other social scientific disciplines will readily grant the ultimate impossibility of verification. In response, many have embraced an alternative view of the nature and role of scientific experimentation. This view is known as *falsification*. Contemporary falsificationist views are generally directly or indirectly traceable to, or at least compatible with, the best known work on falsification, that of the British philosopher Sir Karl Popper (1959). Popper's essential claim in this regard is that any theory, to be scientific, must be capable of falsification. In the area of empirical science, this means that there must be some state of affairs that would constitute convincing evidence that a theory or hypothesis is false. When this thesis is embodied in an empirical study, the logic would be,

> If Theory A is true then Observation A' will occur.
> Observation A' did not occur.
> Therefore, Theory A is not true.

While this is an oversimplification of experimentation and the larger project of falsification, the simple logical pattern holds. It is, in fact, this logical form that makes falsification compelling and seemingly justifies the view of science as essentially a process of falsification. For many in the social sciences, the hope seems to be that once all false theories or hypotheses are falsified, what remains can be taken as true. This hope falters on two accounts. First, the prospect of falsifying all explanations but one will be, in principle, impossible for the reason explained above—that there are potentially an infinite number of explanations for a given event. Second, and more importantly, the falsification of even a single theory or hypothesis will ultimately fail for logical reasons.

The first logical problem is that the logical argument entailed in a falsification strategy is often fallacious. The fallacy is often called *denying the consequent*, or *modus tollens*. The difficulty can be seen in a brief counter-argument:

> If Smith is a friendly person, then he greets everyone with a smile.
> Smith did not greet me with a smile.
> Therefore, Smith is not a friendly person.

The logic fails because there may be a number of other factors at work to prevent Smith's greeting me with a smile, such as his not noticing me, his struggling with a sudden personal tragedy, my menacing attitude toward Smith, and so forth. Similar limitations attach to the project of the falsification of any theory or explanation of an event (such as the outcome of an experiment). An empirical observation can falsify a theory or explanation only if it is a crucial test. An observation is a crucial test only if all other potential explanations or influential factors have been ruled out, either by the design of the given study or by some number of other previous studies. Reason suggests, however, that this condition can never be met because it would require that any given study have built into it potentially infinite control of all possible influential factors or alternative explanations. In principle, this will never be the case, and if it fails for every single study, it certainly fails for the composite body of studies. This argument is often traced to the work of the 19th- and early 20th-century French philosopher, Pierre-Maurice-Marie Duhem (1906/1954). It is most often referred to today as the Duhem-Quine thesis (Quine, 1953).

Causation in Psychology

In light of this analysis, we are led to conclude that the methods of empirical science cannot ultimately falsify theories or hypotheses. We are again left with the commonsense appeal of science as demonstration. It should be noted, however, that if verification and falsification fail, then empirical science cannot make a convincing case regarding causality. This is the case because the isolation of a cause in a given empirical study is exactly the same problem as the falsification of a hypothesis. The isolation of a cause requires the complete control of other competing causal influences. As we have seen this is an impossible proposition. These issues underscore one of the fundamental historical problems of epistemology. It is that empiricism fails as a basis for noncontingent knowledge, that is, knowledge that can provide a foundation for cross-situational or apodictic truth (see Williams, 2000).

None of the foregoing should lead one to jump to the simplistic conclusion that science is of no value or that it will necessarily fail to provide anything of value. The impressive technology of the past century provides ample evidence of the value of traditional science—at least as it has been applied to the natural world. This success suggests that Sir Francis Bacon (1561–1626) may well have been on to something important when he suggested in the *Novum Organum* (Bacon, 1620, in Andrea & Overfield, 1990) that the purpose of methodical science is to prod nature to take off her mask. This description of science is congenial to what was suggested above, that science provides often impressive demonstrations of what can be done. The foregoing arguments simply demonstrate that other powers often ascribed to science are more problematic—specifically, the verification or falsification of theories and hypotheses, and the establishing of causation. The principle question for psychology, then, is whether the methods of empirical science have been properly applied within the discipline, and whether they are configured in such a way as to achieve the same success when applied to uniquely human problems as they have achieved in the world of strictly natural objects. Any argument that they are is necessarily a rational argument stemming from philosophical assumptions and cannot be addressed or settled by empirical science itself. Thus, alternative assumptions about science and scientific psychology ought not be dismissed casually.

THE PRIMACY OF NUMBERS AS THE BEST
LANGUAGE FOR PSYCHOLOGY

The enthusiasm of psychology for empirical methods is always fueled by an assumption that the proper language of science, and therefore, perhaps, of knowledge itself, is numbers. This notion is at least as old as the Western intellectual tradition, as evidenced in the work of Pythagoras. Mathematics has served as the prime example of a logical system capable of providing certainty. In the work of Descartes, for example, the certainty and clarity of mathematics was contrasted with the uncertainty of metaphysical speculation. Contemporary proponents of an empirical scientific psychology have generally assumed that one of the principle advantages of such was that the results of empirical studies could be expressed and analyzed in the language of numbers, which is more precise and less ambiguous than other symbolic languages and, therefore, able to reveal truths about human behavior that we might otherwise miss or distort.

On one level, it is extremely difficult to argue with this assumption. This is certainly so because numbers seemingly constitute a language of expression so closely constrained by logic that there is, in fact, little ambiguity.[3] Numbers as abstractions have discrete and unambiguous definitions. The relations between and among numbers is likewise straightforward. Of all rational expressions, mathematical expressions appear to be the clearest (e.g., $2 + 2 = 4$). These very properties of numbers form the foundation of our faith in the results of statistical analysis, because statistical analysis simply operates straightforwardly on numerical data, extracting the purely numerical information the numbers hold. It should be pointed out that one of the essential properties of abstract numbers is that they can rightly be understood as the purest form of units of measure. This notion is best illustrated by the counting numbers.

While these properties may hold true of abstract numbers, it is much less clear that they hold for numbers that result from the operationalizations typical in psychological science. The least problematic use of numbers in psychological studies can be seen in cases in which the measured variables are genuinely empirical variables. By this I mean that they can be unambiguously counted in units of measure that not only make intuitive sense but also do not deviate far from the measured phenomena themselves. For example, if the variable of interest in a psychological study is "neuron firings," it seems rather straightforward to simply count them. If the variable of interest is milligrams of a chemical in the bloodstream, a relatively straightforward measure can be derived from counting milligrams. The numbers resulting from such measurements are able to maintain a substantial amount of their abstract properties because the units of measure they represent are intuitively valid and discrete.

This situation rapidly changes, however, when one attempts to measure psychologically interesting variables without clear-cut units of measure. In these cases, the units of measure must be concocted or assumed, and thus, they will be some conceptual distance removed from the phenomena themselves. Examples of these more problematic variables include attitudes, personality traits, emotions, and preferences. Because there are not intuitively obvious discrete units of measure, and because the concocted units are ultimately justified conceptually and are, thus, somewhat removed from the phenomena themselves, numbers assigned by this sort of measuring device lack the precision and the univocal meaning of abstract numbers. They thus also lack the mathematical properties of abstract numbers. This is the case because all attempts to measure human phenomena such as those mentioned here require that investigators make assumptions and decisions about what to "look at," what not to look at, how the phenomena will be understood,

---

[3]This analysis will ignore recent theoretical work that may challenge this assumption about numbers. See, for example, Hersh (1997), Lakoff and Nunez (2000), and Tymoczko (1998).

and how the measurements will be interpreted. They must also make assumptions about how phenomena map onto numerical scales reflecting units of measure. When the measurements are obtained from human subjects through self-report, as in the case of attitude or personality scales, the respondents themselves face interpretive problems in reading the scale and mapping their own cognitions, emotions, or interpretations on the scales provided. Through this process, the numbers will lose their original, abstract, and unambiguous character and take on all the ambiguities resident in the human language through which measurement scales are constructed and applied to meaningful human phenomena.

If this analysis has merit, one is led to the conclusion that, in most applications in areas of psychology devoted to the study of distinctly human phenomena, the language of numbers, when used in such studies, is no more precise than the original language in which human phenomena are experienced and conceptualized in the first place. Statistical analyses that operate on the numbers under assumptions that they contain unambiguous information, of the sort inherent to abstract numbers, will thus be incapable of capturing and accurately conveying much of the real information available in the human phenomena under study. Given this analysis, we can begin to see the rationale underlying the use of qualitative methods of investigation, and why an increasing number of investigators find them attractive alternatives to traditional quantitative methods. Qualitative methods rest on different assumptions about the representation of human phenomena in symbolic languages. (See, for example, the chapters in Denzin & Lincoln, 2000; Polkinghorne, 1983; Taylor & Bogdan, 1998, for good introductions to the theory and practice of qualitative research methods.)

A final observation on the matter of measurement in psychology is in order. It seems axiomatic, if not tautological, that quantitative empirical research requires the quantification of the variables of interest in a study. This process is referred to as *operationalization*. The process of measurement operationalizes a variable by turning it into an observable aspect of the experimenter's experience. On one level, this process can be seen as the embodiment of the agenda of the logical positivists—that every concept must be expressed in empirically verifiable terms if it is to have meaning. On another level, however, the commitment of the contemporary discipline to operationalization seems not to be much informed or driven by consciously made metaphysical and epistemological commitments. Rather, it seems to be a necessary result of a commitment to empirical methods themselves. Thus, in the face of evidence that very many of the most important and meaningful human phenomena, which are of innate interest to psychology, cannot be accurately or adequately captured in measurement or other operationalizations, the defense of the process seems to be simply to invoke the demands of the method itself as justification for carrying on the operationalizing process anyway. This seems to be clearly a case of method dictating what can be and what will be done. In so doing, method drives theory, rather than vice versa. This is an unusual state of affairs for a science (see Koch, 1959, 1999).

UNCOMMON CONCLUSIONS

Having devoted the major part of this chapter to the first part of its title—common assumptions, I end with only a brief mention of the second part—uncommon conclusions. The purpose of the chapter was to lay before the reader one set of common assumptions that underlie psychology's adoption of and devotion to traditional, empirical, scientific methods. I have also tried to articulate, and draw attention to, the assumptions that underlie the application of these methods to the study of psychologically interesting phenomena. The intent was to assist the reader in two intellectual projects. The first is to understand that traditional scientific methods are products of human reason and are based on rationally derived assumptions about the nature of the world and our ability to understand it. These methods, that is to say, science itself, is not monolithic, nor is it unproblematic. It may be very good at helping us deal effectively with some aspects of the world, but it does not guarantee knowledge that is not grounded in our own preunderstandings and theoretical commitments.

The second project is, perhaps, more difficult, and certainly more unfinished. It is to invite the reader to transcend the common assumptions and participate in the formulation of alternative approaches, methods, and understandings. These alternatives have the potential to found a psychology that may be, in many ways, more rewarding, more revealing, and more relevant to the human condition. The pursuit of just these alternatives is the essence of science itself. The following chapter offers some alternatives to the prevailing assumptions discussed and challenged here.

REFERENCES

Adams, D. K. (1937). Note on method. *Psychological Review, 44*, 65–71.

Andrea, A., & Overfield, J. (1990). *The human record: Sources of global history.* Boston: Houghton Mifflin.

Bernstein, R. J. (1983). *Beyond objectivism and relativism: Science, hermeneutics, and praxis.* Philadelphia: University of Pennsylvania Press.

Bohman, J. (1993). *New philosophy of social science.* Cambridge, MA: MIT Press.

Brennan, J. F. (2003). *History and systems of psychology* (6th ed.). Upper Saddle River, NJ: Prentice Hall.

Denzin, N. K., & Lincoln, Y. S. (Eds.). (2000). *The handbook of qualitative research* (2nd ed.). Thousand Oaks, CA: Sage.

Descartes, R. (1986). *Meditations on first philosophy with selections from the objections and replies* (J. Cottingham, Trans.). New York: Cambridge University Press. (Original work published 1641)

Duhem, P. M. M. (1954). *Aim and structure of a physical theory* (P. Wiener, Trans.). Princeton, NJ: Princeton University Press. (Original work published 1906)

Feyerabend, P. (1975). *Against method.* London: Verso Books.

Gadamer, H.-G. (1982). *Truth and method.* New York: Crossroad.

Hersh, R. (1997). *What is mathematics, really?* New York: Oxford University Press.

Koch, S. (1959). Epilogue. In S. Koch (Ed.), *Psychology: A study of a science. Study I: Conceptual and systematic* (Vols. 1–3, pp. 729–788). New York: McGraw-Hill.

Koch, S. (1992). The nature and limits of psychological knowledge: Lessons of a century qua science. In S. Koch & D. E. Leary (Eds.), *A century of psychology as science* (pp. 75–97). Washington, DC: American Psychological Association.

Koch, S. (1999). Psychology's Bridgman versus Bridgman's Bridgman: A study in cognitive pathology. In S. Koch (Ed.), *Psychology in human context: Essays in dissidence and reconstruction* (pp. 366–392). Chicago: University of Chicago Press.

Kuhn, T. (1970). *The structure of scientific revolutions* (2nd ed.). Chicago: University of Chicago Press.

Lakoff, G., & Nunez, R. E. (2000). *Where mathematics comes from.* New York: Basic Books.

Newton-Smith, W. H. (1981). *The rationality of science.* London: Routledge & Kegan Paul.

Polkinghorne, D. (1983). *Methodology for the human sciences: Systems of inquiry.* Albany: State University of New York Press.

Popper, K. (1959). *The logic of scientific discovery.* New York: Basic Books.

Quine, W. V. O. (1953). Two dogmas of empiricism. In W. V. O. Quine (Ed.), *From a logical point of view* (pp. 20–46). Cambridge, MA: Harvard University Press.

Singleton, R. A., Jr., Straits, B. C., & Straits, M. M. (1993). *Approaches to social research* (2nd ed.). New York: Oxford University Press.

Slife, B. D., & Williams, R. N. (1995). *What's behind the research? Discovering hidden assumptions in the behavioral sciences.* Thousand Oaks, CA: Sage.

Stumpf, S. E. (1977). *Philosophy: History and problems* (2nd ed.). New York: McGraw-Hill.

Taylor, S. J., & Bogdan, R. (1998). *Introduction to qualitative research methods* (3rd ed.). New York: Wiley.

Tymoczko, T. (Ed.). (1998). *New directions in the philosophy of mathematics.* Princeton, NJ: Princeton University Press.

Wheelwright, P. (Ed.). (1960). *The presocratics.* Indianapolis, IN: Odyssey Press.

Williams, R. N. (2000). Epistemology. In A. E. Kazdin (Ed.), *Encyclopedia of psychology* (Vol. 3, pp. 225–232). New York: Oxford University Press.

12

TOWARD AN ALTERNATIVE PSYCHOLOGY

JEFF SUGARMAN AND JACK MARTIN

Inspired by the technological success and prestige enjoyed by the natural sciences, psychologists have believed from the beginning of organized psychology that methods modeled on those of natural science are the best means available for the study of psychological phenomena. However, as Williams (see chap. 11, this volume) and many others reveal, this allegiance is based on a number of questionable if not mistaken assumptions. Psychologists may attempt to act like scientists, but it does not necessarily follow that they are practicing good science. While there may be some kinds of psychological questions for which natural scientific methods are justified, most of the things psychologists want to know may be resistant to these methods. If this is indeed the case, how then might we go about psychology? What alternatives are there to the inherited tradition of natural science?

In this chapter, we suggest an alternative that draws from a tradition of thought found in Continental philosophy, and we show how hermeneutics (also discussed in chap. 4, this volume) can inform psychological inquiry. Hermeneutics is concerned with the art and theory of interpretation, particularly with the interpretation of what it is to be human and how human understanding is possible. In contrast to the traditional approach to psychology, which assumes the legitimacy of its method and takes its application as the starting point, hermeneutics begins by attempting to clarify the subject of study. Hermeneutics assumes that psychological study, first and foremost, must be faithful to the particular nature of human existence, and consequently begins by attempting to interpret this nature and the conditions that make it possible. In other words, if we want to know how people think, act, and experience their lives, it is necessary first to have some notion of what it is that thinks, acts, and experiences. What psychologists take people to be dictates what counts as a legitimate psychological question and implicates methodologies appropriate to its study. Any method of psychological inquiry will reflect views about what it means to be human, and questions of meaning inevitably are questions of interpretation. Further, from a hermeneutic perspective, the subject matter of psychology, unlike that of the physical sciences, requires interpretation not only for its comprehension but for its very existence. As we elaborate, in psychology the phenomena of interest and the methods of inquiry are constituted by human interpretive practices and are imbued with meaning and significance in ways that natural phenomena are not.

A BRIEF INTRODUCTION TO HERMENEUTICS

The term *hermeneutics* is derived from the Greek *hermeneia*, which means interpretation or translation. Hermeneutics arose historically with concerns about interpreting sacred texts. A matter of life and death during the Middle Ages, differing interpretations of scripture provoked heresies, persecutions, schisms, and wars. In the early 19th century, Friedrich Schleiermacher (1998) proposed a general hermeneutics as an interpretive method for uncovering the authorial intent in texts and speech. Prior to Schleiermacher, the method of interpretation was believed to depend on the type of text to be interpreted. Legal texts required juridical hermeneutics, scripture required biblical hermeneutics, literary texts required a philological hermeneutics, and so forth. Schleiermacher sought to uncover interpretive principles that function universally in all understanding. Schleiermacher introduced the *hermeneutic circle* as one such principle: Interpretation is a circular movement between part and whole. To understand the whole of a text, it is necessary to understand the parts, whereas to understand the parts, it is necessary to comprehend the whole. Thus, interpreting any text involves a repetitive tacking between parts and whole.

Following Schleiermacher, Wilhelm Dilthey (1894/1927/1977) extended the idea of a general hermeneutic methodology to the interpretive study of all forms of mental and social life. Dilthey argued that understanding human beings and their societies was more similar to interpreting texts than to the experimental study of nature. In his words, "we explain nature, we understand mental life" (see Ermarth, 1978, p. 246). Dilthey described two different ways of experiencing the world. One is to stand back and observe the world as a collection of external, natural objects and events to be explained. But there is another more immediate mode of experience that comes of being a person living in the world. Human life, Dilthey claimed, is a seamless lived reality that precedes conceptual distinctions between mind and body, self and world. As living beings, we never can step outside our own existence to offer an impartial interpretation of it. Dilthey argued that the starting point for psychology is not observing external objects at a distance but observing our involved lived experience.

Schleiermacher and Dilthey had aimed to establish hermeneutics as an epistemological foundation for objective knowledge in the human sciences. Martin Heidegger initiated a radical shift in hermeneutic theory by elevating ontological considerations over epistemological ones. In his major work, *Being and Time*, Heidegger (1927/1962) directed hermeneutic analysis to uncovering the conditions that underlie all knowledge claims. Beginning with the ancient philosophical "question of being" (i.e., Why is there something rather than nothing?), Heidegger looked to the conditions that allow entities to show up or matter to us in the first place. How is it that we are able to comprehend something as something? Heidegger argued that traditional conceptions of human understanding overemphasize our capacity for abstract theorizing and detached reflection and overlook its more primordial nature. Heidegger set about describing our "average everydayness" in a way that undermines the Cartesian picture of understanding as the result of individual minds, separated from the world, observing external objects and representing their perceived properties.

Heidegger described how much of our everyday practical activity is prereflective, in which things are tacitly rather than explicitly understood. For example, when we reach to open a door, we do not first discern its handle, hinges, and lock; deduce that it is a door; and then open it. Rather, the door presents itself to us as something to be opened, and only then do we abstract its properties, if at all. What shows up for us is not a "door-thing" with properties but a way of entering or exiting depending on our particular purposes. The door is encountered in terms of a context of functionality. It is situated in a context of relations, not only with other things but also with our purposes in using it. Things are intelligible to us because they exist in a web of meaningful relations with other entities and human purposes, and it is only by virtue of this context of meaning that we are able to comprehend something as something.

However, this context of meaning most often is not made explicit and operates in the background of understanding. Much of our activity in daily life occurs without a great deal of self-conscious reflection or questioning. We seem to understand what we are doing even though we are not explicitly interpreting our actions and the world around us. Heidegger referred to this practical, prereflective understanding in our activities as *preunderstanding*. It is only when we encounter an obstacle to what we are attempting to do that we become self-consciously concerned and reflective, such as if we were unexpectedly to find the door locked and required a key to open it.

In Heidegger's view, what is most basic to our existing as a kind of understanding is neither the reflective capacity of individual humans nor a world of material external objects. Rather, it is the forms that human existence takes as a consequence of the background of social and cultural practices in which we are embedded and from which we draw possibilities for living. From birth, we are "thrown" into worlds not of our own choosing, and our individual being as human agents is shaped with others in the sociocultural contexts in which we find ourselves. The ways in which we learn to interpret ourselves and our experiences are rooted in language and other relational practices that constitute shared understandings among those sharing a form of life. This background of understandings we share with others creates what Heidegger called a *clearing,* in which things make sense in our form of life and show up as mattering to us. We understand ourselves in terms of a public world of shared significance and culturally available possibilities that constitute an ever-present background that lends meaning to our motivations, actions, and experiences. Try, for example, to imagine the self-defining sacrifice of the martyr or the discipline of the aspiring musician in the absence of political conflicts or historically accumulated musical works, respectively, all of which are important elements in the relevant sociocultural, public practices that constitute these and other forms of self-definition and identity.

According to Heidegger, we are so deeply embedded in the shared practices and understandings of our sociocultural world that we never can escape them completely. However, while possibilities for acting and living are appropriated from the sociocultural contexts in which we are embedded, this does not mean that we are entirely determined by them. Rather, our embeddedness in these contexts provides the means that allow us to achieve personhood and develop meaningful individual identities. We appropriate certain possibilities for living sustained in cultural practices, and in the process of interpreting and enacting these possibilities we create our individual lives. According to Heidegger, being human is an event or "happening," not a substance or property. There is no particular substance or essence that makes us what we are. As self-interpreting beings, humans are just what they make of themselves by incorporating and projectively pursuing possibilities for being in living their lives. For example, Martin Luther King both lived and understood himself in terms of the race-related practices in which he developed and acted to overcome. In this way, the forms our selfhood and personhood take are subject to, and change as a function of, the way we see ourselves across our life span, within a particular historical era. The present generation will understand itself differently than a past generation and will interpret the past generation's place in history with hindsight in ways different from the past generation's account of itself.

An important aspect of Heidegger's account is his notion of *care* (see Division I of *Being and Time*; see also Dreyfus, 1991). Heidegger claimed that what it means to be human is to care deeply about one's life and how to live it. Caring about who we are and what we are puts our lives "at stake" or "in question" for us. As self-interpreting beings, we care about our own lives, and the meaning and worth of our lives always are at issue for us. Care constitutes all our involvements in the world. It is the significance that things have for us, the concern we have about our lives, and the sense we make of our existence as a whole. As a consequence of care, we project ourselves as a possible way of being, and our motivations, actions, and experiences find meaning as part of this projection. As the projection of being toward possibilities in living, we are constantly oriented toward the future and the meaning of our lives as a whole. In this way, our lives are projects that take a narrative or storied structure. Just as we make sense of the parts of a story by anticipating the overall plot, we make sense of episodes and events in our lives by relating them to a developing vision of our lives as a whole. All our motivations and actions find meaning in this projection, or *life project*, and things have meaning only to the extent they are part of it. Taking a stand on our own being, we constitute our identity through what we do. Whereas nonhuman objects are defined by their physical properties, we humans are defined by our care, and the way it is manifested in choices and actions that relate to possibilities we encounter in the course of living our lives. The meaning and significance we find in the world depends on a preunderstanding of how things can count for us, and this prereflective understanding is shaped by the clearings created in the language and practices of a culture. Our knowledge of ourselves is not presuppositionless and objectively sanitized of our interests and concerns.

Hans-Georg Gadamer continued Heidegger's line of thought, sharing Heidegger's view of understanding not just as one kind of behavior, but as the human mode of being that creates our whole experience of existing in the world. As Williams (see chap. 11, this volume) mentions, an important contribution of Gadamer's work is his attempt to clarify the preunderstanding and conditions of possibility that guide human science. In *Truth and Method*, Gadamer (1960/1989) argued against the belief that the success of social scientific explanations should be measured by their conformity with the standards of natural science and that the pressing task for the human sciences is to uncover methodological foundations that can assure objective truth. According to Gadamer, the primary problem is not an epistemological one, that is, how to ground findings and knowledge claims. Rather, it is the ontological question of what the human sciences are, aside from the particular methods they use. Gadamer noted that the human sciences are part of history and the human world they study. They do not stand outside of human existence but have emerged as part of it. They draw on cultural and historical traditions and are forms of knowledge that express and develop the historical tradition of which they are part.

Gadamer argued that all understanding, including scientific understanding, arises out of our preunderstanding and embeddedness in historical traditions. Our interpretations of ourselves and others are so deeply embedded in historical traditions as to be largely invisible to us. All understanding requires what Gadamer referred to as a *horizon* of language and other shared practices that comprise tradition and provide a background of meaning and intelligibility. Horizon is a metaphor Gadamer used to describe a context of meaning. It consists of meanings of which one is not presently aware, and which must remain beyond awareness if there is to be a selective focus of attention. Nonetheless, one's horizon serves as the context in terms of which the object of attention is made meaningful. While Heidegger saw our preunderstanding and horizons of meaning tied to a particular period of time, Gadamer saw them as rooted more deeply in history and the unfolding of traditions. Not only do our lives develop with others in specific cultures, times, and places, but our capacities for knowledge and understanding, sustained by cultural practices, are carried forward from one generation to the next by historical tradition. The projections of meaning necessary to understanding are part of traditions that have developed over the course of human history. Consider, for example, the etymology of words we use to express meanings and how the meanings they convey have been carried forward or transformed over time. According to Gadamer, participating in tradition is a principal condition and limit for human understanding.

The aim of interpretation, Gadamer asserted, is not to free ourselves from historical limitation but to accept traditions and cultural prejudices as a necessary condition for understanding. Gadamer's use of the term *prejudice* does not carry the pejorative connotation ordinarily assumed in English. Prejudice, for Gadamer, refers to our particular cultural perspective, steeped in language and tradition, and indispensable to all understanding. According to Gadamer, our prejudices do not prevent us from understanding but are a gateway to it. Prejudices are not narrow-minded biases but form the horizons of meaning that orient us and are brought to bear whenever we attempt to understand. There is never a point when we are totally free from the prejudice and prejudgments of tradition that constitute our horizons of meaning. Understanding cannot occur, Gadamer claimed, outside the tradition in which it is meaningful. However, tradition never can be completely articulated. It exists in the countless unarticulated prejudices we bring forward in dealing with the world. Tradition is the sum of all these prejudices and prejudgments, and each person, living and past, manifests the historically constituted tradition of his or her culture. For example, the *dignitas* of the Roman senator, or the self-respect of the high school senior, resides in complex and subtle cultural and subcultural assumptions and understandings concerning what is appropriate and laudatory.

Gadamer argued against what he called the *prejudice against prejudice*. Since the 17th century, science has been wed to the idea that scientific method requires extricating ourselves from any biases and assumptions seen to arise from our peculiarities as human beings. The formulation and testing of hypotheses, tools of measurement, replicability, and techniques of isolation and control are intended to eliminate subjective intrusions thought to threaten objectivity. However, because all understanding involves prejudices and preunderstandings, Gadamer argued that the scientific method cannot ensure truth in this way. This is especially so in the human sciences in which the inquirer's own being is involved dynamically with the phenomenon being studied. In psychology, for example, we are simultaneously the phenomenon to be understood and the medium for understanding. Further, because understanding is essentially historical, our cultural perspective is continually shifting, and thus there is no such thing as timeless or final truth in interpreting human life. The questions we ask and the answers we interpret depend on our vantage point in history. Gadamer recast the ideal of scientific understanding from visualizing an inquirer without preconceptions to a recognition that all understanding arises out of our preconceptions and our position in a historical tradition.

Although there is no scientific method by which we can completely overcome our prejudices and attain absolute objectivity, Gadamer suggested that we can revise our prejudices in dialogue with others and with texts, and thereby access knowledge. As already mentioned, this knowledge never can be final. It is always partial and always involves historical horizons, as the inquirer is immersed in history that can never be escaped. The present is only understood through the past, with which it has living continuity. As a hermeneutic circle, the past provides us with tradition that contributes possibilities for understanding the present, whereas our present interpretations of those possibilities rebound against historical tradition by indicating how the past can make sense to us. For example, we understand current international conflicts by invoking "lessons" from past conflicts, even as our understanding of past conflicts is altered by our current concerns and interpretations.

Gadamer asserted that to understand another person or a text, we must merge or fuse our horizon with that of the person or text being studied because it is these historical cultural horizons that steer and constitute our individual understandings and experiences. Understanding occurs when our horizon of historical meanings and assumptions fuses with the horizon of the other person or text we are attempting to interpret. The implication is that in any act of interpretation, there is mutual influence between the interpreter and the subject of interpretation as the horizons of each intermingle. When horizons fuse, it is because one's own prejudices have been brought into view, and this makes it possible to comprehend the context in which other perspectives are made meaningful. In revealing one's own prejudices, one becomes capable of grasping those of another. Further, when horizons of meaning are brought together, the outcome will be new meaning not entailed in either of the original perspectives. Such fusions of meaning are all around us, from scientific advances that bring together previously disparate insights from different disciplines to sociopolitical compromises that incorporate bits and pieces of what initially were perceived as irreconcilably oppositional views. According to Gadamer, in such instances, we understand differently if we understand at all. The critical insight is that reaching an understanding of, or with, another is not a matter of observation through the application of an impartial method intended to ensure objectivity. Nor is it a matter of empathetically reconstructing the other's mental processes and private experiences. Instead it involves being open to and integrating another's horizon of meaning in such a way that one's own perspective is altered in the process.

Gadamer emphasized the importance of language and dialogue as a definitive feature of understanding. A valid meaning is one that has been constructed in language and is accepted by a community of interpreters. Meaning is expressed in language, and the possible limits of something being made meaningful are stipulated by the limits of language. When we come to understand something explicitly, it is because we have put into words some previously unexamined aspect of tradition. However, Gadamer asserted that when we understand something explicitly, its meaning not only is acquired from what is said but also from what remains unsaid. Each event of understanding is furnished with meaning by a largely unexpressed context. As we bring one possibility of interpretation forward, others recede into the background. Nonetheless, the background or horizon remains significant in the production of meaning. In this way, understanding is as much a process of "concealment" as "revealment." Thus, Gadamer argued, understanding something explicitly not only involves grasping what is said but also comprehending the tradition sufficiently to grasp relations between what is said and what is not being said.

Gadamer's project in *Truth and Method* (1960/1989) is to challenge accepted notions of truth and method as they are applied in scientific approaches to understanding human life. Our capacity to discern truths about human life does not owe to a detached, neutral process of observing objective facts. Rather, Gadamer claimed, the truth of human life is not separate from us. Understanding ourselves requires recognizing that by existing we are already the truth of human life. The task is to articulate the significant features of our being. Gadamer opposed the idea of formal method. Our only avenue to understanding is to engage in genuine dialogue with others in ways that allow us to encounter and cast light on our prejudices and the effects of our historical traditions. This requires not detachment, but rather a genuine openness to hearing what others and texts have to say, a willingness to examine critically our own preconceptions, and a readiness to abandon those of our beliefs shown to be faulty or inadequate.

IMPLICATIONS FOR A HERMENEUTIC PSYCHOLOGY

Hermeneutics presents a view of psychological phenomena strongly at variance with the ways in which they traditionally have been conceived and studied in disciplinary psychology. First, from a hermeneutic perspective, the subject matter of psychology is interpretive, historical, social, cultural, and saturated with human interests and values. A psychology informed by hermeneutics assumes that human motivations, thoughts, actions, and experiences emerge within a context of historical traditions and sociocultural practices, and any psychological inquiry adequate to its subject matter must recognize and interpret human activity against and within the background of human meanings and significance that structures and orients us as psychological beings. In this light, hermeneutic psychology can be expected to be historical, sociocultural, moral, and political in ways that even the most social of mainstream psychology is not. Such a broadening of the focus of psychology beyond the individual to include history, culture, and politics would seem to require a different kind of education of psychologists than is now advocated and practiced by most organizations and departments of psychology. However, embracing a broader liberal education in the humanities, sciences, and social sciences also might challenge psychology's status as a separate and readily identifiable discipline in its own right. In this way and more generally, a hermeneutic perspective on psychological phenomena may threaten to subordinate psychology to historical, political, and cultural studies.

Second, hermeneutic psychology accepts a distinctive reality of sociocultural and psychological phenomena. Sociocultural and psychological phenomena are created and transformed dynamically as a consequence of individual and collective human activity over time. Unlike natural phenomena, the phenomena psychologists study do not remain fixed, unchanging, and resistant to human history. However, just because these phenomena are socioculturally and psychologically constructed, and constantly evolving, does not mean they are not real. Sociocultural and psychological phenomena are real. They exert undeniable influence in human life, and both make possible and constrain themselves and our interpretations of them. Such influence, while not concretely tangible or static, should not be dismissed. This particular aspect of the hermeneutic approach has caused many psychologists to worry about the way in which hermeneutics erodes the possibility of establishing psychological laws and theories that cross cultural boundaries and lay claim to universality.

Third, in recognizing the constitutive force of historical traditions and sociocultural practices in the expression of human agency, a hermeneutically informed psychology opposes the naturalism and reductionism common to much mainstream psychological theory and research. Once the psychological importance of historical sociocultural contexts is realized, it makes little sense to believe that human psychology is reducible to neurophysiological blueprints that predetermine the nature of human psychology. There are neurophysiological, chemical, and biological requirements necessary to psychological development. But requirement is not equality. Just, for example, as it is a mistake to equate musical performance with the architecture and properties of musical instruments, it is a mistake to equate human actions and experiences with those neurophysiological, chemical, and biological phenomena they require. Psychological development would be impossible without the embeddedness of biological individuals in sociocultural contexts and practices. To think otherwise is like attempting to explain the behavior of baseball players without reference to the rules, regulations, and conventions of the game.

At the same time, while hermeneutics emphasizes the historical and sociocultural constitution of psychological phenomena, it also affirms their irreducibility. Persons and selves are not reducible entirely to their historical and sociocultural constitution. As agents, human beings are able to exercise some degree of individual self-determination. Once a psychologically capable person has emerged developmentally, his or her interpretations will be active in the further constitution of his or her personhood. Individuals' interpretations can create possibilities for present and future understanding and action that are not entirely constrained by past and present sociocultural circumstances. By championing a psychological agency in this way, hermeneutic psychologists resist the hard determinism that has been, and continues to be, a hallmark of scientific psychology for many psychologists.

Fourth, from a hermeneutic perspective, psychological study is an interpretive practice. Psychological phenomena cannot be understood apart from the history of interpretations and descriptions given them. The discipline of psychology belongs to the history of ways human beings have developed for interpreting themselves psychologically, and it is precisely this history that has constituted the objects of psychological study. Not only are the objects of psychological study constituted interpretively, but so are the methods of study. Hermeneutic inquiry depends on our ability to recognize that our truths are made possible by a shared background of life into which we are initiated and to which we contribute through our dialogues and interactions with others. It is only by virtue of participating in human life as self-interpreting beings that we can make sense of it. Psychologists also are self-interpreting, and it is only by being "insiders" with a preunderstanding of the meanings and values they seek to interpret that psychological study is possible. For many psychologists, the idea that psychology is one among many formal and informal practices through which we attempt to understand ourselves erodes the status of psychology as a domain of particular expertise that somehow stands apart from, and is therefore uniquely capable of objectively evaluating, other practices of human self-understanding (Danziger, 1997a; Dawda & Martin, 2001).

Fifth, while psychological study is inherently interpretive, this does not mean that psychological phenomena can be interpreted in any manner whatsoever. Interpretations are subject to the historical and sociocultural perspective of the interpreter. As such, they are always perspectival, partial, fallible, and never final or absolute. There is always room for reinterpretation. However, interpretations are grounded in social, cultural, linguistic, and historical conventions and traditions and must make sense within these contexts. Not all interpretations are equally viable. They must cohere with what we already know and resonate with our self-understandings. It is also the case that our interpretations can transform our understandings of ourselves and engender different or new possibilities of thinking, acting, and experiencing. For instance, one need not look very far to see the powerful influence disciplinary psychology has exerted on the ordinary language contemporary persons use to describe and understand themselves. Of course, underlying this interpretivist, perspectivist, fallibilist, and transformative view of knowledge is a commitment to, and valuing of, understanding itself as a human achievement and tool that carries ontological, epistemological, and moral force. That understanding in general, and psychological understanding in particular, always have a moral aspect has proved to be especially difficult for many scientifically minded psychologists to accept.

Sixth, dialogue is the central means of psychological study. Psychological interpretation finds meaning within a hermeneutic circle of dialogue between specific readings of thoughts, actions, and experiences and an understanding of human life as a whole. Our only course of action is to offer interpretations of phenomena of interest and to develop or critique them by appeals to further interpretations. Psychological study is the attempt to devise language that articulates our understanding of the human existential condition, complete with possibilities and constraints supplied by our sociocultural histories and embodiment. The merits of our interpretations rest largely on the clarity and cogency with which they are expressed, and the degree to which others find them compelling and informative with respect to shared concerns in living. This explicit recognition of the inevitably rhetorical basis for the pronouncements of scientific and professional psychology also has been difficult for many traditionally minded psychologists to sanction.

APPLICATIONS

From the foregoing discussion, it is clear that hermeneutics does not prescribe methods for psychology in the same way that naturalism insinuates the methods of natural science. In light of hermeneutics, once serious attention is paid to conceptualizing psychological phenomena, particularly their historical, sociocultural, and emergent qualities, and the ways in which they are transformative in creating new forms of themselves through understanding, it is clear that psychological study is not amenable to the kind of highly deterministic and prescriptive theorizing and methodology that is feasible in natural science.

This being said, hermeneutic psychologists have used a variety of methods and strategies within a hermeneutic framework. A general strategy is the investigation of everyday experience as a basis for psychological research. Our "average everydayness" is not seen as an impediment to objectivity, but rather an entrance to the assumptions and biases resident in the preunderstanding every inquirer brings to bear in studying psychological phenomena, and particularly the role such prejudgments might play in the interpretation of psychological data or formulation of results. By tacking between their initially inadequate understandings of specific phenomena and interpretations of these phenomena that emerge as their inquiries proceed, hermeneutic psychologists make use of yet another circle of interpretation in which different phases of their inquiries take on meaning and significance in relation to the concerns that motivated them.

Other strategies include the uncovering or "unconcealment" not only of present possibilities of interpretation but also of those that have been closed off or hidden by the prejudices of our preunderstanding; looking at anomalies, disturbances, contradictions, or unique cases as opportunities for uncovering new meanings and significance; examining narratives and other forms of thought in which understanding is expressed; constantly tacking between particular and general contexts; sincerely and openly engaging other perspectives in ways that fusions might reveal the merits of rival views; and examining beliefs and practices at different historical times and locations to reveal the historical, sociocultural, emergent, and transformative features of our contemporary practices within and outside of disciplinary psychology. Additionally, moral and political positions are not ignored or denied but recognized as inescapable and constitutive features of psychological being. Our moral and political sensibilities make claims on us in ways that command our attention and concern.

The foregoing strategies are to be seen as aids to interpretive psychological inquiry. They are not intended prescriptively, nor should their status be elevated above the phenomena at which they are directed. All psychological inquiry is conducted within broader cultural and historical traditions that support the assumptions, biases, theories, interpretations, and investigative strategies and methodologies of researchers. Hermeneutic inquiry is no exception. In hermeneutic psychology it is subject matter, not methodology, that steers inquiry and is of greatest concern.

At this juncture, we turn to an example that we hope might aid the reader to see more clearly the kinds of endeavors in which hermeneutic psychology consists. However, before doing so, we mention that there are a number of notable and varied applications of hermeneutic scholarship in psychology that we encourage the interested reader to explore (e.g., Chessick, 1990; Christopher, 2001; Cushman, 1995; Danziger, 1990, 1997b; Guignon, 1993; Martin & Sugarman, 1999; Martin, Sugarman, & Thompson, 2003; Messer, Sass, & Woolfolk, 1988; Packer, 1985a, 1985b; Packer & Addison, 1989; Polkinghorne, 2000; Richardson, Fowers, & Guignon, 1999; Rose, 1998; Slife & Williams, 1995; Woolfolk, 1998; Young & Collin, 1992).[1]

Philip Cushman's (1995) illuminating and expansive account of the historical development of psychotherapy in the United States is a striking example of the kind of cultural, historical, and critical scholarship advocated by hermeneutic psychologists. Cushman's work illustrates the interpretive strategies of tacking between particular and general contexts as parts and whole of a hermeneutic circle, unconcealment, attending to our everyday understandings, situating objects of psychological study in the context of their historical emergence and development, and the importance of inquirers attending critically to their own cultural frames of reference. Cushman argues that to understand the practice of psychotherapy it is necessary to consider the historical, social, cultural, economic, moral, and political conditions under which it has emerged. Psychotherapy both reflects these conditions and provides a window to understanding American society and the beliefs we hold about ourselves. In other words, the history of psychotherapy is not just the history of a professional practice. As a human artifact, it poses a much broader anthropological opportunity such that Cushman's (1995) aim "is to understand psychotherapy by understanding America and vice versa" (p. 24). In light of numerous historical and contemporary examples, Cushman reveals how and why psychotherapy emerged, the functions it serves, and how it has come to have such strong influence in today's society.

According to Cushman, each historical era in the development of American society has sustained a particular understanding not only of what it is to be a person but also corresponding notions of what constitutes mental illness and dysfunction, how these are to be treated, and who should be officially sanctioned to provide treatment. In tracing the development of psychotherapy in light of the cultural, historical, economic, and political influences of each era, Cushman shows how psychotherapy has promoted particular views of the proper way to be human. Of particular interest is Cushman's assertion that psychotherapy has participated in the rise of consumerism and market capitalism, and currently supports what he called the *empty self* of contemporary American society. As Cushman (1995) described,

> The empty self is a way of being human; it is characterized by a pervasive sense of personal emptiness and is committed to the values of self-liberation through consumption. The empty self is the perfect complement to

[1]It is important to note that while some of the authors cited might not identify their work explicitly as hermeneutic, its character is such that we believe the label justified.

Dreyfus, H. L. (1991). *Being-in-the-world: A commentary on Heidegger's Being and Time, Division I*. Cambridge, MA: MIT Press.

Ermarth, M. (1978). *Wilhelm Dilthey: The critique of historical reason*. Chicago: University of Chicago Press.

Gadamer, H.-G. (1989). *Truth and method* (2nd ed., rev.) (J. Weinsheimer & D. G. Marshall, Trans.). New York: Continuum. (Original work published 1960)

Guignon, C. B. (1993). Authenticity, moral values, and psychotherapy. In C. B. Guignon (Ed.), *The Cambridge companion to Heidegger*. Cambridge, MA: Cambridge University Press.

Heidegger, M. (1962). *Being and time* (J. Macquarrie & E. Robinson, Trans.). New York: Harper & Row. (Original work published 1927)

Martin, J., & Sugarman, J. (1999). *The psychology of human possibility and constraint*. Albany, NY: SUNY Press.

Martin, J., Sugarman, J., & Thompson, J. (2003). *Psychology and the question of agency*. Albany, NY: SUNY Press.

Messer, S. M., Sass, L. A., & Woolfolk, R. L. (Eds.). (1988). *Hermeneutics and psychological theory*. New Brunswick, NJ: Rutgers University Press.

Packer, M. (1985a). Hermeneutic inquiry in the study of human conduct. *American Psychologist, 40*, 1081–1093.

Packer, M. (1985b). *The structure of moral action: A hermeneutic study of moral conflict*. Basel, Switzerland: Karger.

Packer, M., & Addison, R. B. (Eds.). (1989). *Entering the circle: Hermeneutic investigation in psychology*. Albany, NY: SUNY Press.

Polkinghorne, D. (2000). Psychological inquiry and the pragmatic and hermeneutic traditions. *Theory & Psychology, 10*, 453–480.

Richardson, F. C., Fowers, B. J., & Guignon, C. (1999). *Renewing psychology: Beyond scientism and constructionism*. San Francisco: Jossey-Bass.

Rose, N. (1998). *Inventing ourselves: Psychology, power, and personhood*. Cambridge, England: Cambridge University Press.

Schleiermacher, F. (1998). *Hermeneutics and criticism* (A. Bowie, Ed. & Trans.). Cambridge, England: Cambridge University Press.

Slife, B. D., & Williams, R. N. (1995). *What's behind the research? Discovering hidden assumptions in the behavioral sciences*. Thousand Oaks, CA: Sage.

Woolfolk, R. L. (1998). *The cure of souls: Science, values, and psychotherapy*. San Francisco: Jossey-Bass.

Young, R. A., & Collin, A. (1992). *Interpreting career: Hermeneutical studies of lives in context*. Westport, CT: Praeger Publishers.

CONCLUSION:
TOWARD CRITICAL OPENNESS

SUZANNE R. KIRSCHNER

When students are first exposed to the research questions and methods of psychology, it crosses the minds of many of them that there may be other ways to think about, and to investigate, human nature and social life. For example, in research methods courses it is stressed that all questions must be operationalized and investigated through experimental manipulation. Yet many students wonder, at least initially, whether human experience and action can really be adequately studied in this way. Many were drawn to psychology in the first place because they thought it would give them the means to explore human experience as it is lived and felt, and thus they are often surprised and disappointed that psychology's methods do not seem well suited to studying human beings as the complex, meaning-making creatures that we are. Similarly, students are taught (often implicitly) that all human behavior ultimately needs to be understood as determined by antecedent forces and causes. Yet it certainly occurs to many to wonder whether a completely deterministic framework is really necessary, let alone desirable—whether, in other words, there might be room in models of behavior for a vision of humans as agents, possessing free will and bearing some responsibility for their actions.

Most of the time, such critical internal voices, and the questions and challenges that those voices pose, become ever muter as students move farther along in their psychological studies. Indeed, part of becoming well socialized as a psychology student, and then as a psychologist, is to learn to suppress such questions and doubts, so that in the end one comes not to think in such terms at all. This is ironic, because it means that our very enculturation as psychologists entails the suppression of crucial elements of what it means to be a critical thinker. In other words, one learns that to become a successful psychology student, and then a successful psychological researcher or practitioner, one has to stifle the capacity to ask certain kinds of deep and challenging questions.

This book is an attempt to keep those critical voices and sensibilities alive in students of psychology. The contributors demonstrate that many of the questions and criticisms that students have when they are first studying the discipline are indeed legitimate, and that a number of past and present-day psychologists have posed similar challenges to the disciplinary "status quo." Those psychologists have also explored alternative ways of conceiving of the subject matter and methods of psychology (some which have deep roots in the history of psychological and social theory), demonstrating that they are often equally viable and robust. The contributors to this volume thus want to encourage new generations of psychology students to trust their own concerns, to see that others have shared them, and to explore sophisticated and fertile alternatives.

Just as fundamentally, these chapters call attention to the fact that *all* psychological research is structured in terms of assumptions—assumptions both about the nature of the phenomena we study and about what it means to *know* these phenomena. These assumptions are rarely acknowledged either by the researchers themselves or by those who aim to critically evaluate such work. By examining these assumptions, and juxtaposing them against equally (in some cases, more) plausible alternatives, the authors of this volume open up new horizons for psychological inquiry and for the role of critical thinking within such inquiry.

The awareness that assumptions necessarily structure all human inquiry—the questions we ask, the methods we use, and how we interpret what we find—has been a dominant theme in philosophy and social theory for many decades. During the latter half of the 20th century, a number of theoretical developments in the philosophy of language, the philosophy of science, and other fields have challenged *objectivist* (Bernstein, 1983) views of knowledge and of how it is acquired (Derrida, 1976; Heidegger, 1962; Kuhn, 1970; Wittgenstein, 1953). Though diverse in many ways, these philosophical critiques have converged in undermining the objectivist view that knowledge is best understood as a mirror of the world, and that "knowledge is achieved when a subject [the knower] correctly mirrors or represents objective reality" (Bernstein, 1983, p. 9). In place of objectivism, these approaches have promoted an appreciation of the degree to which our ostensibly "objective" and "empirically derived" knowledge is structured in terms of preexisting assumptions, values, narrative structures, and metaphors.

These theoretical developments have been taken very much to heart in some of the other social sciences, most notably sociology and anthropology. Hence, during the past quarter century, there has been far greater penetration into these other disciplines of the awareness that assumptions, values, and "frames" invariably structure both laypersons' and social scientists' ideas about the world (Rabinow & Sullivan, 1979; Seidman & Wagner, 1992). Some psychologists have also heeded these philosophical critiques and have promoted nonobjectivist views of psychological knowledge (Danziger, 1990a; Graumann & Gergen, 1996; Kirschner, 1996; Leary, 1990a, 1990b; Richardson, Fowers, & Guignon, 1999; Slife & Williams, 1995). Philosophical critiques of objectivism have been particularly influential in the work of a number of psychologists who study the construction of gender differences in psychology (Bohan, 1992; Hare-Mustin & Marecek, 1990; Morawski, 1999). Yet in spite of these few notable exceptions, this self-awareness has not pervaded the discipline of psychology as a whole. The dominant tendency has been to retain an uncritical objectivism. As the historian of psychology Kurt Danziger (1990b) put it, psychologists tend to unreflectively assume that "psychological events have fixed natural forms, which a few lucky philosophers and an army of systematic investigators have found and labeled" (pp. 334–335).

No doubt there are a variety of reasons for this disciplinary mind-set and lack of attentiveness to the far-reaching critiques noted above. But many of these reasons are related to the fact that at both institutional and ideological levels, psychologists have sought legitimation for their discipline through its being considered a "science." This is hardly surprising, because in our society, fields of inquiry that are so designated enjoy the highest status and authority, and the greatest access to material resources. However, this scientistic stance within psychology has several undesirable aspects. First, it tends to use an understanding of "science" that is overly simplistic and concrete (Williams, chap. 11). Second, because much of human experience and activity cannot gracefully fit into the experimental or quasi-experimental models that psychologists tend to favor (Williams, chap. 11; Sugarman & Martin, chap. 12), there is often a great deal of distortion and simplification of the phenomena that are ostensibly under scrutiny. As Williams noted in his chapter, "method drives theory" (see p. 248).

Although the chapters in this book deal with diverse branches of contemporary psychology, there are some common themes that appear in nearly all of them. Below I focus on several of the assumptions inherent in psychological research that are highlighted by these authors: objectivism, empiricism, materialism, determinism, and individualism. I then briefly discuss the alternative vision that likewise runs through many of the chapters. This alternative is a more meaning-centered, holistic version of human science.

ASSUMPTIONS: COMMON THREADS

Much psychological research is informed by assumptions that are not only taken for granted by psychologists but are also pervasive in laypersons' everyday understandings of the mind and human nature. This makes it all the more challenging to recognize that they are, in fact, assumptions. One such taken-for-granted idea is the objectivist orientation described above. Thus, for example, psychologists tend to assume that the methods they use can and should provide a view of "objective reality" that is untainted by "contaminating" influences such as the cultural and intellectual traditions in which such research takes form (Williams, chap. 11). Objectivism also influences the assumptions that psychologists make about the nature of the mind and its contents. For example, cognitive psychologists generally believe that mental structures stand for what we know about the world outside of our minds (Bishop, chap. 7).

In addition to such objectivist premises, it is also clear from these chapters that various empiricist assumptions underlie most psychologists' methods. Empiricism (like objectivism) is both a set of descriptive assumptions about the nature of the mind and how it "knows" and a set of prescriptions regarding how we should go about doing scientific inquiry. Such assumptions thus structure both the types of questions asked and the ways psychologists go about trying to answer them. While a number of empiricist assumptions are highlighted in this book, one of the most striking and recurring empiricist themes is that of atomism. At the most abstract and general level, atomism is a tendency either to conceptualize phenomena as being composed of relatively simple, discrete elements or else to "decompose" and "decontextualize" phenomena so that they can be studied in terms of such discrete elements. Atomism thus has implications both for how psychologists conceive of what they study and for the methods that they use. Its influence is detectable in a variety of subfields. For example, the assumption in cognitive psychology (what Yanchar, chap. 8, terms *information atomism*) is that "perception and mental activity are accomplished through the decontextualization and decomposition of . . . holistic experience into independent elements for processing " (see p. 172–173). An analogous assumption underlying the study of social behavior, *social atomism* (Yanchar, chap. 8), holds that we must explain behaviors and interactions solely in terms of properties inherent in individuals (Reber & Osbeck, chap. 3). In other words, there is little room in social psychology for explanations that are framed in terms of "emergent" or "relational" properties, that is, properties that inhere in the whole system or relationship that is being studied. Such social atomism is related to another assumption, individualism, which is discussed later in this chapter.

Methodologically, atomism supports the legitimation of psychology as a science because it directs psychologists to break data down into empirically manipulable bits and pieces, thereby enabling them to cast their research questions into experimental or quasi-experimental form. However, as has been noted, this begs the more general question of whether such atomistic treatments are adequate for the study of experience, behavior, and social life or whether they in fact distort and obscure as much as (or more than) they illuminate.

Much psychological research is also uncritically informed by a family of materialistic and mechanistic assumptions about human nature. Materialism can be defined as the proposition that all psychological phenomena are ultimately reducible to some aspect of matter or material being. Not surprisingly, these assumptions are most evident in neuroscience, as is illustrated in Hedges' and Burchfield's (chap. 5) discussion of the prevailing, unreflectively reductionist model of depression. Under the influence of such presuppositions, psychiatric research is increasingly moving in directions in which contextual and sociocultural factors are viewed as irrelevant (Healy, 1997; Luhrmann, 2000). One of the most prominent implications of materialist reductionism is efficient causal determinism, which for psychologists is the belief that behavioral and mental processes must be preceded by some prior physical cause. Such determinism is evident not only in biological psychology but also in cognitive psychology's information-processing metaphor (Bishop, chap. 7; Yanchar, chap. 8). It is hardly surprising that as psychologists proceed along such reductionist paths, there is generally little room for agency—for choice, responsibility, and free will—in accounts of human behavior.

A related type of reductionism is what Reber and Osbeck (chap. 3) call *naturalism*, or the explanation of human behavior in terms of our similarity to other animals. A currently popular version of such naturalism is evolutionary psychology, but this general approach has taken a number of different forms ever since the Darwinian revolution. In fact, the mid-20th century was dominated by a quite different, but no less influential, rendering of such naturalistic reductionism: behaviorism.

A final, very pervasive assumption that is highlighted by many of these authors is individualism. Individualistic assumptions about human nature, social life, and research methods pervade social, clinical, cognitive, and developmental psychology. They are so taken for granted that they tend not to be explicitly acknowledged by psychologists at all. One aspect of individualism has to do with motivation: People are viewed as fundamentally selfish and egoistic. They are seen to be driven mainly by the desire to realize instrumental goals (Reber & Osbeck, chap. 3; Bishop, chap. 7) and to achieve self-fulfillment (Richardson, chap. 1; Fowers, chap. 2; Christopher, chap. 10).

Another aspect of individualism in psychology is moral: This is the notion that people can and should develop toward autonomy. As Vandenberg and O'Connor (chap. 9) point out, the primary goal of psychological development is to exert mastery and control over the world and ourselves. Finally, as noted earlier, a methodological implication of individualism is what Reber and Osbeck (chap. 3) call *social atomism*: This is the assumption that all behavior (indeed, all social interaction) must be explained solely with reference to properties inherent in the individual. Psychologists tend not to be aware of the degree to which these individualistic beliefs and values are distinctively modern and particularly associated with versions of modernity characteristic of Protestant culture areas (Bellah, Madsen, Sullivan, Swidler, & Tipton, 1985; Kirschner, 1996; Taylor, 1989).

ALTERNATIVES: HUMANS AS MEANING-MAKERS, CONTEXT AS FUNDAMENTAL

The contributors to this volume all see a clear need to promote alternative visions of human nature and human science. Running through all the various alternatives is the message that material reductionist approaches will never be entirely adequate to account for psychological and sociocultural phenomena. Such meaning-centered visions of human science are often called *interpretive* or *cultural* psychology (Bruner, 1990; Shweder, 1990; Valsiner, 2000). Postmodern psychology (Gergen, 1994; Kvale, 1992) overlaps in important ways with the some of these approaches, though there are also some significant differences (Kirschner, 2000).

The cornerstone of such an interpretive or cultural psychology is a conception of human beings as meaning-makers. Such a conception of human beings, and of human science, has long been part of the sociological and anthropological canon. These more genuinely "social" sciences have always retained an awareness that human action is best understood as meaningful, and, indeed, that a defining characteristic of human beings is that we are meaning-makers (Geertz, 1973; Schutz, 1970; Weber, 1958). To be sure, there have also been voices within our own field that have long argued for such a "second psychology" (Cahan & White, 1992). And recently, there have been a number of efforts to launch a truly cultural psychology (Bruner, 1990; Cole, 1996; Valsiner, 1998; Wertsch, 1998). However, this family of traditions has never been dominant within the discipline and, as is made clear in this book, some of the most prominent contemporary areas and trends in psychology remain uninfluenced by it.

The purpose of cultural psychology is less prediction and control than it is the achievement of an increasingly adequate (though never perfect, timeless, or unambiguous) understanding of phenomena of interest. Thus, meaning-centered methods tend to be qualitative: Chiefly, they involve some type of phenomenological, ethnographic (i.e., utilizing interviews and participant observation), or textual analysis. Quantitative methods are not ruled out; but at the very least, qualitative understanding is seen to be a crucial first step to ensure that researchers understand the meanings and contexts of the phenomena they may then want to also study quantitatively (Harwood, Miller, & Iriarry, 1995; Tobin, Wu, & Davidson, 1989). The goal of much of this research can best be understood as achieving the capacity to communicate, or converse, with the people we are studying (Geertz, 1973). This is in contrast to the old (but still widely accepted) metaphor put forward by early modern philosopher of science Francis Bacon, in which the goal of science was held to be to "carve nature at her joints."

While there is a great deal of overlap and commonality in the visions of humans as meaning-makers expounded by the contributors to this volume, it is interesting to note that the "meaning-centered" theme is taken in somewhat different directions by different authors. For example, Slife and Hopkins (chap. 6), as well as Yanchar (chap. 8), sketch out a meaning-centered model that emphasizes the possibility of human freedom and choice. A key point they make is that even in the case of contemporary psychiatry and cognitive science, which are currently very mechanistic and deterministic, it is possible (even desirable) to emphasize the prospects for humans' capacity to make choices and to exercise self-determination. In fact, they demonstrate, it actually helps to account for some phenomena better than do the prevailing models.

By contrast, Richardson (chap. 1), Fowers (chap. 2), and (in a different way) Gantt (chap. 4) are less concerned with opening up new prospects for human freedom than they are with promoting recognition that human beings may, in a sense, be less "free" than we think we are. These authors demonstrate that modern liberal individualist ideologies obscure the degree to which we are all deeply embedded in moral traditions, communities, and relationships. Hence, they highlight how the shared meanings that we live by (indeed, that constitute our very identities) can and should be a source of moral guidance, existential sustenance, and social solidarity. These authors, then, are less concerned with pointing out that we are free to make choices than they are with demonstrating that in contemporary society we may have *too many* choices, much to the detriment of both the individual and the community.

These two variations on the theme of humans as meaning-makers may not be ultimately irreconcilable. Moreover, a common value uniting both of these versions of cultural psychology is an emphasis on humans' responsibility to others and to their society. But the divergence in their emphases does underscore the fact that there is no single "party line" that one must follow if one endorses, and works within, a broad cultural psychology framework.

Such cultural and phenomenological approaches to human nature and action, with their emphasis on meaning and responsibility, render intelligible the notion that human action need not, and likely should not, be accounted for solely in terms of efficient causation (the blind action of forces on objects). Cultural psychology promotes an image of humans as goal-oriented and future-oriented. It thereby clears a space for the notion of final causation (the idea that to explain the causes of behavior, people's purposes and goals must be taken into account) as a supplement or alternative to material efficient causation.

Just as these authors propose alternatives to psychology's dominant materialist and mechanistic vision, so also they challenge its individualistic and atomistic assumptions. They do so chiefly by proposing holistic and contextualist alternatives. Drawing inspiration from some already-existing traditions in psychology and social science, they all emphasize the fundamental theme that in order to adequately understand a phenomenon (be it depression, thinking processes, or intimate love relationships), psychologists need to frame it in terms of wider contexts or systems. One consequence of adopting a contextualist framework is that efficient causal determinism no longer need rule the day in psychological explanation. Formal causation—that is, the influence of contextual effects and interactions—can now be considered a viable alternative or supplement to more linear, mechanistic accounts of causality.

Such a holistic or contextualist reenvisioning of psychology is not simply a matter of factoring in context as another variable. Rather, it leads to a radical undoing of the dualisms and bifurcations that are generally unchallenged in psychological research. These bifurcations include those between subject and object, mind and body, and self and others or self and society. For example, Yanchar's (chap. 8) contextualist cognitive psychology demonstrates how it is possible to conceive of experience such that there is no "fundamental split between an outer reality of sensory stimuli and a private, inner world" (p. 175), by invoking the phenomenologists' premise that the *lifeworld*—the world as experienced—is fundamental. To adopt this premise would be to "undo" the generally assumed split between subject (the knower) and object (the known), and thus would have far-reaching implications for both psychology's theory of mind and its methodologies. Similarly, in the realm of neuroscience, Slife and Hopkins (chap. 6) propose a radical reenvisioning of the relationship of mind and body, such that they are construed as part of a larger system in which they mutually constitute one another.

Another generally unquestioned dualism in psychology—that between self and culture, or self and society—is likewise reenvisioned by a number of these authors (Richardson, chap. 1; Fowers, chap. 2; Gantt, chap. 4; Bishop, chap. 7; Christopher, chap. 10) in contextualist terms. They explore how the overly individualistic ideology of American culture has permeated our ideas about the goals and methods of psychology, obscuring the degree to which people are in fact constituted by social and cultural traditions and relationships. These authors also explore the ethical implications that such a changed understanding of the human condition would entail. For Fowers (chap. 2), the development of one's "best" self in psychotherapy thus turns out to involve a recognition of one's embeddedness in community and relationships, and a concomitant acknowledgment that living a worthy life must be understood in terms that go beyond a narrow understanding of self-interest and self-expression. Perhaps the most radical ethical implications of all follow from Gantt's (chap. 4) social psychology, which is predicated on the Levinasian assumption that we are relational beings, and that life is fundamentally a "being-for-the-other" (Levinas, 1969). If such an assumption is adopted, then the conventional social psychological "problem of altruism" recedes from the horizon, while human selfishness and egoism come to be seen as the puzzles that must be investigated.

CONCLUSION: TOWARD CRITICAL OPENNESS AND THE CAPACITY FOR DIALOGUE

Beyond the uncovering of assumptions and the proposing of alternatives, the contributors to this volume are advocating a fundamental attitude toward psychological inquiry. This stance, which has moral as well as epistemological dimensions, entails what I call a *critical openness*. It involves an awareness that assumptions and commitments inescapably structure and direct theory and research. Yet it also involves the somewhat paradoxical recognition that this need not result in a stalemate between perspectives. Rather, it leads to a model in which the ideal knower/researcher is aware of her or his own assumptions and commitments, yet simultaneously is open to trying to grasp perspectives and models that are different from her or his own. This dialogical or conversational model, which is often used as a metaphor for cultural or hermeneutic research, also works well as a model of the encounter between exponents of different assumptions or paradigms in psychological knowledge. As Richardson (chap. 1) points out, such an open attitude toward the encounter with difference and "otherness" can actually deepen and enrich one's own self-awareness. It may even lead to a strengthening of one's convictions, but on more self-conscious and philosophically sophisticated grounds. At the same time, it entails a continuing humility, because such a hermeneutic approach assumes that one's grasp of the "truth," no matter how firmly held, is always partial and imperfect.

Thus, a central message of this book is that learning to be a good critical thinker in psychology is in some ways like learning to be a good conversation partner. For in a good conversation, both partners listen carefully to each other and may well come away from their encounter with a deeper appreciation of the other's perspective. It is very possible that each partner will be changed in some way by virtue of the dialogue, though it is likely that neither's beliefs will be completely transformed, and in the end they may be reaffirmed or even strengthened. The purpose of this volume, thus, is less to convert readers to a particular set of assumptions than it is to invite them to frame their own critical encounters with the material they study in terms of a respectful and attentive, yet probingly honest, conversation. Surely such a model can lead to critical thinking at its most constructive.

REFERENCES

Bellah, R., Madsen, R., Sullivan, W., Swidler, A., & Tipton, S. (1985). *Habits of the heart: Individualism and commitment in American life.* Berkeley: University of California Press.

Bernstein, R. J. (1983). *Beyond objectivism and relativism.* Philadelphia: University of Pennsylvania Press.

Bohan, J. (1992). *Seldom seen, rarely heard: Women's place in psychology.* Boulder, CO: Westview Press.

Bruner, J. (1990). *Acts of meaning.* Cambridge, MA: Harvard University Press.

Cahan, E. D., & White, S. H. (1992). Proposals for a second psychology. *American Psychologist, 47,* 224–235.

Cole, M. (1996). *Cultural psychology: A once and future discipline.* Cambridge, MA: Harvard University Press.

Danziger, K. (1990a). *Constructing the subject.* Cambridge, England: Cambridge University Press.

Danziger, K. (1990b). Generative metaphor in the history of psychology. In D. E. Leary (Ed.), *Metaphors in the history of psychology* (pp. 331–356). Cambridge, England: Cambridge University Press.

Derrida, J. (1976). *Of grammatology* (G. Spivak, Trans.). Baltimore: Johns Hopkins University Press.

Geertz, C. (1973). From the native's point of view: On the nature of anthropological understanding. In R. A. Shweder & R. A. LeVine (Eds.), *Culture theory: Essays on mind, self and emotion* (pp. 123–135). Cambridge, England: Cambridge University Press.

Gergen, K. J. (1994). *Realities and relationships: Soundings in social construction.* Cambridge, MA: Harvard University Press.

Graumann, C. F., & Gergen, K. J. (1996). *Historical dimensions of psychological discourse.* New York: Cambridge University Press.

Hare-Mustin, R. T. & Marecek, J. (1990). *Making a difference: Psychology and the construction of gender.* New Haven, CT: Yale University Press.

Harwood, R. L., Miller, J. G., & Iriarry, N. L. (1995). *Culture and attachment: Perceptions of the child in context.* New York: Guilford Press.

Healy, D. (1997). *The antidepressant era.* Cambridge, MA: Harvard University Press.

Heidegger, M. (1962). *Being and time* (J. Macquarrie & E. Robinson, Trans.). New York: Harper & Row.

Kirschner, S. R. (1996). *The religious and romantic origins of psychoanalysis: Individuation and integration in post-Freudian theory.* Cambridge, England: Cambridge University Press.

Kirschner, S. R. (2000). Postmodern psychology. In A. Kazdin (Ed.), *Encyclopedia of psychology* (Vol. 6, pp. 246–249). New York: American Psychological Association and Oxford University Press.

Kuhn, T. (1970). *The structure of scientific revolutions* (2nd ed.). Chicago: University of Chicago Press.

Kvale, S. (Ed.). (1992). *Psychology and postmodernism*. Thousand Oaks, CA: Sage.

Leary, D. E. (1990a). Metaphor, theory and practice in the history of psychology. In D. E. Leary (Ed.), *Metaphors in the history of psychology* (pp. 357–367). Cambridge, England: Cambridge University Press.

Leary, D. E. (1990b). Psyche's muse: The role of metaphor in the history of psychology. In D. E. Leary (Ed.), *Metaphors in the history of psychology* (pp. 1–78). Cambridge, England: Cambridge University Press.

Levinas, E. (1969). *Totality and infinity* (A. Lingis, Trans.). Pittsburgh, PA: Duquesne University Press. (Original work published 1961)

Luhrmann, T. M. (2000). *Of two minds: The growing disorder in American psychiatry*. New York: Knopf.

Morawski, J. G. (1999). *Practicing feminisms, reconstructing psychology: Notes on a liminal science*. Ann Arbor: University of Michigan Press.

Rabinow, P., & Sullivan, W. M. (Eds.). (1979). *Interpretive social science: A reader*. Berkeley: University of California Press.

Richardson, F. C., Fowers, B., & Guignon, C. (1999). *Reenvisioning psychology*. San Francisco: Jossey-Bass.

Schutz, A. (1970). *On phenomenology and social relations*. Chicago: University of Chicago Press.

Seidman, S., & Wagner, D. (Eds.). (1992). *Postmodernism and social theory*. Cambridge, MA: Basil Blackwell.

Shweder, R. (1990). Cultural psychology: What is it? In J. Stigler, R. Shweder, & G. Herdt (Eds.), *Cultural psychology* (pp. 1–43). Cambridge, England: Cambridge University Press.

Slife, B. D., & Williams, R. N. (1995). *What's behind the research: Discovering hidden assumptions in the behavioral sciences*. Thousand Oaks, CA: Sage.

Taylor, C. (1989). *Sources of the self*. Cambridge, MA: Harvard University Press.

Tobin, J., Wu, D. Y. H., & Davidson, D. (1989). *Preschool in three cultures: China, Japan, and the United States*. New Haven, CT: Yale University Press.

Valsiner, J. (1998). *The guided mind*. Cambridge, MA: Harvard University Press.

Valsiner, J. (2000). Cultural psychology. In A. Kazdin (Ed.), *Encyclopedia of psychology* (pp. 389–392). New York: American Psychological Association and Oxford University Press.

Weber, M. (1958). *From Max Weber: Essays in sociology* (H. Gerth & C. Wright Mills, Eds. & Trans.). New York: Oxford University Press.

Wertsch, J. (1998). *Mind as action*. New York: Oxford University Press.

Wittgenstein, L. (1953). *Philosophical investigations* (G. Anscombe, Trans.). Oxford, England: Basil Blackwell.

AUTHOR INDEX

Numbers in italics refer to entries in the reference sections.

SUBJECT INDEX

Deference, 160–161
Deliberation, 56
DeLoache, J. S., 224
Democratic government, 45
Denying the consequent, 244
Depression, 99–116
    and culture, 140
    factors of, 134
    historical perspective on, 101–105
    and materialism, 100–101
    materialistic assumptions in research on, 108–114
    materialistic explanations of, 106–107
    and morbidity, 101–102
    neurobiological findings associated with, 105–106
    and one-sided dualism, 114–115
Descartes, René, 128–129, 138, 209, 212, 220, 237–240, 245
Destructive obedience, 64
Determinism, 271
    and efficient causation, 157
    and free will, 127–128
    material causal, 108–110
Development, stages of, 192
Developmental psychology
    and culture, 208–210
    and existential issues, 200–203
    and higher levels of knowing, 218–220
    and implicitness, 215
    limitations/future of, 203–204
    and moral vision, 220–224
    and Jean Piaget, 190–192
    and procedural knowing/being-in-the-world, 210–213
    shortcomings of, 207–210
    and social practices, 213–215
Dialogue, 261
Dilthey, Wilhelm, 252–253
Disenchanted universe, 27
Disguised ideologies, 30–32
Disposition, 53–54
Divine accommodation, 198
Doherty, William, 35
Doubt, 237–239
Duhem, Pierre-Maurice-Marie, 244
Duhem-Quine thesis, 244
Dunn, J., 223

Early subject withdrawal, 112
Ecological cognition, 180

Ecological model of human development, 214
Effectiveness, meaning of, 7–8
Efficient causal determinism, 271
Efficient causation, 153–157, 164, 274
Egoism, 73–76
Elections, 213–214
Emancipatory, 27
Embeddedness, 254, 256, 275
Embodied agency, 137–140
Emotions, virtue and, 51–53
Empirically supported treatments (ESTs), 6–7, 25
Empirical science, 239n.1, 240–243, 245
Empiricism, 106–107, 168, 270
Emptiness, 21
Empty self, 263–264
Enactive memory, 211
Encoding specificity, 181
Engaged agents, 213
Engagement, 165–166
The Enlightenment, 213n.1
Ennis, Robert, 4
Episodic memory, 211
Epistemology, 236–238
Erikson, E. H., 219
Eschatology, 199
ESTs. *See* Empirically supported treatments
Ethical phenomenology, 90–94
Ethos, 221
Event memory, 211
Evolutionary psychology, 69–72, 271
Evolutionary theory, 197
Existential individualism, 31–32, 34
Existential issues, 200–203
Experience
    and depression, 115
    therapist's, 55
Experimental social psychology, 87–90
Expressive individualism, 31
External ends, 46
External goals, 49
External good, 46–49

Fairness, 29
Falsifiability, 71
Falsification assumption, 243–244
Fancher, Robert, 28
Feyerabend, Paul, 240n.2
Final causation, 156, 157, 166
Fisher, A. M., 179
Fisher, Helen, 69

Flax, Jane, 32n.6
Flourishing, 43–44
Folk psychologies, 221–222
Formal causation, 155, 156, 166
Formal logic, 237
Formal operational thought, 192
Fossils, 195
Frank, Jerome, 19–20, 30
Frankfurt School, 158
Freedom, ambiguity of, 33
Free will, 125–128, 138. *See also* Agency
Freud, Sigmund, 71, 102–103
Freudian psychoanalytic theory, 30, 31, 102–104, 132
Friere, Paolo, 226
Fromm, Erich, 7, 33
Fully engaged agency, 218
Fundamentals of Cognition (Mark Ashcraft), 154

Gadamer, Hans-Georg, 240, 255–258
Galileo Galilei, 193, 194
Garsten, Ed, 72
Geertz, C., 209, 214, 215, 221
Gender, 102
Generosity, 40, 50, 53, 54
Genes, 125n.3
Genetic epistemology, 191
Genovese, Kitty, 72–74
Geology, 195–196
Gergen, David, 17
Gergen, K. J., 82–85
Gergen, Kenneth, 24
Gestalt, temporal, 179
Gestalten, 174
Gestalt psychology, 67, 174, 180, 181
Goals
    awareness of, 137n.7
    formation/selection of, 218
    identifying/clarifying, 53
    internal vs. external, 49
Goal seeking, 48
God, 193–199
    and biology, 196–197
    and cosmology, 193–195
    and geology, 195–196
    and historiography, 197–199
The Good
    communal, 45
    external, 46–49
    highest, 43
    and individualism, 44–46

internal, 47, 49
pursuit of, 52
shared, 45–46
Good deeds, 140
Goodnow, J. J., 214, 223
Gottlieb, A., 224
Gravity, 194, 195
Greeks, ancient, 40, 236
Guignon, C. B., 47
Guilt, 74

Habermas, Jürgen, 7, 32–33
Handy, Charles, 17
Harlow, Harry, 67–68
Harmony, 52
Hawi, Z., 122, 123, 125
Healthy narcissism, 31
Healy, David, 102
Heidegger, Martin, 211–213, 220, 253–255
Heiman, G. W., 87–88
Helping behavior, 72–76
Hermeneutic circle, 252, 257
Hermeneutic–phenomenological psychology, 180, 211
Hermeneutic psychology, 259–261
Hermeneutics, 85–90, 251–265
    average everydayness in, 253, 262
    care in, 255
    clearing in, 254
    embeddedness in, 254, 256
    empty self in, 263–264
    horizon of language in, 256–258
    and prejudice, 256–258
    preunderstanding in, 254–256
    and psychology, 259–261
    and truth, 258
    unconcealment in, 262
Hidden assumptions, 21–34
Highest good, 43
Hillman, James, 20, 21
Historiography, 197–199
Hobbes, Thomas, 73
Hoffman, I. Z., 29
Holism, 133–134, 172–175
Holistic monism, 130–143
    and causation/method, 134–136
    and context, 139–141
    mind and body as, 136–141
    research implications of, 141–142
Honesty, 40, 49, 50, 54–55
Horizon of language, 256–258
Human agency. *See* Agency

Prejudice against prejudice, 257
Preoperational understanding, 192
Preunderstanding, 254–256
Problem solving, 181–182
Procedural justice, 29
Procedural knowledge, 211
Profane history, 197–199
Progressive development, 200–201
Progressive evolution, 202
Psychoanalysis, 18
Psychological society, 17
Psychology
    cognitive. *See* Cognitive psychology
    cultural, 272–274
    evolutionary, 69–72
    Gestalt, 67, 174, 180, 181
    hermeneutic, 259–261
    interpretive, 272
    and science, 236–239
    scientific methods in, 189
    social. *See* Social psychology
Psychotherapy, 17–36
    concerns about, 18–21
    golden years of, 35
    hidden assumptions in, 21–34
    individualism in, 26–32
    instrumentalism in, 32–34
    value-freedom in, 22–26
Punctual self, 161, 164, 165, 209–210
Pythagoras, 245

Qualitative methods of investigation, 90, 142, 247
Quantitative methods, 247
Question of being, 253

Rational freedom, 129n.5
Reconstructive memory, 181
Reflective abstraction, 210, 218–219
Reiff, Philip, 17
Relational beings, 91, 275
Relational context, 70–71
Relational properties, 67
Relational self, 82
Relativism, 25–26, 84–85, 89–90
Religious beliefs, 201
Representational knowledge, 160
Responsibility
    acceptance of, 51
    for actions, 55
    and human agency, 127–128
    and material causal determinism, 109

    to others, 273
    and relationships, 91
Richardson, F. C., 159, 213n.1
Ricoeur, P., 113
Rigorous thinking, 4–7, 9, 10
Risk, 73, 75
Rogers, A., 213n.1
Romanticism, 31

Sacred history, 197–199
Sandel, Michael, 30
Sartre, J., 31
Schafer, Roy, 31–32
Schleiermacher, Friedrich, 252
Schumaker, John, 7
Science
    assumptions about, 235–236
    and nature, 245, 273
    objectifying outlook of, 27
    and social constructionism, 85
    and value-freedom, 23–24
Scientific method, 236–240, 257
Scientific stage of human history, 199
Self
    autonomous, 21
    and culture, 215
    explicit knowledge of, 218
    in Japanese culture, 209
    sense of, 211
    and the world, 162
Self-concept, 64
Self-contained individualism, 32
Self-determination, 273
Self-determinism, 128, 161
Self-fulfillment, 271
Selfhood, 224
Self-interpreting beings, 254–255, 260
Selfishness, 73
Self-objects, 31
Self-reflection, 42
Self-representation, 219
Self-responsibility, 42
Sensorimotor intelligence, 192, 211
Settled disposition, 53–55
Shared goals, 48
Shared good, 45–46
Shared meanings, 273
Sherif, M., 64
Shopping, 213
Shweder, R. A., 223–224
Situated cognition, 180
Skepticism, 238

Slife, B., 22–23, 25–26, 179
Smith, A., 22
Social atomism, 164–166, 270–272
Social cognition, 65
Social communication, 223–224
Social constructionism, 82–85, 89–90, 102
Social exchange theory, 65
Sociality of human beings, 64–67, 92, 163n.6
Social practices, 213–215
Social psychology, 63–77, 81–94
    alternative foundations of, 81–94
    and ethical phenomenology, 90–94
    experimental, 87–90
    and helping others, 72–76
    and hermeneutics, 85–90
    and love, 67–72
    and social constructionism, 82–85
    and sociality of human beings, 64–67
Social sciences, 24, 162, 241, 244, 257
Social systems, 28
Sociology, 199
Solar system, 193–195
Speech, 252
Sponsorship effects, 113
Statistical analysis, 246–247
Stratigraphic models of the self, 214
The strong sense, 165–166
Subjectivity, 27
Subject–object ontology, 27
Sufficiency, 122–123, 132, 135–136
Suicide, 101–102

Tacit messages, 223
Taylor, Charles, 161, 163n.6, 165, 209, 218,
    222–224
Technical eclecticism, 25
Temperance, 53, 54
Temporal gestalt, 179
Tenney, T. F., 55
Theological stage of human history, 199
Therapeutic situation, 55–56
Therapists, virtue ethics and, 44
Theresa, Mother, 75, 76
Thinking Critically About Research Methods (J.
    G. Benjafield), 8
Titchener, Edward, 151
Toulmin, Stephen, 129n.5, 200
Tradition, 256, 257
Treatise on Insanity (Phillipe Pinel), 103
Triplett, Norm, 63
Trust, 53
Truth, 84–85, 239–241, 258
Truth and Method (Hans-Georg Gadamer),
    255, 258

Tversky, A., 182
Twinship experiences, 31

Unblinding, 112
Unconcealment, 262
Underdeterminism, 113–114
United Kingdom, antidepressant use in the,
    112
United States, depression in the, 102
Utilitarian individualism, 30

Valenstein, Elliot S., 113, 122–123, 140
Value convergence, 23
Value-freedom, 22–26
Values about values, 219
Variation and selection constructivism, 211
Ventura, Michael, 20, 21
Verification assumption, 242–243
Verificationism, 242
Vico, Giambattista, 199
Virtue, 39–58
    as action, 49–50
    case example of, 41–42, 48–55
    and cognition, 50–51
    defining, 40–41
    and emotions, 51–53
    and flourishing, 43–44
    and the good life, 42–48
    and individualism, 44–46
    and internal/external goods, 46–48
    and practical wisdom, 55–57
    as a settled disposition, 53–55
Virtue ethics, 40, 44
Volcanoes, 195, 196

Wachtel, Paul, 8
Wash out, 112
Weaving metaphor, 215
Weber, Max, 27
Webs of significance, 221
Weltanschauung, 221
Wertheimer, M., 180
Western culture, 162, 164, 175, 209, 211,
    225
*We've Had a Hundred Years of Psychotherapy
    and the World's Getting Worse* (James
    Hillman and Michael Ventura), 20
White, S. H., 200
Withdrawal symptoms, 113
Word, Deletha, 72, 74–75
Worldview, 221, 222
World War II, 75
Wright, Robert, 89
Wundt, Wilhelm, 151, 189

ABOUT THE EDITORS

Brent D. Slife, PhD, is currently professor of psychology at Brigham Young University, where he chairs the doctoral program in theoretical and philosophical psychology and is a member of the doctoral program in clinical psychology. Recently honored with the Karl G. Maeser Award for Outstanding Scholarship, he was also distinguished as "Teacher of the Year" by the university and "Most Outstanding Professor" by the National Honor Society in Psychology, Psi Chi. He is a fellow of several professional organizations, including the American Psychological Association, and he recently served as the president of Division 24 (Theoretical and Philosophical Psychology). He has authored numerous articles and books, including *Taking Sides, What's Behind the Research, Time and Psychological Explanation,* and *Critical Issues in Psychotherapy.*

Jeffrey S. Reber, PhD, is assistant professor of psychology at the State University of West Georgia. His PhD is in general psychology with dual emphasis in theoretical/philosophical psychology and applied social psychology. His scholarly publications have emphasized the assumptions and implications of evolutionary psychology, the meaning and possibility of altruism, and the philosophical underpinnings of eclectic psychotherapy. His current research focuses on a social psychology that treats human relationships as fundamental.

Frank C. Richardson, PhD, is professor of educational psychology at the University of Texas at Austin. He has coauthored (with Robert Woolfolk) *Stress, Sanity, and Survival* and (with Blaine Fowers and Charles Guignon) *Re-Envisioning Psychology.* He has published numerous articles and chapters on topics in psychotherapy theory and the philosophy of social science and is a recent past president of Division 24 (Theoretical and Philosophical Psychology) of the American Psychological Association.

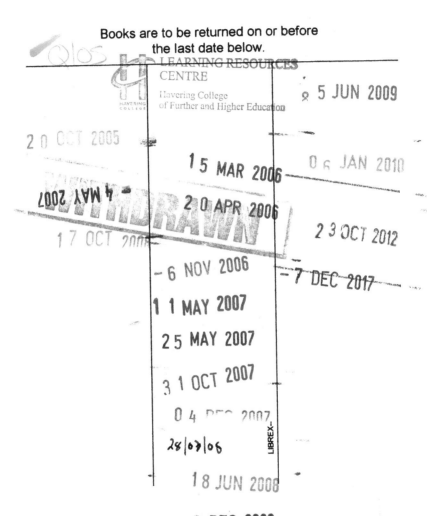